Understanding Chinese Company Law

Understanding Chinese Company Law

Third Edition

Gu Minkang

HKU PRESS
香港大學出版社

Hong Kong University Press
The University of Hong Kong
Pok Fu Lam Road
Hong Kong
https://hkupress.hku.hk

ISBN 978-988-8390-52-6 (*Hardback*)

British Library Cataloguing-in-Publication Data
A catalogue record for this book is available from the British Library.

Digitally printed

Contents

Preface to the Third Edition

As I noted in the Preface to the Second Edition, it is tough to teach Chinese laws in English because they are constantly evolving to suit the needs of implementing economic reform and open-door policy in China. I firmly believe that those who teach Chinese laws in English outside China deserve more appreciation for several reasons: (1) they have spent a considerable amount of time going through the vast amount of Chinese law materials and translating them into English; (2) they have attempted to enhance Chinese company law by adopting multiple approaches aimed towards achieving fair comparison of Chinese company law and company laws in other jurisdictions; and (3) they have contributed greatly by introducing Chinese laws to people in other jurisdictions. Indeed, Chinese laws keep changing, but they are changing for the better, and are becoming more rational and reasonable. It is widely accepted that economic development in China will inevitably encourage the development of more freedom and democracy in the country. Chinese company law, together with other civil or commercial laws, supports at least two important freedoms of Chinese people: the freedom to exercise private property ownership and the freedom to conduct trade business. Thus, if we say that the 2005 Company Law gives more freedom to shareholders to decide important matters through the articles of association, the 2013 Company Law provides capital contribution subscription ("zero capital system") in order to enable the easy establishment of companies in China. This zero capital system is evidence of revolutionary change in the history of Chinese company law and is a major reason behind amending this book.

Certainly, this book must also be updated for other reasons. Firstly, the old Hong Kong Companies Ordinance (now Cap. 622) has had many amendments made to it, so it begs that the relevant comparisons need to be updated accordingly. Secondly, a great number of new discussions have sprung up in the past few years regarding Chinese company law and they need to be reflected in this book. Thus, issues of guiding ideologies, shareholders' right to know, and right to profits and human rights of legal persons are fairly addressed. Thirdly, some colleagues of mine who teach Chinese company law in other jurisdictions have adopted this book as their textbook or reference book and have encouraged me to publish a newer version to reflect the recent changes in China.

This book has been widely used since 2005. I hope that it can continue to help readers understand Chinese company law better, and invite readers to develop deeper thoughts and arguments. For the sake of consistency, even though the contents of this book have been revised, the structure largely remains the same. No matter how much effort was invested into writing this book, mistakes can never be avoided, so I sincerely hope that readers can offer their comments and criticisms in order for improvements to be made in the future.

As a general practice, I want to again thank the staff of Hong Kong University Press, especially Dr Susie Han, acquisitions editor, for their great support to this third edition. I want to thank the Faculty of Law at the National University of Singapore for offering me a chance to conduct my research and compose my thoughts on its beautiful campus. Finally, I want to thank my wife and daughter for their love and support.

Gu Minkang
25 May 2016

Preface to the Second Edition

Doing research on the subject of law is a very difficult task. Doing research on the subject of Chinese law, however, is even tougher and time-consuming because Chinese laws have been constantly changing for the last thirty years. Therefore, in order to give their students the most updated information, those who teach Chinese laws in English must spend huge amounts of time collecting, translating and organizing the relevant laws, rules and regulations.

The frequent change of Chinese laws is understandable because along with the substantial change of economic conditions, the relevant laws also need to be greatly changed. It is evident that in China, thirty years of economic reform significantly changes the Chinese legal system and some important human rights have been gradually respected and protected. If we describe the thirty years economic reform as the process of moving from planned economy towards market economy—which emphases on equal market accession and fair competition—then it is correct to say that, from a legal aspect, China is moving from the situation of rule by man (or Party) towards the situation of rule by law or rule of law. Many basic and fundamental rights have thus been guaranteed by laws, even though problems and criticisms are seen and heard from time to time. One piece of evidence is that property owners are now given substantial autonomy to engage in business activities, so long as the relevant laws do not expressly prohibit them from doing so. This is exemplified by the 2005 Company Law which gives more freedoms to investors to decide internal matters. So far it has been observed that more than twenty provisions grant the right to shareholders to freely incorporate in their special desires in the Articles of Association.

This book has been used for more than two years. It was initially demanded by students and other readers because they could, at least, have one English book that offers a systemic and comprehensive introduction to the Chinese company law and they could use this book to develop their thoughts and arguments. However, the first edition was based heavily on the 1993 Company Law and some statements or references are no longer accurate. Against this background, this book must be revised in order to reflect the new changes made by the 2005 Company Law as well as other relevant laws and regulations.

The contents of this book have been largely revised but the structure remains the same. In addition, a chart of comparison between the 1993 Company Law and the 2005 Company Law is provided to facilitate reading and understanding.

Finally, I want to thank Mr Dennis Cheung, the managing editor of Hong Kong University Press for his great support to this second edition.

Gu Minkang
30 March 2010

Preface to the First Edition

It is generally accepted that the Chinese Company Law has played an important role in restructuring state-owned enterprises and in improving the business environment in China. Even though the Chinese Company Law should be a broad topic, this book can only cover the major topics in the area of the Chinese Company Law. The main feature of this book is the description and analysis of company law in a fast changing country of the world. This book contains a historical introduction, evolution of the current company law, discussion of the factors shaping the company law, the treatment of potential changes of the company law, and finally a detailed introduction to the new achievements made in the 2005 Amendment of the Chinese Company Law. One of the advantages of this book is its comparative approach to introducing and analysing the Chinese Company Law. Therefore, the targeted readers of this book are likely to be law students, practitioners, and persons who want to have a good understanding of some aspects of China's company law.

I am indebted to Professor Robert Art who is a well-established American legal scholar in the field of company law. He was the first person to stimulate my interest in and enthusiasm for studying company law. He promised to give his comments when this book is finished. Unfortunately, he passed away a year ago. I dedicate this book to him.

I am indebted to numerous friends who have offered their constant support and friendship when I encountered difficult times, so that I have been able to fight for justice successfully. As the result of their help, I have been able to write again and finally finish this book.

I want to express my thanks to Dr Colin L. Day, the publisher of Hong Kong University Press. Without his kind assistance, this book could not be published so quickly. I also want to thank the Editorial Board of Hong Kong University Press for its supportive decisions. Needless to say, I shall thank the reader of this book (even though I do not know his name) for his or her positive comments and recommendations.

Last but not least, I would like to thank my wife and daughter for their great love and care. I would like to dedicate this book to them too.

Gu Minkang
16 November 2005

1

General Introduction

I. SHORT HISTORY OF CHINESE COMPANY LAW

The People's Republic of China (hereinafter referred to as "China") did not have any formal national company law until the National People's Congress (hereinafter referred to as the "NPC") promulgated the Company Law of the People's Republic of China in 1993 (hereinafter referred to as the "1993 Company Law")[1] and substantially amended it four times.[2]

In the more than twenty years since the implementation of the Chinese company law, many achievements have been made both in theory and in practice. In terms of theoretical research, there are many publications in Chinese and English, addressing various issues related to Chinese company law. However, it is regrettable to see only a few English books comprehensively discussing this particular topic.[3] Furthermore, it is even rarer to see

1. The Company Law of the People's Republic of China (*Zhonghua Renmin Gongheguo Gongsi Fa*) was adopted on 29 December 1993 by the Fifth Session of the Standing Committee of the Eighth NPC and took effect on 1 July 1994.
2. The first amendment was made on 25 December 1999 by the Thirteenth Session of the Standing Committee of the Ninth NPC. The second amendment was made by the Eleventh Session of the Standing Committee of the Tenth NPC on 28 August 2004. The third amendment was made by the Eighteenth Session of the Standing Committee of the Tenth NPC on 27 October 2005. The fourth amendment was made by the Sixth Session of the Standing Committee of the Twelfth NPC on 28 December 2013.
3. At the time of revising this book, a few English books on the Chinese Company Law were discovered in the library at the City University of Hong Kong: (1) Shaowei Lin, *Derivative Actions in Chinese Company Law*, Kluwer Law International (Alphen aan den Rijn, Netherlands), 2015; (2) Jane Fu, *Corporate Disclosure and Corporate Governance in China*, Wolters Kluwer (Alphen aan den Rijn, Netherlands), 2010; (3) Peter Koh Soon Kwang,

an English book discussing Chinese company law using a comparative approach or method. Therefore, due to language constraints and cultural differences, many foreign law students, legal practitioners, and other legal professionals are not able to obtain a comprehensive picture of Chinese company law and cannot fully understand its background.

China's national company law has a short history. However, there is no doubt that the modern concept of the company has played a very important role in standardizing Chinese enterprises, especially state-owned enterprises (hereinafter referred to as "SOEs"). As a modern business form, the company was initially used as a tool to reform SOEs in China.[4] In other words, companies were recommended as an effective way to combine public ownership with the market economy.[5] Even though Chinese company law contains theories and concepts that are similar to those of Western countries, it needs more substantial improvements in the near future, because loopholes and ambiguities have been discovered from time to time. When the 1993 Company Law was promulgated, one author pointed out that although China had spent fifteen years drafting the law, it would need another fifteen years to seriously implement it.[6] His prediction was absolutely right, as evidenced by the four amendments made over the subsequent twenty years. A better interpretation of this statement is that China required time to accumulate sufficient experience of implementing and improving the law, and now it seems that the time is ripe to comprehensively review that law.

Major Issues in Company Law, Sweet & Maxwell (Singapore), 2010; (4) Chao Xi, *Corporate Governance and Legal Reform in China*, Wildy, Simmonds, and Hill Publishing (London), 2009; and (5) Jian Fu and Jie Yuan, *PRC Company and Securities Laws: A Practical Guide*, CCH (Singapore), 2006.

4. Many scholars understand that one of the fatal problems of the 1993 Company Law was its use to specifically restructure SOEs. As a result, although the 1993 Company Law was designed to be suitable for the needs of SOEs, it probably went against the principles of the market economy. See Fang Liufang, "Gain New Insights Through Restudying Old Materials—Comments on Reform of the Company Law" (*Wenguzhixin—tan gongsi fa xiugai*), in Guo Feng and Wang Jian (eds.), *Vertical and Horizontal Discussion on Reform of the Company Law* (*Gongsi fa xiugai zhongheng tan*), The Law Press (Beijing), 2000, p. 40.
5. "The Several Major Decisions of the Central Committee of the Chinese Communist Party regarding the Reform and the Development of SOEs" (*Zhonggong Zhongyang guanyu guoyou qiye gaige he fazhan ruogan zhongda wenti de jueding*), *Guangming Daily*, 27 September 1999, p. 1.
6. "State Enterprise Taking the Corporate Plunge Faces Numerous Difficulties", *South China Morning Post*, 4 June 1994.

II. OVERVIEW OF EXISTING PROBLEMS

The 1993 Company Law cannot be regarded as a well-drafted law for various reasons, such as its short history, insufficient experience, and changeable circumstances during the transitional period. Another major reason was that China needed to protect existing SOEs rather than get rid of them. Thus, many provisions under the 1993 Company Law cannot be considered as compatible as those of developed countries or regions.

Comments have been made that the 1993 Company Law contained at least the following main problems.

- It was the product of a planned economic system and reflected state administrative interference, especially interference in establishing companies.
- It was closely related to SOEs. The 1993 Company Law was used as a justifiable tool to reform the SOEs. Hence, it offered too many advantages and benefits to the SOEs, which were not compatible with the idea of a modern market economy. Other company investors were less protected.
- The threshold for establishing a company was much too high.[7] The minimum statutory registered capital was said to be the highest in the world. Individuals considered that this threshold was a heavy economic burden and provided no incentive to establish their companies. This threshold was fundamentally unsuitable for the quick development of private enterprises in China.
- The 1993 Company Law contained too many systemic problems. For example, it limited a company's ability to invest in other enterprises. The Law required that such investments not exceed 50 per cent of the company's net assets.[8] This kind of limitation was not often seen in other jurisdictions.
- Other problems included a limitation on transferring shares by promoters; a limitation on transferring shares by senior managers; a limitation on the scope of business operations; a compulsory allocation of statutory common reserve funds, which injured the interests of shareholders; a limitation on the statutory powers of boards of directors and managers, which went against the principle of company autonomy; and a weak protection of small shareholders with no clear civil remedies provided in the case where their legal interests were violated.[9]

7. This will be discussed in detail in the following relevant chapters.
8. The 1993 Company Law, Article 12(2).
9. For detailed information, see Guo Feng and Wang Jian (eds.), *Vertical and Horizontal Discussion on Reform of the Company Law (Gongsi fa xiugai zhongheng tan)*, The Law Press (Beijing), 2000.

Fortunately, those problems were seriously addressed and substantially resolved by subsequent amendments in 1999, 2004, 2005, and 2013. Both the 2005 and 2013 amendments are especially important. Hereinafter, they are described as the "2005 Company Law" and the "2013 Company Law", respectively. For convenience, any reference to "Company Law" in this book means the 2013 Amendment.

Despite the existence of the 2005 and 2013 amendments, Chinese company law could still be improved in the following respects: (1) to enhance the checks-and-balances relationship between a shareholders' general meeting and a board of directors, (2) to improve the checks-and-balances relationship between a board of directors and a board of supervisors (or a supervisory committee), and (3) to improve the mechanism in place to protect minority shareholders.[10]

Furthermore, it is important to note that Chinese company law is an important achievement from both a pragmatic and an ideological perspective. One would be optimistic to point out two advantages of the law: in the small private sector, it is likely to be highly useful because a corporation is a good tool to promote stable business development; and in the far larger state sector, the effects on SOEs are much more significant, because standardized companies are competent enough to compete with their rivals in the international markets.

III. RESEARCH METHODOLOGY OF THIS BOOK

Chinese company law could be better understood through a wide range of comparisons between it and company law in other jurisdictions. Thus, a method of comparative law is applied throughout this book. As a term of art, "comparative law" must rank as one of the most unique tools within the scenario of legal research and study.[11] Furthermore, comparative law is primarily a method of study rather than a legal body of rules.[12] As Zweiaert and Koetz point out, "The primary aim of comparative law, as of all sciences, is knowledge. If one accepts that legal science includes not only the techniques of interpreting the texts, principles, rules and standards of a national system, but also the discovery of models for preventing or resolving social conflicts, then it is clear that the method of comparative law can provide

10. Liu Junhai, "Entry of WTO and Perfection of the Company Law", *Legal Daily*, 16 January 2000, p. 3.
11. Peter de Cruz, *Comparative Law in a Changing World* (2nd ed.), Cavendish Publishing Limited (London), 1999, p. 1.
12. Ibid., p. 5.

a much richer range of model solutions than a legal science devoted to a single nation, simply because the different systems of the world can offer a greater variety of solutions than could be thought up in a lifetime by even the most imaginative jurist who was corralled in his own system."[13]

Certainly, the use of a comparative method never implies that foreign experiences should be simply transplanted onto Chinese soil. One must seriously examine whether there exists a proper cultural or economic background. Thus, according to the theory of selective adaptation, learning from the legal regime of foreign jurisdictions involves a complex process of selectively adapting foreign norms and institutions.[14] Thus, comparison for the purpose of establishing differences is one thing and comparison for the purpose of adopting foreign norms and institutions is another.

This book emphasizes comparisons between Chinese company law and company law in the United States, Hong Kong, and Taiwan. It is understandable that company law in the United States has a major influence on the whole world because it is considered to be advanced with many innovations. Hong Kong company law bears resemblances to the company law of the United Kingdom on the one hand, and has exercised a great influence on the Chinese company law on the other hand. It has been observed that many of the principles stated in Chinese company law are borrowed from Taiwanese company law. Company law in other jurisdictions such as the United Kingdom, Germany, France, and Japan are mentioned from time to time in order to interpret particular provisions of the Chinese company law. In this regard, it is necessary to briefly introduce company law as it is practised in the United States, Hong Kong, and Taiwan.

IV. THE EVOLUTION OF CHINESE COMPANY LAW

From a legal perspective, China did not have a concept of a "company" or a "corporation" until the end of the Qing Dynasty, when the government promulgated the first Chinese corporation law, the *Da Qing Gongsi Lü*, in 1904.[15] Although many scholars have argued that only family businesses

---

13. K. Zweiaert and H. Koetz, *An Introduction to Comparative Law*, Clarendon Press (Oxford), 1998, p. 15.
14. Pitman B. Potter, "Globalization and Economic Regulation in China: Selective Adaptation of Globalized Norms and Practices", *Washington University Global Study Law Review*, Vol. 2, 2003, p. 120.
15. The contents of *Da Qing Gongsi Lü* can be found in Wang Baoshu and Cui Qingzhi, *The Principles of the Chinese Company Law (Zhongguo gongsi fa yuanli)*, The Social Science Documents Press (Beijing), 1998, pp. 7–8.

existed in China before 1904,[16] several have noted that many traditional families were really "corporations" in an economic sense: the members of large clans worked together not merely out of affection for their kin, but also to accumulate capital and pursue profit more effectively.[17] Even if this argument is persuasive, it is important to note that so-called "modern" business enterprises[18] only came into existence in China after 1840, the year the British government launched the Opium War against China and forced the Qing dynasty to open China's doors to foreign investment and businesses. Data indicate that in 1913 Western businessmen invested in 136 enterprises in China. Each enterprise had more than US$100,000 invested in it, and the total investment amounted to US$103 million. Among those enterprises, ninety-six were solely financed by Western businessmen and forty were financed through the form of joint ventures.[19] From the very beginning, foreign companies in China were translated using the Chinese word *yanghang*, such as Jardine, Matheson & Co. (Yi He Yanghang). This was also the case in Hong Kong and Macao. This term can still be seen today.

As mentioned previously, the term "company" became a formal legal term in China in 1903 when the Qing dynasty published its *Da Qing Gongsi Lü*. The purposes for publishing this law were bifurcate. One was to use the law as a tool to promote China's industrial development. At that time, it was recognized that the establishment of a modern business structure was the only way to compete with foreign counterparts. On the other hand, the Qing government had no other choice in order to get rid of extraterritorial legal systems. During that time, many Western "big powers" (*lieqiang*) imposed their various influences on China. England, Japan, America, and other countries promised the Qing government that they would give up their "consular jurisdictional power" (*lingshi caipanquan*) if the Qing government would abolish its cruel punishment system and agree to establish another legal system. In order to maintain political control, the Qing government began the reform of its legal system with a consideration of adopting other legal

16. Max Weber said that in the absence of a law governing voluntary associations most businesses were "merely" family businesses. Teemu Ruskola, "Conceptualizing Corporations and Kinship: Comparative Law and Development Theory in a Chinese Perspective", *Stanford Law Review*, Vol. 52, No. 1599, 2000, p. 1605.
17. Hill Gates, "China's Motor: A Thousand Years of Petty Capitalism, citing Teemu Ruskola, Conceptualizing Corporations and Kinship: Comparative Law and Development Theory in a Chinese Perspective", *Stanford Law Review*, Vol. 52, No. 1599, 2000, p. 1605, n. 15.
18. "Modern business enterprises" were created in Western jurisdictions in the forms of companies, partnerships, and sole proprietorships along with notions of the separate legal entity and limited liability of shareholders.
19. Liu Fengming, *Joint Stock Company and Joint Venture Enterprise Laws* (*Gufen gongsi yu zezi qiye fa*), The China University of Politics and Law Press (Beijing), 1998, p. 1.

systems, specifically those of European countries, the United States, Japan, and other countries. For this reason, the *Da Qing Gongsi Lü* was drafted based primarily on the British Joint Stock Company Act (1856), the British Company Act (1862), and the Japanese Commercial Code (1899). Thus, the *Da Qing Gongsi Lü* was a combination of the traditions of both common and continental law jurisdictions.[20] The comparatively modern Chinese company law was created in 1929 by the Guomindang (Kuomintang) government, which was under the influence of German and Japanese Commercial Codes. The relevant law has been amended many times and is still applied in Taiwan today.[21]

Following the establishment of the People's Republic of China in 1949, the development of company law can be divided into three periods.

Firstly, between 1949 and 1956, in order to encourage private enterprises to continue their operations in China and to protect their legal status, the government passed the Provisional Regulations on Private Enterprises (1950) and Implementing Methods for the Provisional Regulations on Private Enterprises (1951). At that time, there were five forms of companies in the country:

(a) unlimited liability companies (*wuxian gongsi*);
(b) limited liability companies (*youxian zeren gongsi*; hereinafter referred to as "LLCs");
(c) companies limited by shares (*gufen youxian gongsi*);
(d) companies formed by one or more shareholders with unlimited liability and one or more shareholders with limited liability (*lianghe gongsi*); and
(e) companies formed by one or more shareholders having unlimited liability and one or more shareholders having liability limited to their share contributions, plus the company capital was divided into equal shares (*gufen lianghe gongsi*).

In 1954, the Provisional Regulations on Joint Venture Enterprises by Public Ownership and Private Ownership were issued. The enterprises established under these Regulations were more or less like LLCs. However, when China completed its socialist reformation in 1956, those company forms disappeared across the country. SOEs (formerly state-run enterprises)

20. Common law is a case law (or judge-made law) system, and its two major representative countries are the United Kingdom and United States. Continental law is a written law (codified law) system, and its two major representative countries are Germany and France. Before World War II, Japanese law was heavily influenced by continental law traditions.

21. Jiang Ping (ed.), *New Company Law Textbook* (*Xin gongsi fa jiaocheng*), The Law Press (Beijing), 1997, p. 16.

and collectively owned enterprises[22] became predominant business forms in China until 1992, when local regulations on companies appeared in Shanghai and Shenzhen.

Secondly, during 1957 to 1978, there existed only SOEs and collectively owned enterprises in China. According to the Working Regulation on State-Owned Industry Enterprise (1961), all factories had to establish co-operational relations if they manufactured similar products or had similar needs. Some special companies in charge of factories making the same or similar products were established. Although at that time the word "company" (*gongsi*) was used for these special companies, it did not contain the same meaning as in Western countries. Indeed, those special companies were not established for the purpose of operating for profit, but were administrative institutions that were mainly responsible for organizing production and sales in line with the state plan.[23]

Thirdly, during 1979 to 1993, companies under a modern concept became in demand in China. The state recognized the need to establish modern companies in order to implement the economic reform in China. One of the major tasks of the economic reform was for the state to release the heavy burden of poorly managed SOEs. It was believed that companies were one of the best business forms to realize the goal of decreasing government intervention and to separate investors from direct management. Thus, several important laws enacted during this period must be mentioned.

- The Enterprise Bankruptcy Law of the PRC (For Trial Implementation) was adopted on 2 December 1986 and took effect on 1 November 1988.[24]
- The Law of the PRC on Industrial Enterprises Owned by the Whole People was adopted on 13 April 1988.

22. In China, the term "collectively owned enterprises" refers to business organizations in which all of the production materials are owned by workers or economic organizations with a collective nature. All workers work together and enjoy compensation based on their contributions. These enterprises are autonomously managed and responsible for profits and losses. Unlike SOEs, collectively owned enterprises can elect to either hold or refuse legal person status. For detailed information, see Gan Peizhong, *Legal Science on Enterprises and Companies* (*Qiye yu gongsi faxue*), Beijing University Press (Beijing), 1998, p. 152.
23. For detailed information, see Jiang, supra note 22, p. 16.
24. The long-awaited new Enterprise Bankruptcy Law of the People's Republic of China was finally promulgated by the Twenty-third Session of the Standing Committee of the Tenth NPC and took effect on 1 June 2007.

- The State Council also promulgated several important regulations such as the Provisional Regulations on Management of Company Registration (1985) and the Provisional Regulations on Private Enterprises.
- On 29 December 1993, the 1993 Company Law was adopted, and it has since been substantially amended several times.

Like much of the recent legislation, the Chinese company law uses forms and conventions drawn from company law in the United States and other Western countries. This approach represents an important step towards engaging in international business practices. For example, Chinese company law provides for stocks and dividends; shareholders with limited liability, pre-emptive rights, and the power to elect directors; and directors with fiduciary duties and the power to appoint officers.[25] Those features enable foreigners to grasp the major ideas of Chinese company law, even though some of the concepts must be interpreted by taking into account Chinese culture and tradition.

V. A BRIEF INTRODUCTION TO HONG KONG COMPANY LAW

Although Hong Kong was returned to Chinese sovereignty on 1 July 1997, company law in Hong Kong has taken a substantially different approach from that of China, mainly because of their different legal backgrounds and philosophies. It is necessary to introduce Hong Kong company law, as it has exercised a great influence on the Chinese company law.

In Hong Kong, the Companies Ordinance (Cap. 32) was the most important legislation regulating companies in Hong Kong for more than five decades. Among the other company law legislation, the Companies Ordinance was considered one of the largest and most complex statutes. The new Companies Ordinance (Cap. 622) took effect on 3 March 2014, superseding a substantial amount of the provisions in the old Companies Ordinance (Cap. 32).

The new Companies Ordinance is supplemented by subsidiary legislation, including the Companies (Words and Expressions in Company Names) Order, Companies (Disclosure of Company Name and Liability Status) Regulation, Companies (Accounting Standards (Prescribed Body)) Regulation, Companies (Directors' Report) Regulation, Companies (Summary Financial Reports) Regulation, Companies (Model Articles) Notice, Company Records (Inspection and Provision of Copies) Regulation,

25. Robert C. Art and Minkang Gu, "China Incorporated: The First Corporation Law of the PRC", *Yale Journal of International Law*, Vol. 20, No. 2, 1995, p. 273.

Companies (Revision of Financial Statements and Reports) Regulation, Companies (Disclosure of Benefits about Directors) Regulation, Companies (Fees) Regulation, Companies (Unfair Prejudice Proceedings) Rules, and Companies (Non-Hong Kong Companies) Regulation.[26]

The development of Hong Kong company law has a close connection with Hong Kong's historical status as a colony of the United Kingdom. The development of company law in Hong Kong can be traced back to four distinct periods. The first period covers 1865 to 1948, during which the first Company Ordinance was implemented; the second period covers 1948 to 1984, during which the Companies (Amendment) Ordinance 1984 was introduced; the third period covers 1984 to 2013, during which "a thorough review of the Companies Ordinance was called for in 1994" and "a comprehensive rewrite of the Companies Ordinance was launched in mid-2006"; and the fourth period covers 2014 to today, during which the new Companies Ordinance (Cap. 622) was implemented.[27]

It has been said that Hong Kong company law has been intentionally kept similar to British company law. The Companies Ordinance of 1865 mirrored the English Companies Act of 1862, which incorporated both the Joint Stock Companies Registration and Regulation Act of 1844 and the Limited Liability Act of 1855.[28] The Companies (Amendment) Ordinance of 1991 mirrored the corresponding legislative provisions of the British Companies Act of 1985 with respect to share buybacks, redeemable shares, and dividends, differing only slightly with respect to the issue of financial assistance, which was extended to all public companies in Hong Kong regardless of whether they were listed or not.

However, it is reasonable to think that Hong Kong and British company law will move in different directions in the near future. Hong Kong has become a part of China, and the different legal systems in Hong Kong and on the mainland will be further harmonized. On the other hand, as still a member of the European Union (hereinafter referred to as the "EU"), British legislators will have to modify existing company law in order to accommodate the different legal demands imposed by the EU. As has been observed, EU laws were established predominantly based on continental legal traditions represented by Germany and France. Furthermore, the initial countries that established the European Community (hereinafter referred to

26. Stefan H. C. Lo and Charles Z. Qu, *Law of Companies in Hong Kong*, Sweet & Maxwell (Hong Kong), 2013, pp. 52–53.
27. Ada L. L. Chung, *Charting a New Course*, retrieved from http://www.cr.gov.hk/en/publications/docs/studyreport-foreword-e.pdf on 10 September 2015.
28. K. Arjunan and C. K. Low, *Liption and Herzberg's Understanding Company Law in Hong Kong*, LBC Information Services (North Ryde), 1996, p. 3.

as the "EC") were France, Germany, Italy, Belgium, the Netherlands, and Luxembourg. These countries represent the continental legal system. The United Kingdom was not accepted as a member of the EC until December 1969 (twelve years later).[29] In this situation, the United Kingdom will have to compromise its position of maintaining its own common law system.

Furthermore, according to the Basic Law, company law in Hong Kong will generally remain the same as before even though it became a part of China after 1 July 1997. Under the policy of "One Country, Two Systems", it will be quite difficult to establish a unified economic system shared by both Hong Kong and the mainland; this will not happen for at least fifty years.[30] In this situation, the governments on both sides will have to operate with limitations on their administrative authority. For example, companies in mainland China can be listed on the Hong Kong Stock Exchanges. According to Hong Kong's securities law, those companies should be supervised by the Hong Kong authorities. However, authorities in mainland China also have the power to supervise the companies because they are registered in mainland China. This raises two questions: What would happen if the companies or enterprises of mainland China were to become major listed companies or enterprises on the Hong Kong Stock Exchange, and how would the powers and functions between the Securities and Futures Commission of Hong Kong and Securities Regulatory Commission of China be divided?[31] It would not be desirable for Hong Kong's securities market to become overwhelmingly occupied by companies and enterprises from mainland China, as this would hinder the diversified share listings in Hong Kong. On the other hand, it is necessary to see the convergence and inter-influence between Hong Kong company law and company law in the mainland.

In Hong Kong, company laws are reviewed by the Law Reform Commission from time to time. The Commission was established in January

---

29. Cao Jianming, *The Law of the European Union*, Zhejiang People's Publishing House (Hangzhou), 2000, pp. 6, 8, 83–84. On 23 June 2016, the people of Britain voted for a British exit from the EU through a historic referendum. However, the exit talk between the UK and the EU has not been started to date.
30. Article 5 of the Basic Law states that the socialist system and policies shall not be practised in Hong Kong and the previous capitalist system and way of life shall remain unchanged for fifty years.
31. Zhou Bajun, "The Major Conflicts of a Unified Economy between Hong Kong and Mainland China", *Xinpao Financial News*, 12 April 1999, p. 24. The prediction was made fifteen years ago and the situation has gradually become more worrisome. According to the data released on 31 August 2015, the Hong Kong Stock Exchange had 1,810 listed companies (Main Board or Growth Enterprise Market), with 920 from mainland China, 788 from local jurisdictions, and 102 from other jurisdictions. See HKEx, "Our Markets", retrieved from http://www.hkex.com.hk/eng/listing/listhk/our_markets.htm on 10 September 2015.

1980 and survived after the handover. It considers such reforms of the laws of Hong Kong as may be referred to it by the Secretary for Justice or the Chief Justice. The members of the Commission at present are legal professionals from various institutions and organizations.[32]

It is important to know that company law reformers in Hong Kong will have to consider certain elements. Firstly, Hong Kong is not an easy place to introduce fundamental law changes because of its diverse background and historical past. Secondly, Hong Kong cannot avoid the strong influence of mainland China in the near future. Thus, it is necessary to consider the future of Hong Kong company law and its harmonized relationship with company law in mainland China. One thing is certain: commercial law in both Hong Kong and mainland China became more similar following the adoption of the "Closer Economic Partnership Arrangement" on 30 June 2003 and the mutual recognition and enforcement of judgments in civil and commercial matters in July 2006.[33]

For example, Tsingtao Brewery, the largest brewer in China, is listed in both Hong Kong and Shanghai. Anheuser-Busch, the world's largest brewer, is increasing its ownership in Tsingtao by subscribing US$182 million worth of convertible bonds. Thus, Anheuser-Busch will increase its holding in Tsingtao to 27 per cent over a period of up to seven years.[34] As Tsingtao is listed in both Hong Kong and Shanghai, the deal has takeover implications under both the Hong Kong Takeover Code and the takeover rules on the mainland. The takeover rules in both places should be similar to encourage famous companies to list their shares on both the Hong Kong and Shanghai (or Shenzhen) Stock Exchanges.

VI. A BRIEF INTRODUCTION TO TAIWANESE COMPANY LAW

Company law in Taiwan was developed based on company law in the Qing dynasty (hereinafter referred to as the "Qing Company Law"), which was heavily influenced by the German Commercial Code and Japanese Commercial Code. According to Lin Faxin, the Taiwanese company law has gone through three stages.

32. The Law Reform Commission of Hong Kong, "Commission Members and Staff", retrieved from http://www.hkreform.gov.hk/en/members/members.htm on 10 September 2015.
33. In June 1999, the arrangement to mutually enforce arbitral awards was signed between Hong Kong and the mainland. See Department of Justice, "Enforcement of Civil and Commercial Judgments between Hong Kong and the Mainland", retrieved from http://www.doj.gov.hk/eng/public/enforcement.html on 10 September 2015.
34. David Barbozadec, "World's Largest Brewer Increases China Stake", *Asian Legal Business*, June 2003, p. 6.

The first stage was to invoke the Qing Company Law. On 10 January 1911, the Temporary Government issued an order to the whole country that provisions of the Qing Company Law would be applied if they did not conflict with the existing systems.

The second stage was to make a Company Ordinance (*Gongsi Tiaoli*). In 1941, the government made the Company Ordinance based on amendments to the Qing Company Law. The Company Ordinance was published on 13 January 1914 and contained 251 provisions. Nevertheless, it was adopted through a legislative process and could only be referred to as an "ordinance".

The third stage was to promulgate and reform the Company Law. The Company Law, which is still implemented in Taiwan today, was promulgated on 26 December 1929. The contents of the Company Law indicate that it was a continuation of the Qing Company Law and made based on the Company Ordinance.[35]

Since 1929, Taiwanese Company Law has been modified many times in order to adapt to changing situations. Nevertheless, it has been recognized as having a continental law tradition.

Taiwanese company law has had a great influence on the formation of Chinese company law. For example, the three important principles (the principle of maintaining capital, the principle of not changing capital and the principle of identifying capital) stated in Chinese company law are copied from Taiwanese company law.[36] This situation is understandable, because when the Chinese company law was established, many scholars looked for references only from Taiwan for two reasons: they shared the same culture and traditions, and most mainland scholars at that time were not proficient in foreign languages.

VII. A BRIEF INTRODUCTION TO AMERICAN COMPANY LAW

The United States is one representative country to adopt the common law system. The source of US law is British common law. On the other hand, US laws have been developed independently,[37] and most of its commercial laws have played a leading role around the world.

35. Lin Faxin, *The Comparison of Company Systems in Taiwan and the Mainland* (*Haixia liang'an gongsi zhidu zhi bijiao*), the People's Court Press (Beijing), 1997, pp. 17–18.
36. Fang Liufang, *Gain New Insights through Restudying Old Materials: Comments on Reform of the Company Law*, Guo and Wang, supra note 9, p. 41.
37. There are two aspects showing the independence. Firstly, courts frequently re-explain precedents to adapt to the real circumstance, and the Federal Supreme Court can overrule the precedents it previously made (the United Kingdom started this practice in

In the United States, company law was uncommon before 1800. One author pointed out that "almost all of the colonial corporations were churches, charities or cities or small towns".[38] Before the middle of the nineteenth century, most commercial enterprises took the form of partnerships. These partnerships were small in size and involved two or three partners who were relatives.[39] However, following economic development, entrepreneurs paid more attention to the corporation form because it "was a more efficient way to structure and finance their ventures".[40] In this situation, the special charter system became more troublesome: "It was a waste of the legislature's time as well—or would have been, if in fact each charter was carefully scrutinized".[41] Therefore, the general incorporation laws became in high demand.[42]

The most significant point of United States company law is that incorporation is handled by individual states rather than by the federal government. Each state has the right to promulgate its own company law. Among state company laws, Delaware Corporation Law is the most famous one because of its flexibility, simple procedures, and lower taxes and fees. One scholar pointed out that the United States had a national corporation law: "it is the law of Delaware".[43] In 1950, the American Bar Association proposed a standard company law, which was called the Model Business Corporation Act (which has since been revised). The purpose was to provide a standardized company law for the whole country. So far, substantial contents of the Model Business Corporation Act have been adopted by the majority of US states.

There was a new development in corporate law following the collapse of Enron[44] and other big companies. Because of these scandals, the Sarbanes-Oxley Act of 2002 (hereinafter the "2002 Act") was adopted to govern accountants and directors of public companies in even more restrictive ways

1966). Secondly, many written laws were promulgated at the beginning of independence. See Pan Huafang, *English and American Common Law* (*Ying Mei fa lun*), The Chinese University of Politics and Law (Beijing), 1997, pp. 48–49; and Dong Maoyun, "The Tradition of Case Law of the Common Law System" (*Putong faxi de panli fa chuantong*), retrieved from http://www.gongfa.com/dongmypanlifa.htm on 10 September 2015.

38. Lawrence Friedman, "A History of American Law", in Jesse H. Choper, Hohn C. Coffee, and C. Robert Morris (eds.), *Cases and Materials on Corporations* (3rd ed.), Little, Brown and Company (Boston), 1989, p. 9.
39. Ibid.
40. Ibid.
41. Ibid.
42. Ibid.
43. Lewis S. Black, Jr., "Why Corporations Choose Delaware", retrieved from https://corp.delaware.gov/pdfs/whycorporations_english.pdf on 10 September 2015.
44. The story of Enron is available at CNN Library, Enron Fast Facts, at http://edition.cnn.com/2013/07/02/us/enron-fast-facts/ (10 September 2015).

to prevent public companies from engaging in fraudulent activities. The 2002 Act not only had a great effect on United States companies, but also was significant to China's development of its company and securities law. Dr Wang Jianxi, Deputy Secretary General of the China Securities Regulatory Commission, listed three ways in which the 2002 Act was important to China: "it is important to accounting practice, to the regulation of the capital market and to the Chinese companies listed in the USA."[45] The 2002 Act states that foreign firms are subject to its regulations, and as many Chinese companies engaging in oil, telecommunications, power, and Internet businesses are listed on the New York Stock Exchange and Nasdaq, these companies cannot be exempted from its impact.[46] Thus, it is fair to state that the problem for China becomes more than a corporate governance issue. One important resolution made was to further cope with the market economy in order to survive various challenges in foreign markets. Nevertheless, it must be noted that the 2002 Act will help to establish even healthier corporate governance and set a good example for the whole world.

45. "Corporate Governance in the Wake of Enron: From Failure to Reform", retrieved from http://www6.cityu.edu.hk/puo/CityUMember/Story/Story.aspx?id=20040903000016 on 10 September 2015.
46. Ibid.

2

Nature of Companies

I. DEFINITION OF COMPANIES

1. Differences between a "Company" and a "Corporation"

In common law jurisdictions, differences may exist between a company and a corporation. The word "company" does not contain certain legal meaning. In fact, every association that is formed for certain goals can be called a company regardless of whether it intends to make profits or not, and whether it is a legal person or not. Sometimes, the term "company" can be used to refer to not only a big corporation with legal person status, but also a partnership organization or another association.[1]

However, the word "corporation" is often regarded as a legal term, which may contain following four meanings:

- it is a municipal corporation established by the state and has bi-legal status under both public and private law;
- it is a corporate sole formed by one person or his or her heir to obtain a legal competency or some privileges, such as an archbishop or a cardinal;

1. In Hong Kong, partnership firms are often referred to as companies. Article 1(4) of the Agreement between Japan and the People's Republic of China concerning the Encouragement and Reciprocal Protection of Investment defines companies as: (a) in relation to Japan, corporations, partnerships, companies and associations whether or not with limited liability, whether or not with legal personality and whether or not for pecuniary profit; and (b) in relation to the People's Republic of China, enterprises, other economic organizations and associations.

- it is a non-profit corporation formed to engage in a charity, education or scientific research; and
- it is a business corporation formed with the goal of making profit.

Today, people use these two words ("company" and "corporation") interchangeably. For example, the Delaware General Corporation Law provides that the name of a corporation shall contain one of the following words: "association, company, corporation, club, foundation, fund, incorporated, institute, society, union, syndicate, or limited" [Sec. 102(a)(1)]. Nevertheless, it is necessary to bear in mind that only a business corporation or a business company is the focus of this book.

2. The Legal Definitions of "Company"

Reading Chinese company law, one cannot possibly determine the specific definition of a company. Article 2 of the 2013 Company Law provides the following description:

> The term "company" as mentioned in this Law refers to a limited liability company or a joint stock company limited set up within the territory of the People's Republic of China according to the provisions of this Law.

Interestingly, the Hong Kong Companies Ordinance adopts the same approach by not defining the meaning of a company. Section 2(1) of the Companies Ordinance states that the term "companies" shall mean companies formed and registered under the Ordinance or existing companies. In the United States, the Revised Modern Business Corporation Act states that a corporation is a for-profit corporation, which is not a foreign corporation, incorporated under or subject to the provisions of the act [Sec. 1.40(1)]. This simple definition is not helpful for the purpose of theoretic research. From the perspective of written law tradition, it is a rare situation when a written law fails to define the concept of a company. The only possible reason is that the legislators want to leave more room for defining various business associations. Normally, the duties of a company are imposed on a business association if it is deemed to be a company.

However, the silence of both the Chinese company law and the Hong Kong company law on the concept of a company does not mean that it is impossible to obtain a definition of a company. For example, Article 2 of the Provisional Regulations on Management of Company Registration[2]

2. This law was issued by the State Council in 1985.

(hereinafter referred to as the "Registration Regulations") defines a company as an economic entity formed in accordance with the Registration Regulations to engage in production and services. Furthermore, a company has an independent property right and autonomy in management and shall take full responsibility for its profits and losses. Here, however, one problem remains. It is evident that under Article 2 of the Law of the People's Republic of China on Industrial Enterprises Owned by the Whole People, that the definition of a wholly state-owned enterprise is almost the same as the definition of a company. In other words, the definition provided by the Registration Regulations does not necessarily reflect the exact meaning of a company.

The comparative law approach may help to clarify the true meaning of a company. Firstly, Taiwanese company law provides a clear definition of a company. Article 1 states that a company is an organization with legal person status (*shetuan faren*) organized, registered, and established in accordance with the Law for the purpose of profit. Other Western countries, especially continental countries, treat a company as a for-profit enterprise formed under national company law. For example, the French Civil Code states that a company is an enterprise formed by more than two persons through an agreement under which all the parties of the agreement are required to make their investments in the form of property or skills, and all the parties share the profits and interests generated by the operation.[3]

Based on the above descriptions, it is possible to conclude that a company should contain at least four elements.

(1) Domestic Company Law Is the Controlling Law

A company is formed under a particular national company law.[4] All companies must be established in accordance with relevant national company law because they are traditionally subjected to control by a national sovereignty. Furthermore, the establishment of a company requires a registration process. For example, Article 3 of the Administrative Rules of the People's Republic of China Governing the Registration of Companies states, "A company shall be granted legal person status only after it has been registered and issued with a 'Corporate Business Licence' subject to an examination and approval by a company registration authority in accordance with this Law."

3. Article 1832. The translation was carried out in accordance with the Chinese version of the French Civil Code. See Bian Yaowu (ed.), *Contemporary Foreign Company Law* (*Dangdai waiguo gongsifa*), The Law Press (Beijing), 1996, p. 367.
4. In the United States, state corporate law is the governing law.

Having stated this, it is necessary to know that there is a tendency to internationalize domestic company laws. One example is that company laws in the Member States of the European Union (hereinafter referred to as the "EU") have to be compatible with the EU Company Law.[5] Another example is that the Organization for Economic Cooperation and Development (hereinafter referred to as the "OECD") promotes its Principles of Corporate Governance, which all of its Member States should consider.[6]

(2) A Company Is an Independent Legal Person

It is generally recognized that every company should be granted legal person status. However, it is not correct to state that other business organizations cannot be treated as legal persons because diversity remains when defining a legal person. This is due to the different legal systems in common law jurisdictions and in continental law jurisdictions. In common law jurisdictions, it is true that only a company can be regarded as an independent legal person, while a partnership or a sole proprietorship does not enjoy legal person status.[7] However, in continental law jurisdictions, the definition of a legal person may broadly include not only companies, but also other business associations. This may be a matter of vocabulary because in common law jurisdictions differences exist between a company and a firm, and the latter cannot qualify as a company. In continental law jurisdictions such as France and Germany, the word "*société*" or "*Gesellschaft*" may include not only companies but also partnerships. Furthermore, in France, a *société* can also enjoy legal person status. For this reason, Article 48 of the Treaty Establishing the European Community states, "Companies or firms means companies or firms constituted under civil or commercial law, including co-operative societies, and other legal persons governed by public or private law, save for those which are nonprofit-making."

In China, a legal person has a unique character, and the term can refer to either a company or a State-owned enterprise, which is established under laws other than the Chinese company law. Furthermore, a legal person can be considered as either an enterprise legal person, which operates for profit, or an institutional legal person, which is a non-profit institution. Thus,

5. It has been well established in the EU that when there is a conflict between EU law and the law of the Member States, the EU law prevails.
6. The full text of the OECD Principles of Corporate Governance is available online. OECD, "G20/OECD Principles of Corporate Governance", retrieved from http://www.oecd.org/corporate/principles-corporate-governance.htm on 11 September 2015.
7. Please see the relevant changes in this chapter.

when the term "legal person" is used, it is necessary to identify whether it refers to a company or another association.

(3) A Company Is a Business Corporation

A company shall be considered as a business corporation, which is generally established by two or more shareholders. However, this element has been challenged recently because one-person companies have become more popular in many jurisdictions.[8] In China, there are disguised one-person companies, i.e., wholly state-owned companies, which are invested in solely by the state. The 2005 Company Law for the first time authorizes the establishment of one-person LLCs, and this will rapidly stimulate the quick development of the market economy. Many Western countries used to hold a negative attitude towards one-person LLCs because of their obvious flaws, such as their lack of a checks-and-balances mechanism, the easy mixture of shareholders' own property with the company's property and their abuse of corporate legal person status. That is why company law in the United Kingdom and other jurisdictions provides the doctrine of lifting the corporate veil. In continent law jurisdictions, commercial laws usually define a company as a juridical association. Even though the Chinese Civil Law does not use this term, scholars use it frequently. The negative attitude towards one-person companies also resulted due to a worry that the definition of a juridical association would change.

Nevertheless, one-person LLCs are now widely adopted by more and more countries and regions. That shows the existing value of this type of company. It is further believed that perfecting the corporate system will make it possible to prevent this type of company from being abused.

In the next chapter, wholly state-owned and one-person companies are discussed in detail.

(4) A Company Is Formed to Make a Profit

In China, non-profit-making companies are not the target of the Chinese company law even though in some other jurisdictions (for example in Hong Kong) company law may cover some non-profit-making companies.

8. Examples of a one-person company can be seen in several countries, such as Germany, France, Japan, Canada, and Denmark. Furthermore, it is important to note that in Germany, Japan, and Canada, a one-person company is allowed for both LLCs and joint stock companies.

Nevertheless, it is certain that the non-profit-making companies cannot be regarded as traditional business companies.

3. A Company versus a Partnership

Since 1993, three internationally recognized business vehicles have been formally adopted in China: the sole proprietorship, partnership, and company. Each can be used based on different intentions and financial conditions. In other words, different business forms are chosen because each may contain advantages and disadvantages.

The Law of Sole Proprietorship Enterprises of the People's Republic of China[9] defines a sole proprietorship as a business entity established within China and invested in by one natural person. The property of a sole proprietorship is personally owned by the investor, who shall assume unlimited liabilities for the debts of the enterprise with his or her personal property.[10]

So far in China, the sole proprietorship is considered the simplest and most flexible business form for running business activities simply due to its easy formation and operation. Certainly, the most important advantage is its single taxation. According to relevant rules, the taxable amount shall be the remainder after the deduction of costs, expenses, and losses from its gross income in a tax year with reference to the standard of individual income tax rates.[11]

On the other hand, the disadvantages of the sole proprietorship are obvious. Firstly, the owner's liability is unlimited, and the business owner is personally liable for the debts of his or her business enterprise. Secondly, the sole proprietorship is chosen mainly due to the limitations of investor assets. Therefore, the size of an enterprise may exclude its possibility of raising capital. Thirdly, there is a limit life to the enterprise. The enterprise will be terminated as soon as the owner is incapable or dead.

It is generally recognized that companies are developed from partnership businesses. It has been said that without sole proprietorships, there would be no partnerships; furthermore, without partnerships, it would be impossible to create companies.[12] What is a partnership then? Article 30 of

9. The Law of Sole Proprietorship Enterprises of the People's Republic of China was adopted at the eleventh meeting of the Standing Committee of the Ninth NPC on 30 August 1999 and promulgated on the same day.
10. The Law of Sole Proprietorship Enterprises of the People's Republic of China, Article 2.
11. The Circular of the State Council concerning Issues of Taxation of Sole Proprietorship and Partnership, published in 2000.
12. Liu Xinghu, *Research on Legal Issues of Joint Stock Companies (Gufen youxian gongsi falü wenti yanjiu)*, The Chinese Procuratorial Press (Beijing), 1998, p. 2.

the Chinese Civil Law[13] states that the term "partnership of individuals" shall mean two or more persons, who in accordance with an agreement contribute funds, property, skills, and the like and operate in partnership and work jointly in a business. This is a very narrow and perhaps incorrect definition. In general, a partnership shall mean a business entity established by more than two persons (who may also be legal persons) to engage in business with a view to making a profit. On 23 February 1997, the first national partnership law, the Partnership Enterprise Law of the People's Republic of China (hereinafter referred to as the "Partnership Law") was promulgated.[14] Article 2 of the Partnership Law provided the definition of a partnership enterprise, which was similar to the general idea of a partnership in that it referred to a profit-making organization established within Chinese territory in accordance with the provisions of the Law. However, when the Partnership Law was promulgated, it made no reference to the Ministry of Foreign Trade and Economic Cooperation,[15] and neither did it address the relationship between the partnership enterprises and existing foreign-involved cooperative joint ventures. An additional problem was that this Law indicated the government would tax partnerships. Thus, in China, partners had to undertake unlimited liability while being subject to taxation at two levels.[16] Obviously, this tax provision was not consistent with the general theory of a partnership in other jurisdictions, where unlimited liability was accepted as the price for avoiding double taxation. The Partnership Law was amended in 2006, and the new Article 2 states that the term "partnership enterprise" refers to the general and limited liability partnership enterprises established within China by natural persons, legal persons and other organizations in accordance with the Law. At the same time, Article 6 confirms that "for the production and business operation incomes and other incomes of a partnership enterprise, the partners shall pay their respective income tax in accordance with the relevant tax provisions of the state". This means that the single tax applies to partnership enterprises today.

As discussed before, the company system was developed based on the partnership system because they share the following similarities.

13. The General Principles of the Civil Law of the People's Republic of China was adopted by the fourth session of the sixth NPC on 12 April 1986 and amended on 27 August 2009.
14. It was amended at the twenty-third session of the Standing Committee of the Tenth NPC on 27 August 2006.
15. It has been absorbed by a newly established authority, the Ministry of Commerce.
16. N. C. Howson, "Flood Legislation Clears the Way for a New Corporation Form—But Are They Worth It?" *China Joint Venture*, July/August 1997, p. 11.

- Both systems were established for the purpose of making a profit.
- Both systems may require two or more persons[17] to contribute a certain amount of capital, although in the situation of a partnership the capital contribution may be more flexible. Thus, the members in a partnership are named "partners" and the members in a company are named "shareholders".
- The profits shall be shared by members in both entities in accordance with their capital contributions or agreements.
- Both unlimited companies and partnerships share similar structures and liabilities. Therefore, in some countries, unlimited companies are allowed to apply regulations to partnerships (as in Germany and England).

However, there are many differences between a company and a partnership.

(1) Establishment

A company is established through registration in accordance with national company law. It must comply with a number of statutory formalities, such as the preparation of a written memorandum of association (and/or the articles of association) and the payment of a registration fee. A partnership is created by an agreement between partners. No fees are payable other than those that must be paid by all business enterprises under the relevant laws regardless of their corporate status. The partnership agreement needs not be in writing, although in practice many partnerships prefer to rely on written agreements, which in those cases must be adopted by all partners.

(2) Legal Status

A company is recognized as a legal person with a separate legal identity. Compared with a partnership, it has the following effects.

(a) In a company situation, all property contributed by shareholders is vested in the company, and once shareholders invest their property in a company, they are no longer the owners of the property. In a partnership situation, all of the property continues to belong to the individual partners.

17. Except one-person companies.

(b) A company can make contracts and incur debts on its own behalf, and that is why a company can be called an artificial person. A partnership does not act on its own behalf and every partner is jointly and severally liable for the firm's debts and contracts.
(c) Unless a company is wound up or made bankrupt, it has a perpetual succession. However, the continuation of a partnership depends on the terms of the partnership agreement. If no agreement to the contrary is made, then the partnership is dissolved upon the death or bankruptcy of any partner.
(d) A company can sue and be sued in its own name due to its legal person status. In contrast, even if the firm's name can be used in any legal action, the partners are jointly and severally liable. Therefore, a partnership is not a legal person. (In France, Article 1842 of the French Civil Code gives a partnership a legal person status. This is considered an exception.)

(3) Transfer of Ownership

Shares in a public company can be freely transferred and their ownership by shareholders can change hands easily. On the other hand, private companies are more restricted, as they must impose certain limitations on the transfer of shares in the articles of association. Despite those limitations, the ownership of shareholders can nevertheless be changed if certain conditions are satisfied. In the partnership situation, new partners cannot be added unless all of the partners agree to such changes.

(4) Management

Members of a company have no automatic right to be involved in the management of the company unless they are elected as directors or supervisors. Although members do have the right to vote on certain resolutions, including the appointment of directors or supervisors, in practice the members of a small private company are often the managers of the business. Members of a public company are often completely divorced from the management of the company and regard their shares as an investment rather than as a stake in the ownership of the business. The partners, on the other hand, run a partnership in a democratic manner, subject to the terms of the partnership agreement. Usually all partners will be fully involved in the management process.

(5) Agent and Principal

A member of a company is not automatically an agent of the company unless he or she acts under a separate agent agreement. In the partnership situation, each partner is the agent of the other partners and the firm.

(6) Termination

It is commonly recognized that one member alone cannot wind up a company while a single member can dissolve a partnership.

In general, a company is a comparatively higher level business form but not a perfect one. There are, however, several disadvantages for incorporating companies. All registered companies are required to disclose certain information to the public, and this may lead to administrative expenses in the form of registration and filing fees. Most importantly, all companies are bound to have their accounts audited annually, and there is a need to pay audit fees.[18] Thus, individuals need to consider both the advantages and disadvantages before they choose a suitable business vehicle.

II. TYPES OF COMPANIES

1. Companies in China

As mentioned in the previous chapter, there were five forms of companies in China during the 1950s. When the first national company law was being drafted, however, many people suggested the provision of unlimited companies and joint liability companies in addition to the two popular company forms, i.e., LLCs and joint stock companies (known to some as companies limited by shares). Some people suggested that since China had already had certain amounts of private enterprises formed by individuals and families, those enterprises should be treated as unlimited companies. Some also suggested adding into the Chinese company law joint stock cooperative companies,[19] which first appeared in towns and villages in the 1980s. Eventually, these suggestions were not adopted by legislators on the

18. Vanessa Stott, *Hong Kong Company Law* (9th ed.), Financial Times (Hong Kong), 2000, p. 14.
19. Joint stock cooperative companies are the new form of enterprise organization in China. It is not yet fully developed or well understood outside the country, but it is uniquely well suited to Chinese ideological and economic characteristics. This book does not formally discuss this type of company. For detailed information, see Gu Minkang, "The Joint Stock Cooperative Enterprise: A New Independent Legal Entity in China", *The Hastings International and Comparative Law Review*, Vol. 23, No. 1, 1999, pp. 125–48.

basis that unlimited companies and joint liability companies had almost no practical benefit in China, while joint stock co-operative companies had just emerged in the country and there was not enough experience to deal with them. From a legal standpoint, Chinese company law deals with only two types of company. However, it is not correct to say that other types of company created later by other rules and regulations will have nothing to do with the Chinese company law. Apparently, the Chinese company law has not been amended to account for other company forms. For example, joint stock cooperative companies have been officially endorsed in China since the Fifteenth Party Congress in 1997. So far, there is no sign that the Chinese company law will be used to govern joint stock cooperative companies, because they are currently governed by various national and local regulations. Thus, determining how to reconcile this situation is important and significant for the future development of Chinese company law.

An LLC is usually recognized as a "private" or "closed" company, and a joint stock company is recognized as a "public" or "open" company. Furthermore, it is important to note that a "public company" is different from a "listed company". A listed company is one whose shares are traded on the stock exchanges, while a public company is one whose shares are issued to the public but are not necessary traded on the stock exchanges. Because of this difference, it is correct to say that every listed company is a public company, but not vice versa. As will be discussed later, the term "limited liability company" has different meanings in Hong Kong and mainland China. Without identifying this difference, Hong Kong businesspeople would be confused when they engage in businesses or corporate activities in mainland China.

In line with the 2013 Company Law, an LLC is a company whose shareholders assume an amount equivalent to the amount of contributed capital to offset its total assets against the responsibility assumed for company debt (Article 3). On the other hand, a joint stock company is a company whose total capital is divided equally with shares of equivalent value to offset its total assets against the responsibility assumed for company debt (Article 3). In addition to these two types of company, a listed company is a joint stock company whose shares will be traded over stock exchanges (Article 120). Thus, a listed company must satisfy not only the requirements of a joint stock company, but also the following additional requirements:

(a) it must have a complete and well-operated organization;
(b) it must have the capability of making profits continuously and maintaining a sound financial status;

(c) it must have no false record in its financial statements over the previous three years and no other major irregularity; and
(d) it must meet any other requirements as prescribed by the securities regulatory authority approved by the State Council.[20]

2. Companies in Hong Kong

According to Sections 7, 8, 9, and 10 of the Hong Kong Companies Ordinance (Cap. 622), companies can be divided into limited companies and unlimited companies. Limited companies can be further divided into companies limited by shares and companies limited by guarantee.

(1) A Company Limited by Shares

A company limited by shares is formed on the principle that the liability of its members is limited by the amount of shares for which they promised to pay. As the members of a company limited by shares have limited liability, the creditors of such a company do not have access to the personal property of the members to satisfy their debts.

(2) A Company Limited by Guarantee

In Hong Kong, a company limited by guarantee refers to a company whose shareholders guarantee their contribution but are required to make such a contribution only upon the request of the company. It can be further divided into the following companies.

(a) A Company with No Share Capital

This company is formed based on the principle of having the liability of its members limited by the company's articles to the respective amounts that the members undertake to contribute to the property of the company in the event of it being wound up. Members are not required to contribute capital while the company is operating. However, in the event of the company being wound up and its assets being insufficient to meet its liabilities, its members are liable to pay up to the amount specified in the articles as the members guaranteed. Such companies are very rarely used for the purpose of trading, as they do not raise initial or working capital from their members. However, this type of company may be convenient for clubs and other non-trading

20. Securities Law of the People's Republic of China (2014 Amendment), Article 13.

companies (charities and quasi-charitable organizations such as schools and hospitals), whose capital needs can be met from outside courses, subscriptions, and social activities. This type of company is usually engaged in non-profit activities and does not require a large amount of money. Thus, by soliciting a promise or a guarantee from its members, the company can acquire sufficient credibility to engage in its relevant activities.

(b) A Company with Share Capital

In the past, Hong Kong allowed this type of company. A member of such a company was liable to pay the amount, if any, unpaid on any shares he or she held, in addition to meeting his or her guaranteed contribution of a specified amount in the event the company was wound up. However, in practice, such companies were rare, and based on the recommendation of the Standing Committee on Company Law Reform, this type of company was abolished after 13 February 2004.[21]

(3) Unlimited Liability Companies

When a company is registered as an unlimited company, its members are personally liable for the debts of the company without limit. An unlimited company may be preferable to a partnership because of its perpetual succession and organizational structure. In comparison, it is hard to understand why businesspeople would want to form a company with unlimited liability today. Company law experts have said that the motivation for establishing this type of company was to maintain the gentleman's mentality. In the old days, many companies were formed by gentlemen who did not want to shield their liability for their companies. They wanted to be responsible for all of the consequences caused by their activities. Today, unlimited liability companies have lost all of their advantages and are rarely seen.

In Hong Kong, companies can also be divided into private companies and public companies. Private companies are suitable tools for engaging in small business and are intended for situations where the members are also the managers of the company. A private company is defined by Section 11(1) as a company which by its articles:

(a) restricts the right to transfer its shares;
(b) limits the number of its members to fifty;[22] and

21. Stefan H. C. Lo and Charles Z. Qu, *Law of Companies in Hong Kong*, Sweet & Maxwell (Hong Kong), 2013, pp. 87–88.
22. Section 29(1)(b) of old Companies Ordinance (Cap. 32) states that fifty members were "not including employees of the company and former employees who were members of

(c) prohibits any invitation to the public to subscribe for any shares or debentures in the company.

If a company's articles of association fail to satisfy the requirements of Section 11(1), then it is a public company, although the term "public company" is not actually used in or defined by the Ordinance. In fact, a "public company" is a company "held by members of the general public".[23]

3. Companies in the United States

There have traditionally been two types of company in the United States: closely held companies (similar to private companies in Hong Kong) and publically held companies. It is true that the double tax structure applicable to corporations resulted in serious increases in economic costs in the United States. This should be the major motivation to create new company forms, i.e., S corporations and LLCs in addition to C corporations.

Very differently, an LLC is treated as an unincorporated business entity with two or more owners (called members) that is organized under an LLC statute. It affords all its members corporate-like limited liability, can allow its members to actively participate in the management of the business and can be structured to be taxed like a partnership for federal and state income tax purposes (there is a single "pass through" tax at the individual rates, i.e., only owners of the business pay the tax).[24] In 1957, the US Congress created a special tax election for certain closely held corporations, the so-called S corporation election. This election permits most corporations with fewer than thirty-five shareholders to elect to be taxed in a manner that generally permits income to be passed through the corporation and shareholders are taxed directly. To be eligible for subchapter S, a corporation must meet the following conditions on the date of election:

(a) it must be a domestic corporation;
(b) it must not be part of an affiliated group of corporations;
(c) it must have no more than seventy-five shareholders;

the company whilst employed and who have continued to be members". It is unclear whether this exception is no longer available.

23. Robert W. Hamilton, *The Law of Corporations in a Nutshell* (4th ed.), West Publishing (St. Paul, MN), 1996, p. 22.

24. One author believed this was "the most astonishing development in the area of business forms in the 1990s". Robert W. Hamilton, *Business Organizations: Unincorporated Businesses and Closely Held Corporations*, Aspen Law & Business (New York), 1996, p. 123. This type of company is introduced in a subsequent chapter.

(d) each shareholder must be an individual, a descendant's estate, or a certain type of trust and no shareholder may be a non-resident alien; and
(e) it may have only one class of stock outstanding.[25]

Therefore, a corporation that is ineligible for or has not elected to be an "S corporation" is called a "C corporation". A C corporation must pay "double tax", but it has no limitation on the number of shareholders or the types of shareholder, and it can have either subsidiaries or corporate shareholders.

4. Companies in Taiwan

In Taiwan, there are four types of company, i.e., unlimited liability companies, LLCs, companies formed by one or more shareholders with unlimited liability and one or more shareholders with limited liability (*lianghe gongsi*), and joint stock companies. Before 1980, some companies in Taiwan were formed by one or more shareholders with unlimited liability and one or more shareholders with liability limited to their share contributions, and the company capital was divided into equal shares (*gufen lianghe gongsi*). Because of their unpopularity, these companies were eventually abolished in Taiwan.[26]

5. Summary and Comments

Both in Hong Kong and mainland China, the term "company limited by shares" is used but means different things. In Hong Kong, a company limited by shares can be a private company (a closed company) or a public company (an open company), while in mainland China a company limited by shares (or a joint stock company) is legally a public company. In addition, an LLC in mainland China is a typical closed company that is different from an American LLC. Readers should develop a clear picture of the differences when studying the Chinese company law.

It is also clear that the choice of company forms in China is relatively limited, perhaps due to the short history of the Chinese company law.

25. Ibid., p. 271.
26. One can still see this type of company in Germany and France. Lin Faxin, *The Comparison of Company Systems in Taiwan and the Mainland* (*Haixia liang an gongsi zhidu zhi bijiao*), The People's Court Press (Beijing), 1997, p. 34.

There used to be a hot debate on whether China should adopt American-type LLCs. It is generally accepted that the American LLC is a hybrid of a company, a partnership, and a sole proprietorship. These LLCs were first seen in the Wyoming in 1977 and were created based on the idea of German GmbH (*Gesellschaft mit beschränkter Haftung*).[27] According to the Wyoming LLC Act, an LLC shall possess the following characteristics: (1) limited liability, (2) full juristic personality, (3) limited membership, and (4) dissolution by the death of a member.[28] The American LLC is attractive because it boasts the following obvious advantages:

- there is no limit to the membership of an LLC and it can be established by one natural person, which is similar to a one-person company in China;
- members enjoy limit liability;
- LLCs are not subject to double taxation;
- members may need not to give administrative power to the board of directors, and shareholders' meetings may not be held once a year: there are a few administrative documents and records; and
- members can transfer their interests amongst themselves.

Despite those advantages, the LLC in the United States is a relatively new business form and has received legal reorganization in all states only for several years. Therefore, LLCs may vary across the states because there is no uniform understanding of their nature. In some states, LLCs are given a full juristic personality (e.g., see the Virginia LLC Act) while in other states, case law may not consider LLCs as having legal person status (e.g., cases in Washington, DC). Some other disadvantages exist: (1) in order to establish an LLC, special fees must be paid to the state to enjoy the benefit of limited liability; (2) LLCs may face difficulty in raising financial capital due to the small size of their operations; (3) even though an operating agreement is not required, operating without it may create more disputes; (4) operation without a board of directors may cause corporate governance problems; and (5) the principals use different titles such as member, managing member, managing director, chief executive officer, and president, which may cause confusion as outsiders may not be able to identify who has the power to enter into contracts on behalf of the LLC.[29]

---

27. "LLC History", retrieved from http://www.llc-reporter.com/16.htm on 13 September 2015.
28. For detailed information, please see "Wyoming LLC Act", retrieved from https://www.wyomingra.com/wyoming-limited-liability-company-act/ on 13 September 2015.
29. Wikipedia, "Limited Liability Company", retrieved from http://en.wikipedia.org/wiki/Limited_liability_company on 13 September 2015.

Thus, it is obvious that American LLCs are different from Chinese LLCs. More precisely, Chinese LLCs are similar to American closed companies, for which "there is no established way for an outside investor to invest in the business and no assurance that current owners can sell their ownership interests and exit from the business".[30] Scholars have pointed out three additional characteristics. (1) Unlike public companies, a closed company is usually run by one majority shareholder (or a group of shareholders who cooperatively form the majority) and its board of directors is controlled by the majority shareholder. (2) Unlike the shareholders of public companies, the shareholders of closed companies own only the shares of closed companies, rather than diversified securities portfolios. (3) Unlike public companies, highly personal and family relationships often have an influence on corporate decisions, a unique feature of closed companies.[31]

In comparison, there are several differences between American LLCs and Chinese LLCs. (1) Members of Chinese LLCs cannot exceed the shareholder limit. Article 24 of the 2013 Company Law allows a maximum of fifty shareholders. On the contrary, American LLCs can have hundreds or thousands of members.[32] (2) Chinese LLCs require the establishment of an internal administrative structure. In a normal situation, an LLC shall establish a shareholders' meeting, a board of directors and a board of supervisors.[33] On the other hand, an American LLC may choose to be managed by either members or managers.[34] (3) Chinese LLCs need to pay double taxes while single tax is the main purpose of establishing American LLCs. (4) Chinese LLCs have a perpetual life while American LLCs are relatively unstable.

Following this detailed introduction, it is necessary to consider whether China should adopt American LLCs.

Generally, the market economy may require diversified business forms to suit the needs of different businesspeople. However, this does not necessarily mean that American LLCs should be imported into China immediately. One important consideration is that the Chinese company law has a short history and needs more time to develop healthily. In addition, China has allowed the existence of one-person LLCs, sole proprietorship enterprises, and limited liability partnership enterprises. If American LLCs had been blindly imported, the existing structure between companies and

30. Robert W. Hamilton and Richard A. Booth, *Business Basics for Law Students* (2nd ed.), Aspen Law & Business (New York), 1998, p. 259.
31. Hamilton, supra note 25, pp. 185–86.
32. Ibid., p. 124.
33. The 2013 Company Law, Chapter 2.
34. Wikipedia, supra note 29.

non-corporate enterprises would have been dramatically shaken and the tax system would have been abnormally affected.

Furthermore, various forms of business enterprise have been established thanks to the open door policy and the creation of relevant rules and regulations. However, permission for the co-existence of different types of business enterprises, which are governed by three different sets of laws and regulations, has created a chaotic situation. The first series of laws and regulations governs business enterprises based on the nature of their ownership, i.e., whether they are state, collectively, or privately owned. The second series of laws and regulations governs business enterprises that are similar to those in other jurisdictions, i.e., companies, partnerships, and sole proprietorships. The third series of laws and regulations governs business enterprises that involve foreign investors, e.g., equity joint ventures, contractual joint ventures, and wholly foreign-owned enterprises.[35] Following the accession to the WTO and implementation of the market economy, China will inevitably restructure those laws and regulations to create uniform business laws and regulations. Before this goal can be achieved, the importation of American LLCs may produce further confusion without good preparation.

On the other hand, after the LLC was adopted in Wyoming, the Internal Revenue Service "took over ten years to acknowledge the consequences of its own tax classification regulations",[36] and as a result of this LLCs have been adopted across the whole country. In 1997, the Japanese Commercial Law Society, for the first time, suggested the adoption of American LLC. However, the adoption took ten years of preparation. On 1 May 2006, the Japanese Company Law formally adopted the American LLC and renamed it the "Contractual Company".[37] However, the Law lists only three requirements: (1) the company must have the legal person qualification, (2) its shareholders must bear limited liability, and (3) its internal structure can be freely decided. Interestingly, the requirement that only shareholders pay tax was put in the Annex of Law Commission of the Upper House and treated

35. Gu Minkang, "Chinese Business Enterprise Law in the Twenty-first Century", in Joseph Y. S. Cheng (ed.), *China's Challenges in the Twenty-first Century*, City University of Hong Kong Press (Hong Kong), 2003, pp. 452–53.
36. Daniel S. Kleinberger, "Two Decades of 'Alternative Entities': From Tax Rationalization through Alphabet Soup to Contract as Deity", paper presented to the 21st Century Commercial Law Forum: Modern Development of the Law of Non-incorporated Enterprises, organized by Tsinghua University (Beijing) on 20–21 October 2007, p. 5.
37. Yoshida Masayuki, "The Introduction to Contractual Company in Japan", paper presented to the 21st Century Commercial Law Forum: Modern Development of the Law of Non-incorporated Enterprises, organized by Tsinghua University (Beijing) on 20–21 October 2007, p. 424.

as a special consideration.[38] South Korea decided to follow the Japanese way to adopt the American LLC. However, it could not avoid a theoretical problem: under Chapter 3 of the Korean Commercial Law, only the LLC can enjoy the tax treatment as a partnership, and other companies cannot enjoy this benefit solely due to their legal person status.[39] A recent study commissioned by the Dutch Ministry of Justice concluded that there was no need for the introduction of hybrid legal forms for the following reasons.

Firstly, the introduction of a new legal form requires a clear definition which could differentiate from existing forms. As seen in the United States, the distinction between an LLP and an LLC is an important question.

Secondly, it is not expedient to introduce one or more new business forms at a time when the law is made subject to reforms.[40]

The Dutch position is useful to China because China is also facing the problem of improving its business laws. Furthermore, America has not only destroyed the clear distinction between various business forms, but also, through the contractual nature of the LLC, abandoned the important concept of fiduciary duty. For example, Section 18-1101(b) of the Delaware Limited Liability Company Act states that "it is the policy of this chapter to give the maximum effect to the principle of freedom of contract and to the enforceability of limited liability company agreements". It is generally recognized that fiduciary duty is the most important part of traditional company law. Through the agreements, members of LLCs are able to eliminate fiduciary duty. Because of this change, it is not clear what the future direction of company law theory is. Therefore, it is possible to say that the creation of an LLC may to some degree harm the interests of creditors, as well as of other members of companies. Those parties must be well educated by the concept of *caveat emptor*.

Another acceptable theory against the adoption of the American LLC is that the German LLC was used as the model when the LLC was created in the United States. It is not proper to import this hybrid form, which would affect the current company framework. In other words, just because the US company law does not provide a supervisory board system does not

38. Ibid.
39. Junesun Choi, "Introduction of New Types of Business Organization in Korea", paper presented to the 21st Century Commercial Law Forum: Modern Development of the Law of Non-incorporated Enterprises, organized by Tsinghua University (Beijing) on 20–21 October 2007, p. 116.
40. Loes Lennarts, "A Dutch View on the Need for Hybrid Legal Forms", paper presented to the 21st Century Commercial Law Forum: Modern Development of the Law of Non-incorporated Enterprises, organized by Tsinghua University (Beijing) on 20–21 October 2007, p. 159.

mean that Chinese company law must follow the approach by abolishing supervisory boards.

Last but not least, the LLC in the USA is also in the process of developing. Sometimes, when a LLC's status is not clear, courts in the United States consider the principles of company or partnership law. Sometime, because the LLCs can be divided into two types, i.e., member-managed LLCs and manager-managed LLCs, it may be uncertain whether securities law could be applied to LLCs because in the situation of a member-managed LLC, it would be considered as partnership and the agreement signed by partners would not be considered as an "investment contract", which is a part of securities.[41]

Thus, China should carefully consider the importation of the American LLC at this stage.

III. NATURE OF COMPANIES

1. Legal Definition

Article 3 of the 2013 Company Law provides that a "limited liability company" or "joint stock company" is an enterprise legal person.

Article 41 of the Chinese Civil Law mentions only two types of enterprise legal persons (state-owned and collectively-owned enterprises), which are considered outdated. In this circumstance, the Chinese company law and other relevant laws shall be utilized to fill in the gap. Currently in China, there exist many different types of enterprise legal persons, i.e., state-owned enterprises, collectively owned enterprises, privately owned enterprises, jointly owned enterprises, and foreign-invested enterprises. China has adopted a bi-system for different business organizations. State-owned enterprises, collectively owned enterprises, and privately owned enterprises are based on the ownership of investors, while companies, partnerships, and sole proprietorships are relatively new business forms created in the 1990s.

Furthermore, readers should bear in mind that the intention of forming an enterprise legal person is to engage in economic activities and make profits. Therefore, the enterprise legal person should be different from other types of legal persons. For example, Article 50 of the Chinese Civil Law states, "A government agency with independent funds enjoys the status of a legal person from the day when it is established; that an institution or association which satisfies the requirements for legal persons, and is not required by law to register as a legal person, acquires the status of a legal

41. *Williamson* v. *Tucker*, 645 F.2d 404 (5th Cir.), cert. denied, 454 U.S. 897, 102 S. Ct. 296 (1981).

person from the day when it is established; if it is by law required to register as a legal person, it acquires the status of a legal person upon approval and registration."

2. An Enterprise Legal Person

To qualify as an enterprise legal person, the following requirements must be met in accordance with relevant Chinese laws.

(1) A Company Owns its Assets

The property of a company comes from the contributions or investments of its shareholders. Once the property is transferred from the shareholders to the company, the property is owned by the company legally. Shareholders have no right to control the property directly or to take back their investments after the company has been incorporated. They may enjoy the rights only based on the shares they own. From this point, one important concept is recognized by traditional company law theory, i.e., the "separation of a company's property and shareholders' personal property", which is discussed further in the relevant chapter.

(2) A Company Enjoys the Rights and Fulfils Its Duties on Its Own Behalf

A company can sign a contract with a third party and use its own assets to guarantee transactions with the third party. Shareholders are not liable for the company's debts owed to third parties (usually creditors). The doctrine of "lifting the corporate veil", which is popular in common law jurisdictions, was introduced by the 2005 Company Law, and the real implementation of this doctrine may require the publication of detailed rules. Therefore, in cases involving fraudulent trading (discussed later), the responsible persons may be ordered to bear personal liability. In addition, the responsible persons are subject to administrative sanctions if they improperly manage the company and cause its undercapitalization. The criminal punishment is also available if the circumstances are serious. For example, if a director uses his official powers to accept bribes or other illegal incomes or to seize company property, the illegal incomes shall be confiscated, the company property shall be returned and the company shall impose sanctions on him or her. If a criminal offence is constituted, then criminal liability shall be pursued according to the Chinese Criminal Law.[42]

42. The 2005 Company Law, Article 216.

(3) A Company Can Sue and Be Sued

A company is a legal person, which is an artificial person. It can sue somebody or be sued on its own behalf. In other words, if a company is involved in a lawsuit, the third party can only sue the company but usually cannot sue its shareholders unless there are circumstances that allow the corporate veil to be lifted.

(4) A Company Has Its Own Management Rights

Usually management rights are held by the directors or managers of a company. In a large company, shareholders are not directly involved in day-to-day management. However, one may see the Shareholders' General Meeting has been given different powers under the company law, which will be addressed in a subsequent chapter.

IV. INCORPORATION VERSUS INCORPORATED

The terms "incorporation" (*sheli*) and "incorporated" (*chengli*) may reflect different natures of operation. Incorporation usually refers to the procedures of establishing a company. It is a civil legal action and reflects the will of a promoter. For example, the incorporation of LLCs should be done by way of promotion while the incorporation of joint stock companies can be done through either a promoter's method or a share offering method. Article 29 of the 2013 Company Law does not mention the word "promoter" and instead uses the words "a representative designated by all the shareholders or by an agent jointly entrusted by them". However, one may conclude through careful interpretation of these words that the "representative" or "agent" in this case plays more or less the same role as a promoter. In common law jurisdictions, persons who prepare the incorporation are called promoters. Furthermore, promoters are usually liable for contracts entered into in their own names or in the name of a company to be formed. A detailed discussion of this issue is given in the relevant chapter.

However, the word "incorporated" simply refers to an administrative action. The very important sign of this action can be seen in Article 6 of the 2013 Company Law, which states as follows:

> In order to establish a company, one shall submit an application for registration of incorporation according to relevant laws and regulations. The Company Registration Authority shall grant registration and issue a business license to a company that meets the requirements stipulated in this Law; the Company Registration Authority shall not register a company failing to meet the requirements stipulated in this Law.

Article 7 further states that the date of the issuance of the company business license shall be the date of the incorporation of a company.

Thus, it is certain that only from the time at which it obtains a "business license" can a company obtain legal person status. The remaining issue is whether before a company is incorporated it could be regarded as an incorporating company, which may have a limited civil capacity. In China, many scholars have argued that an incorporating company should be treated as an economic entity with no legal person status. Thus, it may entrust its agent (usually a promoter) to conduct certain civil activities and assume all of its liabilities before it has been fully established. This topic is further examined in the next chapter.

V. BRANCH COMPANIES AND SUBSIDIARY COMPANIES

The 2013 Company Law contains only one provision dealing with branch companies and subsidiary companies. Under Article 14, a company may establish branch companies that have no legal person status, and their civil liability shall be borne by the company. In accordance with the same provision, a company may establish subsidiary companies that have legal person status and shall bear civil liability independently. Since subsidiary companies are independent legal persons, all provisions of the Chinese company law that apply to regular companies shall apply to subsidiary companies as well. On the other hand, because the doctrine of "piercing the corporate veil" is formally established by the 2005 Company Law, it is possible to impose liabilities on parent companies if they abuse their shareholders' rights in subsidiary companies.

VI. FOREIGN COMPANIES

Foreign companies are those companies established and registered outside the territory of China and are subject to control by foreign company laws.[43] Thus, foreign companies are foreign legal persons permitted to engage in production and business operations by way of establishing branch companies in China. Foreign branch companies in China do not have legal person status, and foreign companies shall bear civil responsibility for the operational activities of their branch companies. Foreign companies are different from foreign-invested companies, which are registered in China. Furthermore, foreign-invested companies are Chinese legal persons; they

43. The 2013 Company Law, Article 217.

are incorporated either by foreign investors alone or by taking the form of joint ventures with Chinese partners in accordance with Chinese foreign investment laws and relevant regulations. They are Chinese legal persons. In the relevant chapter, a brief introduction to foreign invested companies will be given.

3

Constitution of Companies

I. A COMPANY'S CONSTITUTION

1. Different Names of Constitution

Generally, articles of association (or by-laws) are recognized as the "constitution" of a company. Using the term "constitution" makes it clear that articles of association are so important for the overall operation of companies. In China, a company's constitution refers only to its articles of association (*gongsi zhangcheng*). This approach is the same as that of Taiwan.[1] However, in the United States, different names have been used to describe companies' constitutions, such as "articles of incorporation", "certificates of incorporation", "company by-laws", and "charters". Here, it is important to point out a distinction between articles of incorporation and by-laws in the United States. The former are usually filed with the appropriate state agency for the purpose of incorporation, while the latter are the internal documents of a company. One unique feature is that the amendment of articles of incorporation is more difficult than the amendment of by-laws, i.e., any amendments made to articles of incorporation generally require approval by specified votes of shareholders following a favourable recommendation made by the board of directors. By-laws, on the other hand, may be amended either by the board of directors, acting alone, or by the shareholders.[2]

1. China might have copied this approach from Taiwan.
2. Robert W. Hamilton, *Business Organizations: Essential Terms and Concepts*, Aspen Law & Business (New York), 1996, p. 208.

In Hong Kong, companies used to adopt two constitutional documents, i.e., the Memorandum of Association and the Articles of Association. Section 23 of the old Companies Ordinance (Cap. 32) stipulated that "subject to the provisions of this Ordinance, the memorandum and articles shall, when registered, bind the company and its members thereof to the same extent as if they respectively had been signed and sealed by each member, and contained covenants on the part of each member to observe all the provisions of the memorandum and articles". Like that in the United States, the memorandum serves a function similar to that of articles of incorporation, while articles of association are similar to bylaws. However, the new Hong Kong Companies Ordinance (Cap. 622) abolishes the memorandum and requires only articles of association.[3]

Hong Kong company law used to require companies to provide their objects in the memorandum, and companies could only operate legally if their operations were based solely on those objects, exercising only those powers set out in the object clauses. Operations outside those objects would be the subject of legal action based on the doctrine of *ultra vires*. The rationale of this doctrine was to protect a company against any improper conduct by its management so as to safeguard the legitimate interests of its members and creditors. However, beginning on 10 February 1997, this doctrine became optional.[4] In fact, the term "optional" gives two choices to regular companies: if a company chooses not to state its objects, it has the capacity, rights, powers, and privileges of a natural person who can do almost everything legally. However, if a company does state its objects, it cannot carry on any business or exercise any power that is not authorized by the articles of association, and a member of the company may bring proceedings to restrain the company from acting outside the objects.[5]

Through comparison, one can see that the single constitution system adopted in China is considered as a common practice. In fact, the single constitution system could easily achieve the purpose of a dual constitution system. In the following chapter, the new changes concerning the articles of association are fairly covered.

3. "The decision to abolish the memorandum of association was made on the basis of the diminution of the need for such a document." See Stefan H. C. Lo and Charles Z. Qu, *Law of Companies in Hong Kong*, Sweet & Maxwell (Hong Kong), 2013, p. 161.
4. The Companies Ordinance (Cap. 32), s. 5(1A)(b); the Companies Ordinance (Cap. 622), s. 82.
5. The Companies Ordinance (Cap. 622), s. 115 and s. 116.

2. The Articles of Association in China

According to the Chinese company law, articles of association are used for both internal and external purposes. The preparation of the articles of association is a "must" before a company can be registered or established. The articles of association shall be signed and affixed with the shareholders' seals. Furthermore, the following items must be contained in the articles of association:

(a) name and address of the company;
(b) scope of business operations of the company;
(c) registered capital of the company;
(d) names and titles of shareholders;
(e) methods, amounts, and time of capital contributions by the various shareholders;
(f) the company's organizations, establishment methods, duties, and rules of procedure;
(g) legal representative of the company; and
(h) other items deemed necessary by the shareholders to be stipulated.[6]

Here, it is necessary to pay attention to the term "shall" (*yingdang*) stated in Articles 25 and 81 of the Chinese Company Law. In Chinese, *yingdang* is a term of art that is equivalent to the word "must" (*bixu*). If the word "must" is defined as meaning that people shall do something absolutely, then the articles of association "must" contain the above statutory items. However, both in practice and in theory, the term *yingdang* has been interpreted differently. Firstly, it is suggested that some items listed in Articles 25 or 81 must be included in the articles of association. Those items include the company's name, domicile, scope of business, and registered capital; the names of its shareholders; its forms and amounts of contribution; its internal organizations; and its methods of establishment. Secondly, it is suggested that some items are relatively important but not listed in Articles 25 and 81, such as the rights and duties of shareholders, functions and powers of a company, legal representative of a company, and dissolution and liquidation of a company. Although these items are not listed under Articles 25 and 81, that does not mean they are not important. In fact, the Chinese company law separately deals with these issues. For example, Articles 20 and 35 deal

6. The 2013 Chinese Company Law, Article 25. However, Article 25 controls only limited liability companies. In the case of joint stock companies, the Articles of Association shall require additional contents: (1) methods of profit distribution, (2) reasons for company dissolution and methods of liquidation, and (3) methods of making company notices or announcements. See Article 81.

with the obligations and rights of shareholders; Articles 36, 40, and 51 deal with three important organizations (the shareholders' meeting, the board of directors, and the board of supervisors); and Article 13 deals with the legal representative. Thus, it is necessary to clear up the confusion that the items listed in Articles 25 or 81 are not exclusive and that the items not mentioned by these two provisions are still somewhat important under the Chinese company law. Thirdly, it is suggested that some items not listed by Articles 25 and 81 are discretionary and could be included by shareholders in the articles of association.[7] These interpretations make some sense but are not consistent with the meaning of *yingdang*. In any event, this may reflect the fact that the Chinese company law needs to reconcile these different interpretations. On the other hand, it is necessary to observe that the Chinese company law gives more freedoms to companies. So far it is observed that more than twenty provisions grant the right to shareholders to freely incorporate their special desires into the articles of association so long as those desires do not contradict the relevant laws and regulations. Therefore, they can (1) decide the scope of business (Art. 12); (2) decide the ceiling of providing guarantee (Art. 16); (3) decide the notice period (Art. 41); (4) decide how to exercise voting rights (Art. 42); (5) decide the deliberation and voting procedures of the annual shareholders' meeting (Art. 43); (6) decide the term of directorship (Art. 45); (7) decide the powers and functions of the board of directors (Art. 46); (8) decide the deliberation and voting procedures of the board of directors (Art. 48); (9) decide the powers and functions of the supervisory board (Art. 53); (10) decide the deliberation and voting procedures of the supervisory board (Art. 55); (11) decide the procedures for transferring stock ownership (Art. 71); (12) decide the term of operation for the company (Art. 74); (13) decide the matter of succession (Art. 75); (14) decide the subscription of shares by promoters (Art. 83); (15) decide the situations for holding an interim shareholders' meeting (Art. 100); (16) decide the major assets transition (Art. 104); (17) decide the limits of transferring shares by directors, supervisors, and senior executives (Art. 141); (18) decide the specific duties of directors, supervisors, and senior executives (Art. 147); (19) decide the time limit for submitting financial statements to shareholders (Art. 165); (20) decide the distribution of profits (Art. 166) and (21) decide the meaning of "senior executives"

7. By reading both Kong Xiangjun and others, *New Interpretation of Company Law and Relevant Regulations* (*Gongsi fa ji peitao guiding xin shi xin jie*) (First Part), The People's Court Press (Beijing), 1997, p. 291, and Jiang Daxing, *The Intensive Studies on Company Law* (*Gongsi fa de zhankai yu pingpan*), The Law Press (Beijing), 2001, p. 337, one may conclude that there is no uniform interpretation of the term "*yingdang*". Furthermore, this issue has not been resolved by the company law itself.

(Art. 216). Many of these freedoms were not available under the 1993 Company Law.

II. THE NATURE OF THE ARTICLES OF ASSOCIATION

In accordance with Article 11, the articles of association must be formulated in accordance with the Chinese company law when a company is being incorporated. A company's articles of association shall have a binding force over the company and its shareholders, directors, supervisors, and managers. Therefore, this suggests that the articles of association in China also serve as a "contract" between the company and its shareholders, directors, supervisors, and managers. People from common law jurisdictions may not fully understand this provision because the articles of association are usually considered as a contract between a company and its members or between members in their jurisdictions. In order to explain this confusion, it is necessary to examine the nature of the articles of association in common law jurisdictions, taking the Hong Kong Companies Ordinance as one example.

In Hong Kong, the legal effect of the articles of association is provided by Section 86 of the Companies Ordinance (Cap. 622):

> (1) Subject to this Ordinance, a company's articles, once registered under this Ordinance or a former Companies Ordinance—
> (a) have effect as a contract under seal—
> (i) between the company and each member; and
> (ii) between a member and each other member; and
> (b) are to be regarded as containing covenants on the part of the company and of each member to observe all the provisions of the articles.
> (2) Without limiting subsection (1), the articles are enforceable—
> (a) by the company against each member;
> (b) by a member against the company; and
> (c) by a member against each other member.
> (3) Money payable by a member to the company under the articles—
> (a) is a debt due from the member to the company; and
> (b) is of the nature of a specialty debt.

Generally, in Hong Kong "members" refer to shareholders only. Shareholders are the investors in a company and have the right to formulate the articles of association as a contract, which will create a legally binding force between the company and its shareholders and between the members themselves. On the other hand, directors, supervisors, and managers are the employees of a company and cannot enforce the contract in their capacities as directors, supervisors, and managers. This may be the same even if they are concurrently shareholders, as long as they do not try to enforce the contract in their capacity as shareholders.

In *Eley v Positive Life Assurance Co* (1867) in the United Kingdom, the company's articles of association provided that "Eley shall be the solicitor of the company . . . and shall not be removed from office except for misconduct." Eley, who was also a shareholder of the company, sued the company for breach of contract for not employing him as the solicitor of the company. The judgment was that the articles of association did not create a contract between Eley and the company in terms of its employment of a solicitor.

In China, articles of association may have a different meaning. The Chinese company law states that articles of association can bind a company and its shareholders, directors, supervisors, and managers. In other words, the company and its shareholders, directors, supervisors, and managers could treat the articles of association as a "contract" and enforce the "contract" in their capacities as shareholders, directors, supervisors, and managers. Thus, from a legal standpoint, if Eley had brought forward the same case in China under the Chinese company law, he would have won his case without being challenged in his capacity as a solicitor. However, a possible argument is that the Chinese company law does not mention solicitors or other personnel and thus is a third party of the "contract". In this case, there would have been no privity of contract, and Eley might not have been able to enforce the articles of association in China either.

Which approach is better? It is really a matter of legal tradition. In most common law jurisdictions, articles of association have been treated as a binding contract, while in most continental law jurisdictions articles of association are treated as internal rules (at least this is true in China). In this situation, all members as well as other employees such as directors, supervisors, and managers should obey these internal rules.

One point of difficultly is that even if they are in line with the Chinese Company Law, articles of association are signed and sealed only by shareholders and not directors, supervisors, or managers.[8] If the articles of association are treated as a contract, the parties who have not signed them should not be bound by the contract because there is no privity of contract. If the articles of association are treated as the internal rules of a company and the company's directors, supervisors, and managers are bound by these internal rules,[9] the logical conclusion is that directors, supervisors, and managers

8. The 2013 Chinese Company Law, Article 25(2).
9. Article 11 of the 2013 Chinese Company Law states clearly that directors, supervisors, and managers shall abide by the company's articles of association.

shall not be allowed to stop the alteration of the articles of association as long as the alteration itself is lawful or complies with legal procedures.

Thus, in both common law jurisdictions and continental law jurisdictions, directors, supervisors, and managers should not be treated as members of a company. Furthermore, shareholders can, through shareholders' meetings, provide in the articles of association the duties and obligations of directors, supervisors, and managers. The purpose of doing so is to ensure that directors, supervisors, and managers observe those internal rules and are liable for their misconduct. Directors, supervisors, and managers can protect their legitimate interests by invoking other legal devices.

One British example may explain this situation better. Shirlaw was, by a written agreement, appointed as the managing director of a company for ten years. Three years into the contract, another company acquired the company. The company's articles of association were amended to include the power to remove any directors by written instrument. Shirlaw was removed under this provision. Shirlaw sued and won his case. It was held that removing Shirlaw as director, albeit on the grounds laid down by the articles of association, was a breach of contract by the company [*Southern Foundries* v *Shirlaw* (1940) A. C. 701].

In this leading British case, Shirlaw was protected by his ten-year employment contract even though he had no right to stop the alteration of the articles of association.

Thus, the logical conclusion is that under the Chinese company law, directors, supervisors, and managers are bound by the articles of association as they are by internal rules, but they should not be permitted to enforce the articles of association as a contract.

III. ARTICLES OF ASSOCIATION SHOULD BE FILED OR APPROVED IN CHINA

In both the United States and Hong Kong, articles of association are usually made valid through the process of filing or registration. In the United States, every state requires that the articles of association be filed with a state official, usually the secretary of each state. At the same time, there is a need to pay a filing fee. The traditional manner of filing the articles of association is to mail them in, deliver them by overnight mail service or deliver them by messenger or courier to the secretary of a state. Many state filing offices now also permit electronic filing and have set up fax machines and numbers for that purpose. In the near future, computer filing will be more convenient and could become a predominant filing method.

In China, the articles of association usually need to be approved by the relevant authorities in order to be valid. Article 12 of the Company Law provides that "a company's scope of business shall be defined in its articles of association and registered in accordance with the law. Items within the company's scope of business' that are subject to restrictions under laws, administrative rules and regulations shall be approved in accordance with the law." One could say, based on this provision, that the incorporation of some companies in China is still considered to be a privilege rather than a right.

IV. POWERS OF SHAREHOLDERS UNDER THE ARTICLES OF ASSOCIATION

The shareholders of a company are authorized to formulate the articles of association. Furthermore, shareholders' rights are not only stipulated by the Chinese company law, but also exercised through the formulation of the articles of association. The next question is whether shareholders could, through the articles of association, delegate some of their powers to the board of directors despite those powers being vested in the shareholders. In the following case, the negative answer was given, but the underlying reasons are still the subject of further debate.

The plaintiff, Zhang Hong, was a shareholder of Shanghai Shenhua Industry and Commerce Joint Stock Company (hereinafter referred to as the "Shenhua Company"). On 28 April 1994, the Shenhua Company held a regular shareholders' meeting at which the company's articles of association were passed. Article 18 of the articles of association was the pertinent provision in this case. It stated that "when the shareholders' meeting is not in session but there is a need to change directors, the board of directors shall have the right to decide the changes, provided that the number of directors newly appointed shall not exceed one third of the total number of directors." On 25 February 1995, the Shenhua Company held a board of directors' meeting and passed resolutions Nos. 5 and 6 in line with Article 18 of the articles of association. Both resolutions added Ma Jun and Mo Quanfu as directors. On 12 August 1995, the Shenhua Company held another board of directors' meeting, and resolution No. 7 was passed to add Li Weirong as a director.

The plaintiff brought a lawsuit in a people's court claiming that Article 18 of the articles of association did not comply with Article 103 of the 1993 Company Law, which stated that the election and change of directors were rights solely vested in the shareholders' meeting. The plaintiff asserted that all three resolutions infringed upon the legal interests of shareholders and asked the court to set aside the resolutions.

The Shenhua Company, the defendant in this case, responded that the three resolutions to add Li Weirong, Ma Jun, and Mo Quanfu as directors were made in accordance with Article 18 of the articles of association, which were passed by the shareholders' general meeting. Thus, it asked the court to announce the validity of the three resolutions.

Li Weirong, Ma Jun, and Mo Quanfu acted as the third parties in this case and submitted their opinions that they were fully supporting the defendant's position. Furthermore, they had acted as directors and exercised functions and duties as directors (*de facto* directors). Thus, they asked the court to dismiss the plaintiff's claim.

The court of first instance supported the plaintiff's claim. It ruled that the three resolutions to add the three directors were invalid. The defendant appealed the case. The court of second instance upheld the original judgment.[10]

In fact, the Company Law (2013 Amendment) still gives the power to elect and change the directors and supervisors assumed by non-representatives of the employees (Articles 37.1 and 99). One must consider the important issue in this case, i.e., the extent to which the shareholders' general meeting could exercise its powers or rights. It has been recognized that shareholders' rights are built on their property rights.[11] Generally, shareholders have three major rights, namely the right to vote, the right to obtain information, and the right to sue. As far as the right to vote is concerned, it is not certain whether the law granting the right to vote is also the obligation to vote. On the one hand, the right to vote is of great importance for shareholders because it enables them to voice their views and to decide crucial matters of the company.[12] Therefore, the issue of whether the right to vote can be delegated through the formation of articles of association must be evaluated by taking the interests of shareholders, company, and creditors into account.

Bearing this standard in mind, several flaws in the judgment can be identified.

---

10. Shanghai Pudong New District People's Court (1996), No. 5940, Civil First Trial; and Shanghai No. One Intermediate People's Court (1998), No. 282, Civil Final Trial. This case is cited from Jiang, supra note 7, pp. 280–81.
11. Richard R. Ellsworth, *Leading with Purpose: The New Corporate Realities*, Stanford University Press (Stanford), 2002, p. 182.
12. T. Baums and E. Wymeersch, *Shareholder Voting Rights and Practices in Europe and the United States, Kluwer Law International* (The Hague), 1999, p. 110.

In this case, the shareholders' general meeting passed the articles of association and empowered the board of directors to make limited changes of directors. This case was decided in accordance with the 1993 Company Law, and the Company Law (2013 Amendment) does not offer any new solution. Even though both Articles 37.1(2) and 99 still give the power of electing and replacing directors to the shareholders' meeting, the law does not expressly state that such power cannot be delegated to the board of directors. Thus, it may be argued that the shareholders' meeting can delegate limited power to the board of directors. It has been admitted that the said clause certainly limits the right to vote, but the scope of authorization is rather marginal because the board of directors is allowed to vote only in a particular situation and one-third of the total directors.

Secondly, shareholders' right to vote is exercised for the purpose of making a profit. The achievement of this purpose may heavily rely on the proper and efficient decisions of the board of directors.

Thirdly, shareholders may still exercise their right to vote when the annual meeting is in session, and they have ample opportunity to examine whether the directors chosen by the board of directors are suitable candidates. Furthermore, if shareholders do not like the new change of directors, they can exercise their power to make a necessary correction when the chance comes (through either a regular shareholders' meeting or a provisional shareholders' meeting).

Fourthly, this position may be further supported by the legal practice in other jurisdictions. Taking Hong Kong company law as one example, although the general power to appoint directors is vested in the members in a general meeting, Table A of the old Companies Ordinance (Cap. 32) gave directors the power to fill any casual vacancy and to make additional appointments, provided the maximum number of directors was not exceeded.[13] Another example is Section 8(10) of the American Revised Model Business Corporation Act, which states the following:

13. Article 97 of Table A states, "the directors shall have power at any time, and from time to time, to appoint any person to be a director, either to fill a casual vacancy or as an addition to the existing directors, but so that the total number of directors shall not at any time exceed the number fixed in accordance with these regulations. Any director so appointed shall hold office only until the next following annual general meeting, and shall then be eligible for re-election but shall not be taken into account in determining the directors who are to retire by rotation at such meeting." Now, the same ideas can be seen in the new Model Articles. For example, see Model Articles (private companies), Article 22; Model Articles (public companies), Article 23.

(a) Unless the articles of incorporation provide otherwise, if a vacancy occurs on a board of directors, including a vacancy resulting from an increase in the number of directors:
   (1) the shareholders may fill the vacancy;
   (2) the board of directors may fill the vacancy; or
   (3) if the directors remaining in office constitute fewer than a quorum of the board, they may fill the vacancy by the affirmative vote of a majority of all the directors remaining in office;

(b) If the vacant office was held by a director elected by a voting group of shareholders, only the holders of shares of that voting group are entitled to vote to fill the vacancy if it is filled by the shareholders.

(c) A vacancy that will occur at a specific later date (by reason of a resignation effective at a later date under Section 8.07(b)[14] or otherwise) may be filled before the vacancy occurs but the new director may not take office until the vacancy occurs.

Obviously, the Chinese company law is not flexible enough to address this particular issue. The Chinese judiciary does not have sufficient experience to handle this type of case, and the relevant cases have not been decided satisfactorily.

Now, let us turn to the next case, which happened in China in 1998.

The Tianjin Dagang Oilfield (Group) Limited Liability Company and its related enterprises (hereinafter referred to as the "Dagang Company") purchased shares of Shanghai Aishi Joint Stock Company (hereinafter referred to as the "Aishi Company") four times through the Shanghai Stock Exchange during July and August of 1998. People, however, did not understand why the Aishi Company did not take any counteraction at that point. As reported on 8 August 1998, the Dagang Company held 12,144,680 shares of the Aishi Company, which amounted to 10.0116 per cent of the total shares of the Aishi Company. Because of this acquisition, the Dagang Company became the biggest shareholder of the Aishi Company. Subsequently, the Dagang Company demanded the holding of a shareholders' meeting and intended to change the board of directors. However, the Dagang Company was soon frustrated by Article 67 of the Aishi Company's articles of association,[15]

14. Section 8.07 deals with resignation of directors.
15. Article 67 of the articles of association states:
"The board of directors puts forward (or nominates) candidates of directors and supervisors on the condition that the opinions of shareholders have been sought. The candidate list will be sent as a motion to the shareholders' meeting for discussion and approval.
Shareholders who individually or jointly hold more than 10 per cent of total voting shares of the company (not including share proxy) and have held those shares for more than 6 months shall, if they want to nominate their representatives to the board of

which stated that the methods and procedures for nominating directors and supervisors were as follows:

> Shareholders who want to nominate directors must hold shares of the Aishi Company for at least 6 months; newly elected directors cannot exceed more than half of the total number of existing directors.

If this provision was considered a valid one, the Dagang Company would have to wait for six months to nominate new directors, and, even if it satisfied the requirement, it would not effectively control the board of directors of the Aishi Company. Because of this provision, the Dagang Company could not quickly achieve its goal of controlling the management of the Aishi Company, and its takeover costs thus dramatically increased.

Both the Dagang Company and the Aishi Company hired experts to address the legality of Article 67 of the articles of association. Supporters of Article 67 held the view that it was a valid provision because it was just a so-called "shark repellent tactic" that was popular in Western countries[16] and could serve as an effective measure against the takeover. Opponents of Article 67 held the view that this provision did not comply with Article 4 of the 1993 Company Law.[17] Finally, the CSRC decided that the Aishi Company's articles of association were not "standard" and gave an instruction to the Shanghai Securities Administrative Office to conduct conversations with existing directors of the Aishi Company. Under heavy pressure, the Aishi Company gave in over its Article 67. A provisional shareholders' meeting was convened on 31 October 1998. Article 67 was amended and six persons were nominated by the Dagang Company to be the new directors.[18]

---

directors or the board of supervisors, submit written nominations together with necessary materials to the board of directors 20 days before the shareholders' meeting is held.

When the term of the board of directors or board of supervisors has expired and there is a need to form a new one, the number of new directors or supervisors shall not exceed half of the total number that is necessary to form the board of directors or the board of supervisors.

The procedures for creating candidates of directors or supervisors: (1) the board of directors holds a meeting with shareholders and listens to their suggestions; (2) the board of directors holds a meeting to examine the qualifications of those candidates, to discuss and decide the list of candidates; (3) the board of directors submits the list of candidates to the shareholders' meeting together with their resume and basic information."

16. The "shark repellent tactic" can be summarized into the following categories: (1) supermajority provisions, (2) "fair price" amendments, and (3) staggered board provisions. For detailed information, see Hamilton, supra note 2, pp. 1123–26.
17. Article 4 of the 1993 Company Law stated, "As investors, the shareholders of a company shall, according to their share of capital invested in the company, enjoy rights and interests as part owners of the company, such as gaining benefits from its assets, major decision making and selection of management personnel."
18. This case was cited from Jiang, supra note 7, pp. 303–5.

This case was decided under Article 4 of the 1993 Company Law, which is the same as Article 4 of the 2005 Company Law. Firstly, Article 4 mentions only the shareholders' right to choose management personnel. The choice of management personnel means two things: (1) the nomination of management personnel, and (2) the election of management personnel. The nomination of management personnel is a procedurally related right, while the election of management personnel is a more substantive right. One could argue that these two rights can be delegated. Secondly, neither the Chinese Company Law nor other regulations provide any guidelines concerning the methods and procedures for nominating directors or supervisors. On the other hand, the limitation of nomination in Article 67 of the Aishi Company's articles of association is an internationally popular anti-takeover measure that should be endorsed and encouraged.

It was suggested that Article 115(2) of the 1993 Company Law was also an obstacle that prevented the Dagang Company from taking control of the Aishi Company smoothly. In line with Article 115(2), a shareholders' meeting shall not be permitted to remove a director from his or her post without proper reason if the term of the director has not expired. At the time when the Dagang Company became the biggest shareholder and tried to take control of the Aishi Company, the terms of all thirteen existing directors had not yet expired. As a result of pressure being applied, the articles of association were amended to change the number of directors from thirteen to nineteen, with six directors nominated by the Dagang Company.[19]

This was obviously a compromise. Following this approach, it is clear that the relevant provisions should be modified. In Western countries, shareholders are considered as investors in a company and are authorized to appoint or dismiss directors anytime they want, so long as they follow the relevant legal procedures. Thus, Eley could not stop shareholders from removing him from his post even though he was capable in this post and had not committed any misconduct. This idea is accepted by the Company Law (2005 Amendment).

V. CONTENTS OF THE ARTICLES OF ASSOCIATION

In China, the contents of articles of association are usually similar because most companies choose to follow the items listed by Chinese company law. The similarity of the contents may indicate that Chinese companies are not sophisticated enough to develop their own articles of association and that

19. Jiang, supra note 7, pp. 216–317.

Chinese company law offers them opportunities to outline their own wishes in addition to the required items. Nevertheless, in order to offer a clear picture of the contents, it is necessary to introduce the contents by following the order of the list required by Chinese company law.

1. Name and Domicile of a Company

(1) Name of a Company

The name of a company is a sign of the company. It is important to have a name for two reasons.

(a) A name indicates the type, size, and credibility of a company.
(b) A name is relevant to protecting a company's legal interests. The name of a company is usually a part of the property of the company, especially when the company has established its goodwill.

Thus, a company shall have an exclusive right to its own particular name. In China, a name carries the following limitations.

Firstly, one company can have only one name.[20] However, in the United States, a corporation, like an individual, may engage in its business under an assumed name (e.g., the ABC Company can use an assumed name such as the "XYZ Company") so long as the purpose is not fraudulent and it does not constitute unfair competition. Also in the United States, many states have assumed name statutes that require a person, whether an individual or a corporation, who is conducting business under an assumed name to file a statement (usually at the county level) disclosing who is conducting business under that assumed name.[21] The possible advantage is that people can keep lower profiles when using assumed company names. Nevertheless, it seems that the use of an assumed name may reduce the reputation of a company because it is impossible to know who the actual operator is.

Secondly, any other companies established later cannot use the same or a similar name that already exists for unfair competition purposes. According to the Chinese Regulations on Registration of Enterprises' Name, which was issued by the State Administrative Bureau for Industry and Commerce on 14 June 2004, there is a limitation on the exclusive use of company names

20. The Regulations on the Administration of Company Registration of the PRC (*Zhonghua Renmin Gongheguo Gongsi Dengji Guanli Tiaoli*) issued by the State Council on 24 June 1994, Article 11. The said Regulations were amended by the State Council on 18 December 2005.
21. Hamilton, supra note 2, pp. 51–52.

(Article 3). The exclusion applies only to the same area instead of different areas. For example, in both Shanghai and Zhejiang, the use of the same name may be allowed. However, one problem remains under this interpretation. If the same names are permitted in different areas, the legal interest of a company with a nationally famous name could be seriously injured. The best solution may be to apply the trademark for the key name in order to avoid this problem. Certainly, this is a topic beyond the scope of this book, and it is urged that the relevant laws or regulations should resolve this problem as quickly as possible.

Thirdly, in China a pre-check of a company's name should be conducted systemically before the company can be registered. Article 14 of the Regulations on Administration of Company Registration of the PRC provides this requirement. The company registry will decide whether or not to approve a proposed name. If the decision allows the name suggested, then a Notice of Approval valid for 6 months will be issued.[22] The principle of "first in, first in service" will be applied if there is any dispute.

Fourthly, the company's name shall include the following elements:

(1) The nature of the company, i.e., an indication of whether it is a limited liability company or a joint stock company.
(2) The level of company registry, i.e., if a name contains "China or Chinese", it indicates that the company is registered with the National Registry. The same principle applies to a name with a provincial name such as "Shanghai" or "Zhejiang," which means a company is registered with the Shanghai or Zhejiang Registry. However, foreign investment enterprises, famous enterprises, enterprises with a long history, and national enterprises are not subject to this limitation.[23]
(3) The type of business, such as "food production" or "cloth-making".

Fifthly, the name shall not contain ideas or words (a) that will harm State interests or public interests; (b) that are misleading; (c) that are the names of foreign States or the names of international institutions; (d) that are the names of parties, governments, military institutions, social groups, and so on; or (e) that are *pinyin* (except in English) or a number.[24]

22. The Regulations on Administration of Company Registration of the PRC, Article 16.
23. Those enterprises are usually registered with the State Administration of Industry and Commerce. For example, Article 6(4) of the Regulations on Administration of Company Registration of the PRC states that a limited liability company shall register with the State Administration of Industry and Commerce.
24. Jiang Ping (ed.), *New Textbook of Company Law* (in Chinese), Law Publishing House, Beijing, pp. 59–62 (1994).

In early 1990, one company (hereinafter referred to as the "A Company") registered its name as "X City Jin Lang Restaurant Company Limited". The name "Jin Lang Restaurant" occupied its nameplate. In November of the same year, another company (hereinafter referred to as the "B Company") registered and operated its business as a restaurant on another street using the same name as the A Company. These two companies were located on different streets, but there was only a distance of 100 metres between them. Even though they were not far from each other, they belonged to different districts of a city and were registered with different company registries. When the A Company discovered that the B Company was using the same name, it initiated a lawsuit against the B Company in a people's court.

The A Company claimed that it had used the name since February 1990 after its registration was approved. The B Company had never used the name until December 1990. For this reason, the B Company had infringed upon the good fame of the A Company and caused certain bad consequences. Therefore, the A Company asked the court to issue an injunction to order (1) B Company not to use the same name again, and (2) the B Company to bear civil responsibility, make an apology, and restore the reputation of the A Company.

The B Company claimed that it used the name "Jin Lang Restaurant" before 1949. In 1992, in order to attract customers, it decided to reuse the old name, which had a long history and good fame. It used the name after a formal registration process, as it was approved by the company registry of its district. The company had spent several hundred thousand yuan to change the name and logo and to produce advertisements. For these reasons, the B Company claimed that it had not infringed upon the interests of the A Company and that furthermore only passing off or usurping the name would constitute infringement. The B Company went through formal procedures to use the name, which made it lawful. Moreover, the business scope of the A Company was food and drink, while the business scope of the B Company was the hotel business. Therefore, the B Company argued that the same name could be used by different enterprises conducting different businesses.[25]

The court held that the B Company infringed upon the A Company's rights and should stop using the same name.

The Regulations Concerning Registration of the Name of Enterprises were the most relevant authority in this case. Article 7 states that an enterprise can only use one name that should not be the same as or similar to the

25. The case is cited from Xu Wusheng, *Company Law: Case Analysis and Practice*, The Economic Daily Press (Beijing), June 1994, pp. 14–15.

name of another enterprise already registered within the same jurisdiction of a company registry. Article 4 states that the company registry shall have the right to correct the name of an enterprise that is registered improperly.

In this case, the A Company legally registered its name earlier, thus it should have had the right to use the name "Jin Lang Restaurant" exclusively. The B Company subsequently registered the same name in a different district, which was still within the jurisdiction of the same company registry at the county level. The B Company was 100 metres from the A Company and should have been aware of the existing name of the A Company. The B Company further claimed that it engaged in a different business from the A Company's business, so the use of the same name would not harm the legal interests of the A Company. This argument could not be supported. In line with the relevant provision of the Chinese Trademark Law (2014 Amendment), this was an obvious "passing off" that would easily confuse customers (Art. 13). The company registry in the B Company's district exercised its name examination carelessly and should have borne a proportion of the economic losses suffered by the B Company. Finally, the fact that the B Company used the name before 1949 did not help the company. After 1949, all enterprises went through socialist reforms, and the name "Jin Lang Restaurant" did not qualify as a famous trademark deserving special protection under the Unfair Competition Law of the PRC.[26]

(2) Domicile of a Company

Article 10 of the Company Law states that the domicile of a company shall be the place where its main administrative organization is located. In China, one company can have only one domicile, even though it may operate in different places.[27] There are three legal significances of the domicile:

(a) Indication of a jurisdiction. In case there is a lawsuit, the plaintiff shall bring the case to the court that has jurisdiction over the defendant
(b) For the purpose of delivering legal documents, such as the court's judgments
(c) To locate the place where the defendant needs to perform his or her duties

The situation is the same in Hong Kong. It is required that the company's actual address of its registered office be given to the Registrar of Companies within fourteen days of its incorporation. It provides a place

26. Unfair Competition Law of the PRC, Article 5(3).
27. It is also true that a company can operate its business in more than one place.

where legal documents, notices, and other communications can be served on the company. Various registers and documents must be kept at the company's registered office.

2. The Scope of Business of Companies

Traditionally, a company is required to register its scope of business for several reasons. Firstly, shareholders can foresee their investment risks in order to make their investment decisions properly. Through its articles of association, a company promises its shareholders to use the invested money for the projects or operations stated in the articles of association. Secondly, the power and function of the directors or managers shall comply with the business scope. Any nonconformity to the business scope will be sued for *ultra vires*. Thirdly, a third party, through the articles of association, can know basic information about the company and make their proper decisions when dealing with it.

Before addressing this issue in detail, it is necessary to read about one case and to consider the possible consequences.

In July 1992, a joint venture company (hereinafter referred to as the "JV Company") was formed and registered by four parties: Hong Kong Mingyao Sound Designing Company, X City Security Bureau in Neimenggu (Inner Mongolia), Y City Special Lights Factory, and Z City Financial Bureau. The approved business scope of the JV Company included the following items: production and sale of special light bulbs, lights for decoration of advertisement boards, and lights for stagecraft. Thereafter, the JV Company was waiting for the beginning of its operation because the Hong Kong Company failed to invest its portion of the agreed-upon investment. In May 1993, Mr Lee, the general manager of the JV Company, gave the official seal to Ms Yan, the part-time accountant of the JV Company who was also the accountant of X City Security Bureau, and asked her to pass the seal to Mr Dong, the manager of the JV Company, to handle the procedural matters of land-use rights for the factory building as well as the customs declaration. Later that month, Mr Liu, an officer of X City Security Bureau, received information that the Shandong Taian Company was looking for a buyer of plywood. Mr Liu also knew that the Ningxia Board Production Factory (hereinafter referred to as the "Ningxia Factory") needed a certain amount of plywood. On 27 May 1993, Mr Liu had a discussion with four personnel of X City Security Bureau and decided to sign a contract with the Shandong Taian Company on behalf of the JV Company to buy 2,000 pieces of plywood at ¥45.5 per piece. According to the contract, the JV Company had to pay the Shandong Taian Company 30 per cent of the total price (¥280,000) as a deposit. On 28 May 1993, the director of the Ningxia Factory went to Neimenggu. After he examined the business licence of the JV Company, he signed a contract to buy plywood and paid ¥300,000 as the deposit. The parties who represented the JV Company were four personnel of X City Security Bureau, among whom only one person was the part-time accountant of the JV Company. After the contract was signed, Mr Liu received a cheque in the amount of ¥300,000 from the Ningxia Factory and managed to transfer that amount of money to the account of X City Security Bureau. On 29 May 1993, Mr Liu demanded to see the goods of the Shandong Taian Company. In fact, the Shandong Taian Company had no plywood at all. Mr Liu immediately asked someone (S) who was not an employee of the JV Company to send the cheque in the amount of ¥300,000 back to the Ningxia Factory. However, the director of the Ningxia Factory refused to accept the cheque and insisted on receiving the plywood. The director also drafted a notice regarding the change of contractual price and amount of plywood and gave it to S. S did not give this notice to the JV Company. On 19 June 1993, Mr Liu, knowing that the Ningxia Factory had refused to accept the cheque, called the director of the factory. The director agreed to accept the cheque over the phone. On 23 June 1993, the Ningxia Factory sent a formal notice to the JV Company that stated the following:

> The deadline for performing the contract is 22 June 1993 and today is the day the JV Company has breached the contract. The JV Company has sent one regular personnel member to our factory to inform us orally that no plywood can be offered, and to return the cheque with no explanation for the breach. Since the breach has caused serious economic loss to our factory, we formally urge you to send a responsible personnel member to our factory to solve the problem. Otherwise, we will sue your company in a people's court. As regarding the cheque, we will hold it until all the disputes are resolved.

This notice was again sent to and signed by S. In fact, S did not give this notice to the JV Company. On 8 July 1993, the Ningxia Factory sued the JV Company in a people's court and asked the JV Company to return the deposit. Until this moment, S had sent two written notices to the JV Company.

The court held that this was a typical case of *ultra vires*. The JV Company could only engage in business for the production and sale of special light bulbs, lights for decoration of advertisement boards, and lights for stagecraft. The contract for selling plywood was outside the scope of business and should be deemed an invalid contract. Thus, the JV Company should bear major responsibility for the losses of the Ningxia Factory, while the

Ningxia Factory should bear a certain percentage of the losses because it failed to cash the returned cheque and thereby enlarged the damages.[28]

According to Article 11(3) of the 1993 Company Law, companies shall engage in business activities within their registered scope of business. A company may change its scope of business by amending the articles of association in accordance with statutory procedures and registering such amendments with the Company Registration Authority. In China, the relevant government authorities were quite focused on the scope of business of an enterprise. Very often, an enterprise was given a limited scope of business. This was implemented due to the remaining idea of the planned economy. However, this situation has been relatively changed because Article 12 of the 2005 Company Law requires only the scope of the business to be registered properly.

Having said this, it is not certain whether the government's control in this area is totally removed and whether shareholders are given more freedom to decide the scope of the business of their companies.[29] This is evident in Article 12(2) of the 2005 Company Law, which states that the "relevant legal procedures" in practice include approval by the government. The difficulty in changing the scope of business is equally predictable. Thus, unless there is a further economic reform and more freedom is given to entrepreneurs, "*ultra vires*" (acting outside the line of business) will remain a problem if a business decision is made outside the scope of business.

In Western countries, an *ultra vires* act is one engaged in beyond the purposes or powers of a corporation. It is firmly grounded on the notion that a corporation possesses only limited power. The rationale of this doctrine is to protect the company against its management so as to safeguard the interests of its members and creditors. However, this doctrine has caused many hardships and has especially become a trap for innocent victims who are not aware of their counterpart's business scope.

Therefore, before the concept of business scope was officially abolished, people in practice tried to develop the following body of principles for use when the *ultra vires* defence might have been asserted.

---

28. A brief introduction of this case could be seen at Liu Zhixin (ed.), *Comments on China's Typical Commercial Cases* (*Zhongguo dianxing shangshi anli pingxi*), The Law Press (Beijing), January 1998, pp. 13–20. It can be inferred that this case involves not only the issue of ultra vires, but also the issue of a valid representative of the JV Company. This is discussed in the relevant part.
29. Guiguo Wang and Roman Tomasic, *China's Company Law (An Annotation)*, Butterworths (Hong Kong), 1994, p. 18.

(a) An *ultra vires* transaction might have been ratified by all of the shareholders. Ratification could be expressed or implied, e.g., by the receipt of benefits without objection. The ratification, however, had to be made by unanimous consent.
(b) The doctrine of estoppel usually precluded reliance on the *ultra vires* defence in cases where the transaction was fully performed by one party.
(c) A transaction fully performed by both parties could not be attacked.
(d) If the contract was fully executable, the *ultra vires* defence might have been raised by either party.
(e) If an agent of the corporation committed a tort within the scope of his or her employment, the corporation could not defend itself on the grounds that the act was *ultra vires*. This conclusion was reached because of the overriding necessity of protecting innocent third parties from corporate abuse over which they had no means of control.

At the same time in Hong Kong, the doctrine of constructive notice was created to work hand in hand with the doctrine of *ultra vires*.[30] Under the doctrine of constructive notice, it is assumed that a third party who is dealing with the company should be aware of the company's objects because the memorandum and articles of association are filed with the company registry and are available for examination. As a result, the third party who fails to examine the objects of the company is bound by the doctrine of *ultra vires*.

Several modern developments relating to corporate formation are helpful in avoiding *ultra vires* acts. Thus, the development of multiple-purpose and general clauses permitting corporations to "engage in any lawful business" indirectly limits the role of the doctrine.[31]

Beginning on 10 February 1997, the objects of a company became optional in Hong Kong.[32] If a company chooses not to state its objects, it has the capacity, rights, powers, and privileges of a natural person.[33] Certainly, if a company decides to state its objects in its articles of association, then its power to carry on business is restrained by the objects.[34] Furthermore,

30. Justice Susan Kwan and others (eds.), *Company Law in Hong Kong: Practice and Procedure*, Sweet & Maxwell Asia (Hong Kong), 2007, p. 9008.
31. Stephen J. Leacock, "The Rise and Fall of the Ultra Vires Doctrine in United States, United Kingdom, and Commonwealth Caribbean Corporate Common Law: A Triumph of Experience over Logic", *DePaul Business and Commercial Law Journal*, Vol. 5, 2006, p. 67.
32. Cap. 32, s. 5(1A); Cap. 622, s. 82(2).
33. Cap. 32, s. 5A; Cap. 622, s. 115.
34. Cap. 32, s. 5B(1); Cap. 622, s. 116(1).

an act of the company is not invalid by reason that it is not within its objects or powers.[35] In other words, the *ultra vires* doctrine is virtually abolished. This may indicate that a company can engage in any business so long as it is lawful.

In China, the *ultra vires* doctrine is still a valid one. However, the justification of the doctrine is rooted more in State interests. During the period of the "planned economy", there was no concept such as "shares" or "shareholder". Most enterprises were State-owned or collectively owned. Their major task was to perform their obligations as pre-planned by the State. At that time, resources were extremely limited, and the scope of business served State plans to balance the supply and market needs. Thus, the economic plan was the major purpose of adopting the doctrine of *ultra vires*.

At the time when the 1993 Company Law was promulgated, China did not move fast enough towards the market economy and the doctrine of *ultra vires* was kept. Thus, in a case involving *ultra vires*, a relevant contract is deemed to be an invalid one. Furthermore, there are some other legal consequences if an *ultra vires* act is involved. Firstly, Article 73 of the Administrative Rules of the PRC Governing the Registration of Companies states (2005 Amendment), "if a company is found to have conducted business activities beyond its scope of business operation as approved and registered, the competent company registration authority shall order the company to rectify the situation and impose a fine of ¥10,000 to ¥100,000 on the company. If the case is very serious, its business licence shall be revoked." In accordance with this provision, it is clear that a company that commits an *ultra vires* act will be punished. When the Administrative Rules of the PRC Governing the Registration of Companies were amended again in 2014, this provision was kept and renumbered as Article 69.

Secondly, an *ultra vires* act will render the contracts entered into by the company with a third party invalid. Thus, both contracting parties will be ordered to go back to their original positions, i.e., the contract is made invalid from its beginning. If there is any economic loss, the loss should be handled in accordance with the civil law principle concerning a civil wrong. That means that both parties shall bear the losses based on the percentage of their faults. Based on the rule of equity, which is very popular in common law jurisdictions, the application of the doctrine is not fair for a third party who does business in good faith.

China is now moving towards having a "market economy". Under the market economy, supply and demand are supposed to be balanced by the

35. Cap. 32, s. 5B(3); Cap. 622, s. 116(5).

market instead of by the State. Companies are independent entities aimed at making a profit. In this situation, companies should be given the liberty to freely adjust their objects with the changes in supply and demand in the markets, investing their capital in the most profitable businesses.

In fact, subsequent legislation tried to remedy this kind of situation. Firstly, Article 50 of the PRC Contract Law states that even if a legal representative is acting *ultra vires*, a contract signed by him or her may still be valid in order to protect a *bona fide* party on the other side. This is a new change made by the Contract Law rather than by the Chinese Company Law. It indicates that an *ultra vires* case will be brought against a company if it purposefully or intentionally committed an *ultra vires* act. Secondly, the Supreme People's Court (hereinafter referred to as the "SPC") issued the Interpretation to Questions Concerning the Application of the PRC Contract on 29 December 1999. Article 10 states, "Where the parties concluded a contract beyond their scope of business, the People's Court shall not find the contract void on that ground, unless the parties have violated provisions whereby the State restricts or requires special permission of a business activity or whereby laws or administrative regulations prohibit a business activity." This apparently indicates that the situation of strictly enforcing the doctrine of *ultra vires* has been relaxed.

Fair attention should also be paid to Article 12 of the 2005 Company Law, which omits specific language, i.e., "a company shall conduct business activities within its registered business scope", contained in Article 11(3) of the 1993 Company Law. This omission may be interpreted as the legislators' intention to narrow the application of the *ultra vires* doctrine.

Certainly, this is an optimistic interpretation. One must keep in mind that this is a grey area so far for the following reasons. Firstly, the Chinese company law still requires a company to provide the scope of its business in its articles of association. Secondly, the business scope can be amended, but it must follow the procedure of reregistration. Thirdly, some business activities must be approved in advance if they are required by laws and administrative regulations. Thus, some commentators may be right in holding that China still adopts the doctrine.[36]

36. Jian Fu and Jie Yuan, *PRC Company & Securities Laws: A Practical Guide*, CCH Asia Pte Limited (Singapore), 2006, p. 41.

3. Registered Capital of a Company

(1) Significance of Registered Capital

The capital of a company is important in several aspects. It is a symbol of the financial capacity of a company, and it is an indispensable condition for a company to operate its business. Unlike the 1993 Company Law, which allowed capital to take the forms of cash, goods, industrial property rights, technology with non-patented rights or land-use rights,[37] the 2005 Company Law defines the forms of capital as cash, goods, intellectual property, and land-use rights.[38] In comparison, there is no big difference in the form of capital contribution. In line with the existing legislation, labour or human capital is not considered as investment capital, and it may be too early to consider them as the composition of capital. The basic obstacle is the language of Article 27 of the Company Law, i.e., "properties that may be **assessed** on the basis of currency and may be **transferred** according to the law". The legislators may believe that labour or human capital cannot be assessed and transferred. If the Chinese company law could be further liberalized and give the power of assessment to boards of directors, this may change the labour or human capital situation.

Issue one is whether the contributed currency can include illegally obtained currency. It is true that money obtained through criminal activities should not be used as a capital contribution because such a contribution would be deemed money laundering and the investors would be charged with violating criminal law.[39] However, it is not clear whether disputed money, especially money obtained through an invalid contract, can be used as invested capital. In Jiang's view, the investor should be permitted to use that money as invested capital even though the investor still owes a duty to return the same amount (maybe plus interest) to another party.[40]

Issue two is whether borrowed money can be used as the invested capital. Generally, borrowed money can be used as invested capital because under a loan contract the lender transfers the ownership of the money to the borrower subject to the condition that the same amount of money (maybe plus interest) should be returned on a fixed due date. The problem is that in reality some people may use the borrowed money to satisfy the registered capital requirement in order to obtain a business licence. After the

---

37. The 1993 Company Law, Article 24.
38. The 2005 Company Law, Article 27.
39. For example, see Article 191 of the Chinese Criminal Law.
40. Jiang, supra note 5, pp. 30–32.

company is successfully incorporated, the borrowed money is returned to the lender immediately. This activity is definitely inconsistent with the registered capital requirement and constitutes a falsified capital contribution. In another situation, an investor may provide company assets as security for borrowed money and use that money as invested capital. Many scholars believe that such money cannot be used as invested capital.[41] In order to support their position, they often cite Article 3 of the Certain Regulations on the Subscription of Capital by the Parties to Sino-foreign Joint Equity Enterprises, which were promulgated on 1 January 1988:

> No party to a joint equity enterprise may use as its own, investment loans, leased equipment or other property obtained in the name of the joint equity enterprise or the property of a party other than the joint equity party, nor may the property or rights and interests of the joint equity enterprise or of another party to the joint equity enterprise be used as security on its capital investment.

A few scholars hold the view that money borrowed in this situation can still be used as invested capital because the borrower has obtained the ownership of that amount of money. Even though Article 148.1(3) of the Company Law (2013 amendment) provides that a director or a senior manager shall not be permitted to lend the company's capital to other persons or use company assets to provide guarantees for personal (including the investor's) debts payable by other persons, this provision does not deprive the borrower's ownership of the borrowed money, and in fact the borrower can still use that money as invested capital. In order to support this position, they cite Article 214(3) of the 1993 Company Law, which states, "If a director or manager is found to have violated this Law by using the company's property to provide collateral for the debts of shareholders or other individuals, he or she shall be ordered to cancel that collateral and shall bear liability for compensation in accordance with the law, and the proceeds gained by illegally providing the collateral shall be owned by the company. If a case is serious, the person in question shall be punished by the company." This provision addresses only the cancellation of guarantees and return of proceeds, but not the cancellation of the invested capital.[42] Interestingly, this provision is omitted by the 2005 Company Law for unknown reasons.

The above two issues are relatively novel and should be carefully examined in the near future.

41. Shi Shaoxia (ed.), *The Textbook of Company Law (Gongsi Fa Jiaocheng)*, The China University of Politics and Law Press (Beijing), 1999, p. 109.
42. Jiang, supra note 5, pp. 35–36.

(2) Legal Meanings of Registered Capital

According to the Chinese company law, "registered capital" means several things.

Firstly, registered capital must be written in the articles of association (Arts. 25 and 82) so it is possible for both the company registry and a third party to know the real financial situation of a company.

Secondly, one important change made by the 2013 Amendment that could be considered as a leading innovation within continental law jurisdictions is that a company is no longer required to pay a certain amount of actual capital in order to be registered or established.[43] Thus, since the 1993 Company Law, the capital requirement has gone through two "big leaps" within twenty years.

The 1993 Company Law required that full and actual payment be made before the establishment of a company. The first leap is that the 2005 Company Law allows shareholders to initially pay 20 per cent of the total registered capital and pay the rest within two years after the company is formed.[44] For the first time, domestic investors are enjoying the same benefit granted to foreign investors many years ago. For example, Article 4 of the Certain Regulations on the Subscription of Capital by the Parties to Sino-foreign Joint Equity Enterprises[45] states, "If the joint equity venture stipulates that capital is to be fully subscribed in one payment only, the respective joint venture parties shall settle their contributions in full within six months of the day of issue of the Business Licence. If the joint venture contract stipulates that capital is to be paid up in instalments, the first payment by the respective joint venture parties shall be paid within three months of the day of issue of the Business Licence." The 2005 Company Law has dramatically reduced the economic burden of investors, as they may not have sufficient capital before the company is established or they may need capital for other investment purposes. Even though the 2005 Company Law dramatically reduces the amount of minimum registered capital, the required amount is still considered on the high side. Ironically, when Bill Gates formed his Microsoft Company, it has been said that he did not have property or

43. Article 26 of the Company Law (2013 Amendment) states, "the registered capital of a limited liability company shall be the amount of capital contributions **subscribed** for by all its shareholders as registered with the company registration authority" (emphasis is added by the author).

44. The 2005 Company Law, Article 26. Please note that under the 2005 Company Law, the 20 per cent rule is not applicable to one-person limited liability companies. See Article 59.

45. It was approved on 30 December 1987 by the State Council and jointly promulgated on 1 January 1988 by the Ministry of Foreign Economic Relations and Trade and the State Administration for Industry and Commerce.

money equivalent to ¥30,000. At that time, he had only US$500 (about ¥4,000). He never would have been able to form his company in China if the minimum capital requirement had applied to him. Thus, a technological revolution that affects almost all human beings would have been prevented.[46] Therefore, the threshold of registered capital in China does need to be further reduced in order to follow the international trend.

The second leap taken by the 2013 Company Law is a completed leap because it allows "zero capital contribution" before a company is established. In other words, the 2013 Company Law authorizes a so-called "capital subscription system" decided by the articles of association. Under this system, Chinese company law no longer requires a minimum capital contribution, which is also applicable to one-person companies. From this point, it is correct to say that China's capital system is very similar to the authorized capital system, which is popular in common law jurisdictions.

In the two representative countries of civil law jurisdiction, reforms have been done to change the minimum capital requirement. In France, the Economic Initiative Act (*Loi pour l'initiative économique*) was promulgated on 1 August 2003, abolishing the minimum capital requirement of €7,500 for the *Société à responsabilité limitée* (SARL) and making it possible to form a limited liability company for capital of one Euro.[47] Germany is going to follow the model of France. In Germany, the minimum registered capital for establishing a *Gesellschaft mit beschränkter Haftung* (GmbH) is €25,000. At the time of registration, at least €12,500 must be actually and verifiably contributed to a bank account.[48] However, on 1 November 2008, the GmbH Act was amended to allow the establishment of a new category of limited liability company, a "Mini-GmbH", which could have minimum registered capital totalling only one Euro.[49] One Euro of capital is quite a nominal requirement and could be considered as part of a move from the continental law approach to the common law approach, a point discussed subsequently. Nevertheless, in both France and Germany, the establishment of a joint stock company still requires €37,000 and €50,000 in minimum capital, respectively.

46. See Fang Liufang, "Gain New Insights Through Restudying Old Materials: Comments on Reform of the Company Law", in Guo Feng and Wang Jian (eds.), *Vertical and Horizontal Discussion on Reform of the Company Law*, The Law Press (Beijing, 2000), p. 42.
47. "Société à responsabilité limitée", retrieved from http://en.wikipedia.org/wiki/Soci%C3%A9t%C3%A9_%C3%A0_responsabilit%C3%A9_limit%C3%A9e on 29 September 2015.
48. "Private Limited Liability Company (GmbH)", retrieved from https://en.wikipedia.org/wiki/Gesellschaft_mit_beschr%C3%A4nkter_Haftung on 29 September 2015.
49. Ibid.

Fourthly, under the capital subscription system, "each shareholder shall make full payment for the capital contributions he has subscribed to according to the bylaw".[50] Thus, it is clear that the capital subscription system is only prolonging the time of payment and it never involves subscription without the obligation of payment. Further, according to the Reform Plan on the Registered Capital Registration System issued by the State Council on 7 February 2014, each enterprise shall, through the National Enterprise Credit Information Publicity System, submit an annual report to the State Administration for Industry and Commerce within a pre-decided time period. The annual report shall include information on the enterprise's actual capital contribution.[51] Also, according to the Interim Regulation on Enterprise Information Disclosure issued by the State Council on 23 July 2014, the contents of the annual report of an enterprise shall include "shareholders or promoters' amount of subscription or actual contribution, time of contribution and form of contribution".[52]

This significant change is also applicable to foreign-invested enterprises. According to the Circular of the Ministry of Commerce on Improving the Administration of Foreign Investment Approval issued by the Ministry of Commerce of the People's Republic of China on 17 June 2014, most foreign-invested enterprises are given the same treatment as domestic enterprises. In other words, the minimum capital contribution, ratio of initial capital contribution, ratio of monetary capital contribution and time limit for capital contribution have been removed.[53]

In reality, the total amount of investment is always more than the registered capital. For example, Article 3 of the Provisional Regulations of the State Administration for Industry and Commerce on the Ratio between the Registered Capital and Total Investment of Sino-Foreign Joint Equity Enterprises once stated that (1) where the total investment is US$3 million or less, its registered capital shall be at least 70 per cent of its total investment; (2) where the total investment is between US$3 million and US$10 million, its registered capital shall be at least half of its total investment. Where the total investment is less than US$4.2 million, its registered capital may not be less than US$2.1 million; (3) where the total investment is between US$10 million and US$30 million, its registered capital shall be at least

50. The 2013 Company Law, Article 28(1).
51. The Reform Plan on the Registered Capital Registration System, Article 2(2).
52. The Interim Regulation on Enterprise Information Disclosure, Article 9(4).
53. The Circular of the Ministry of Commerce on Improving the Administration of Foreign Investment Approval, Article 1.1(1)(2).

40 per cent of its total investment. Fortunately, foreign invested enterprises will no longer be subjected to this requirement.

Fifthly, Article 26(2) of the 2013 Company Law still requires certain companies to follow the paid-in registered capital or the minimum amount of registered capital.[54] In reality, those limited liability companies are usually referred to banks, insurance companies, and so on. Companies engaged in those specific industries may require huge amounts of capital. For example, Article 13 of the Chinese Commercial Bank Law states that the minimum amount of registered capital necessary for the establishment of a commercial bank shall be ¥1 billion. The minimum amount of registered capital for an urban cooperative commercial bank shall be ¥100 million, and the minimum amount of registered capital for a rural cooperative commercial bank shall be ¥50 million.

Thus, it is reasonable to foresee that false capital contribution and other illegal activities will still be punished in accordance with the Chinese Criminal Law. For example, Article 158 of the Chinese Criminal Law states, "using forged certifications to apply for company registration or using other fraudulent means to falsely declare registered capital with intent to deceive company registration departments, where the registered capital so falsely declared is large in figure with serious consequences or of a severe nature, shall be punished by imprisonment or criminal detention of less than three years, with a fine or a separately imposed fine of over 1 per cent but less than 5 per cent of the falsely declared registered capital." It is equally important to know that the criminal liabilities under Articles 158 and 159 are no longer applicable to companies implementing the capital subscription system. However, it is not logical to say that by implementing the capital subscription system China will eliminate the phenomenon of false capital contribution. After the 1960s, more and more jurisdictions adopted "authorized capital". In comparison, authorized capital may provide some

54. The Annex of The Reform Plan on the Registered Capital Registration System lists out 27 types of companies that are not allowed to implement the capital subscription system: (1) joint stock companies set up by way of fund raising; (2) commercial banks; (3) foreign-funded banks; (4) financial asset management companies; (5) trust companies; (6) financial companies; (7) financial leasing companies; (8) auto finance companies; (9) consumer finance companies; (10) currency brokerage companies; (11) rural banks; (12) loan companies; (13) rural credit cooperative associations; (14) rural mutual cooperatives; (15) securities companies; (16) futures companies; (17) fund management companies; (18) insurance companies; (19) professional insurance agencies, insurance brokerages; (20) foreign-funded insurance companies; (21) direct selling enterprises; (22) foreign labour cooperation enterprises; (23) financing guarantee companies; (24) labour dispatch companies; (25) pawn shops; (26) insurance asset management companies; and (27) small loan companies.

flexibility, as investors do not need to put all of their money in one company and can keep enough money for other investment purposes.

On the other hand, it seems that a compromised capital system is created to avoid the negative aspects of the authorized capital system.[55] For example, Article 75 of the French Company Law provides that before a company is formed, the subscription of capital shall be one fourth of the total shares. The board of directors of the company shall collect the remaining subscription within five years after the company is established.[56] In fact, the 2005 Company Law followed this approach, but the 2013 Company Law quickly adopted the "zero capital system".

There is a substantial difference between the authorized capital system and the capital subscription system. Under the authorized capital system, the company's articles of association authorize the board of directors to issue shares from time to time within the range of the authorization. But under the capital subscription system, shareholders promise to subscribe certain amount of shares and to make contributions within the agreed-upon time period. The board of directors obviously has not been given a similar power of issuing shares.

4. Names and Titles of Shareholders

The names and titles of shareholders will help to determine the details of each shareholder and in particular the big shareholders. In line with the Chinese company law, shareholders could be either natural persons or legal persons. If a shareholder is a legal person, it shall supply its titles. In reality, both a partnership and a sole proprietorship can become the shareholders of a company with a limitation, i.e., the company shall register their individual names and indicate the nature of the partnership.

5. Rights and Obligations of Shareholders

Shareholders' rights can be divided into statutory rights and agreed rights. The same applies to shareholders' obligations. Statutory rights refer to the rights that are created by the Chinese company law and relevant regulations. Agreed rights refer to the rights that are created by shareholders based on

55. Shi Shaoxiao, *The Theory of Company Law (Gongsi faxue)*, The Chinese University of Political Science and Law Press, 2012, pp. 92–93.
56. Citing Jiang Ping and Fang Liufang, *New Company Law Textbook (Xin Gongsi fa jiaocheng)*, 7th ed., The Law Press (Beijing), 1997, p. 74.

the principles of fairness, legality, honesty, and trust. This part is discussed in detail when discussing the shareholders' meeting.

6. Form and Amount of Capital Contribution

Capital contribution usually means payment in the forms of money or material objects, intellectual property rights, and land-use rights at their appraised value. In terms of cash contributions, China has gone through several stages. Under the 1993 Company Law, the percentage of cash contributions was not mentioned, but Article 24(2) stated that if the investment took the form of industrial property rights and non-patented technology, their appraised value should not exceed 20 per cent of the registered capital. On 25 December 1999, the NPC Standing Committee decided to amend the Company Law and to add one provision to Article 229. Thus, Article 229(2) provides that the State Council shall promulgate separate rules concerning the percentage of the capital contribution in the form of industrial property rights or technology with non-patent rights by the promoters of a high-tech joint stock company as well as the conditions of issuing new shares or listing shares. Under Article 27(3) of the 2005 Company Law, the amount of cash contributions must be no less than 30 per cent of the total registered capital. This means that China no longer limits the percentage of other forms of capital contribution. Now, under the 2013 Company Law, there is no percentage requirement for any form of capital contribution. This literally means that shareholders are given the freedom to choose their form of capital contribution.

As for the liability towards capital contributions, differences exist between a limited liability company and a joint stock company, as seen in Article 3(2) of the Company Law. Article 3(2) provides the definitions of these two companies. Shareholders in a limited liability company assume a liability that is equivalent to the "amount of capital contribution", while shareholders in a joint stock company assume a liability that is equivalent to the number of shares held and each share has equal value. The question is whether the capital contribution in a limited liability company can be divided into equal amounts.

So far, three methods have been adopted around the world to deal with the amount of capital contribution in an LLC. (1) The total capital is divided into equal portions and each shareholder can subscribe one or more portions. For example, Article 10 of the Japanese Limited Liability Company Law states that each share should be equal in amount and total at least 1,000 yen. (2) The total capital is divided into unequal portions and each shareholder subscribes one portion. The Taiwanese Company

Law provides this method. (3) The compromised approach: Article 5 of the German GmbH Act provides that the minimum capital of a company shall be 50,000 marks (about €25,000). The basic contribution of each shareholder shall be 500 marks (about €250). Each shareholder can make only one basic contribution, but the company can provide different amounts of the basic contribution in multiples of 100 marks (about €50).

The Chinese Company Law does not state a method of capital contribution. It is assumed that a limited liability company can choose any method it thinks fit.[57] But in any event, the shareholders in a limited liability company can hold only a proof of contribution that is not tradable, like share certificates (*gupiao*).

7. Conditions for Transferring Capital Contributions[58]

According to Article 35 of the Company Law, once a company is registered, its shareholders cannot withdraw their capital contributions. Furthermore, in comparison with a joint stock company, the transfer of capital contributions is more limited for the shareholders in a limited liability company. Article 71(2) of the Company Law states that if a shareholder intends to assign its capital contribution to persons who are not shareholders, the consent of over half of all other shareholders must be secured. Those shareholders who disapprove of the assignment shall purchase the capital contribution to be assigned. If such shareholders do not make the purchase, they shall be deemed to have consented to the assignment.

According to this provision, one shareholder can freely transfer his or her capital contribution to other shareholders, but cannot freely transfer that capital contribution to persons who are not shareholders. If a shareholder wants to transfer his or her capital contribution to outsiders, he or she must get consent (whether it is express consent or implied consent) from other shareholders. Furthermore, the consent must be given from more than half of the shareholders instead of shareholders who hold more than half of the votes. However, if more than half of the shareholders reject the transfer of capital contribution to persons who are not shareholders, they should purchase that capital contribution. In the case of a Sino-foreign joint venture, the transfer of capital contribution to a third party is even more

57. Kong Junxiang et al. (eds.), *The Company Law and the Relevant Set of Rules, New Interpretations (First Part)*, The People's Court Press (Beijing), 1997, pp. 307–8.
58. This item is removed in the 2013 Company Law. Please see Article 25 for details. However, for the sake of consistency, this book keeps this item.

limited. The assignor should not only get consent from other party(s) in the joint venture, but also seek an approval from the relevant authorities.[59]

Certainly, one has to pay attention to Article 71(4) because it authorizes shareholders to put special provisions concerning the transfer of their capital contribution into the articles of association. Shareholders are advised to take advantage of this provision when the articles of association are formulated.

8. Organizations of the Company, Method of Creation, Functions, and Powers, and the Rules of Procedure

There are several important institutions in China that must be discussed in one special chapter. Those institutions include the shareholders' meeting, board of directors, and board of supervisors. In addition to these institutions, other organs are discussed, such as newly emerged independent directors, managers, the working union, and the primary organizations of the Communist Party of China (hereinafter referred to as the "CPC").

9. The Legal Representative of a Company

The concept of the "legal representative" (*fading daibiao ren*) may not be understood by people from common law jurisdictions, but it is a unique concept under the Chinese company law. A legal representative is usually a natural person authorized to act on behalf of his or her company in a manner similar to that of the "agent" in American corporation law. The Chinese legal representative, however, serves an expanded role, bearing greater risks than an agent under the common law. The legal representative of a company is usually the chairman of the board of directors, executive director or manager.

In China, a legal representative may be given considerable power to control his or her company, but he or she is also subjected to sanctions for the legal person's misconduct. For example, the legal representative is personally at risk if the corporation engages in business beyond its authorized scope, conceals facts from registration and tax authorities or hides property to evade repayment of debts. While the legal representative is not personally liable for corporate debts, the extent of responsibility is nevertheless serious. He or she may be fined or subjected to administrative sanctions, including warnings, reprimands, probation, and dismissal from office, with

59. Article 20 of the Regulations for Implementing the Equity Joint Ventures Law of the PRC (*Zhonghua Renmin Gongheguo Zhongwai Hezi Jingying Qiye Fa Shishi Tiaoli*), which was amended on 22 July 2001.

attendant losses of prestige, status, and face. Moreover, if the offence constitutes a crime, the legal representative may be prosecuted.[60]

In the relevant part, the nature, powers, advantages, and disadvantages of a legal representative are discussed and suggestions are made to improve this system in the near future.

10. Reasons for Dissolution and Methods of Liquidation[61]

"Dissolution" is a broad concept. It involves statutory dissolution and voluntary dissolution. It is certainly important if the articles of association stipulate the detailed reason for voluntary dissolution in order to avoid any dispute. In a separate chapter, issues concerning bankruptcy and liquidation are examined.

11. Other Items That Shareholders Consider Necessary to Be Specified

Shareholders should have the discretion to provide any necessary items in the articles of association. For example, shareholders can provide the names and number of directors and quorums for a shareholders' meeting or a board of directors' meeting. However, it is proposed that any items other than the aforementioned can be freely included in the articles of association, so long as they are not specifically prohibited by the relevant laws and regulations.

60. Robert C. Art and Minkang Gu, "China Incorporated: The First Corporation Law of the PRC", *Yale Journal of International Law*, Vol. 20, 1995, p. 294.
61. This item is removed in the 2013 Company Law. Please see Article 25 for details. However, for the sake of consistency, this book keeps this item.

4

Establishment of Limited Liability Companies

I. INTRODUCTION

"Limited liability company" (*youxian zeren gongsi*) is a special term used to describe one of two forms of company in China. Contrarily, in common law jurisdictions, an LLC can be broadly interpreted as a company in which shareholders' liability is limited to the total amount of their capital contributions (including guaranteed capital contributions). Thus, an LLC may be interpreted as either a private company or a public company. In comparison, a Chinese LLC is equivalent to a private company or a closed company, which are popular in the United States and Hong Kong.

In Hong Kong, a private company is defined as a company in its articles of association, which (1) restrict the right to transfer its shares; (2) limit the number of members to fifty, not including employees of the company and former employees who were members of the company whilst employed and who have continued to be members; and (3) prohibit any invitation to the public to subscribe to any shares or debentures in the company.[1] If the articles of association fail to satisfy these requirements, the company is regarded as a public company.

In the United States, a closed company is defined as a company that provides "no established way for an outside investor to invest in the business and no assurance that current owners can sell their ownership interests

1. Cap. 622, s. 11(1).

and exit from the business".[2] In comparison with joint stock companies, closed companies may possess the following characteristics.

(1) The use of professional managers is common in public companies, rarely appearing in closed companies. Typically, one majority shareholder is actively involved in the management of the business. He or she alone may be regarded as the board of directors. As such, he or she oversees the operation of the business in much the same way a proprietor does.
(2) Another difference is that the shareholders of a closed company rarely own diversified portfolios of securities; they usually own shares of the closed company.
(3) The shareholders and managers of a closed company usually deal with each other outside the business, and these external dealings may influence how they handle business transactions.[3]

It is important to note that there is no direct connection between LLCs in China, Hong Kong (mentioned in the previous chapter), and the United States. In the United States, as discussed in the previous chapter, LLCs were created in the 1990s and developed quickly thereafter. Although it bears the same name, an LLC in the United States is considered as a hybrid business form basically arising from its combination of desirable tax and business features, including (1) limited liability for all of its members; (2) the pass-through tax treatment and capital structure of a partnership; and (3) almost complete internal flexibility in terms of management and control.[4] It is a hybrid business form because it is neither a corporation nor a limited partnership or perhaps a business form between a company and a partnership. In any event, one must be careful when using the term "limited liability company" in China, Hong Kong, or the United States.

Article 3(2) of the Company Law provides the "definition" of an LLC: shareholders shall assume liability towards the company to the extent of their respective capital contributions. In other words, the company shall be liable for its debts to the extent of all of its assets. Strictly speaking, this cannot be considered a proper definition because it only points out the shareholders' scope of liability and not the special characteristics of an LLC.

---

2. Of course, negotiated purchases or sales of interests in closely held businesses are always possible and occur all the time, but there is no established trading market. See Robert W. Hamilton and Richard A. Booth, *Business Basics for Law Students* (2nd ed.), Aspen Law & Business (New York), 1998, p. 259.
3. For details, see Robert W. Hamilton, *Business Organizations: Unincorporated Business and Closely Held Corporations*, Aspen Law & Business (New York), 1996, pp. 187–88.
4. Hamilton and Booth, supra note 2, p. 281.

Therefore, it cannot substantially show the differences between an LLC and a joint stock company.

LLCs were created far later than joint stock companies. Joint stock companies existed at the beginning of the seventeenth century, whereas LLCs were created in Germany with the promulgation of the Limited Liability Companies Act on 20 April 1892.[5] This type of company had the advantages of both joint stock companies and unlimited liability companies: on the one hand, the liability of all shareholders was limited to the total amount of their capital contribution (the advantage of joint stock companies); and on the other hand, the incorporation procedures and internal structures were comparatively simple and easy (the advantage of unlimited liability companies).

It is true that all LLCs mainly focus on certain numbers of shareholders and their good relationships. In other words, all LLCs focus on personal relationships more than on capital contributions. That is why shareholders in LLCs are allowed to take a hostile attitude towards outsiders or strangers. This is even true when a shareholder wants to transfer his or her capital contribution to any person who is not an existing shareholder, i.e., the right to transfer a capital contribution is not without limitation.

Since the personal relationship is a major consideration for most LLCs, it is important that every LLC be of reasonable size. In accordance with Article 24 of the Company Law, an LLC shall be jointly invested in and incorporated by no more than fifty shareholders. This provision is somewhat different from Article 20 of the 1993 Company Law, which required both minimum (two members) and maximum (fifty members). This is presumably because the Company Law has officially authorized one-person LLCs since 2005. However, one-person LLCs can only be considered as a special form of company. As far as a regular LLC is concerned, it is necessary to require minimum members in order to differentiate it from a one-person LLC. After all, the personal relationship is one of the main considerations in forming an LLC. One possible interpretation is that a regular LLC may require at least two members through the articles of association.

Roughly speaking, fifty shareholders in an LLC is an acceptable size around the world. In some jurisdictions, however, variation exists. For example, Article 98(1) of the Taiwanese Company Law states, "An LLC shall have no less than five and no more than twenty shareholders. Among those shareholders, more than half of the shareholders shall be citizens of Taiwan and have domiciles in Taiwan. In addition to that, the total of

5. Lei Xinghu, *Research on Legal Issues of Joint Stock Companies* (*Gufen youxian gongsi falü wenti yanjiu*), The China's Prosecution Press (Beijing), 1998, p. 33.

their capital contributions shall be more than a half of the company's total capital." Article 98(2) of the Taiwanese Company Law further states, "If the number of shareholders of an LLC is changed because of heritage or gift by will, the number shall not be limited by twenty shareholders provided in the preceding paragraph."

In comparison, Article 24 of the Chinese Company Law is still not comprehensive enough to deal with the change in shareholder numbers and legal consequences of non-conformity. Thus, the Chinese company law should be improved in at least two respects. (1) An exception should be provided under Article 24 that allows the number of shareholders to exceed fifty in some special situations provided approval is sought from the relevant authorities immediately. (2) Legal consequences should be provided if the number of shareholders does not comply with a relevant law.[6]

II. ESTABLISHMENT

In China, the procedures for establishing an LLC are relatively simple. Article 23 of the Company Law requires satisfaction of the following conditions:

(1) the number of shareholders constitutes the quorum;
(2) the amount of capital contributions subscribed to by all shareholders is in compliance with the company's articles of association;
(3) the articles of association have been jointly formed by all shareholders;
(4) the company has a name and its organizational structure complies with that of an LLC; and
(5) there is a proper company domicile.

Because most LLCs are middle- or small-sized enterprises, they have limited numbers of shareholders and no shares are issued to the public. Thus, LLCs may receive less affection from the public at large than joint stock companies. In fact, almost all company laws in different jurisdictions provide less restrictive procedures concerning the establishment of LLCs.[7] In the previous chapter, a company's articles of association, name and domicile are fairly discussed. In the following chapter, a company's organizational structure is addressed in detail. Hence, the introduction of this chapter focuses on the number of shareholders and capital contributions.

---

6. Kong Xiangjun et al. (eds.), *New Interpretation of Company Law and Relevant Rules (Gongsi fa ji peitao guiding xin shi xin jie) (Part One)*, The People's Court Press (Beijing), 1998, p. 286.
7. Liu Ruifu, *Chinese Company Law*, Joint Publishing (Hong Kong), 1998.

1. The Number of Shareholders Constitutes the Quorum

Most jurisdictions provide requirements for the number and quality of LLC shareholders through their company laws. Regarding the number of shareholders, there are two popular limitations seen worldwide.

Firstly, there is a limitation on either the minimum number or maximum number of shareholders. For example, the company laws of Germany, Austria, Italy, Switzerland, Holland, and Denmark provide no limitation on the maximum number of shareholders. There is only a minimum number of shareholders, i.e., at the time an LLC is established, the number of shareholders must be two and thereafter can be only one.[8] On the other hand, company laws in the United States, the United Kingdom, Japan, France and Belgium provide a limitation only on the maximum number of shareholders. For example, Article 8 of the Japanese Law on LLCs provides that in principle the maximum number of shareholders shall not exceed fifty. Article 36 of the French Law on Commercial Companies states that the number of shareholders in an LLC shall not exceed fifty, and if the number of shareholders exceeds fifty, the company shall be switched to a joint stock company within two years unless the number has been reduced to fifty during that period of time.[9]

Secondly, there is a limitation on both the minimum and maximum numbers of shareholders. The 1993 Company Law adopted this method. However, the 2005 Company Law provides a limitation on only the maximum number of shareholders. Apparently, there is a tendency not to provide the minimum number of shareholders that accompanies the recognition of a one-person company.

The Chinese company law is silent on the qualifications of shareholders in an LLC. In accordance with the existing practice, government institutions, legal persons and natural persons are all permitted to be shareholders in an LLC. Generally, individuals must, in accordance with the Chinese Civil Law Principles, have civil capacity in order to become shareholders, i.e., an individual must attain majority at the age of eighteen and have no mental problems.[10] This general requirement, however, became very controversial in the following case.

Li, Zhang, and Wang decided to form an LLC in order to engage in a typewriting and copying business. Zhang and Wang were both nineteen

---

8. Jiang Ping, *The New Text Book of Company Law (Xinbian gongsi fa jiaocheng)*, The Law Press (Beijing), 1997, p. 125.
9. Citing Xu Yan, *The Principle of Company Law (Gongsi fa yuanli)*, The Law Press (Beijing), 1997, p. 107.
10. The Chinese Civil Law Principles, Article 11.

years old and contributed their capital in the form of a computer and a copy machine given to them by their parents. Li was only fifteen at the time he became a shareholder in the LLC. His uncle gave him ¥40,000 as a gift, and Li decided to use the money as the capital contribution. The relevant company registry refused the registration based solely on the reason that Li was only fifteen years old and was deemed to be a person with a limited capacity for civil acts.[11] Li held the view that the Chinese company law did not clearly prohibit a person of limited capacity from establishing a company and that it was unlawful to refuse the registration of the LLC.[12]

In this case, whether Li could have acted as a promoter is arguable. In China, the traditional view is that a person of limited capacity or a person of no capacity cannot act as a promoter, even though the Chinese company law is silent on this matter. Obviously, the relevant company registry took this general view, which was reflected in this case. However, Jiang holds a sharply different view. He believes that if a law does not expressly prohibit one particular act, people should have the freedom to do so. He lists several examples in order to support his position: (1) in Japan, there is no special limitation on the qualifications of a promoter, and a person of limited capacity is also permitted to be a promoter; (2) in South Korea, a person of limited capacity can be a promoter for either an LLC or a joint stock company; and (3) on 12 July 1999, France created a new company law (SAS) that permitted individuals (including a person of limited capacity) to be shareholders.[13] However, Jiang admits that a person of limited capacity should act through his or her agent(s).[14] In this case, there is no indication that Li had an agent. Presumably, Li failed to handle the incorporation business through his agent(s). Thus, it seems that the relevant company registry correctly refused the registration.

As is discussed in detail shortly, a promoter is a person who arranges for someone to be a director, to place shares, to negotiate preliminary agreements or to prepare the company's prospectus. Taking a contract as one example, Section 4(1) of the Hong Kong Sale of Goods Ordinance states, *inter alia*, that where necessities are sold and delivered to a minor or an infant, the minor or infant must pay a reasonable price. In other words,

11. Article 12 of the Chinese Civil Law Principles is pertinent here. It states, "A minor of ten or more years of age is a person of limited capacity for civil acts and may engage in civil activities commensurate with his age and intellect. In other civil activities he is to be represented by his legal agent or obtain the consent of the legal agent."
12. The case was cited from Jiang Daxing, *Intensive Studies on Company Law (Gongsi fa de zhankai he pingpan)*, The Law Press (Beijing), December 2001, p. 2.
13. Ibid., pp. 8–9.
14. Ibid., p. 4.

only executed contracts for sale of necessities are binding on minors and infants. According to Section 4(2) of the same law, "necessities" refer to goods suitable for the condition in life of an infant or a minor and to his or her actual requirements at the time of sale and delivery.[15] Thus, without assistance from his agent(s), Li was not permitted to engage in the incorporation, which was clearly outside the scope of "necessities".

In China, legal persons can become shareholders of other companies. Under the 1993 Company Law, one company's investment in other companies should be subject to a limitation of investment amount.[16] Many scholars and experts criticized this provision heavily for its unreasonable restriction. At the time the provision was drafted, China was facing a situation where most enterprises were moving from "production" or "focusing on cost" to "operation" or "focusing on profits". The concept of an "investment-oriented company" did not exist during that period. In addition, the accounting system was based on an old "capital balance sheet" system, i.e., if an enterprise intended to make investments in the form of currency or goods in its subordinate legal person enterprise, that amount of assets had to be taken away from the original capital of the investor. Otherwise, both a parent company and its subsidiary would have calculated the same amount of capital twice. This system absolutely denied the fact that the long-term investment was part of the capital of an investing company.[17]

The 2005 Company Law abolished this limitation and offered two options to investment companies: (1) the investment should be approved by the resolutions of either the board of directors or shareholders' meeting; (2) if the maximum amount of investment has been articulated by the articles of association, the investment should be limited to that maximum amount.[18] The 2013 Company Law is even more flexible: a company may invest in other enterprises with a condition that it cannot become a capital contributor that shall bear several and joint liabilities for the debts of the enterprises in which it invests.[19]

15. D. K. Srivastava (ed.), *Business Law in Hong Kong*, Sweet & Maxwell Asia (Hong Kong), 2002, p. 127.
16. Article 12(2) of the 1993 Company Law stated that the amount of accumulated investment shall not exceed 50 per cent of the amount of the company's net capital. Furthermore, after the investment has been made, the increase of capital transferred through accepting the profit from the invested companies shall not be included in the investment amount.
17. Liu Jipeng, "Ten Suggestions for Amending the Chinese Company Law" (*Dui gongsi fa xiugai de shi dian jianyi*), in Guo Feng and Wang Jian (eds.), *Intensive Comments on Amending Company Law* (*Gongsi fa xiugai zhongheng tan*), The Law Press (Beijing), December 2000, p. 87.
18. The 2005 Company Law, Article 16.
19. Ibid., Article 15.

Thus, a related issue is whether companies can become the members of unlimited companies or partnership enterprises. It is suggested that companies should not become members who enjoy unlimited liability, i.e., they cannot become the members of unlimited liability companies and partnership enterprises because the unlimited liability is too risky for those companies, their members and creditors. Since the Chinese company law does not provide unlimited liability companies based on the fact that they have become less and less popular around the world, the focus here is whether companies can become members of partnership enterprises. Article 52 of the Chinese Civil Law Principles has a relevant provision to deal with joint operations between different enterprises. It states, "Where enterprises or an enterprise and institution join for business purposes without fulfilling the criteria of a legal person, each party to the joint operation shall, in accordance with its proportion of contributed funds or the provisions of an agreement, assume civil liability with its respective property or with the property for operation and management. Where joint liability is to be borne according to law or the terms of an agreement, the parties shall assume joint liability." Thus, it is possible to conclude that companies can become partners in joint operations. Furthermore, Article 40 of the SPC's Opinion on Implementing the Chinese Civil Procedures Law (1990) also endorses this type of "partnership joint venture". For this reason, the 2005 Company Law abolished Article 12 of the 1993 Company Law.[20]

This approach is supported for three reasons. Firstly, it is recognized that in the situation of either LLCs or joint stock companies, the term "limited liability" means only that the liability of shareholders is limited to the amount of their capital contributions. The company's liability is never limited. Companies shall exhaust all assets to pay off their debts. Secondly, it is the decision of companies whether to make investments in partnership enterprises, so long as the decision is approved by the shareholders' meeting or, if authorized, by the board of directors. Thirdly, creditors of those companies are always advised to take the status of secured creditors for obvious reasons. That is to say, the investing companies cannot use mortgaged property as a capital contribution when they decide to invest in partnership enterprises. Most importantly, secured creditors are protected in case the investing companies are subject to bankruptcy proceedings. Fourthly, allowing investment in partnership enterprises and especially in limited

20. Article 12(1) of the 1993 Company Law states that a company may invest in other limited liability companies or joint stock companies. This provision does not mention partnership joint ventures.

partnership enterprises facilitates the development of venture capital market and private equity funds.

The Chinese company law does not provide a clear limitation on the nationalities and domiciles of the shareholders in an LLC, even though this is not a case of being a joint stock company. This potential conflict may indicate that LLCs focus only on personal relationships rather than their nationalities or domiciles.

2. The Amount of Capital Contributions Subscribed to by All Shareholders

Unlike the company law practice in most jurisdictions, the Chinese company law has gone through several stages to regulate capital contributions.

(1) The Minimum Registered Capital

As is mentioned in the previous chapter, the 2005 Company Law substantially reduced the threshold for minimum registered capital, from ¥30,000 for establishing regular LLCs to ¥5 million for establishing joint stock companies. Certainly, this should be considered as major progress compared with the original high threshold provided by the 1993 Company Law. In fact, the high threshold of the 1993 Company Law was provided for several important reasons. At the time the Company Law was drafted, these high thresholds might have been provided in order to prevent people from establishing a company without sensible consideration. In other words, incorporation in China was considered as a privilege rather than a right.

Furthermore, under the 2005 Company Law, if shareholders failed to contribute the minimum registered capital, the company could not be registered or established. However, as is mentioned in the previous chapter, the 2013 Company Law formally establishes a "zero capital system", i.e., shareholders subscribe an amount of share contributions but do not need to pay in the contributions immediately. Because of this flexibility, one company may register a huge amount of subscribed capital contributions, even though the due date for paying in the contributions is many years later.

(2) Forms of Capital Contribution

Article 27 of the Company Law provides that a shareholder may make capital contributions to a company in currency or by contributing goods, intellectual property rights and land-use rights at their appraised value. Labour and credit are not considered acceptable forms of capital contribution. In the

United States, however, there is usually no limitation on contributions in the forms of labour and credit, perhaps because the board of directors is given the power to deal with this matter.

Interestingly, the 2005 Company Law took a step further by allowing investment in forms other than currency at their appraised value to a maximum of 70 per cent of the registered capital of an LLC. The relaxed percentage of the non-cash form of investment was understandable because under the 2005 Company Law, investors had an obligation to make an initial capital contribution up to 20 per cent.[21] Today, under the 2013 Company Law, there is no percentage limitation for any form of capital contribution so long as a company can be operated. This clearly indicates that investors are given more freedom to decide their investment.

Finally, after shareholders have paid in their capital contribution, the full amount of such capital contribution shall be deposited in the interim bank account opened by the LLC to be established.[22] Where a shareholder makes a capital contribution in the form of goods, intellectual property rights or land-use rights, the transfer procedures for the property rights shall be handled in accordance with the law. For example, the transfer of land-use rights shall go through not only an agreement, but also a registration process.

(3) Asset Evaluation

The next important process is the evaluation when the capital contributions are made in forms other than currency. Unlike the practice in the United States, directors in China are not responsible for evaluating contributions in forms other than currency. In practice, the evaluation is conducted by officially established institutions and certified public valuers.[23]

Asset valuation institutions shall be established based on the Interim Measures on Administration of Asset Valuation Institutes, which were issued by the State Bureau of State-owned Assets Administration on 27 October 1993. They are basically asset valuation companies (or firms), accounting firms, or auditing firms. Asset valuers (*zichan pinggu ren*) are the most important persons to secure an accurate asset valuation. In line with the

21. The 2005 Company Law, Article 26.
22. The 2013 Company Law, Article 28.
23. Article 29 of the 2005 Company Law states that after a capital contribution has been made, such capital shall be verified by a capital verification organ established lawfully and capital verification certificates shall be issued. Interestingly, Article 27(2) of the 2013 Company Law states only that "the value of the non-monetary properties as capital contributions shall be assessed and verified". It does not specify whether it should be done so by a capital verification organ. Presumably, the capital verification organ is the best choice to avoid future potential disputes.

Interim Rules on Qualifications of Registered Asset Valuers issued jointly by the Ministry of Human Resources and the State Bureau of State-owned Assets Administration on 10 May 1995, those who have passed examinations and been registered are named as Certified Public Valuers. Those who have had administrative sanctions or criminal punishments imposed because of serious mistakes they committed during an asset evaluation shall not be registered as Certified Public Valuers.[24]

Purposeful under-evaluation or over-evaluation or providing a falsified capital verification certificate is also punishable. Article 207 of the Company Law states:

> Where any institution that undertakes the evaluation or verification of assets or the verification of certificates provides any false materials, its illegal proceeds shall be confiscated by the company registration authority, and be fined 1 up to 5 times of the illegal proceeds, and may be ordered by the competent administrative department to suspend its business operation or to withdraw the qualification certificates of the directly liable persons, and revoke its business license.
>
> Where any institution that undertakes the evaluation or verification of assets or the verification of certificates makes any important omission in the report it submits, it shall be ordered by the company registration authority to make rectifications; if the circumstances are serious, it shall be fined 1 up to 5 times of the proceeds it has obtained, and may be ordered by the competent administrative department to suspend its business operation and to withdraw the qualification certificates of the directly liable persons, and revoke its business license.
>
> Where the evaluation result or proof of asset verification or certificate verification, as provided by any institution that undertakes the evaluation or verification of assets or the verification of certificates, is proved to be untrue, which has caused any loss to the creditors of the company, it shall bear the compensation liabilities within the sum which is found to be untrue, unless it can prove that it has no fault in the incurrence of the loss.

Furthermore, if a case is serious enough to constitute a crime, criminal liability shall be pursued in accordance with the relevant law.[25]

In practice, civil liability for false capital evaluation by valuers is pursued in three forms.

24. For detailed information, see Tang Dehua, *Legal Practice of Establishment and Internal Operation of Joint Stock Companies (Gufen youxian gongsi sheli yu neibu yunzuo falü shiwu) (Part One)*, The People's Court Press, 1998, pp. 231–43.
25. The 2013 Company Law, Article 215.

(a) Valuers Should Bear Civil Liability in Subsequent Order

In May 1996, Zhang Yu and Zhang Chi were going to form a company called X LLC (hereinafter referred to as "the X Company"). Both parties signed the articles of association, under which the registered capital was ¥500,000. Zhang Yu agreed to contribute ¥300,000 while Zhang Chi agreed to contribute ¥200,000. Among Zhang Chi's capital contributions was ¥180,000 in the form of cash and ¥20,000 in the forms of one motorcycle and one telephone. In order to satisfy the capital evaluation, Zhang Chi managed to get a certificate of capital issued by Y Bank Branch through the help of his friend Mr Xu, who was in charge of Y Bank Branch. The certificate was sealed and stated the following:

> To Accounting Firm: we hereby certify that the X Company (legal representative is Zhang Yu) has deposited ¥480,000 in our bank.

This certificate turned out to be false. On the same day, Z Accounting Firm relied solely on the false certificate and issued a capital evaluation report that stated that up to 13 May 1996, the X Company had paid capital totalling ¥500,000. In fact, the amount of ¥480,000 did not exist at that time. On 17 May 1996, the X Company was registered and given its business operation licence. Subsequently, the X Company was dissolved in October 1998 but the subsequent registration for cancellation was not done.

On 1 May 1997, the X Company borrowed ¥4,000 from Mr Wang and promised to pay back the money within one month. When the due date came, the X Company failed to pay the money back to Mr Wang. On 18 June 1998, the X Company issued a promissory note to Mr Wang and agreed that ¥4,000 plus bank interest in the amount of ¥540 would be paid back to Mr Wang on 24 June 1998. On the same day, the X Company again borrowed ¥25,000 from Mr Wang and promised to pay back the money by the end of July 1998. However, the bank interest for the second loan was not decided. Again, when the due date came, the X Company failed to pay back the two debts to Mr Wang. In this situation, Mr Wang sued the X Company on 6 January 1999 and demanded that the X Company pay back the two debts in the amount of ¥29,000 and total bank interest in the amount of ¥1,720.08. Mr Wang further demanded that Y Bank Branch and Z Accounting Firm bear the civil liability within the amount of money falsely certified.

Y Bank Branch argued that the certificate was issued by Mr Xu, who violated the banking regulations. Because it was his individual act, the certificate was invalid and Mr Xu should bear the relevant legal responsibility. Z Accounting Firm argued that its capital evaluation report was issued based on the certificate issued by Y Bank Branch. Since the firm was not at fault in this case, it should not be liable for the plaintiff, Mr Wang.

The court of first instance held that it was true that the X Company owed ¥29,000 to Mr Wang and thus that Mr Wang's claim should be supported and the X Company should pay back the principal debts plus bank interest. At the time of the company's registration, both Zhang Yu and Zhang Chi made false capital contributions as shareholders. The actual capital contribution was ¥20,000. Since the X Company failed to satisfy the statutory requirement of minimum registered capital, it should not have been granted legal person status. When the capital of the X Company was not sufficient to pay off the debts, both Zhang Yu and Zhang Chi should bear joint liability. Y Bank Branch knew that the X Company had not deposited money in the bank, but issued a false certificate of ¥480,000. Thus, Y Bank Branch should bear civil liability within the amount certified if both Zhang Yu and Zhang Chi could not fully compensate Mr Wang. Z Accounting Firm failed to follow the relevant rules to verify the certificate issued by Y Bank Branch and issued a false capital evaluation report. Thus, it also had to bear civil liability after Y Bank Branch could not fully pay off the debts within the amount evaluated.

In line with Articles 84(2) and 90 of the 1993 Company Law[26] and relevant rules, the judgment was as follows.

(a) The X Company had to pay back ¥32,575.02. (The principal debt was ¥29,000 and the bank interest amount was ¥3,575.02).
(b) If the X Company could not fully pay back the debts, then both Zhang Yu and Zhang Chi had to bear joint liability.
(c) If the X Company, Zhang Yu and Zhang Chi could not fully pay back the debts, then Y Bank Branch was liable to compensate Mr Wang within ¥480,000.
(d) If the X Company, Zhang Yu, Zhang Chi and Y Bank Branch could not fully pay back the debts, then Z Accounting Firm was liable to compensate Mr Wang within ¥480,000.

The judgment was upheld by the court of second instance.[27]

Firstly, there is no doubt that all of the defendants were liable for their civil wrongs. Secondly, the court tried to establish a payment order that valuers had to bear civil liability within the amount of capital evaluated if the principal wrongdoers could not fully pay off the debts. In other words, the valuers served as a backup for the principal wrongdoers. Although in

26. Now Article 207 of the 2013 Company Law.
27. Citing Jiang, supra note 12, pp. 259–61.

this case Z Accounting Firm might not have needed to pay anything because Y Bank Branch should have had sufficient money to pay off the debts, the court established the principle that valuers should also bear civil liability if they gave a false evaluation.

(b) Valuer Shall Take a Percentage Liability

In this case, the defendant was the same as in the previous case, i.e., the X Company. On 17 December 1996, the X Company borrowed ¥100,000 from N Bank. The X Company failed to pay back the debt when it was due. N Bank brought the case to the same court of first instance. The court ruled that the X Company should pay back a total ¥100,992 (the bank interest was counted until 28 May 1998). After the judgment was effective, the court enforced only ¥32,000, which was the total capital of the X Company. Because the X Company had no more property left, the court decided to stay the judgment enforcement. On 7 January 2000, N Bank sued Zhang Yu and Zhang Chi in the same court and demanded they both pay off the remaining debts in the amount of ¥90,298.56. (Bank interest was counted until 20 February 2000.) If they could not fully pay off the debts, Y Bank Branch should compensate N Bank within the limit of ¥480,000, and Z Accounting Firm should compensate N Bank within the limit of ¥480,000.

The court of first instance ruled differently even though the underlying reasons were the same as in the previous case:

(a) Zhang Yu and Zhang Chi should bear joint liability for paying back ¥88,265.81 (including bank interest) to N Bank.
(b) If Zhang Yu and Zhang Chi could not fully pay back the debts, Y Bank Branch should bear 70 per cent liability within the limit of ¥480,000 and Z Accounting Firm should bear 30 per cent liability within the limit of ¥480,000.

The court of second instance upheld the judgment and held that in this case Y Bank Branch had committed a greater civil wrong than did Z Accounting Firm.[28]

Obviously in this case, the valuer, Z Accounting Firm, was ordered to bear a percentage of liability. Percentage liability may be a better approach. However, different outcomes of similar cases reflect the problem that the same court cannot make consistent judgments.

28. Citing Jiang, supra note 12, pp. 262–64.

(c) Valuer Shall Take Joint Liability

In June 1995, the Jianglong Company borrowed ¥500,000 from the Tiandi Company to purchase rabbit furs. However, due to its unsuccessful business operation, the Jianglong Company could only return ¥100,000 to the Tiandi Company. The Tiandi Company had several times without success asked the Jianglong Company to return the remaining ¥400,000 and ultimately sued the Jianglong Company in October 1997. The court discovered that the Jianglong Company had no cash in its account. The court further discovered that at the time of incorporation, the investor, the Jianglong Group, did not make an actual capital contribution. In this situation, the court decided to add the Jianglong Group; A Bank, which issued the deposit certificate to the Jianglong Company; and FZ Accounting Firm, which issued the capital evaluation report for the Jianglong Company, as joint defendants.

The Jianglong Group argued that when the Jianglong Company was incorporated in August 1994, even though the Jianglong Group did not invest ¥400,000 in accordance with the articles of association, it invested in the Jianglong Company's house, tower crane, and one car, which were worth ¥400,000. Those assets were evaluated and confirmed by FZ Accounting Firm. For this reason, it should not bear any civil liability.

A Bank argued that when the Jianglong Company was established, even though it issued a certificate of deposit, the certificate was not fully false and it should have been further examined by FZ Accounting Firm. For this reason, it should not have borne any civil liability.

FZ Accounting Firm argued that at the time the Jianglong Company was established, it strictly followed the legal procedures to evaluate the assets of the Jianglong Company. The articles of association stated that the registered capital was ¥600,000, of which the Jianglong Group should invest ¥400,000 and another ten individuals should invest ¥200,000. FZ Accounting Firm evaluated two pieces of important evidence. One piece comprised eleven invoices issued by the Jianglong Company to the Jianglong Group and ten individuals, which indicated that investors made capital contributions in July 1994. Although these invoices bore no financial chop of the Jianglong Company (because the company had not been officially established), they were signed by the relevant persons. Furthermore, the investment amount complied with the articles of association. The second piece of evidence comprised two certificates issued by A Bank in order to prove that both the Jianglong Group and ten individuals had deposited ¥400,000 and ¥200,000, respectively. FZ Accounting Firm, based on the evidence, issued a capital evaluation report. Although these documents were proven false, FZ Accounting Firm could not have discovered them at that time. Thus, it should not have borne any civil liability.

The court ruled as follows:

(a) The loan contract between the Tiandi Company and the Jianglong Company was an illegal private loan and the contract should be invalid. Since both parties were at fault, the Jianglong Company should pay back the principal debt to the Tiandi Company but the interest should be confiscated.
(b) The Defendant, the Jianglong Group, did not actually make a capital contribution when the Jianglong Company was established, and thus it should bear joint liability. However, considering that it had made up the capital contribution, its liability could be excused.
(c) The Defendant, A Bank, did issue a false certificate of creditworthiness, and thus it should bear joint liability.
(d) The Defendant, FZ Accounting Firm, failed to carefully examine the certificate of creditworthiness and caused the Jianglong Company to be registered, and thus it should bear joint liability.[29]

In this case, the court tried to create a new approach, i.e., joint liability of valuers. It may be that joint liability is not a good approach when there is no evidence that valuers have conspired with the principal wrongdoers. If it is clear that promoters are the principal wrongdoers in a case of false capital contribution, then they should be subject to major civil liability in addition to administrative sanctions or criminal responsibility. Although there may be some faults on the part of a valuer, their liability shall be a limited one rather than a joint liability. In conclusion, it is believed that percentage liability is a better approach, while joint liability could be adopted if there is clear evidence of conspiracy. Thus, the relevant legislation should solve this inconsistency in the near future.

(4) Payment Method

According to the 1993 Company Law, shareholders were not allowed to pay their contribution by way of instalment, or more specifically by way of a compromised approach, a point discussed subsequently in this book. The underlying purpose was to ensure the healthy development of companies and to protect against companies being established without proper consideration. However, when an LLC was formed by foreign investors, it was treated differently, and although payment by instalment was allowed, the first payment could not be less than 15 per cent of the total capital. The 2005 Company Law made a remarkable change to allow payment by instalment.

29. Citing Jiang, supra note 12, pp. 267–69.

The 2013 Company Law made a revolutionary change by allowing "zero capital" contributions, even though it is not the same as an authorized capital system. Thus, shareholders are given more freedom to arrange their capital contributions.

III. ONE-PERSON COMPANY

Generally, a one-person company is a company that has only one shareholder (either a natural person or a legal person), whose liability is limited to the amount of his or her capital contribution. Traditional company law requires that a company have at least two shareholders for the simple reason that one shareholder may easily abuse the doctrine of a separate legal entity and use the company to escape his or her personal liability.[30] Many Western countries used to hold a negative attitude towards one-person LLCs because of their obvious flaws, including the lack of a checks-and-balances mechanism, the easy mixture of shareholders' own property with the company's property, the abuse of corporate legal person status, and so on. This situation, however, has changed and one-person companies are allowed in many developed countries such as the United States, Japan, France, Germany, and the United Kingdom. This shows the existing value of this type of company. It may be a correct conclusion that "being flexible and able to implement decisions without having to worry about the 'internal political players' is a driving force",[31] and at the same time the shareholder can enjoy the benefit of limited liability.

Why is the one-person company welcome? Does the one-person company challenge the well-established theoretical foundation? In continental law jurisdictions, commercial laws usually define a company as a juridical association (similar to a legal person in common law jurisdictions).[32] After a one-person company is adopted, following a major company law theory, can the company still be called a juridical association? One thing is

30. This was the typical argument in *Salomon v A Salomon & Co Ltd* [1897] AC 22, although in that case there were more shareholders.
31. Other reasons may include: (1) the desire for personal freedom that allows them to adopt the lifestyle of choice; (2) the drive and passion to implement a business plan and to fulfill their personal dreams; (3) the willingness to go the extra mile and desire to succeed; (4) they are very passionate about what they do; (5) they are committed to their venture; and (6) they are comfortable working alone and are above average users of new technologies such as the Internet or voiceover IP. See Christoph Puetz, "The One Person Company", retrieved from http://ezinearticles.com/?The-One-Person-Company&id=96448 on 5 October 2015.
32. Although the Civil Law Principles of the PRC does not adopt this term, Chinese scholars use this term frequently.

certain: the concept of the traditional company must be changed following the adoption of a one-person company. Professor Jiang once described the one-person company as an irrevocable tendency in China: in a joint participant company, regardless of what type of shareholding system is arranged, the controlling power will eventually be centralized in the hands of a few shareholders who make decisions, while other shareholders are in fact the puppets. Thus, the character of the Chinese people lacks the group type of personality.[33] This conclusion must be subjected to further discussion simply because the one-person company was developed later in China.

Under the 1993 Company Law, individuals were not allowed to establish a one-person company because a regular LLC had to be formed by at least two persons. This restriction was removed by the 2005 Company Law in order to give people more freedom and autonomy to run their business and to decide the way to run their business.

In China, the first one-person company was established in Wenzhou City, Zhejiang Province, which is the birthplace of China's private economy. Wang Yicheng, an individual businessman, received an operation licence from the local administrative bureau for industry and commerce for operating his computer leasing company with registered capital of ¥100,000 (about US$12,345).[34] This marked the beginning of the one-person company in China.

Technically, if one natural person wants to do business in more than ten cities, a one-person company is a better choice than a sole proprietorship in terms of limited liability. Furthermore, the one-person company is a stable business form and can easily pass its business to the next generation. Today, technology is developing quickly, and many hi-tech products such as software, electronic and communication products are coming from one-person companies. Those hi-tech products need key technologies controlled by only a few persons and can be put into production or authorize others to produce through licensing agreements. A one-person company can also easily protect its trade secrets.

However, due to the nature of the one-person company, it is important to prevent the sole shareholder from abusing the company by utilizing limited liability as a shield. The best way to do so is to endorse the old doctrine of lifting (or piercing) the corporate veil, which is popular in common law jurisdictions.

---

33. Jiang Daxing, *Company Concepts and Interpretation (Gongsi fa de guannian he jieshi) (I)*, The Law Press (2009), p. 116.
34. "1st One-Person Firm Set Up in Wenzhou", retrieved from http://english1.people.com.cn/200601/03/eng20060103_232374.html on 5 October 2015.

In the Salomon case, the House of Lords established two important concepts that continue to be widely accepted today: one is the concept of separate legal entity and the other is the concept of limited liability. However, in reality, there is a danger that a company can be used by some shareholders as a shield to escape their personal liability. Therefore, from time to time, courts in common law jurisdictions decide to ignore the company as a veil in order to impose personal liability on an individual investor.

So far in common law jurisdictions, lifting the corporate veil is an available option under both case law and statute. Under case law, there are some "established grounds" to justify the courts' attempts to pierce the corporate veil:

- Fraud: one may use the company as a device, a stratagem or a mask in order to perpetrate fraud.
- Group enterprises: even subsidiary companies are considered as separate legal entities. The veil of a subsidiary company can be pierced if the subsidiary company has been treated as the part of same economic entity or group.
- Agency: the company is nothing but an agent of the investor.
- Trust: sometimes if a trustee holds the shares of the company concerned, the court may ignore the veil in order to see the characteristics of relevant shareholders.
- Enemy character: during wartime, a court may pierce the veil in order to see its shareholdings.[35]

Under the statute, a corporate veil is pierced in the following situations in Hong Kong:

- fraudulent trading; and
- abuse of company names or employment of disqualified directors.

Obviously, Chinese legislators have foreseen the potential danger of a one-person company being abused by one shareholder. Thus, Article 63 of the Company Law provides that the shareholder of a one-person company shall be jointly liable for the debts of the company if he or she fails to prove the separation of his or her own property from the company's property. Article 20(3) further provides that if a shareholder is found to escape debts by abusing his or her legal person status and limited liability, to cause serious damages to creditors of the company, he or she should be jointly

35. For detailed information, please see Anusuya Sadhu, "Lifting the Corporate Veil", retrieved from http://www.legalserviceindia.com/articles/corporate.htm on 5 October 2015.

liable for the debts of the company. This provision, in fact, is quite close to the doctrine of lifting the corporate veil. However, due to the fact that China does not implement a case law system, judges may encounter difficulties in dealing with relevant cases without a sophisticated list of types of behaviour that may be adopted to pierce the corporate veil.

IV. ESTABLISHMENT OF A SPECIAL LLC: A WHOLLY STATE-OWNED COMPANY

1. Definition

A wholly state-owned company (hereinafter referred to as a "WSC") refers to an LLC invested in solely by the state. The State Assets Regulatory and Management Institution (*Guoyou zichan jiandu guanli jigou*, hereinafter referred to as the "SARMI"), authorized by the State Council or local people's governments, shall exercise rights and bear duties as a capital contributor.[36] This definition basically contains two major elements. Firstly, a WSC is formed by a special investor, i.e., the state through the authorization of the SARMI.[37] Hence, WSCs are formed by the state rather than other legal persons or individuals. Because there is only one promoter and one shareholder, it can literally be called a "one-person company". Certainly, under the 1993 Company Law, this type of company was specially authorized and had the sole purpose of maintaining the state ownership of large companies converted from state-owned enterprises (hereinafter referred to as "SOEs"). In this situation, special treatment was given to SOEs. This is a typical example where the main motivation for promulgating the 1993 Company Law was to rescue the SOEs.

However, it has been suggested that the special chapter dealing with WSCs should be taken away from the Chinese company law and that there

36. The Company Law, Article 64(2). However, from the perspective of statistics, WSCs would be divided into three categories: (1) WSCs are controlled 100 per cent by the State; (2) WSCs' majority shares (more than 50 per cent) are controlled by the State; and (3) WSCs' shares are partly owned by the State. See the Letter of State Statistics to Determine State-owned Companies, which was issued on 18 April 2003. In this book, the term "WSCs" refers only to companies that are controlled 100 per cent by the State.

37. The relevant Regulations on Management of State-owned Assets state clearly that only the Administrative Bureau of State-owned Assets should be the investor in WSCs. It is not difficult to infer from the Chinese tradition that the relevant investment institutions or departments could easily acquire authorization from the Administrative Bureau of State-owned Assets. It should be noted that the new organ, the Commission on Supervision and Administration of State-owned Assets, was approved to be established by the first session of the Tenth National People's Congress.

should be a separate law to specially deal with WSCs.[38] The underlining argument is that under the Chinese company law all investors should be subject to consistent and equal requirements. Furthermore, there is a need to build up healthy conditions for fair competition among various market players.

All WSCs take the form of LLCs. Because of this, WSCs have to follow procedures of establishment similar to that of regular LLCs. Furthermore, because they are LLCs, the state is liable only for the amount of their capital contributions instead of bearing unlimited liability. In this situation, the state successfully gets rid of its unlimited liability when a business enterprise is deemed to be a WSC. On the other hand, because WSCs are still invested in by the state, the state retains its substantial control over them.

2. Application for Establishing WSCs

Article 64 of the 1993 Company Law pointed out that WSCs were suitable only for some special enterprises, i.e., "companies which manufacture special products determined by the State Council or companies that belong to the category of specialized trades shall adopt the form of WSCs". Although the 2005 Company Law ceased using the same language, it is understandable that only some special enterprises were qualified for organizing this type of company. The provision is consistent with China's emphasis that the public ownership system should take a dominant position and that the state should control some important enterprises directly. It is observed that those important and giant enterprises are usually engaging in businesses such as energy, communication, postage, military products, aerospace and steel. Many of them are under the direct leadership of the Central Government. So far, this type of WSC numbers 110, representing a 50 per cent reduction from the number in 2003, the year such WSCs were established. However, China's central government issued a Guideline to Deepen Reforms of State-owned Enterprises on 13 September 2015 and intended to "improve the competence of SOEs and turn them into fully independent market entities".[39] In order to achieve this goal, senior managers should be given more decision power. This may mean that the Company Law relating to WSCs will be amended in the near future. Today, senior managers are still appointed by the SARMI or by the SARMI and the Organization Department

38. Gu Gongyun, "Basic Thoughts of Completely Revising the Chinese Company Law" (*Quanmian xiuding gongsi fa de jiben silu*), in Guo and Wang, supra note 17, p. 109.
39. Xinhua, "China Issues Guideline to Deepen SOE Reforms", retrieved from http://news.xinhuanet.com/english/2015-09/13/c_134620039.htm on 5 October 2015.

of the Central Committee of the CPC if they are CPC members. On the other hand, the SOEs that are less important will be allowed to convert into either regular LLCs or joint stock companies.

3. Special Features of WSCs

(1) *Special Shareholders*

It is clear that only special shareholders can make investments in WSCs. As mentioned previously, so far only state-authorized investment institutions or departments are considered as investors. At present, government departments at all levels and the various kinds of organizations established by the governments at all levels may be authorized to form WSCs. Furthermore, the establishment of WSCs will obviously require the approval of the state or the SARMI, authorized by the State Council, local people's governments or the relevant government authorities.[40]

(2) *The Internal Structure*

Firstly, because the ultimate investor is the state, a WSC has only one shareholder and there is no need to have a shareholders' meeting. As a result of this, the articles of association of WSCs are formulated by the SARMI or by the board of directors with one precondition: that the formulated articles of association be approved by the SARMI.[41] Some major powers are given to the board of directors, but the issues of mergers, divisions, dissolutions, increases or reductions of capital and issuances of company bonds must be decided by the SARMI.[42] The underlying reason is to protect state-owned assets.

Secondly, there is a special board of directors. Most directors are appointed and replaced by the SARMI, but the directors who are representatives of the employees are elected through the Workers Representatives Assembly (*Zhigong daibiao dahui*).[43] The Company Law does not indicate whether workers' representatives are mandatory. However, in accordance with the Administrative Rules on Implementing Worker Directors within Wholly State-owned Companies (on a trial basis) issued by the Commission on Supervision and Administration of State-owned Assets on 3 March 2006,

40. The Company Law, Article 64(2).
41. Ibid., Article 65.
42. Ibid., Article 66.
43. Ibid., Article 67(2).

at least one director shall be the worker representative.[44] The board of directors shall exercise its functions and powers in accordance with the provisions of Articles 46 and 66 of the Company Law, which are discussed in detail subsequently.

Thirdly, a WSC has one manager who shall exercise his or her functions and powers in accordance with Article 49 of the 2005 Company Law. Legally, a director can serve concurrently as a manager if it is approved by the SARMI.[45]

Fourthly, a board of supervisors has become a compulsory organ of WSCs. On 25 December 1999, the Standing Committee of the NPC passed a decision amending the 1993 Company Law. Article 67 requires that a board of supervisors should be established within a WSC in order to supervise its operation. One unique feature is that the board of supervisors is mainly composed of representatives, who are elected by the Workers Representative Assembly. The members of the board must number at least five, and at least one third should be worker representatives. The board exercises its powers and functions in accordance with Articles 53(1), 53(2) and 53(3), i.e., the right to investigate the company's financial affairs; the right to supervise acts conducted by directors and managers during the performance of their duties on whether they are violating the law, statutory regulations or the company's articles of association; and the right to demand the correction of wrongful conduct of directors and senior management personnel. Supervisors attend meetings of the board of directors but have no voting power. Directors and management personnel are not allowed to take the position of supervisor concurrently. Detailed issues concerning the role and functions of supervisors are discussed in the subsequent chapter.

V. FOREIGN-INVESTED ENTITIES THAT ARE LLCS

It is worth giving a brief introduction to some foreign-invested entities that take the form of LLCs for better comparison and understanding. What follows is a selection of foreign-invested entities for introduction purposes. These foreign-invested companies can also be divided into two major categories, i.e., LLCs and enterprises with no legal person status. Given the diversity of foreign-invested companies in various business areas, the following introduction cannot be exhaustive. Furthermore, it is important to note that when the Company Law was amended in 2013, the legislators

44. The Administrative Rules on Implementing Worker Directors within Wholly State-owned Companies (on a trial basis), Article 4.
45. The Company Law, Article 68(2).

decided to keep Article 217 unchanged, i.e., "the limited liability companies and joint stock limited companies invested by foreign investors shall be governed by this Law. Where there are otherwise different provisions in any law regarding foreign investment, such provisions shall prevail". This clearly means that the relevant laws concerning foreign-invested enterprises are still valid even though they may contradict and conflict with the Company Law.

1. Traditional Foreign-Invested Companies

Initially, foreign investment in China took three traditional forms, i.e., Sino-foreign equity joint ventures (hereinafter referred to as "EJVs"), Sino-foreign contractual joint ventures (hereinafter referred to as "CJVs") and wholly foreign-owned enterprises (hereinafter referred to as "WFOEs").

EJVs are usually foreign companies, enterprises and other economic entities or individuals (hereinafter referred to as "foreign parties") forming joint venture enterprises within the territory of China with Chinese companies, enterprises or other economic entities (hereinafter referred to as "Chinese parties"). In line with the Sino-Foreign Equity Joint Venture Law of the PRC, all EJVs shall take the form of LLCs (Art. 4), and thus all EJVs are Chinese legal persons and governed and protected by relevant Chinese law.

Both foreign parties and Chinese parties shall invest mutually in EJVs. Usually, foreign participants are encouraged to invest high technology and capital (Art. 5). Regarding the percentage of investment, foreign participants are usually required to invest not less than 25 per cent.[46] However, following the amendment of the Company Law in 2013, the Ministry of Commerce issued the Notice on Improving the Administration of Foreign Investment Review on 17 June 2014. The important message of this Notice is that "requirements for or provisions on proportions of initial capital contribution, proportions of monetary contribution and fulfilment periods of capital

46. In the past, 25 per cent foreign-held shares was the indicator of a foreign-invested enterprise. Thus, if a foreign-invested enterprise does not satisfy the requirement of 25 per cent foreign-held shares, whether the enterprise can still be considered as a foreign-invested enterprise is questionable. On 17 July 2003, a Notice concerning examination and approval of the situation where the contribution of foreign investors is less than 25 per cent was jointly issued by the MOFTEC, the State Tax Bureau, the State Administrative Bureau for Industry and Commerce and the State Bureau for Foreign Currency. The Notice points out that since the beginning of 2004, if the capital contribution of foreign investors is less than 25 per cent, then the wording "Less than 25 per cent Foreign Investment" must appear in the Approving Certificate and Business Licence. Most importantly, the enterprise established shall not be permitted to enjoy tax advantages given to foreign-invested enterprises.

contribution to a foreign-funded company (including a company funded by investors from Taiwan, Hong Kong or Macao) shall be cancelled". In other words, those issues are confirmed through contracts or bylaws. On the other hand, the Notice states that "the proportion between a company's registered capital and total investment shall conform to the Interim Provisions on the Proportion between Registered Capital and Total Investment of a Chinese-Foreign Equity Joint Venture and other existing provisions which are effective".[47]

Although there is no limitation on the maximum investment by foreign investors, according to the Provisional Regulations on Foreign Investment and Guideline Catalogue of Foreign Investment Industries, in some investment areas the Chinese participant must take the absolute or relative majority. The parties to an EJV shall set the time limit in their joint venture contract for paying up their respective investment contributions, and they shall pay their respective investment contributions fully within the time limit stipulated in the contract. Delay or partial delay in payment shall be subject to a payment of the investment in arrears or compensation for the loss as defined in the contract. If the joint venture contract stipulates that investment contributions shall be paid by instalments, the first instalment shall not be less than 15 per cent of the total amount of their respective investment contributions.

One of the unique features of EJVs is their internal structure. EJVs do not have to set up shareholders' meetings for the simple reason that there is a Chinese party on one side and a foreign party on the other side. EJVs shall establish boards of directors, the size and composition of which shall be determined through negotiations between the parties to the EJVs. Boards of directors shall have the right to decide all major matters of the EJVs. However, the Chinese and foreign parties must agree:

- to amend the articles of association;
- to stop or dissolve the EJVs;
- to increase or decrease the registered capital;
- to merge or divide the EJVs; and
- on other matters articulated in the articles of association.

On the other hand, CJVs are enterprises formed under contract terms in accordance with Article 2 of the Sino-Foreign Contractual Joint Venture Law of the PRC. The most important advantage of forming a CJV is that

47. The Interim Provisions on the Proportion between Registered Capital and Total Investment of a Chinese-Foreign Equity Joint Venture, Article 3.

the Chinese party may contribute capital in the forms of cash, land-use rights or labour. Most importantly, the rights and duties of each party are not calculated based on investment percentage; rather, they are decided by the joint venture contract. In the situation of EJVs, the Chinese party has to contribute a certain percentage of cash. Furthermore, in the situation of CJVs, the foreign party is allowed to take back its investment by way of depreciation fees. In the situation of EJVs, the investment cannot be taken back during the operation.

A CJV may choose to become a legal or non-legal person. In the situation where a CJV chooses not to become a legal person, it is naturally treated as a partnership enterprise and the liabilities of each party are joint and several.

As mentioned previously, the rights, responsibilities, profit distributions and risk bearing are decided by the joint venture contract but not based on the investment. Both parties may distribute earnings by means of distributing profits or products or by other means agreed upon by the parties. For example, if a CJV running a real estate business wants to sell apartments, the parties can sell them either jointly or separately based on the joint venture contract. Furthermore, on the expiry of the duration of the term of the enterprise, all permanent assets of the CJV shall be reverted to the ownership of the Chinese party without any compensation or payment. However, the foreign party may apply to recover its investment during the term of operation by the following means: (1) a stipulation in the contract increases the earnings distribution ratio of the foreign party, with the distribution occurring in accordance with the proportion of investment or terms of cooperation; and (2) subject to examination and approval by the finance and taxation organs under the relevant state taxation provisions, the foreign partner recovers its investment before the payment of income tax.

If a CJV takes the status of a legal person, its internal structure is similar to that of an EJV.

Today, CJVs are becoming less and less attractive because more and more foreign investors are focusing on long-term investment and controlling their investments effectively. As such, they choose either EJVs or WFOEs.

The most important advantage of establishing a WFOE is that foreign investors obtain 100 per cent control of the enterprise, making it easy to control its technology and commercial secrets. Therefore, WFOEs are welcome by foreign investors. This held true even after China joined the World Trade Organization.

WFOEs are different from foreign enterprises because the latter are enterprises established in foreign jurisdictions. According to Article 8 of the Wholly Foreign-owned Enterprise Law of the PRC, WFOEs can adopt either a legal person form or a non-legal person form. If a legal person form is adopted, a WFOE is deemed to be an LLC (could be another type of one-person LLC). On the other hand, if a non-legal person form is adopted, a WFOE can be treated as either a partnership or a sole proprietorship.

With regard to EJVs and CJVs, most application matters can be handled by the Chinese partners (e.g., the Chinese partners also arrange land-use right, raw material and energy supply transactions and hire employees). When a WFOE is formed, foreign investors have to entrust a Chinese agency to assist in all application matters.

2. The Establishment of Investment-Type Companies

Investment-type companies with foreign investment are also called "foreign-funded holding companies". When China promulgated the 1993 Company Law, nothing was mentioned in that Law regarding this type of company. For the purpose of improving the environment for foreign investment, on 4 April 1995, the then Ministry of Foreign Trade and Economic Co-operation (hereinafter referred to as "MOFTEC", now the Ministry of Commerce) promulgated the Interim Provisions on the Establishment of Investment Companies by Foreign Investors. Subsequently, this legal document was supplemented or revised several times by the following legal documents: Explanations of Relevant Questions of the Interim Provisions on the Establishment of Investment Companies by Foreign Investors (1996), the Supplemented Rules for the Interim Provisions on the Establishment of Investment Companies by Foreign Investors (1999), the Supplemented Rules (Second Part) for the Interim Provisions on the Establishment of Investment Companies by Foreign Investors (2001), and the Decision on Revising the Interim Provisions on the Establishment of Investment Companies by Foreign Investors and Supplemental Rules (2003). Finally, the Ministry of Commerce issued the Rules on the Establishment of Investment Companies by Foreign Investors (hereinafter referred to as the "Regulations on Investment Companies") on 10 June 2003. Again, the Ministry of Commerce amended the Regulations on Investment Companies on 13 February 2004 and 26 May 2006, respectively. The relevant introduction is based on the Regulations on Investment Companies.

(1) Definition

Foreign-funded holding companies usually engage in investment activities (direct investment). They are LLCs, which are established in China by a foreign investor in the form of either a wholly foreign-owned company or a Sino-foreign joint venture company (Art. 2).

(2) Conditions of Establishment

It is unclear whether the Circular of the Ministry of Commerce on Improving the Administration of Foreign Investment Approval issued by the Ministry of Commerce of the People's Republic of China on 17 June 2014 would apply to foreign-funded holding companies. Presumably, these companies are considered special companies and have to follow the capital requirement stipulated by the Regulations on Investment Companies.

Firstly, foreign-funded holding companies must have minimum registered capital of US$30 million (Art. 3.3).

Secondly, foreign investors shall have a good creditworthiness and a strong financial capability. Only those that have satisfied the conditions and fall into one of the following categories may apply to establish an investment company in China:

(A) the foreign investor that has a total asset value of no less than US$400 million in the year prior to the application, has established foreign investment enterprises in China with a paid-up capital contribution of more than US$10 million, and has had three or more investment project proposals approved; or
(B) the foreign investor that has already established ten or more foreign investment enterprises that are engaged in production or infrastructure projects with a paid-up capital contribution of more than US$30 million (Art. 3.1).

Thirdly, if the investment companies are established in the form of joint ventures, the Chinese parties shall have good creditworthiness and a strong financial capability. Furthermore, the Chinese parties shall have a total asset value of no less than ¥100 million in the year prior to the application (Art. 3.2).

(3) Procedures of Establishment

Clearly, the establishment of a foreign-funded holding company must follow the procedures for their establishment, which are similar to those of other foreign-invested enterprises. The most important thing is that a foreign-funded holding company must be approved by the Ministry of Commerce before its establishment (Art. 10).

(4) *Enterprises Invested in by Investment Companies*

Firstly, if an enterprise is invested in by an investment company directly or in conjunction with other foreign and/or Chinese investors, the capital contribution by the investment company or by the investment company in conjunction with other foreign investors shall account for 25 per cent or more of the registered capital of such an enterprise (Art. 11.1).

Secondly, if an established enterprise in China whose interests, owned by the investors or the associated companies of an investment company and other foreign investors, are partly or entirely acquired by such an investment company, the capital contributions by the investment company and other foreign investors shall account for 25 per cent or more of the registered capital of such an enterprise (Art. 11.2).

Thirdly, if an enterprise is invested in by an investment company directly, 10 per cent of the registered capital of that enterprise shall be contributed by the investment company (Art. 11.3).

(5) *New Changes*

According to the Regulations on Investment Companies, foreign-invested companies shall be allowed to engage in a broad scope of business. They can provide the enterprises they invest in with management services.[48] They can also provide a wide range of consultation services to their affiliated companies (Art. 10). In addition, they can enjoy preferential treatment if permission is given by the Ministry of Commerce.

3. Establishment of Joint Equity Foreign Trade Companies

On 30 September 1996, MOFTEC issued the Provisional Measures on the Trial Establishment of Sino-foreign Joint Equity Foreign Trade Companies (hereinafter referred to as the "Measures"). The Measures were replaced by the New Measures issued by MOFTEC on 31 January 2003. Furthermore, the Ministry of Commerce issued the Supplementary Rules for the New Measures on 7 December 2003.

According to the New Measures, foreign companies or enterprises and Chinese companies or enterprises can form foreign trade companies (hereinafter referred to as "FTCs"). Due to the nature of foreign trade, individuals

48. Before 2004, they could provide only consultation services to the enterprises they invested in.

are not permitted to engage in this area alone. Furthermore, parties wishing to form an FTC are subject to selection. Both the foreign partner and Chinese partner must satisfy the conditions stipulated in the Measures.

(1) Special Contribution

Although the requirement of 25 per cent is relaxed, the total amount of investment is still an obligation, i.e., within two years after the licence is issued, the invested capital shall be at least ¥30 million, and the rest of the capital shall be paid within five years after the licence is issued (Art. 1 of the 2006 Amendment). However, as of 11 December 2003, the Chinese partner is no longer required to hold more than 51 per cent of the registered capital and to appoint the legal representative (Art. 16).

(2) Financial Conditions of Investors

Foreign investors shall have engaged in trade with China in the average amount of more than US$30 million within three years prior to the application (Art. 4.1).

(3) Special Chinese Partners

The Chinese partner shall have obtained permission to engage in foreign trade, and its average amount of imports and exports shall be more than US$30 million within three years prior to the application (Art. 4.2).

(4) Registered Capital

The registered capital for a joint equity FTC must be at least ¥50 million (Art. 4.3).

(5) New Changes

Under the New Measures, the scope of business is no longer specified. That means that every FTC can import and export goods and technologies as long as the goods and technologies are not subject to a quota system or a licence system (Art. 9). Unlike the old Measures, the New Measures remove the limitations placed on the location of the FTC.

The Supplementary Rules try to respond to the Closer Economic Partnership Arrangement between mainland China, Hong Kong, and

Macao. Thus, investors from Hong Kong or Macao have been able to, since 1 January 2004, establish FTCs in the forms of equity joint ventures, contractual joint ventures and sole ownership ventures. In addition, investors in Hong Kong or Macao are required only to have engaged in trade with China in the average amount of more than US$10 million within 3 years prior to the application (Art. 2). Finally, the registered capital of the FTCs established by investors from Hong Kong or Macao should be no less than ¥20 million (Art. 3).

4. Foreign-Funded Commercial Enterprises

On 25 June 1999, both MOFTEC and the State Economic and Trade Commission jointly issued the Regulations on Establishment of Pilot Projects of Foreign-Funded Commercial Enterprises. The Regulations were replaced by the Administrative Measures on Foreign Investment in the Commercial Areas (hereinafter referred to as the "Administrative Measures") issued by the Ministry of Commerce on 9 April 2004.

Under the Administrative Measures, a foreign-funded commercial enterprise (hereinafter referred to as an "FFCE") is allowed to be established between foreign companies and enterprises (foreign partners) and Chinese companies and enterprises (Chinese partners). Article 21 of the Administrative Measures allows the establishment of wholly FFCEs in China after 11 December 2004.

(1) Form of Cooperation

Every FFCE can be formed by way of either an equity joint venture or a contractual joint venture. As of 11 December 2004, wholly foreign-owned commercial enterprises are permitted to be established (Art. 21).

(2) Financial Condition of Investors

This is also relevant to registered capital. Any FFCE shall satisfy the minimum registered capital in accordance with the Chinese company law. For example, the minimum registered capital for retail commercial enterprises shall be not less than ¥50 million. The minimum registered capital for wholesale commercial enterprises shall be bigger even though the Chinese Company Law is silent on this matter (Art. 7.1). Presumably, in the situation of a joint venture, foreign investors shall contribute at least 25 per cent of the total registered capital.

(3) Fixed Duration

The period of operation of an FFEC shall not exceed thirty years (forty years for those based in the central and western parts of China).

(4) Scope of Business

An FFCE doing retail commercial business can engage in retail (including the retail of goods on a commission basis and the consignment of goods for sale on commission), organize the export of Chinese goods, import and export goods for its own operation and operate any relevant auxiliary services. An FFCE doing wholesale commercial business can engage in the wholesale of Chinese goods in China and imported goods for its own commercial operation and organize the export of Chinese goods.

FFCEs are no longer subject to limitations placed on location. Furthermore, investors from Hong Kong or Macao may enjoy preferential treatment in accordance with the Closer Economic Partnership Arrangement. One of the noticeable benefits is that Chinese citizens who are permanent residents of Hong Kong or Macao are allowed to engage in commercial retail business by forming an individual household for commerce and industry (Art. 25.4).

5. Foreign Resident Representative Offices of Foreign Companies

On 30 October 1980, the State Council issued the Interim Regulations of the State Council of the PRC concerning the Control of Resident Representative Offices of Foreign Enterprises. The National Administration for Commerce and Industry issued the Measures for Managing the Registration of Resident Representative Office of Foreign Enterprises (1983) and MOFTEC issued the Detailed Implementation Rules for Examination and Management of Resident Representative Offices of Foreign Enterprises in the same year. Under these legal documents, foreign companies are allowed to carry out business activities in China provided they have obtained approval and completed registration procedures. So far, most foreign resident representative offices of foreign companies (hereinafter referred to as "RROFCs") established in the whole of China have been located mainly in Beijing and Shanghai. According to the Chinese company law, RROFCs do not have legal person status and foreign companies shall bear civil responsibility for their operational activities.

6. Disputes under Foreign Investment Laws

Disputes arising out of foreign investment can be handled through either arbitration or adjudication. In order to resolve the disputes, one must consider not only the relevant foreign investment laws and regulations, but also the Chinese company law and other laws (e.g., the Chinese Labour Law and the Labour Contract Law). Although the resolution of such disputes is not the major concern of this book, the following case is offered for a concrete understanding.

In April 1991, businessmen from the United States and Japan invested in an LLC (hereinafter referred to as "the F Company") and signed an employment contract with Zhao Hai. The contract did not mention the specific time of termination. Zhao was appointed as a vice general manager in charge of marketing. On 25 February 1992, the general management decided to terminate the service contract with Zhao for the reason that he was not capable of doing his job. Both sides signed the termination document. On 25 March 1992, however, Zhao lodged a claim against the F Company in the City Labour Arbitration Committee (hereinafter referred to as the "CLAC") and required the dispute to be settled. Zhao demanded that the general manager withdraw his termination decision, restore his position and reimburse him his wage during the application for arbitration. On 16 August 1992, the CLAC decided not to support Zhao's claim. Zhao then filed the case to a district court.

Zhao argued that without the approval of the board of directors the general manager had no right to fire him as vice general manager, in accordance with provisions of the Chinese company law. The general manager argued that he was responsible for the board of directors and should have the right to fire Zhao based on the constitution of the company.

In this case, the court had to consider the powers of the general manager under both the Chinese company law and relevant foreign investment laws. In accordance with the Chinese company law, the general manager shall be responsible for the board of directors and shall exercise one of the powers of office to propose the appointment and dismissal of the company's deputy manager (Article 50). The word "proposal" clearly indicates that the general manager had no power to simply fire Zhao. This conclusion is also supported by Article 37 of the Implemental Rules for Sino-foreign Equity Joint Venture Law issued by the State Council on 22 July 2001, which provides pertinent language indicating that the general manager and vice general manager(s) shall be appointed by the board of directors. One may argue that the board of directors could have authorized the general manager to fire Zhao. This argument, however, would not have succeeded in this case. Firstly, there was no evidence of authorization. Secondly, all relevant provisions stipulate that only the board of directors can appoint the general manager or vice general manager(s). It is strongly indicated that the appointment and dismissal of a general manager or vice general managers are two sides of a coin; hence, the general manager should not exercise the dismissal without a reasonably clear authorization of the board of directors.

5

Establishment of Joint Stock Companies

I. INTRODUCTION

In China, joint stock companies (hereinafter referred to as "JSCs") could also be called companies limited by shares (*gufen youxian gongsi*). The establishment of a JSC must follow specific procedures provided under the Chinese company law. For example, an LLC can only be established by adopting the promoter method, while a JSC may be established by either the promoter method or share-offering method.[1] Furthermore, a JSC is a typical company form used to gather capital from the public so that the public interest can be seriously protected. For this reason, the Chinese company law deals with JSCs more restrictively than it does with LLCs. The 1993 Company Law, through its Article 77, required that the incorporation of a JSC be subject to the examination and approval of a department authorized by the State Council (usually the CSRC) or of a people's government department at the provincial level. In this situation, the current Chinese approach is comparable to the "special" incorporation process, which was popular in the United Kingdom and the United States until the early 1800s. During that time, each incorporation required special legislation (or permission).

1. According to Article 77(2) of the Company Law, the promoter method reflects a situation where "the promoters establish a company by subscribing to all of the shares that should be issued by the company". Furthermore, according to Article 77(3) of the Company Law, the share-offering method is a situation where "the promoters establish a company by subscribing to some of the shares that should be issued by the company and offering the remaining shares to the general public or to a group of specified people for subscription".

Current American policy, in contrast, grants corporate status to any enterprise fulfilling nominal filing requirements.[2]

One needs to understand that at the time when the 1993 Company Law was drafted and promulgated, there was no rich experience in handling incorporation. Restrictive control was seen to be an effective way to prevent people from forming JSCs without due consideration.

The 2005 Company Law, in contrast, basically repealed the mode of permission to the circumstance of intensive development in China. In other words, to form a JSC becomes a regular investment decision for regular individuals so long as they meet other mandatory requirements. However, the 2005 Company Law requires that the company concerned shall submit the approval document of the CSRC to the company registry if it intends to adopt the share-offering method (now Article 92.2 of the 2013 Company Law). This is even harder for the list companies. The good news is that China will soon adopt a new system, i.e., the "registration-based IPO", which is quite similar to a Western-style system for the purpose of simplifying the listing process but emphasizes post-supervision.[3]

II. ISSUES CONCERNING PROMOTERS

It is admitted that the concept of the promoter can be interpreted differently in common law jurisdictions and in continental law jurisdictions, especially in China. In continental law jurisdictions, promoters need to handle all preparatory matters. In addition to those matters, promoters are required to subscribe shares of their company in order to prevent promoters from committing any corporate fraud. Therefore, according to the Supreme People's Court, "whoever concludes the articles of association for the purpose of establishing a company, subscribes to capital contributions or shares and performs the duties of establishing the company shall be deemed as a promoter of the company, including the shareholders at the time of establishment of a limited liability company".[4] However, in common law

2. Robert C. Art and Minkang Gu, "China Incorporated: The First Corporation Law of the PRC", *Yale Journal of International Law*, Vol. 20, No. 2, 1995, p. 289.
3. Xie Yu, "China Ushers in New IPO Registration System but it's Likely to Come with 'Chinese characteristics'", retrieved from http://www.scmp.com/business/markets/article/1888910/china-ushers-new-ipo-registration-system-its-likely-come-chinese on 9 December 2015.
4. Provisions of the Supreme People's Court on Several Issues concerning the Application of the Company Law of the People's Republic of China (III) (2014 Amendment), Article 1.

jurisdictions, promoters are not required to subscribe shares and their job is to handle corporate matters only.[5]

In order to understand the concept of the promoter thoroughly, it is necessary to examine the major differences between promoters and shareholders.

- Promoters usually exist before the establishment of a company, but shareholders exist after the company is established.[6]
- Promoters may not necessarily become shareholders later on, but promoters may always have the opportunity to be shareholders or directors if they want because they are quite influential.
- Promoters' rights and duties are different from those of shareholders.

Based on those differences, promoters must be subject to different duties, a point discussed later on.

1. Qualifications and Number of Promoters

Promoters (some may call them "sponsors") are very important to the successful establishment of companies. Promoters are persons who arrange for someone to be a director, place shares, negotiate preliminary agreements or prepare prospectuses and so on. Thus, promoters usually work to accomplish three things: (1) to arrange for the necessary capital for a company to be established; (2) to obtain necessary assistant personnel so that the company can be operated after it has been formed; and (3) to arrange for the formation of the company itself. In common law jurisdictions, a person may be regarded as a promoter even though he or she takes only a minor part in organizing the incorporation.[7] The purpose of this recognition is to impose duties and liabilities on promoters if there is any breach.

In every jurisdiction, company law may require promoters to meet several qualifications. The Chinese company law attempts to regulate the qualifications of promoters in the following ways. Firstly, promoters usually possess full civil capacity in order to conduct civil activities. As discussed in the previous chapter, persons who have limited civil capacity should be allowed to conduct a promoter's activities through their agent(s). However,

5. For detailed information, see Xu Yan, *The Principles of Company Law (Gongsi fa yuanli)*, The Law Press (Beijing), 1997, pp. 141–42.
6. However, in the situation where the share offering method is adopted, shareholders can exist when the company is not formally registered.
7. Vanessa Stott, *Hong Kong Company Law* (9th ed.), Financial Times, 2000, p. 24.

the agent in this scenario must be highly regulated as he or she may abuse the principal-agent relationship for his or her personal gain.

Secondly, promoters usually have their domiciles in China. The 2005 Company Law follows the approach taken by the 1993 Company Law, which required more than half of promoters to have domiciles inside Chinese territory. Some authors narrowly interpreted this requirement because they believed that it served the main purpose of communicating with those promoters whose domiciles were certain.[8] The requirement, however, must be interpreted differently. In fact, this requirement was very important because it was the only provision in the Chinese company law to open the door to foreign investors to participate in the formation of JSCs. Furthermore, it served as a legal base for the promulgation of the Regulations on Foreign Investment Joint Stock Company in 1995.[9]

Thirdly, promoters could be either natural persons or legal persons.[10] So far, the Chinese company law does not prohibit a JSC promoted by family members jointly or by a parent company and its subsidiaries jointly. However, in the former situation, a potential problem may occur when China promulgates the law for tax on gifts or law for estate duty because the source of income would be circumvented. In the latter situation, a potential conflict may be triggered under the current arrangement of equal status between the parent company and its subsidiaries.

Fourthly, even though the Chinese company law is silent on whether foreign investors can be the promoters of JSCs, this problem was resolved after 1995, when the Regulations on Foreign Investment Joint Stock Company were promulgated.

Most jurisdictions require a minimum number of promoters for JSCs. For example, England, France and Japan require more than seven promoters in their company laws, Germany requires at least five promoters and in the United States each state requires three promoters or more. Under the 1993 Company Law, there should be at least five promoters. On the

---

8. Tang Dehua (ed.), *Legal Practice Concerning Establishment and Internal Operation of Joint Stock Companies (Gufen youxian gongsi sheli yu neibu yunzuo falü shiwu) (Part One)*, The People's Court Press (Beijing), December 1998, p. 84.
9. The Interim Rules on Several Issues Concerning the Establishment of Foreign Investment Joint Stock Companies (*Guanyu sheli waishang touzi gufen youxian gongsi ruogan wenti de zhanxing guiding*) was issued by the then Ministry of Foreign Trade and Economic Co-operation in 1995.
10. Before the Chinese company law was promulgated, natural persons were not allowed to become promoters. In 1992, the Standard Opinions on JSCs provided that all promoters should be legal persons. This prohibition was obviously not supported by the 1993 Company Law and 2005 Company Law.

other hand, Article 75(2) of the 1993 Company Law was a special provision that should be specially addressed. Article 75(2) stated that where a SOE was restructured as a JSC, the number of promoters could be less than five. One limitation was that such a company should be incorporated by means of a share offering. The possible reason for this special requirement was that the driving force to convert SOEs to JSCs was to solve the problem of capital shortage by attracting public investments. The promoter method in this context did not benefit SOEs. Furthermore, the minimum number of promoters aimed to guarantee the performance of their obligations, since in the case of SOEs converting to JSCs the promoters were usually government departments or large SOEs and were supposed to have adequate funds and be qualified to serve as promoters. Thus, the reason behind this exemption was more probably to allow the necessary flexibility to encourage the conversion of the SOEs into JSCs.[11] On the other hand, it was argued that the different requirements for the SOEs and individual natural persons would put them in an unequal position, and this was apparently against the principle of equal treatment and fair competition.

Following the deep degree of economic development, this provision seems to be unnecessary. Hence, the 2005 Company Law does not even contain the same or a similar provision. Article 79 of the 2005 Company Law (now Article 78) simply states that the promoters of a JSC shall number at least two and no more than two hundred persons. Presumably, all promoters are treated equally.

In Hong Kong, company law is less restrictive towards promoters. Ordinance (Cap. 622) does not define who is a promoter. Presumably, one has to seek assistance from case law. As a general principle, one has to get permission or approval from the relevant authorities to be a promoter regardless of his or her nationality or domicile, unless he or she intends to engage in banking or insurance business. However, it must be noted that lawyers or accountants who help to form a company shall not be regarded as promoters unless there is clear evidence to prove otherwise. One special situation is that "merchant banks which act as sponsors in the public flotation of a company would likely be regarded as promoters".[12]

11. For detailed information, see Huang Jianchu, "Formation of a Shareholding Enterprise under the New Company Law", in Cheng Dejun, Michael J. Moser, and Wang Shengchang (eds.), *Commercial Laws in the PRC*, Butterworths, 2000.
12. Stefan H. C. Lo and Charles Z. Qu, *Law of Companies in Hong Kong*, Sweet & Maxwell, 2013, p. 102.

2. Duties of Promoters

Unlike the 1993 Company Law, the current Company Law imposes more duties on promoters. The following list of duties is not inclusive:

- duty to prepare for the articles of association (Art. 76.4);
- duty to subscribe all shares issued if the promoter method is used (Art. 77.2);
- duty to subscribe 35 per cent of the total shares issued if the share-offering method is used (Arts. 77.3 and 84);
- duty to make a company's prospectus if the share-offering method is used (Art. 85);
- duty to sign an underwriting agreement with a securities company that is lawfully established if the share-offering method is used (Art. 87);
- duty to sign an agreement with a bank that will collect payments for shares if the share-offering method is used (Art. 88); and
- duty to call for and preside over an inaugural meeting after the share payment is fully made (Art. 89).

However, the promoter's duties shall not just be limited to the preceding activities. Article 147 of the Company Law provides an idea of "fiduciary duty", which is a popular concept in common law jurisdictions. Such a duty may be imposed on promoters. The following relevant part includes a substantial discussion of the theory of fiduciary duty.

Generally, promoters have the duty to act *bona fide* and in the best interests of the company to be formed. However, the Chinese company law is silent on whether promoters can make any profit during the process of promotion. This problem has been resolved perfectly in common law jurisdictions where promoters must ensure to fully disclose an interest in any contract entered into by the promoters. Non-disclosure is a breach of the promoter's duty towards the company to be formed.[13]

3. Pre-incorporation Contract

In the United States, pre-incorporation contracts have been dealt with in at least three different situations.

(a) Contracts executed in the name of the promoter. In this situation, promoters shall take personal liability.

13. K. Arjunan and C. K. Low, *Understanding Company Law in HK*, LBC Information Services, Sydney, 1996, p. 77.

(b) Contracts entered into in the name of the corporation. If promoters enter into a contract with a third party on behalf of the corporation without disclosing that it is not in existence, the promoters are personally liable under the contract. If the corporation is thereafter created and takes over the contract, the promoters have a chance of being relieved of liability, but there is a substantial chance that a court will conclude that no novation was intended and the promoters remain personally liable.

(c) Contracts referring to the fact that the corporation is not yet formed. The tendency is that promoters are not personally liable under such contracts.[14] This is a welcome approach because the third party on notice should never intend to rely on the promoters' performance of the contract and therefore should not be able to hold the promoters personally liable. Most persons assume that even if promoters are initially liable, they are nevertheless released if the corporation is later formed and adopts the contract. This is because those promoters are likely to be directors of the corporation and may persuade the corporation to adopt pre-incorporation contracts.

In Hong Kong, pre-incorporation contracts have been regulated by written law, which provides an idea similar to United States common law. Section 122 of Ordinance (Cap. 622) states:

> (1) This section applies if a contract purports to have been made in the name or on behalf of a company before the company was incorporated.
> (2) Subject to any express agreement to the contrary—
> (a) the contract has effect as a contract entered into by the person purporting to act for the company or as an agent for the company; and
> (b) the person is personally liable on the contract and is entitled to enforce the contract.
> (3) After incorporation, the company may ratify the contract to the same extent as if—
> (a) the company had already been incorporated when the contract was entered into; and
> (b) the contract had been entered into on the company's behalf by an agent acting without the company's authority.

14. Robert W. Hamilton, *The Law of Corporations*, West Publishing Co., St. Paul, Minn., 1996, pp. 83–87.

(4) Despite subsection (2)(b), if the contract is ratified by the company, then on and after the ratification, the liability of the person mentioned in that subsection is not greater than the liability that the person would have incurred if the person had entered into the contract after the company's incorporation as an agent acting without the company's authority.

One significant achievement of this provision is that it has abolished the relevant case law, which held that a contract made in the name of the company before its incorporation could not be ratified by the company after it was incorporated based on the notion that at the time the contract was made there was no principal in existence.[15] The statute, however, leaves this power to the company concerned and is more realistic.

In China, how to deal with pre-incorporation contracts used to be a controversial issue. One notable explanation is that at the time when a pre-incorporation contract is made, there is no company in existence that has a civil capacity and the contract must be void in line with the Chinese Civil Law Principle.[16] In comparison, the Chinese company law provides fewer guidelines regarding the effect of pre-incorporation contracts and who shall ultimately be liable for those contracts. Fortunately, this problem has to be resolved by the SPC through the Provisions of the Supreme People's Court on Several Issues concerning the Application of the Company Law of the People's Republic of China (III) (2014 Amendment).

According to the SPC, pre-incorporation contracts are handled in the following ways. (1) If a promoter concludes a contract with anyone else in his or her own name for the purpose of establishing a company, he or she is personally liable under the contract. However, if the contract is confirmed by the company after its establishment, or if the company has in fact enjoyed the contractual rights or performed contractual obligations, the company shall be liable under the contract.[17] (2) If a promoter concludes a contract with anyone else in the name of a company being established, the company shall be liable under the contract after its establishment. However, the company can escape its liability under the contract if it can prove that the promoter has concluded a contract with anyone else in the name of the company being established for his or her own interest.[18] (3) In any event, if the company fails to be established, all promoters shall bear joint liability

15. Vanessa Stott, *Hong Kong Company Law* (12th ed.), Pearson, 2008, p. 27.
16. Xu, supra note 2, p. 147.
17. Provisions of the Supreme People's Court on Several Issues concerning the Application of the Company Law of the People's Republic of China (III) (2014 Amendment), Article 2.
18. Ibid., Article 3.

under the contract. Normally, all promoters need to share the liabilities according to the agreed-upon accountability proportion; in the absence of an agreed-upon accountability proportion, liabilities shall be shared according to the agreed-upon proportion of capital contributions; and in the absence of an agreed-upon proportion of capital contributions, liabilities shall be shared equally. Certainly, those who are liable for the failure to establish the company shall bear more liability.[19] (4) If a promoter causes any harm to anyone else due to performing the duty of establishing the company, the company shall be liable after its establishment. However, if the company fails to be established, all promoters shall bear joint and several liabilities. Certainly, there is always the chance that a company or promoters not at fault may, after making compensations, that recourse against the promoters at fault.[20]

III. ESTABLISHMENT OF JSCS

1. Articles of Association

The articles of association of JSCs shall have mandatory contents, which bear a strong resemblance to those of LLCs. One minor difference is that in a JSC, all of the promoters rather than the shareholders shall make the articles of association.[21] If a JSC adopts the share-offering method, the articles of association also need to be adopted by the inaugural meeting (Art. 90).

2. Capital Contribution

Many continent law jurisdictions still require minimum capital for establishing a JSC. In Germany, the establishment of a public limited company requires minimum capital of €50,000, one quarter of which must be paid in.[22] In France, the establishment of a JSC (*société anonyme*) requires minimum capital of €37,000, or €225,000 if a public offering is planned. Half of the capital must be paid up at the time of incorporation and the remainder within five years.[23]

19. Ibid., Article 4.
20. Ibid., Article 5.
21. Article 23(3) of the Company Law requires that all shareholders of an LLC jointly formulate the articles of association.
22. PLC Formation, "Public Limited Company Formation from eformations", retrieved from http://www.eformations.co.uk/plc-formation/#sthash.z66fpTS2.dpuf on 6 October 2015.
23. The Economist, "Organising an Investment", retrieved from https://store.eiu.com/article.aspx?productid=480000248&articleid=111962995 on 6 October 2015.

However, company laws in the United States and Hong Kong do not have these requirements. This practice is getting more and more popular around the world today. One study examined the 189 economies in 2014, and 99 had no minimum capital requirements. Furthermore, some economies never required firms to deposit money for incorporation, while thirty-nine have eliminated minimum capital requirements in the past seven years.[24]

In China, the minimum capital was provided by Article 81(3) of the 2005 Company Law, which should be ¥5 million. The 2005 Company Law also abolished the concept of "paid-up share capital",[25] which was adopted by the 1993 Company Law. An additional change was made by the 2013 Company Law, which abolished ¥5 million as the minimum capital requirement. As far as registered capital is concerned, the Company Law offers two options: (1) if a JSC is formed by the promoter method, its registered capital shall be the capital stock subscribed for by all of its promoters; and (2) if a JSC is established by the share-offering method, its registered capital shall be the total actually paid capital stocks.[26] This approach is again different from the theory of "authorized capital".

Regarding the forms of contribution, there is no difference between JSCs and LLCs. The capital contribution may take the forms of cash, goods, intellectual property rights and land-use rights. However, it is important to note that when the amount of capital contributions made by shareholders takes a form other than cash, a statutory capital verification institution shall be commissioned to verify the funds and produce a verification certificate.

Furthermore, if a JSC is formed by the share-offering method, promoters must subscribe for more than 35 per cent of the total shares issued by the company (Art. 84). Before offering shares to the general public for subscription, the promoters must submit an application for share offering to the CSRC, after which the approval documents issued by the CSRC can be used for company registration (Art. 92.2). Finally, promoters and subscribers may not withdraw their shares after paying their subscription money or making their capital contributions as substitutes for subscription money (Art. 91).

---

24. Valentina Saltane and Paula Garcia Serna, "Why Are Minimum Capital Requirements a Concern for Entrepreneurs?" retrieved from http://www.doingbusiness.org/~/media/GIAWB/Doing%20Business/Documents/Annual-Reports/English/DB14-Chapters/DB14-Why-are-minimum-capital-requirements.pdf on 6 October 2015.
25. It basically refers to the capital contribution that shall be fully paid when applying for company registration.
26. The Company Law, Article 80.

3. Inaugural Meeting

The inaugural meeting is a special procedure adopted during the establishment of a JSC. Its powers will end after the JSC is established. The Chinese company law sets out conditions for an inaugural meeting. Firstly, promoters shall notify each subscriber of the date of the inaugural meeting or make a public announcement fifteen days prior to the convening of the meeting (Art. 91.1). Secondly, if promoters fail to hold an inaugural meeting within thirty days after the deadline of subscription or after payment in full is made, the subscribers may claim a refund from the promoters according to the paid-up share subscription money plus bank deposit interest calculated for the same period (Art. 89.2).

The powers of an inaugural meeting are provided by the Company Law. The most important power is to adopt the articles of association of the company and to elect members of the board of directors as well as members of the board of supervisors (Art. 90.2). The Company Law also requires that those resolutions shall be approved by more than half of the voting rights (Art. 90.3).

4. Registration

This is the last important procedure for the establishment of a JSC. The Chinese company law provides very restrictive registration procedures in the Regulations on the Administration of Company Registration, which were promulgated in 1994 and amended in 2005 and again in 2014.

(1) Application for Registration

The board of directors shall be responsible for making an application, together with required documents,[27] to the relevant company registration authority. If the promoter method is adopted, the board of directors can apply for registration immediately after the board of directors is established.

27. Article 92 of the Company Law requires the following documents to be submitted: (1) application for company registration; (2) minutes of the inaugural meeting; (3) the articles of association; (4) certificates of capital verification; (5) certificates of appointing legal representative, directors, supervisors and their identifications; (6) promoters' legal person status or natural person identification; and (7) proof of the company's domicile. However, the Regulations on Administration of Company Registration require more documents to be submitted. For detailed information, see Article 21 of the Regulations on Administration of Company Registration.

If the share-offering method is adopted, the board of directors shall make an application within thirty days after the inaugural meeting.

(2) Procedures of Registration

Following technological development, the method of registration application is no longer sufficient. Today, the registration application can be done through letters, faxes or even emails.[28] The company registration authority shall, after receiving the application for establishing a JSC, make a decision as to whether the registration shall be allowed: (1) the decision of whether the registration is allowed shall be given immediately if the application for registration is made in person and (2) the decision of whether the registration is allowed within fifteen days after the application is received if the application is made through mail.[29]

A company that complies with the provisions of the Chinese company law shall be registered and a company business licence shall be issued thereto. It is assumed that the date of issuance of a company business licence shall be the date of incorporation of the company.

(3) Announcement of Incorporation

Once a company is incorporated, an announcement shall be made publicly so that any third party is aware of the existence of this company.[30]

5. Conversion of LLCs into JSCs

The Chinese Company Law contains one provision dealing with this issue.[31] The provision is quite general in nature. It is uncertain whether the total amount of the shares converted shall be equal to the value of the net assets of the company when an LLC is converted into a JSC, which used to be required by Article 99 of the 1993 Company Law. This old provision was criticized for not being realistic because in practice, when most SOEs (including LLCs) were converted into JSCs, the total amount of shares converted did not equal the value of the net assets of the companies. One view suggested that the total amount of shares converted should be based on the

28. The Regulations on Administration of Company Registration, Article 50.
29. Ibid., Article 53.
30. Ibid., Article 56.
31. The Company Law, Article 9.

net assets confirmed by certified evaluation or audit institutions and that the rate of the total amount of shares converted should be agreed upon by all contributors through negotiation.[32]

In line with the Chinese company law and other regulations, the following steps shall be taken in order for an LLC to be converted into a JSC.

Firstly, the number of shareholders must satisfy the relevant requirements. Generally, at least two to two hundred promoters are required and more than half of the promoters shall have their domiciles in China. In order to ensure this, an LLC can transfer some shares to new shareholders and maintain the original registered capital. An LLC can also apply to increase its registered capital and issue those shares to new shareholders. In practice, it is likely that an LLC may issue shares to the public in order to satisfy the registered capital requirement under the Chinese company law.

Secondly, when an LLC has been approved for transformation into a JSC, the total amount of shares converted should be carefully calculated (Art. 95).

Thirdly, the structure of the shares shall be examined. In China, share classification is done based on the status of holders. Thus, it is important to examine state-owned shares, legal person shares and individual shares, which are addressed in the next part.

Fourthly, the conversion shall be approved by the shareholders' meeting and the relevant authorities.

Finally, re-registration of a JSC must be done accordingly. In line with the Chinese Company Law, it is not necessary to inform the creditors of the conversion because the debts receivable and debts payable by the original LLC shall be assumed by the JSC into which it has been transformed.[33]

6. Conversion of JSCs into LLCs

The Chinese company law also allows a JSC to be converted into an LLC. Presumably, this type of change is rare and not often seen. Nevertheless, it is possible to point out one practical example in the United States. In a leveraged buyout situation, a small group of investors (sometimes including members of a target company's existing management) purchase (usually through a tender offer) the publicly held shares of the targeting company. After the takeover is completed, the targeting company turns into a private

---

32. Liu Jipeng, *Ten Suggestions for Amending the Chinese Company Law* (*Dui gongsi fa xiugai de shi dian jianyi*), in Guo Feng and Wang Jian, pp. 95–96.
33. The Company Law, Article 9(2).

company. The privatization of a public company is seen in Hong Kong from time to time. Certainly, the re-registration shall be done after the conversion has been completed.[34]

IV. FOREIGN-INVESTED JSCS

1. Introduction

Before 1995, most foreign-invested enterprises took the form of LLCs. In comparison with regular LLCs, foreign-invested LLCs are special in several ways: (1) foreign-invested LLCs are joint ventures between a Chinese party and a foreign party or solely owned by foreign investor(s); (2) in the situations of contractual joint ventures or equity joint ventures, the companies do not have shareholders' meetings and the highest decision-making authority is the board of directors or a joint management committee; and (3) major decisions concerning the amendment of articles of association, mergers, dissolutions and increasing and reducing capital must be agreed upon by unanimous decision. These differences are expressly permitted by the Chinese company law. In other words, the Chinese company law applies to foreign-invested LLCs and JSCs, but if other laws contain special provisions dealing with those companies, such provisions shall apply.[35]

It is true that the 1993 Company Law did not foresee the establishment of foreign-invested JSCs (hereinafter referred to as the "FIJSC"). The establishment of FIJSCs was permitted after 1995 based on the Provisional Regulations on Several Issues concerning the Establishment of Foreign Investment Joint Stock Companies (hereinafter referred to as the "FIJSC Regulations"), which were issued by the then MOFTEC on 10 January 1995. Thus, foreign investors are allowed to establish either LLCs or JSCs in China.

Article 2 of the FIJSC Regulations provides that FIJSCs refer to enterprises with corporate status whose total capital is composed of the equivalent value of stock; whose shareholders assume an amount of liability equal to the amount of shares purchased, which offsets its total assets against the responsibility assumed for company debts; and whose company shares jointly held by Sino-foreign shareholders and shares purchased and held by foreign shareholders constitute more than 25 per cent of the company's registered capital. Through this definition, one can see that one unique feature

34. The Regulations on Administration Company Registration, Article 33.
35. The Company Law, Article 217.

of FIJSCs is that foreign investors must hold more than 25 per cent of the issued shares. This is a very important indicator of foreign investment.

2. Establishment

The establishment of an FIJSC is subject to a limitation of its investment area. Article 4 of the FIJSC Regulations states that the establishment of an FIJSC shall comply with the relevant state-stipulated provisions on industrial policies for foreign-invested enterprises. The most pertinent laws are the Regulations on Foreign Investment Guidelines[36] and the Guideline Catalogue of Foreign Investment Industries.[37] The state encourages the establishment of technologically advanced production-type companies in the form of FIJSCs.

Apparently, the FIJSC Regulations try to make a connection with the 1993 Company Law even though the latter did not directly address this issue. Article 6 of the FIJSC Regulations states that if a company is established through the promoter method, it must comply with the conditions applicable to promoters as stipulated in the Chinese company law and, in addition, at least one of the promoters shall be a foreign shareholder.[38] If a company is established through the share-offering method, it must comply with more conditions as mentioned previously. In addition, at least one of the promoters shall have a profit record for the 3 successive years prior to the share offering.

3. Registered Capital

Furthermore, Article 7 of the FIJSC Regulations states that the registered capital of a company shall be the total amount of paid-up share capital registered by the company with the registration authority. The minimum amount of registered capital of a company shall be ¥30 million. As mentioned in the previous chapters, following the Notice on Improving the Administration of Foreign Investment Review on 17 June 2014, there is no minimum amount of registered capital for regular foreign-invested enterprises.

36. *Zhidao Waishang Touzi Fangxiang Guiding*, which was promulgated by the State Council on 11 February 2002 and took effect from 1 April 2002.
37. *Waishang Touzi Chanye Zhidao Mulu*, which was promulgated by the State Council on 11 March 2002. It would be amended from time to time.
38. This is consistent with Article 75 of the 1993 Company Law (now Article 78 of the 2013 Company Law).

4. Broad Participants

Most importantly, the following companies or enterprises can be converted into FIJSCs. Article 15 of the FIJSC Regulations provides that if an established Sino-foreign equity joint venture enterprise, Sino-foreign contractual joint venture enterprise or foreign-owned enterprise (hereinafter referred to as a "foreign-invested enterprise") makes an application to transform into an FIJSC, it must have a profit record for the last three successive years. The agreement and articles of association for the establishment of an FIJSC that have been concluded and signed by investors in the original foreign-invested enterprise acting as the company's promoter (or in conjunction with other promoters) shall be submitted to the examining and approving authority at the location of the original foreign-invested enterprise for preliminary examination. Subject to authorization, the documents shall then be submitted to MOFTEC (now the Ministry of Commerce) for examination and approval. Article 18 of the FIJSC Regulations states that if an SOE or a collectively owned enterprise applies to transform into a FIJSC, it shall, in addition to complying with the provisions of other articles of these Regulations, meet the following criteria: (a) the enterprise has been operating its business for a minimum of 5 years and has a profit record for the last three successive years; (b) shares of the enterprise bought and held by foreign shareholders using freely convertible currency constitute more than 25 per cent of the enterprise's registered capital; and (c) the scope of business operations of the enterprise shall be in conformity with industrial policies for foreign-invested enterprises. Today, this kind of transformation is rare. Articles 20 and 21 state that a regular JSC can also be transferred into that type of company by the public issue of special renminbi-denominated shares (B shares).

Finally, Article 23 of the FIJSC Regulations states that a regular JSC can also be transformed into an FIJSC by listing overseas and issuing overseas listed foreign capital shares (including but not limited to H shares and N shares). This provision sends a strong signal that foreign investors are permitted to take over regular JSCs, especially the current listed companies, if they go through both a concentration review and a national security review under the PRC Competition Law.

5. Differences between FILLCs and FIJSCs

Compared with regular JSCs, FIJSCs may present some advantages. The most important advantage is that the FIJSCs are foreign-invested enterprises. Thus, they shall obtain certain advantages and types of preferential treatment given to foreign-invested enterprises, such as tax exemptions and deductions and privileges related to imports and exports. However, FIJSCs may have drawbacks. One notable limitation is that placed on their transfer of shares. It is true that shareholders of regular JSCs can transfer their shares freely while shareholders of FIJSCs cannot transfer their shares freely for two reasons. Firstly, the transfer of shares shall not destroy the 25 per cent rule, i.e., after the transfer, foreign shareholders must still hold 25 per cent of the total shares. Secondly, the transfer of shares shall not change the majority shareholding status of the Chinese party. Otherwise, there would be a violation of the Investment Guidelines. For example, in line with No. 221 of the Guideline Catalogue of Foreign Investment Industries (2015 Revision), FIJSCs can engage in the manufacturing and repairing of marine engineering equipment (including modules), but Chinese parties shall be the controlling shareholders. Thus, the best way is to seek prior approval from the relevant government authorities before the transfer of shares is made.

Furthermore, in comparison with traditional FILLCs, FIJSCs may have the following advantages.

- While FILLCs can attract investment only from certain investors, an FIJSC can absorb capital from the public through the share-offering method. Thus, FIJSCs are able to extend their scope of capital investment.
- While FILLCs are generally not permitted to transfer a shareholding unless the transfer is agreed upon by the other parties or approved by the relevant approving authorities, FIJSCs are much more flexible in terms of share transfers.
- While FILLCs are subject to a term of operation (usually ten to fifty years), FIJSCs have an unlimited life.[39]

V. LIABILITIES FOR AN INVALID INCORPORATION

1. Conditions for an Invalid Incorporation

"Invalid incorporation" usually refers to a situation where a company cannot be finally incorporated because the incorporation does not meet the statutory requirements or the incorporation violates statutory procedures. The following situations render incorporation invalid.

39. Mu Yaping, *Legal System of International Investment* (*Guoji Touzi de Falu Zhidu*), Guangdong People's Press (Guangdong), 1999, p. 181.

- There is a violation of law or a violation of social order, public interests and customs.
- The conditions to form a company are not satisfied. For example, the number of promoters does not satisfy the statutory requirements, or there is no fixed place for operation.
- There is a violation of incorporation procedures. For example, the articles of association for an LLC are not signed by all shareholders, or the articles of association of a JSC formed by way of the share-offering method are not passed at the inaugural meeting.
- Promoters fail to subscribe the whole amount of the shares if a JSC is formed by way of the promoter method.

2. Legal Responsibilities

"Legal responsibilities" are civil liabilities, administrative liabilities or sometimes criminal liabilities. Chapter 12 of the Chinese Company Law provides administrative and criminal liabilities, and civil liabilities are included in other provisions of the Law.

For example, Article 198 of the Company Law states that where a company obtains its registration by making a false report on its registered capital, submits falsified certificates or resorts to other fraudulent means to conceal important facts in violation of the Law when carrying out company registration, it shall be ordered to make a rectification; where a company makes a false report on its registered capital, it shall be fined an amount of not less than 5 per cent but not more than 15 per cent of the registered capital falsely reported; and where a company submits falsified certificates or resorts to other fraudulent means to conceal important facts, it shall be punished with a fine of not less than ¥50,000 but not more than ¥500,000. If the circumstances are serious, the registration of the company shall be revoked. Article 215 of the Company Law states that relevant criminal liabilities will be pursued if the case is serious enough. Both Articles 158 and 159 deal with crimes of falsely declaring registered capital, making false capital contributions and withdrawing capital contributions. However, following the adoption of the "zero capital system", the Standing Committee of the National People's Congress released the Interpretation on Articles 158 and 159 of the Criminal Law of the People's Republic of China on 24 April 2014, stating that "the provisions of Articles 158 and 159 of the Criminal Law shall only apply to companies subject to the registration of paid-in capital in accordance with the law". Thus, literally speaking, Articles 158 and 159 of the Criminal Law are no longer applicable for companies under the "zero capital system". However, strictly speaking, this interpretation has two problems. On the one hand, the capital subscription system does not mean that shareholders' obligation to pay-in capital contributions is eliminated; it is only a matter of time before shareholders must pay in. Therefore, the crime of making false capital contributions may exist as a matter of evidence. On the other hand, after shareholders pay in their capital contributions, there is always the possibility that they may withdraw their capital contributions illegally. Thus, it is improper to state that "the provisions of Articles 158 and 159 of the Criminal Law shall only apply to companies subject to the registration of paid-in capital in accordance with the law".

Article 214 of the Company Law states that where a company violates the provisions of the Law it should assume civil liability for compensation and pay fines and penalties. If the company's property is insufficient to pay such compensation, fines and penalties, the company shall assume the civil liability for compensation first. It is clear that the civil liability should be borne first before the administrative or criminal liability.

In Xiamen City, Guan, Wang, and Liu decided to form a JSC called Xiahua Electron Co. Ltd. They drafted a promoter's agreement and the company's articles of association. They also partially subscribed the shares, and the rest were sold to the public by a share-floating method. During the process of incorporation, Wang and Liu signed their names on the promoter's agreement and the articles of association. Guan, however, did not sign his name on either document because he was on a business trip in another city temporarily. In fact, Guan had participated in drafting the two documents and subscribed part of the shares according to the agreement. During the period in which shares were sold to the public, Deng decided to subscribe part of the shares and made the first payment. Thereafter, Deng noticed that the company was not formed within a long period of time. For this reason, Deng decided to talk to Guan, Wang and Liu to cancel the subscription and take back the payment. Three promoters refused Deng's demand and claimed that shareholders should not withdraw their investment. In this situation, Deng lodged a claim against the three promoters in a people's court. The court of first instance ruled against the defendant as follows:

(1) The company should not be established and promoters should return the invested capital to Deng.
(2) Only Wang and Liu should return the money to Deng, and Guan should not be liable for the payment but should be liable for the consequence of an unsuccessful incorporation of the company.[40]

40. Citing Xu Wusheng, *Case Analysis and Practice of the Chinese Company Law (Zhonghua Renmin Gongheguo gongsi fa anli pingxi yu shiwu)*, The Economic Daily Press (Beijing), 1994, pp. 46–47.

According to the judgment, there was a partnership relationship between Guan, Wang, and Liu. All three of them should be liable for an invalid incorporation. Furthermore, it was discovered that Wang and Liu had signed the promoter's agreement and the articles of association. Guan did not sign these two documents. Thus, the court correctly decided that only Wang and Liu should be liable to return the money to Deng. The only difference was that Guan did not need to pay Deng but should be liable for the unsuccessful incorporation in line with his agreed-upon capital contribution.

Under the Chinese company law, there are special legal liabilities for promoters:

(1) In the event of the company failing to be incorporated, joint and several liabilities for all debts and expenses incurred in the act of the incorporation.
(2) In the event of the company failing to be incorporated, joint and several liabilities for refunding to the subscribers the paid-up subscription money plus bank deposit interest calculated for the same period of time.
(3) In the event of the interests of the company being damaged during the course of its incorporation due to the fault of the sponsors, liability for compensation to the company.[41]

The share subscribers may claim a refund from the promoters according to their paid-up subscriptions plus bank deposit interest calculated for the same period.

In addition to Article 94, Article 89(2) states that if the number of shares has not been fully subscribed within the time limit specified in the prospectus on the share offer or after payment in full of the subscription money for the total shares is made or if promoters fail to hold an inaugural meeting within thirty days thereafter, then the share subscribers may claim a refund from the sponsors according to the paid-up share subscription money plus the bank deposit interest calculated for the same period.

41. The Company Law, Article 94.

6

Shareholders' Meeting

I. ISSUES OF CORPORATE GOVERNANCE

Corporate governance concerns the exercise of power over corporate entities. It has become one of the central issues in running and regulating modern enterprises today.[1] In order to understand the concept of corporate governance, one must clearly know the entity's internal management structure. Furthermore, one should bear in mind that the purpose of establishing a company is not only to increase its property, but also to increase profits for shareholders.

It has been said that good corporate governance relies on a good internal management structure and a good internal relationship: "Weaker shareholder rights are associated with lower profits, lower sales growth, higher capital expenditures and a higher amount of corporate acquisition."[2] The Association of British Insurers reports that the best corporate governance records have produced returns 18 per cent higher than poor governance records. Furthermore, a breach of governance best practice reduces a company's industry-adjusted return on assets by an average of 1 percentage point a year,[3] and investors who bought firms with the strongest democratic

1. R. I. Tricker, *Corporate Governance*, Ashgate Publishing Limited (London), 2000, p. xiii.
2. Paule A. Gompers, Joy L. Ishii and Andrew Metrick, "Corporate Governance and Equity Prices", retrieved from http://qje.oxfordjournals.org/content/118/1/107.abstract on 8 October 2015.
3. ABI Research, "Corporate Governance Pays for Shareholders and Company Performance", retrieved from https://www.abi.org.uk/News/News-releases/2008/02/ABI-Research-Corporate-governance-pays-for-shareholders-and-company-perfomance on 8 October 2015.

rights and sold them with the weakest rights earned abnormal returns of 8.5 per cent per year during the sample period.[4]

It has been concluded that the worldwide financial crisis, which affected so many people in so many countries, can be attributed to the failures and weaknesses of corporate governance that cannot safeguard against excessive risks. In a number of financial services companies, accounting standards and regulatory requirements are insufficient.[5]

Thus, if the traditional goal of a company is to maximize profit through legal means, that must be enlarged by including a responsibility to society. Thus, the precondition of achieving those goals is to control and manage the company in a proper or effective manner.

Governance structures can be traced back to the British East India Company and the Dutch East India Company, which were established in 1600 and 1602, respectively. The two companies had similar governance structures. There were three typical organs, i.e., a shareholders' meeting (hereinafter referred to as an "SHM") as the highest authority, a board of directors as the decision-making institute and a board of managers as the executive institute.[6] However, people paid little attention to the concept of corporate governance until the 1980s.[7] This clearly suggests that corporate governance is a new topic and deserves more research and debate.

In China, the internal organizations of a company mainly comprise an SHM, a board of directors (hereinafter referred to as a "BOD") and a board of supervisors (hereinafter referred to as a "BOS").[8] On the surface, this type of internal or corporate governance structure is similar to that of Germany or France. However, the German model is much more specialized than that of China because the BOS is given the power to control the BOD. Furthermore, there is a sharp distinction between continental law jurisdictions and common law jurisdictions in terms of internal organization structure. Usually, internal organizations in common law jurisdictions are parts of only two organs. For example, in Hong Kong, the Companies Ordinance does not require a company to form a BOS. In practice, the

4. Gompers, Ishii, and Metrick, supra note 2.
5. Grant Kirkpatrick, "The Corporate Governance Lessons from the Financial Crisis", retrieved from http://www.oecd.org/finance/financial-markets/42229620.pdf on 8 October 2015.
6. Tang Dehua (ed.), *Legal Practice Concerning Establishment and Internal Operation of Joint Stock Companies (Gufen Youxian Gongsi Sheli yu Neibu Yunzuo Falu Shiwu) (Part One)*, The People's Court Press (Beijing), December 1998, p. 345.
7. Tricker, supra note 1, p. xiii.
8. In addition to the three major institutions, there are some other institutions (such as trade unions) that also play an important role inside a company.

function of the BOS is usually exercised by the SHM. However, in the United States, the modern BOD plays a more and more important role than the BOS, a point covered in detail later.

Thus, based on the principle of "separation of powers", the continental law jurisdictions set up the SHM, BOD and BOS within companies and the common law jurisdictions set up only the SHM and BOD within companies (see the chart).[9]

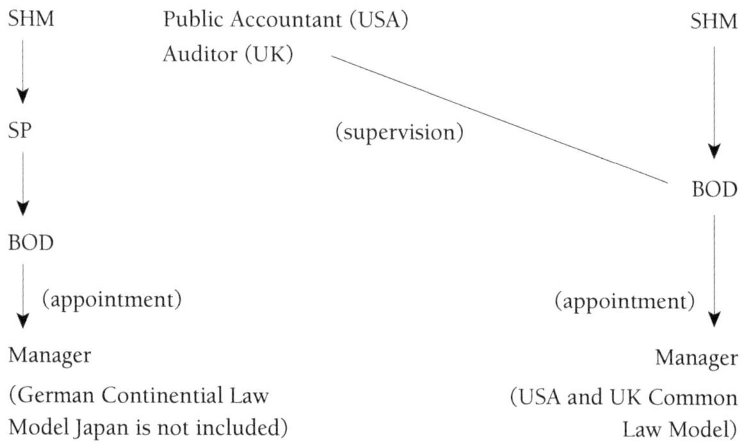

In Japan, almost all large companies are listed companies and their shares are held by other legal persons. For example, the A Company holds shares of the B Company while the B Company holds shares of the A Company. Therefore, among these legal persons, a stable trade relationship and linkage of property rights are firmly held. In this situation, even though the BOD and BOS are elected by the SHM, the company is actually supervised by all representatives of the investing companies. As far as the internal structure is concerned, Japan adopted the German style at the beginning, then learned from the experiences of the United States and finally established a compromised model that has been followed by Taiwan's company law until today.

9. Mei Shenshi, *The Structure of Powers* (*Quanli Gouzao Lun*), The China University of Politics and Law (Beijing), 1996, p. 116.

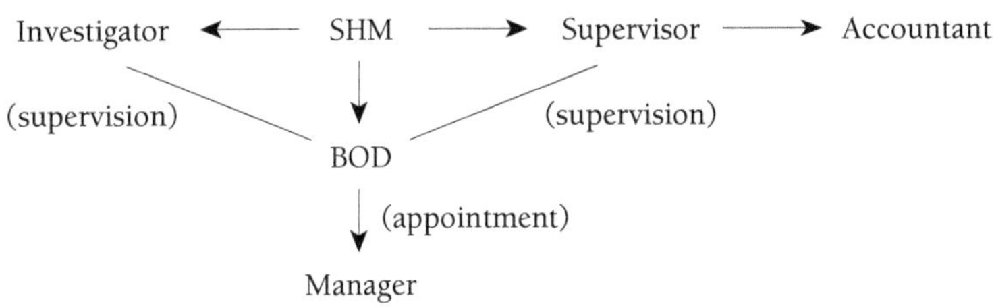

In comparison, China's internal structure of companies has been built up differently. On the face of it, the internal structure is similar to the pattern of the continental law jurisdictions. In reality, the internal structure is problematic, a point discussed thoroughly in the following sections.

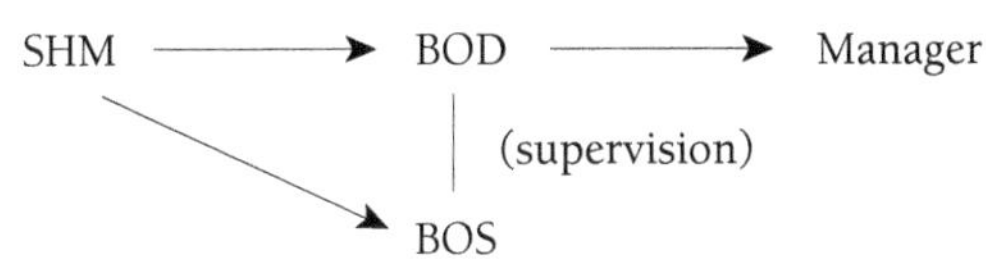

II. SHAREHOLDERS' MEETING

1. The Nature of the Shareholders' Meeting

The SHM is formed by all shareholders of a company. It is recognized as the most powerful authority of a company because shareholders are the capital contributors and without their capital contributions the company cannot be effectively formed or operated.[10] Thus, the SHM must represent the interests of the majority shareholders if not all of the shareholders. Fairly speaking, the interests of the majority shareholders may represent the company's interests, while one shareholder's interests usually cannot be said to reflect the interests of the company. This interpretation may be similar to the idea of "shareholders' democracy". However, in the situation of modern companies, including large-sized JSCs with very many shareholders, shareholders' democracy is not easily realized when the shareholders are located dispersedly. For those shareholders who own only small amounts of shares, internal governance is almost unachievable. In reality, most of the shareholders in JSCs have only a loose expectation of profit returns and their management power is entirely controlled by internal management personnel.

10. Some scholars believe that the SHM is not the highest authority but just an indispensable organ. See Shi Zhimou, *The Company Law* (*Gongsi fa*), San Min Book Co. Ltd. (Taipei), 1991, p. 142.

Although the SHM is the most powerful authority of a company, it should not be treated as a standing authority because it usually holds a meeting once a year to decide the most important matters of the company. Furthermore, although it is regarded as the most powerful authority, it usually does not represent the company because it only decides a company's internal matters and will not deal directly with a third party. Also, in line with general theory, the BOD has already been entrusted to represent the company despite the fact that in reality different jurisdictions may provide different answers.

In accordance with Article 82 of Table A of the Hong Kong Companies Ordinance (Cap. 32, now Part. 2.2 of the Companies [Model Articles] Notice), directors shall manage a company's business. This provision indicates clearly that directors are authorized to represent the company to engage in business with any third party. Although the Chinese company law provides a similar idea, it gives too many powers to the SHM, a point explained as follows.

2. Significance of the Shareholders' List

As one technical system, the shareholders' list plays a very important role in identifying shareholders' qualifications, share transfers and share pledges. It is also crucial if shareholders are allowed to participate in the SHM. However, the Chinese Company Law does not contain reasonable provisions to deal with the shareholders' list. Consider the following case.

A, B, and C jointly contributed to establishing an LLC. Thereafter, without notifying C, A and B held an SHM and passed a resolution to authorize the transfer of all of C's shares to D, an outsider. Both A and B signed the resolution and asked someone, E, to sign the resolution on behalf of C. Then A and B appointed E to sign the agreement on behalf of C to transfer C's shares to D. Then the LLC, by presenting the resolution and share transfer agreement, amended the shareholders' list at the company registry. D was registered on the shareholders' list and C's name was taken off of the list. After C learned about this sequence of events, he lodged a lawsuit in a people's court and asked to invalidate the resolution as well as the share transfer agreement. A and B counterclaimed that C failed to make a capital contribution and that C was not a qualified shareholder. The court of first instance found out that (1) C had not contributed capital, (2) C's part of the contribution was paid by A, and (3) D was a *bona fide* party because he did not know the story before signing the share transfer agreement. The court held that even though the articles of association of the company recorded C as a shareholder, he was unable to show the certificate of share contribution. Thus, C was not qualified as a shareholder under the Company Law, and his identification as a shareholder could not be recognized. As a result, C's claim would not be supported and should be rejected.[11]

(1) Nature of the Shareholders' List

The shareholders' list is a legal document dealing with the relationship between a company and its shareholders. In other words, making a shareholders' list is a legal requirement that deals with the relationship between a company and its shareholders but not the relationship between the company and third parties. To some extent, the shareholders' list may reflect the company's reputation and source of capital, which could be viewed by shareholders, potential investors and creditors.

(2) Function of the Shareholders' List

The shareholders' list is open for review. Furthermore, it serves as a basis for paying dividends to shareholders, registering share transfers, contacting shareholders and accepting inspection from relevant authorities. Article 32 of the Company Law states that an LLC shall prepare a shareholders' list and shall record the following information: (1) the names of all shareholders and their domiciles thereof; (2) the amount of capital contributions made by each shareholder; and (3) the serial numbers for all capital contribution certificates. It seems that the names and amount of the capital contributions are "must-have" information. On the other hand, serial numbers for certificates or dates of obtaining certificates are relevant information because the absence of such records may render the list with no legal force. Furthermore, according to the Chinese Guarantee Law, the pledge contract goes into effect as of the date of the pledged shares on the shareholders' list.[12] Thus, the shareholders' list should also record "other information that is relevant to shareholders' rights and interests".

(3) Shareholders' List v Capital Contribution Certificate

The information contained in the shareholders' list has a presumed power. Even if the list cannot become the basis of determining the whereabouts of shareholders, it can be a *prima facie* qualification of the shareholders.

11. Xiao Long, Sun Xiaoping and Wang Zhong, "Some Issues on Stock Rights Transfer of Limited Liability Company", retrieved from http://pkulaw.cn/(S(21ctss45i13hjxjvmt44tijw))/fulltext_form.aspx?Gid=1510061650&Db=qikan on 24 November 2015.
12. The Guarantee Law, Article 78(3).

In other words, those who are on the list do not need to bear the burden of proving their status as shareholders. On the other hand, the capital contribution certificate (hereinafter referred to as the "certificate") is a legal document that may show that a shareholder of an LLC made his or her capital contribution.[13] Thus, in a normal situation, a shareholder can exercise his or her rights by relying on either the shareholders' list or the certificate. However, if the contents of both the list and certificate are inconsistent, then the contents of the list should prevail. In other words, the list has a legal force with certainty, while the legal force of the certificate is only assumed.

(4) Shareholders' List v Articles of Association

Which one should prevail if the two documents are in conflict with each other? There are divided views. The prevailing view is that if names and titles recorded in the articles of association are conflicting with those on the shareholders' list, then the shareholders whose names are recorded in the articles of association can request the company to change the record of the shareholders' list. The opposite view is that the shareholders' list should prevail over the articles of association. This view may rely on Article 32, which states that an LLC "shall prepare the shareholders' list". The Company Law does not impose such a requirement for the articles of association.[14] This view cannot be supported because it ignores the nature of the articles of association, which are collectively regarded as the constitution of a company and should enjoy a higher status than the shareholders' list.

(5) Shareholders' List v Company's Registration

In reality, registration can be further divided into two types, i.e., registration creating rights and registration for filing purposes. Registration creating rights has a legal effect while registration for filing purposes simply delivers information and does not create a legal relationship between a company and its shareholders or between shareholders. Since registration naturally involves publicity and credibility, if a third party is involved, it should prevail over the shareholders' list. This conclusion is supported by Article 44(2) of the PRC Contract Law, which states that if a contract becomes effective only

13. However, making a capital contribution does not automatically prove the shareholder's status.
14. Lan Liyan, "How to Deal with the Conflicts between Shareholders' List and Articles of Association", retrieved from http://china.findlaw.cn/lawyers/article/d21730.html on 6 November 2015.

after the completion of the approval and registration procedure according to the provisions of law and administrative regulations, such provisions shall govern. Article 32(3) of the Company Law reflects the same idea. In other words, the contract for transferring shares cannot stand up to any third party without modifying the registration.

(6) Seal-Up of the Shareholders' List v Date of Registering Ownership

Normally, the shareholders' list is changed following the transfer of a capital contribution or shares. When a company holds the SHM or decides the distribution of profits, it must be certain as to who the shareholders are. Thus, the seal-up of the shareholders' list and ownership registration date means to decide on a "date", and after the date has expired, those who are on the shareholders' list are considered as shareholders who participate in the SHM or exercise shareholders' rights or pledge rights.

3. Shareholders' Rights and Powers of the SHM

(1) Shareholders' Rights

Shareholders' rights can be summarized into three major rights, i.e., the voting right, the right to sue, and the right to information. The voting right ensures that a shareholder can vote on the important matters of a company, especially when voting for their favoured directors. The right to sue is important in the sense that a shareholder can seek legal remedies in order to protect himself or herself and his or her company's legal interests. The right to information is equally important because it enables a shareholder to make informed decisions. Shareholders' other rights are basically developed from these three rights. The Chinese company law also provides these three rights to shareholders. In summary, the shareholders' rights in either an LLC situation or a JSC situation are listed as follows:

(a) the right to enjoy limited liability (Art. 3);[15]
(b) the right to exercise voting rights (Art. 37);[16]

15. Some authors treat "limited liability" as a duty of shareholders. See Zeng Huaqun and Li Shufeng, *Chinese and Hong Kong Company Law (Zhong Gang gongsi fa shiwu)*, Commercial Press (Hong Kong), 1994, pp. 105–15.
16. The right to vote by proxy is assumed in either LLC or JSC situations. A proxy is a person who is authorized in writing by a shareholder to vote on his or her behalf. The relationship is one of principal and agent. The counterpart words are "to vote in person". In practice, a proxy can be revocable or irrevocable.

(c) the right to elect directors or supervisors or be elected as directors or supervisors (Art. 37);
(d) the right to review minutes of meetings and financial reports (Arts. 33 and 37);
(e) the right to obtain a dividend or bonus according to the proportion of their contributions (Arts. 34);
(f) the right to transfer their shares (Arts. 71 and 137);[17]
(g) the right to exercise pre-emptive rights to get new shares (Art. 133);
(h) the right to get the residue assets when a company is liquidated (Art. 186);
(i) the right to call a temporary meeting if more than 10 per cent of shareholders with voting power or more than one third of the directors or supervisors want to do so (Art. 39);[18] and
(j) the right to take direct actions (Art. 22) or derivative actions (Art. 151).

(2) Shareholders' Right to Know

Article 33 deals with shareholders right to know in an LLC. This right can be further divided into two categories. First, there is an absolute right to know, i.e., the right to review and duplicate the company's bylaw, the minutes of the SHM, the resolutions of the BOD meetings, the resolutions of the BOS meetings as well as the financial reports. Secondly, there is a restricted right to know. Every shareholder may request to review the accounting books, but in order to do so he or she is subjected to some limits, for example, he or she needs to submit a written request showing motivation, but the company can refuse if there is any improper motivation and legitimate interests of the company are impaired. Furthermore, the company may request the shareholder to review the accounting books without extracting or copying. If a company rejects the request of any shareholder to review the books, the shareholder concerned may ask a people's court to order the books to be reviewed. In fact, the right to plead cannot be barred by the statute of limitation because this right is granted during the existence of the company. In practice, if a company fails to follow the court's order, it may be subjected to administrative penalties. Furthermore, a person in charge of books should

17. Shareholders of LLCs can have only a limited right to transfer their shares, i.e., they must obtain consent from other shareholders before the transfer is made. The Company Law, Article 71.
18. The Chinese company law specifies only 10 per cent of the voting rights rather than the number of shareholders. Thus, the number of shareholders could be just one.

provide reasons. Those who fail to do so should bear the consequence of compensation unless the shareholder gives up this piece of information.

If a shareholder is allowed to review the accounting books, can he or she then request to review original vouchers (accounting proofs)? In order to answer this question, it is necessary to review the Accounting Law of the PRC (hereinafter referred to as the "Accounting Law"). There are two provisions that are pertinent here. Article 9 of the Accounting Law states that "all units must fulfil accounting practice, fill in and prepare accounting proofs, record accounting books and work out financial accounting statements according to the economic and business transactions actually taken place". Article 15 states that "entries into accounting books must be based on the examined and verified accounting proofs and comply with the provisions of related laws, administrative regulations and the state's unified accounting system". Based on these two provisions, it is certain that the accounting proofs, accounting books and financial accounting statements are three different concepts. Generally speaking, accounting books should be made based on accounting proofs, while financial accounting statements should be made based on accounting books.

However, in practice, courts may make decisions differently. The Beijing No. 2 Intermediate People's Court received a plead to review original accounting books from Ms Zhang, who was a shareholder of one technological consultation company and decided that the company should make available original accounting proofs from 1996 through 2006. This was the number one case concerning Article 33, and the shareholder was allowed to review both the accounting books and relevant original proofs.[19] On the other hand, Chengdu Intermediate People's Court ruled in 2006 that a company's accounting books sufficiently reflected the company's financial situation. Since Article 33(2) allows only the review of accounting books, the request to review original proofs was not supported by the facts and law and should have been rejected.[20] Which interpretation is reasonable? There are several reasons for Article 33(2) mentioning only accounting books and not accounting proofs: (1) compared to accounting books, accounting proofs contain more trade secrets that should be protected; (2) large companies usually have big amounts of accounting proofs every day, and the request

19. Song Yi, "Beijing No. 2 Intermediate People's Court for the First Time Confirmed the Shareholder's Right to Check Accounting Information", retrieved from http://old.chinacourt.org/public/detail.php?id=213111 on 4 November 2015.

20. Cheng Weibing, "Balancing the Interest of a Company and Shareholders' Right to Know", retrieved from http://www.chinalawedu.com/new/16900a175a2010/2010125lifei11340.shtml on 4 November 2015.

to review may seriously affect daily operations; (3) reviewing accounting proofs may involve huge amounts of labour and cost; and (4) the reviewed proofs may be lost or altered without proper supervision. Thus, it is clear that all of these factors must be considered before a decision can be made. The SPC tries to protect the shareholder's right to know by stating that "when a shareholder of an LLC requests to review company's accounting books and relating original proofs, if the company is unable to provide evidence to show that the shareholder's motivation is not legitimate, the court should rule for the shareholder".[21] However, it is still not clear whether this is an over-interpretation of Article 33(2) and whether this right should be extended to shareholders of a JSC.

One more controversial issue involves whether a shareholder should be allowed to review a BOD's minutes. Apparently, Article 33(1) does not mention a BOD's minutes. Some people say "no" because they believe that a shareholder is not a director or a supervisor and thus cannot participate in a BOD's meetings, which may involve the company's operational strategy, trade secrets and so on. Furthermore, Article 33(1) deals with the situation of LLCs and gives the limited right to know to shareholders. On the other hand, Article 97 of the existing Company Law authorizes a shareholder to review the minutes of a BOD's meetings. What is the rational difference between Articles 33(1) and 97? The answer needs to be discovered.

(3) Shareholders' Right to Profits

The right to profits is very important to shareholders as investors.[22] However, the profits generated by a company cannot be solely distributed to shareholders. Article 166 requires a company, before it distributes its after-tax profits, to draw 10 per cent of the profits as the statutory common reserve, if approved by the SHM, to allocate certain profits to the discretionary common reserve. Until these things have been done, any leftover profits may be distributed to shareholders. The word "possibility" is crucial here because the company's management may decide not to distribute any profits. Thus, it is crucial to comprehensively balance the interests of the company and investment expectations of shareholders.

Certainly, if a shareholder is unhappy about the decision not to distribute profits, he or she has two options to protect his or her legal interests.

---

21. The SPC's Provisions on Certain Issues Concerning the Application of the "Company Law of the People's Republic of China" (IV) (Consultation Paper), Article 11.
22. Article 4 of the Company Law states that the shareholders of a company shall be entitled to enjoy the capital proceeds.

First, he or she could request the company to purchase his or her stock rights at a reasonable price provided that (1) the company has made profits for five consecutive years and (2) the company has failed to distribute any dividends during the five consecutive years.[23] Secondly, he or she could seek a judicial involvement. In other words, he or she could plead to a court to order the company to distribute profits. The question is whether the judicial involvement will injure the company's corporate autonomy or the rights of big shareholders. So far there have been divided views in China. Opposing parties hold the view that if a court ignores the decision of the SHM and makes a decision to distribute profits to the shareholders, the profits may be exhausted and big shareholders' interests may be injured. Furthermore, due to the different economic position, it is almost impossible to achieve absolute equity between big shareholders and small shareholders.[24] On the other hand, supporters believe that a company's autonomy is not absolute. It has been pointed out that the virtual limits hold that if a company's autonomy is out of control by law, it may destroy the interest framework of the parties. Some parties are afraid to participate in a company's gameplay. The tolerance of the company may also be destroyed, in which case the company will eventually move on to self-destruct.[25]

This is again a balancing issue. In the United States, a BOD has the right to decide whether to distribute profits based on the business judgment rule and is generally free from any lawsuit. However, in a special case, if a shareholder can prove that the action taken by the BOD is unreasonable, the court may intervene based on the rule of equity and ask the BOD to distribute profits. This book suggests that the judicial involvement should be strictly controlled and the court should respect the business judgment rule without making unnecessary second guesses.

Judicial involvement must be strictly controlled, especially when a company's SHM has not decided the plan of distribution. Before a resolution of profit distribution is made by the SHM, it is not proper for a shareholder to plead to the court. It is well recognized that a lawsuit launched must have justifiable benefits, which can be seen only after the resolution is made by the SHM. The Company Law states clearly that the decision to distribute profits is vested in the SHM.[26] Before the decision of the SHM is made, the

23. The Company Law, Article 74(1).
24. Yang Zhiqiang, "Judicial Remedy: Right to Dividends for Medium and Small Shareholders in LLCs", retrieved from http://www.148guquan.com/ny.asp?nyid=1598 on 4 November 2015.
25. Hao Lei, "Judicial Remedy for Shareholders' Right to Profits", retrieved from http://old.civillaw.com.cn/article/default.asp?id=53995 on 23 November 2015.
26. The Company Law, Article 37.

decision whether to distribute profits is still within the scope of company's autonomy. If a shareholder believes that his or her rights and interests are injured, he or she can obtain his or her relevant incomes by transferring his or her shares, demanding the purchase of his or her share right by the company before taking the case to a court. The court cannot step into the shoes of the company to decide whether the distribution should be made. Furthermore, the distribution of profits is a business judgment rather than a legal judgement and judicial involvement must be restricted as much as possible.

Assuming that a shareholder petitions a court for profit distribution and the court supports him or her, how does the court determine what amount of profit should be distributed to the shareholder? In China, different courts may adopt different methods. Some courts entrust accountant firms to conduct an audit in order to calculate after-tax profits as a basis, then deduct the statutory common reserve and a certain percentage of the discretionary common reserve, after which the remaining portion is multiplied by the shareholder's percentage of shares in order to figure out the amount of profits that should be paid to him or her. Other courts adopt an arbitrated way to figure out the amount of profits to pay to the shareholder. In one case, the court referred to the profit level in the relevant industry and decided that the company's contracted profits were 30 per cent, and used this as a basis to deduct a 20 per cent statutory common reserve and a 10 per cent discretionary common reserve. The remaining portion was then multiplied by the shareholder's share percentage in order to distribute profits to him. This book holds the view that in order to distribute profits reasonably, it is better to entrust an accountant firm with conducting an audit and determining the proper distribution amount.

(4) Shareholders' Duties

Interestingly, not many company law books discuss shareholders' duties. One possible explanation for this is that most people focus on the duties of directors because it is important to ensure good behaviour of directors. Another possible explanation is that the 1993 Company Law did not have enough provisions discussing shareholders' duties. However, the 2005 Company Law started to pay serious attention to the following duties of shareholders:

(a) to comply with the laws, administrative rules and articles of association (Art. 20);
(b) to exercise their rights lawfully and not abuse their rights (Art. 20);

(c) to not abuse the company's legal person status and limited liability (Art. 20);
(d) to pay capital contributions (Arts. 28 and 30);
(e) to not withdraw their investment after the company is incorporated (Art. 35); and
(f) to not take advantage of an affiliated relationship to damage the interests of the company (Art. 21).[27]

Furthermore, shareholders may have to assume the statutory joint liability in the following situations: (a) the shareholders of a company evade the payment of its debts by abusing the independent status of the legal person or the shareholder's limited liabilities;[28] (b) in the situation of an LLC, the actual value of the capital contributions in non-monetary properties is found to be apparently lower than that set forth in the byelaw of the company;[29] (c) the shareholder of a one-person LLC is unable to prove that the property of the one-person LLC is independent from his or her own property;[30] and (d) when a company's properties are insufficient for the repayment of debts, the shareholders, having not contributed their capital and other shareholders for the formation of the company, shall assume the joint and several liabilities for the debts of the company within the scope of un-contributed capital.[31]

(5) The SHM

Generally, the SHM is held at least once a year. In addition to a mandatory annual meeting, shareholders, directors or supervisors may call special meetings from time to time. The SHM usually exercises the following powers:

(a) to determine a company's business policy and investment plans;
(b) to elect and replace directors and supervisors, who are not worker representatives, and to determine the remunerations of the directors and supervisors;

27. The "affiliate relationship" is defined by Article 216(4) of the Company Law, which states that it "shall mean the relationship between a company's holding shareholders, actual controllers, directors, supervisors, senior executives, and an enterprise directly or indirectly controlled by the forgoing persons, and any relationship that may transfer a company's interests".
28. The Company Law, Article 20(3).
29. Ibid., Article 30.
30. Ibid., Article 63.
31. Provisions of the Supreme People's Court on Several Issues Concerning the Application of the Company Law of the People's Republic of China (II), Article 22(2).

(c) to discuss and approve the reports compiled by the BOD;
(d) to discuss and approve the reports compiled by the BOS or supervisors;
(e) to discuss and approve the company's annual budget plans and final accounting plans;
(f) to discuss and approve the company's profit distribution plans and loss recovery plans;
(g) to pass resolutions on matters such as increases or reductions of the company's registered capital;
(h) to pass resolutions on matters such as issuances of corporate bonds;
(i) to pass resolutions on matters such as company mergers, divisions, restructurings, dissolutions, or liquidations;
(j) to amend the company's articles of association; and
(k) to exercise any other rights stated in the articles of association.[32]

Because the SHM is the highest authority of a company, it is not surprising that it is given many important powers. In practice, however, companies are largely managed or operated by the BOD or managers. It is a worldwide phenomenon that the SHM can only possess several important powers, and it is better to give many other substantial powers to the BOD and managers in order to meet the demands of the fast-changing world. For example, in most common law jurisdictions, the BOD usually exercises the following powers:[33]

(a) to decide the management policy and investment plan of the company and to approve the budget;
(b) to decide the issuance of shares and bonds;[34]
(c) to consider and approve plans for distributing profits and recovering losses; and
(d) to decide whether to issue dividends.

According to Article 37(1) of the Company Law, the SHM has the right to decide the company's business policies and investment plans. Why does China adopt this different approach? This right may be imposed because of

32. Under the 1993 Company Law, the SHM had the right to pass resolutions on shareholders' assignments of capital to parties other than shareholders. However, Article 71 of the Company Law now takes a simple approach by allowing the written request to all other shareholders.
33. American corporate law, in contrast, places these decisions exclusively within the scope of the directors' authority. See Robert C. Art and Minkang Gu, "China Incorporated: The First Corporation Law of the People's Republic of China", *The Yale Journal of International Law*, Vol. 20, 1995, p. 297.
34. In common law jurisdictions, the articles of association usually authorize the amount of shares to be issued, and the BOD will decide to issue shares from time to time.

the special characteristics of the company system in China, i.e., in order to provide greater security for the shareholders' (usually the state is the biggest shareholder) investment, the legislators have tried their best to keep the BOD from abusing its power and require the BOD to be closely responsible to the shareholders. As has been said, the original purpose of promulgating the Chinese company law was to reform and rescue SOEs. Once the SOEs have been converted into companies, the assets of those SOEs remain state-owned. Since the state is the biggest shareholder in most companies, it is reasonable to expect that this important power will be given to the SHM. Thus, the extraordinary power accorded to the SHM is consistent with the Chinese company law's overall approach to rescuing SOEs. The state, as the biggest shareholder in incorporated SOEs, does not intend to relinquish its ownership or ultimate control over China's productive enterprises. Rather, it seeks to remove itself from the micro-management of enterprise decisions. Furthermore, by assigning management authority to the BOD while retaining majority stock ownership and a strong role for shareholders, the government can maintain the level of control that is chosen.[35]

Regardless of which argument prevails, the decision whether to give this power to the SHM needs to be further examined. It may well depend on the size of the company and involvement of the shareholders. However, one could argue that the 2005 Company Law was released after the effects of the economic reform had been deeply felt and that many companies are privately owned. By the end of 2013, the total number of private enterprises exceeded twelve million.[36] The remarkable thing is that the non-public sectors now contribute 60 per cent of the national GDP.[37] Thus, a reasonable suggestion is that the existing Company Law should leave these powers to be decided by the SHM rather than treat them as statutory powers of the SHM.

When dealing with the voting power of shareholders, Article 103 of the Company Law provides that a resolution of the SHM must be passed by more than one-half of the voting rights held by the shareholders present at the meeting. Resolutions by the SHM on the merger, division, or dissolution of the company require more than two-thirds of the voting rights held by the shareholders present at the meeting.

One remaining problem is that neither the 1993 Company Law nor the existing Company Law stipulates the quorum required when deciding these important matters. Obviously, the quorum of shareholders may

35. Art and Gu, supra note 33, pp. 296–97.
36. Sun Tiexiang, "Private Economy Contributed 60% of the GDP in 2013", retrieved from http://news.xinhuanet.com/fortune/2014-02/28/c_119558098.htm on 8 October 2015.
37. Ibid.

substantially affect the true voting power.[38] A possible resolution is to let companies decide a proper quorum through the articles of association.

In the situation of an LLC, a shareholder's voting power may be different from that of a JSC. Under Article 71 of the Company Law, if a shareholder transfers his or her stock rights to parties other than shareholders (i.e., strangers), the approval of a majority of shareholders shall be required. In this situation, the Law adopts the "one shareholder, one vote" system. However, under Article 42, shareholders shall exercise voting rights at the SHM according to the proportion of their contributed capital. In this situation, the law adopts the "voting by percentage of capital contribution" system. Thus, Article 43(2), which states that a resolution passed by the SHM on matters such as increases or reductions of the company's registered capital and company divisions, mergers, dissolutions or transformations shall require the approval of a two-thirds majority of the voting rights of shareholders in order to be valid,[39] can be interpreted to allow a situation where big shareholders successfully control important parts of the company. In comparison, the Taiwanese Company Law adopts a different approach, i.e., each shareholder shall, regardless of how much of a capital contribution is made, have one vote. As an exception, the articles of association may divide votes in accordance with the capital contribution (Article 102). Japan adopts the same approach as that of Taiwan.

Which approach is better? It seems that the "one shareholder, one vote" system (with exceptions) is the better approach. As has been discussed before, an LLC focuses on personal relationships more than capital contributions. The harmonized relationship is more important to the better operation of a company. In this situation, "one shareholder, one vote" can truly reflect the principle of democracy. If the shareholders of an LLC have reached an agreement and decided to divide their voting power based on their capital contributions, they should write this special arrangement into the articles of association.

Article 106 of the Company Law also provides the method of voting by proxy. This method is particularly suitable for most public companies. It is observed that following the emergence of public share ownership, a requirement of personal attendance at meetings became more and more unfeasible because of the geographic dispersion of shareholders and the small sizes

---

38. For example, if a company has one hundred shareholders and only forty shareholders attend the SHM because a quorum is not required, then the majority of the shareholders presenting at the meeting may not be considered as constituting the majority.
39. Article 43(2) of the Company Law does not give shareholders an option to use a different approach.

of their individual investments.[40] Thus, voting by proxy has become very popular and there appears to be a battle for proxies, i.e., directors trying to get as many proxies as possible to vote for certain decisions. In common law jurisdictions, shareholders usually appoint management personnel or directors to be their agents. Today, in fact, the proxy has become a special tool for management personnel to control large companies. In continental law jurisdictions, however, shareholders usually appoint organizational intermediates (such as banks) to be their agents. On the other hand, banks are usually the major shareholders of large companies and transfer the proxy to the BOD. Thus, there are two methods with one direction.

Although the Chinese company law fails to provide special limitations on voting by proxy, it seems that China should adopt the approach of continental law jurisdictions and add a few changes at the same time. It is a good idea to appoint organizational intermediates to be shareholders' agents so they can at least depart from having the same interests as those of directors. On the other hand, it is important to choose independent intermediates that have no substantial connection to the management board of the company.

One related issue is whether China should adopt the voting trust method in the near future. Voting trusts are popular in many common law jurisdictions. Shareholders may by agreement in writing transfer, irrevocably within a certain period of time, their stock rights to a voting trustee, thus enabling the voting trustee to vote uniformly.

There is one major difference between the voting by proxy and voting trust methods. In the case of voting trust, the ownership of shares remains in the hand of the trustee for a certain period of time, but in the case of voting by proxy, the directors will have to seek agreement from shareholders from time to time. Since China has adopted the voting by proxy method, the next logical step is to consider writing the voting trust method into the Chinese company law.

Shareholders also have the right to sue for an injunction plus damages if a decision of the BOD "violates laws and administrative rules (Art. 22.3)." The Chinese Company Law does not specify whether a shareholder's action should be direct (asserting the shareholder's own rights) or derivative (asserting rights on behalf of the corporate entity), or even whether that distinction is recognized. However, it requires that a plaintiff shall provide a guarantee in advance in order to sue (Art. 22.3). The possible reason for this is that the requirement of a guarantee may help to avoid the abuse

40. Jesse H. Choper, John C. Coffee and C. Robert Morris, *Cases and Materials on Corporations* (3rd ed.), Little, Brown and Company (London), 1989, p. 580.

of litigation, and the BOD can conduct its operation without unnecessary interference.

In the following section, shareholders' direct actions and indirect actions are discussed.

4. Majority Rule and the Protection of Minority Shareholders

In the situation of a JSC, the Chinese company law reflects the rule of following the majority shareholders, which is similar to the rule in Western countries. The traditional view is that if the interests of the majority of shareholders are protected, then the interests of a company are also protected. Thus, a company's decisions are made on the basis of majority rule, and in most cases this democratic principle is sufficient to ensure that all decisions are made fairly.[41] Under the Chinese Company Law, the majority rule can be seen in Article 103. Firstly, it ensures that each share held shall represent the equivalent of one voting right. Most importantly, a resolution proposed at the SHM shall require the approval of a one-half majority of the voting rights of shareholders present at the meeting in order to be valid. Secondly, resolutions on amending the articles of association; increasing or reducing the company's registered capital; and mergers, divisions, dissolutions or changes in the nature of company shall require the approval of a two-thirds majority of the voting rights of shareholders present at the meeting in order to be valid.

There is a distinction between majority shareholders and minority or individual shareholders. The legitimate interests of minority shareholders must be protected. Thus, it is important to ensure that majority shareholders shall not abuse their powers, especially when they pass a resolution that adversely affects the interests of their company as well as those of minority or individual shareholders. In order to tackle this problem, the 1993 Company Law provides one catchall provision that offers certain help to minority and individual shareholders.

Article 111 of the 1993 Company Law states:

> Where a resolution of the shareholders' meeting or of the board of directors violates the law, administrative rules and regulations, and thus infringes upon the lawful rights and interests of the shareholders, the shareholders concerned shall have the right to bring a lawsuit

41. Vanessa Stott, *Hong Kong Company Law* (9th ed.), Financial Times (Hong Kong), 2000, p. 154.

> in a people's court demanding that such illegal or infringing action be stopped.

Regrettably, this provision does not clearly indicate whether this should be a direct action or an indirect action. In line with traditional company law theory, shareholders can always sue if their personal legal interests have been harmed. However, if there is an indirect action, whether an individual shareholder can sue becomes a tough question. Before turning to a detailed discussion of this matter, it is necessary to offer an introduction to the relevant theories and practices in other jurisdictions.

In common law jurisdictions, shareholders usually cannot sue directly when a civil wrong is done to a company. In a famous case, *Foss v Harbottle* (1843) 67 ER 189, two shareholders alleged that the company's property had been misapplied and wasted and that certain mortgages over the company's property had been given improperly. They brought an action against the company's five directors and others. They asked the court to declare that the directors were accountable for the company's loss and sought the appointment of a receiver. The court held that the shareholders could not sue because the sole right to bring such proceedings belongs to the company. This is the famous rule of *Foss v Harbottle*.

Behind this rule, there may be two theories. Firstly, if a wrong is done to a company (as a legal entity separate from its members), only the company (as a legal person) can sue. This is the so-called "proper plaintiff" theory. Secondly, the court will not interfere with the internal management of companies acting within their powers. This is the so-called "internal management" theory. These two theories try to encourage people to settle disputes over company policies through the company's established procedures and to prevent multiplicity of actions.

However, there are some exceptions to the rule of *Foss v Harbottle*, i.e., minority shareholders (or individual shareholders) are able to sue even if the directly injured person is the company when the following situations happen:

(a) the resolution is *ultra vires*;
(b) the resolution should be adopted by super-majority votes; or
(c) there is a fraud on the minority.

As mentioned before, even though the *ultra vires* doctrine has become optional in Hong Kong, if a company chooses to provide the *ultra vires* doctrine in its articles of association, a shareholder can sue for a resolution if an *ultra vires* act occurs. Furthermore, if a resolution is not adopted by the required super-majority votes, it is considered a procedural violation that enables a shareholder to sue. However, fraud on the minority is a special concept in common law jurisdictions that deserves the following discussion.

5. Fraud on the Minority and Shareholders' Derivative Action

(1) Derivative Action in General

In Hong Kong, "fraud" has a broader meaning than it does under the law of torts, where the term is used to denote deceitful or dishonest behaviour. "Fraud" means an abuse of power whereby the majority secures an unfair gain at the expense of the minority. If the minority itself is the injured party, it has a personal right of action against both the majority and the company. If the majority commits a fraud on the minority and the injured party is the company, the minority shareholders are permitted to bring an action in the name of the company against the majority in a "derivative action". Thus, some scholars suggest replacing the term "fraud on the minority" with "fraud on the company" in order to clearly differentiate between the direct action and derivative action.[42]

A derivative action is equitable in nature. It is an action brought by one or more shareholders to remedy or prevent a wrong to the corporation. In the United States, this action is usually taken to challenge the management's power.

Before talking about a derivative action, one must consider whether a claim is direct or derivative. In one sense, anything that harms a company also harms shareholders by reducing the value of their shares (or interest). However, differences exist in various aspects. Generally speaking, a lawsuit charging officers and directors with misapplication of corporate assets or other breaches of duty is derivative in nature. Lawsuits that require a controlling shareholder to account for a premium received on the sale of company's shares are also derivative in nature, since the benefit belongs to the corporation.

Sometimes, claims are direct if they (1) violate a special duty (e.g., a contractual duty) owed to the shareholders (even though the action complained of may also significantly injure the corporation) or (2) cause an injury to the shareholders that is separate and distinct from the injury suffered by other shareholders. Thus, a lawsuit claiming that it was improper for a controlling shareholder to vote on a resolution authorizing the

---

42. Stefan H. C. Lo and Charles Z. Qu, *Law of Companies in Hong Kong*, Sweet & Maxwell (Hong Kong), 2013, p. 394.

corporation to issue additional shares to that shareholder is direct in character, since it prevents the dilution of the voting power of the complaining shareholder's shares.[43]

A derivative action is usually initiated by minority shareholders. In Hong Kong, however, there was an attempt to grant the Securities and Futures Commission (hereinafter referred to as the "SFC") the power to initiate a derivative action. On 18 November 2003, Financial Services and the Treasury Bureau (hereinafter referred to as the "FSTB") and the SFC published a consultation on the proposal to empower the SFC to initiate a derivative action against wrongdoers (in relation to a listed company on grounds including fraud, negligence, default in relation to any legislation or breach of fiduciary or statutory duty) without a court's approval.[44] Because limited support was given, the FSTB and SFC had to give up the proposal for the time being.

Further effort led to the enactment of the Companies (Amendment) Ordinance 2004 by the Legislative Council on 22 July 2004, and the Amendment is in force now. One of the distinctive features was its codification of the derivative action in Article 168BA, which empowered a shareholder to take a derivative action on behalf of the company. The court had the power to strike out the action if it was not taken in the best interests of the company or in good faith.[45]

(2) Derivative Action in China

One common view is that the 1993 Company Law did not authorize a derivative action. Article 111 clearly stated, "If resolutions . . . infringe upon the legal rights and interests of shareholders, a shareholder shall have the right to sue." This is a typical direct action. However, some scholars held the view that the 1993 Company Law implied a derivative action. Firstly, Article 14(2) of the 1993 Company Law stated that the legal rights and interests of a company should receive the protection of the law and should not be infringed upon. This provision authorized shareholders to protect the legal rights and interests of the company. Secondly, Article 63 of the 1993 Company Law stated that if a director violated the provisions of the

43. Robert W. Hamilton, *Law of Corporations*, West Publishing (St. Paul, Minn.), 1996, pp. 459–80.

44. FSTB/SFC "Joint Press Release—Consultation on Proposal to Empower SFC to Initiate Derivative Actions", retrieved from http://www.sfc.hk/edistributionWeb/gateway/EN/news-and-announcements/news/doc?refNo=03PR127 on 8 October 2015.

45. Under the new Companies Ordinance (Cap. 622), the statutory derivative action is set out in Part 14 (Division 4) with no substantial change.

law, statutory regulations or the company's articles of association during the performance of duties and thereby caused damage to the company, the director should bear liability for the compensation for such damage. This provision stipulated the civil responsibilities of directors to their company. Thirdly, on 11 December 2002, Mr Li Guoguang, the deputy president of the SPC, gave a speech on the Meeting Concerning China's Court Adjudication Work for Civil and Commercial Affairs. In his speech, Mr Li concluded that courts should accept derivative actions.

In practice, the first derivative action was rejected by Shenzhen Intermediate People's Court on the basis that a derivative action should represent the legal interests of shareholders as a whole; the shareholders who wanted to take derivative action must first obtain consent from all shareholders. In addition, the court held the view that Mr Li's speech on 11 December 2002 could only be treated as a reference but could not be considered as the authority to establish a case. However, the first derivative case, which was successful, was the *Real Estate Operation Company of Nanchang District of Wuxi City and Shanghai Pudong State-owned Assets Investment Management Limited Liability Company* (plaintiffs) v *Hengtong Group Joint Stock Company* (defendant).[46]

In this case, the plaintiffs and defendant jointly established a new stock company in 1993. The defendant held 55 per cent of the shares and was a big shareholder. Both the chairman of the BOD and general management were appointed by the defendant. Thus, the company was in fact controlled by the defendant. Within about five years, the defendant had borrowed or taken away about ¥40 million from the company and used its real estate valued at only ¥11 million as the repayment. The case was adjudicated by one people's court. The court relied on the Principles of Civil Law to decide the case due to the fact that the 1993 Company Law did not authorize the derivative action. The court held that the defendant's conduct injured the legal interest of the company and went against the principle of fairness and honesty and therefore should be invalid. In accordance with Articles 4, 58, and 117, the defendant should pay ¥28 million plus ¥5.6 million in bank interest and other litigation fees.[47]

Thereafter, the SPC issued the "Replying Letter Concerning the Issue of the Chinese Party in a Joint Venture Enterprise Suing on Whose Behalf if

46. Ma Xiaoying, "Suggestions for Importing Shareholder's Derivative Action into China" (*Lun Woguo Yinjing Gudong Paisheng Susong Zhidu Zhi Gouxiang*), retrieved from http://docin.com.cn/p-552339270.html on 8 October 2015.
47. Ibid.

the Enterprise has a Contractual Dispute with a Third Party but the Foreign Party, Who Controls the Enterprise, has Certain Related Interests with the Third Party" on 4 November 1994. According to this Replying Letter, if there is a contractual dispute between the joint venture enterprise as a buyer and the third party as a foreign seller who controls the enterprise and has direct interests with the seller and refuses to convene the BOD meeting and decides to sue the seller on behalf of the enterprise, the Chinese party can sue the seller on behalf of the enterprise.[48]

The 2005 Company Law, for the first time in China, authorized the derivative action. Article 151 of the 2013 Company Law states:

> If any director or senior executive of a company is under the circumstance of Article 149 of this Law, in case of a limited liability company, the shareholders, or in case of a joint stock company, the shareholders separately or jointly holding one percent or more of the company's shares for 180 consecutive days may request in writing the supervisory board or the supervisor of the limited liability company having no supervisory board to bring a lawsuit before the People's Court; where any supervisor of the company is under the circumstances of Article 149 of this Law, the said shareholders may request in writing the board of directors or the executive director of the limited liability company having no board of directors to bring a lawsuit before the People's Court.
>
> If the supervisory board or the supervisor of the limited liability company having no supervisory board, the board of directors or the executive director of the limited liability company having no board of directors, upon its receipt of the shareholders' written request as stipulated in the preceding Paragraph, refuses to sue, or fails to sue within 30 days upon its receipt of such request, or in case of emergency, the company's interests will suffer irreparable damage if no lawsuit is raised immediately, then, the shareholders as stipulated in the preceding Paragraph may, for the benefits of the company, directly bring a lawsuit before the People's Court in their own name.
>
> Where others infringe the lawful rights and interests of a company and cause loss to the company, the shareholders as stipulated in the preceding Paragraph 1 of this Article may sue in accordance with the preceding two Paragraphs.

The derivative action under Article 151 can only be regarded as a derivative action with Chinese characteristics.

---

48. Ibid.

(a) Purpose of a Derivative Action

The purpose of a derivative action is to pursue the civil liability of directors, supervisors and senior executives if they have violated the laws, administrative regulations, or articles of association when performing their functions and thus caused a loss to the company. In the normal situation, those persons have the controlling power and the company concerned will not sue them even if they have abused their power to seek personal gains. Therefore, it is correct to state that the derivative action is an additional weapon to deter the behaviour of those management personnel.[49] In fact, in the situation of an LLC, big shareholders also control their companies and could be the targets of a derivative action in Western countries. Although the Chinese company law is silent on this issue, it is not a serious problem at this stage. A possible suggestion is to treat big shareholders as senior management personnel. This could be subjected to further discussion.

(b) Qualifications of a Plaintiff

Different jurisdictions may require different qualifications. In China, the qualifications are mainly related to the quantity and duration of the shareholding. In the situation of an LLC, there is no requirement for the quantity and duration. In the situation of a JSC, the shareholders are required to separately or jointly hold 1 per cent or more of the company's shares for 180 consecutive days.[50] The different requirements are understandable because of the differing natures of the LLC and JSC. The LLC is a closed company and there is a limitation to transferring one's shareholding to strangers. That is why no duration is required. However, it is not certain why there is no quantity requirement. Does this mean that once an investor becomes a member of an LLC he or she automatically obtains the qualification to sue?[51] Why should the shareholders in the JSC be treated discriminatively? Debate over the issues of quantity and duration continues. One may argue that the requirements of quantity and duration are not necessary

49. It is also because directors or senior executives are usually supervised by supervisors or independent directors.
50. In accordance with Article 5 of the Rules Concerning Several Issues of Applying the Company Law of the PRC (1) issued by the Supreme People's Court on 28 April 2006, the term "180 consecutive days" refers to the 180 consecutive days before the lawsuit is brought before a People's Court.
51. In order to answer this question, one may need to consider Article 23(1) of the American Federal Rules on Civil Procedures, which require a plaintiff to "fairly and adequately represent the interests of shareholders or members who are similarly situated in enforcing the right of the corporation". This means that if the shareholding quantity is not sufficient, the party concerned cannot be the plaintiff.

because the purpose of a derivative action is to monitor and deter the activities of directors or senior executives. If this argument can be established, then one should be allowed to sue even if one holds only one share or becomes a shareholder after the wrongs have been committed. However, others may argue that the purpose of requiring quantity and duration is to avoid the derivative action being abused. For example, in England and Australia, there is a requirement that a plaintiff must be on the shareholder's name list at the time the lawsuit is begun. In Japan, the articles of association may disqualify a plaintiff if his or her share unit (usually 1,000 shares are considered as 1 unit) is not enough.[52] The US laws dealing with derivative actions require the plaintiff to have become a shareholder when the cause of action arose and remained so continuously since that time. Furthermore, it is noted that many US states permit a shareholder to serve as a plaintiff even though he or she is not a shareholder when the cause of action arose if the shareholder can show that he or she acquired the shares in ignorance of the existence of the claim. In this situation, it is possible for a person to "buy a lawsuit". From a positive perspective, the derivative action is a good device to monitor the behaviour of the management personnel and/or majority shareholders. Thus, if a person wants to "buy a lawsuit", he or she should be encouraged because he or she still needs to satisfy other preconditions.

In China, there is a view that the qualification requirement should be relaxed and a shareholder shall be allowed to sue so long as he or she is a member of the company when the wrongs have been done and regardless of the quantity of his or her share amount.[53] This book supports this view based on the lesson learned from Taiwan, where the system of derivative action is hardly used because there are too many restrictions.[54] That is one of the reasons why, starting from 2003, Taiwan has considered adopting "the class action for securities cases",[55] even though the two systems are

52. Qiao Xin and others, *Judicial Remedies for Company's Disputes* (*Gongsi Jiufen de Sifa Jiuji*), The Law Press (Beijing), 2007, p. 52.
53. Shu Xuxia, "Several Issues Concerning the Adjudication of Shareholder Derivative Action" (*Shenli Gudong Paisheng Susong Anjian de Jige Wenti*), retrieved from http://www.chinacourt.org/public/detail.php?id=59176 on 8 October 2015.
54. Taiwan imported the derivative action in 1929, before which no such action was taken. In 1983, its company law was amended again in order to lower the threshold. From 2001 to today, there have been seven derivative actions in total. See Lai Yuanhe, "The System of Shareholder's Derivative Action in Taiwan" (*Taiwan de Gudong Daibiao Zhi Su Zhidu*), in the thesis collection for the 4th Legal Forum for Asian Enterprises held in the East China University for Politics and Law (Shanghai) on 8 June 2007.
55. The Speech made by Zhu Defang at the 4th Legal Forum for Asian Enterprises held in the East China University for Politics and Law (Shanghai) on 8 June 2007.

different in nature. In China, the structure of shareholding is relatively simple and overly harsh requirements may not be encouraging. More sophisticated rules could be developed when the company system has matured enough.

In China, the research on derivative action has just started. In the United States, the technical discussion about the qualifications of a plaintiff is on-going. For example, due to a merger (the use of the shares of one company to change for shares of another company) or other reasons, the plaintiff may lose his or her shareholder status and fail to continue the derivative action.[56] A person who purchases shares in the initial share offering cannot take a derivative action against the directors who decided the offering conditions because the plaintiff must prove that at the time the offering conditions were made he or she was a shareholder in the new company.[57] In one case, the court concluded that if a plaintiff (1) simultaneously holds the shares of both the parent company and wholly-owned subsidiary company, (2) sues the directors of the subsidiary company in the capacity of a shareholder in the parent company (double derivative action), or (3) has lost a plaintiff qualification when the parent company has taken back all shares of the subsidiary company but is still considered as a plaintiff, as a matter of equity, he or she is allowed to take derivative action on behalf of the former subsidiary company, even if the wrongs were committed before the plaintiff had become a shareholder in the subsidiary company.[58]

(c) Preconditions of a Derivative Action

Before a derivative action is taken, the plaintiff must do something. Firstly, if the wrong is committed by directors or senior management personnel, the plaintiff should send a written demand to the BOS asking it to sue those wrongdoers. Secondly, if the wrong is committed by supervisors, the plaintiff should send a written demand to the BOD asking it to sue the wrongdoers (Art. 151.1). This provision may create a false image to potential plaintiffs because it allows the plaintiff to make a written demand automatically. In contrast, in the case where the wrong is committed by the directors, the plaintiff should ask the directors concerned or the BOD to correct the relevant wrong in the first place. If they refuse to correct their wrong, then the written demand can be sent to the BOS. This remains the same in the situation where the wrong is committed by supervisors. This arrangement

56. The relevant cases are Lewis, 477 A.2d at 1049; *Heit v. Tenneco, Inc.*, 319 F. Supp. 884, 886 (D. Del. 1970).
57. *7547 Partners v. Beck*, 682 A.2d 160, 162-63 (Del. 1996).
58. *Shaev v. Wyly*, 1998 Del. Ch. LEXIS 2, 1998 WL 13858 (Del. Ch. Jan. 6, 1998).

is more logical because the demand to correct a wrong is more positive than the demand to sue, and less litigation is good for the normal operation of a company.

(d) Who Should Be the Plaintiff?

Article 151 authorizes the plaintiff to take a derivative action on his or her own behalf, which creates further confusion. The derivative action is different from the direct action because the action is taken to protect the interest of the company. If the action can be taken on his or her own behalf, then the artificial legal person status of a company is ignored and the theoretical basis of the company law is shaken. Only if a plaintiff can take a derivative action on behalf of a company can the wrongdoers return relevant properties or pay compensations to the company rather than to the plaintiff. Certainly, the lawmakers of this provision may insist on authorizing the plaintiff to take this special action on his or her behalf. In this case, it would be proper not to call this action a derivative action. Otherwise, it would be problematic to call this action a derivative action on the one hand and to provide different content on the other hand.

In common law jurisdictions, if a derivative action is taken by a plaintiff, he or she must point out that the action is taken on behalf of the company concerned. This can be seen from the following two examples.

Example One:[59]

> Cyma Siegel, Derivatively on behalf of Nominal Defendant Hypercom Corporation
>
> Plaintiff
>
> v
>
> Christopher S. Alexander, Danile Diethelm, William C. Keiper, Phillip J. Riese, Norman Stout and John W. Smolak
>
> Defendants
>
> and
>
> Hypercom Corporation, Nominal Defendant

59. This case was retrieved from http://www.gardencitygroup.com/cases/pdf/HYP/HYPNotice.pdf on 8 October 2015.

Example Two:[60]

Anthony F. Gonzalez, for and on behalf of Colonial Bank,
Petitioner
v
Joseph V. Chillura, Jr, Alfred T. Rogers, and MCAPITAL II, LLC, A Florida limited liability company,
and
COLONIAL BANK, an Alabama corporation,
Respondents

Furthermore, in common law jurisdictions, a derivative action must put the company concerned as a joint defendant (nominal defendant). On the face of it, there exists one conflict between the company as one plaintiff and the company as one defendant. This kind of arrangement, however, suits a special purpose. Only if the company can be treated as a joint defendant can the decision of the court bind the whole company as well as the management. If without this special arrangement, the decision of the court can be bound only to individual personnel. The management can still make certain decisions that are not in the best interests of the company, even though some wrongdoers have been replaced. Thus, in a derivative action, the company concerned is concurrently a substantial plaintiff and a nominal defendant. This unique feature differentiates a derivative action from a direct action.

For the preceding reason, the view that the company concerned in a derivative action is neither a plaintiff nor a defendant but an independent party is not convincing.[61] Firstly, this view does not have sufficient legal basis. Secondly, if this view is allowed, then the existing civil procedural law must be revised to adopt this type of independent party.

(e) Defendants in a Derivative Action

Article 151 gives a broad right to a plaintiff to choose relevant defendants. Thus, the defendants may include directors, supervisors, managers and

60. Retrieved from http://www.2dca.org/opinion/November%2003,%202004/2D03-5885.pdf on 8 October 2015.
61. Shu, supra note 53.

other senior management personnel. There is a view that in certain situations the defendants may be third parties who have infringed upon the civil rights of the company. The basis of this view is the theory of subrogation power.[62] This view is problematic because it dilutes the focus of the derivative action.

It must be clear that the purpose of a derivative action is to control the conduct of management personnel. Therefore, to broaden the scope of application may not be a good idea. So far, company laws in many countries focus mainly on directors, supervisors, senior officers or controlling shareholders, who are internal persons instead of third parties. In this area, the American type of free legislation does not show its superiority because the majority of derivative actions have targeted the management personnel. Furthermore, to enlarge the scope of application would create an opportunity to abuse the derivative action. As a general rule, the BOD should be entrusted to sue third parties and it is not necessary to give the plaintiff such power. If the BOD fails to do so, it would be considered a breach of fiduciary duty, and relevant directors may be subjected to the derivative action.[63]

How, then, should "other persons" under Article 151(3) be interpreted? If other persons are not third parties, who fits into this category? Although it is difficult to find the legislative intention, it is possible to conclude that "other persons" should refer to "actual controllers" or "controlling shareholders".[64] In other words, even if those persons do not have the titles of directors, supervisors, or senior officers, so long as they perform a decisive function in the operation of the company, the duties or responsibilities of directors, supervisors, or senior officers should be imposed on them.

Even when focus is drawn to the directors, supervisors, senior officers, or controlling shareholders, it must still be considered whether certain conduct should be exempted from the derivative action. In Japan, for example, if a director does not breach the statutory duties but breaches only those duties stipulated by the articles of association, the company is allowed to exempt his or her responsibility. In England, Australia, and Canada, the exempted conduct is not subject to the derivative action.[65] The Chinese

62. Li Xiang, "The Beginning of the Derivative Action" (*Gudong Paisheng Susong Qihang*), retrieved from http://finance.sina.com.cn/stock/t/20060913/15552911651.shtml on 8 October 2015.
63. Niu Haiqin, "The Establishment of the Derivative Action System in China" (*Gudong Paisheng Susong Zhidu zai Woguo de Queli*), retrieved from http://gsf.110.com/gudongquanyi/2010/0428/87245.html on 8 October 2015.
64. Such as "shadow directors" in common law jurisdictions.
65. Qiao Xin et al., *Judicial Remedies for Company's Disputes* (*Gongsi jiufen de sifa jiuji*), The Law Press (Beijing), 2007, p. 76.

company law is silent on this matter. It is expected that this matter is decided by companies through their articles of association. The next logical step is to identify what conduct can be exempted from the derivative action.

(3) Article 151 Should be Further Improved

The existing Company Law contains only one provision to deal with derivative action, which is far from sufficient. There are two solutions to this problem: one is to further improve the Law by adding more provisions, and the other is to publish detailed implementation rules or regulations. Regardless of which solution is adopted, it is necessary to pay attention to the following items.

(a) Exhaustion of Internal Remedy

Article 151 requires that the plaintiff shall exhaust the internal remedy by sending a written demand to either the BOD or the BOS if the wrongdoers are different. The written demand is important because it gives either the supervisory body or the management body an opportunity to decide whether the relevant action should be taken or whether the relevant action is not in the best interest of the company and thus should be refused. As a general rule, "whether a corporation should assert a claim is a business decision ordinarily committed to the business judgment of the board".[66]

Therefore, if a director violates Article 149, the plaintiff shall firstly send the written demand to the BOD asking it to take necessary actions instead of sending the written demand directly to the BOS. The plaintiff may copy the written demand to the BOS for two purposes. Firstly, it encourages the plaintiff to supervise the conduct of directors. Secondly, it solves one logical problem: when the BOD refuses to take necessary action, the BOS must take necessary action. If neither of them takes action, the plaintiff may argue that there is a futility of demand, i.e., the demand is useless.

The existing Company Law does not require the plaintiff to prove the futility of demand in order to sue directly. The futility of demand refers to a situation where a plaintiff has the necessary evidence to show that the written demand required by the Law is useless, and he or she may take the derivative action immediately. In order to do so, the plaintiff needs to show "adequate reasons" for not making the effort, i.e., (1) the wrongdoers hold a majority of the shares and hence a favourable shareholders' action is

66. Joseph M. Mclaughlin, "Directors' and Officers' Liability: Demand Futility in Derivative Actions", retrieved from http://www.stblaw.com/content/Publications/Publication20_0.pdf on 8 October 2015.

impossible; (2) the number of shareholders is so large that it is unreasonable to require the plaintiff to incur the expense of what is essentially a proxy solicitation when there is little chance of success; or (3) the acts complained of cannot be ratified by the majority shareholders, so the action taken by the shareholders is useless. On the other hand, the US courts will examine whether there is a situation of demand futility by using the Aronson Test, i.e., whether there is "a reasonable doubt either that: (1) the directors are disinterested and independent or (2) the challenged transaction otherwise was the product of a valid exercise of business judgment".[67]

(b) Business Judgment Rule in a Derivative Action

Both the 2005 Company Law and the 2013 Company Law do not adopt the business judgment rule, which is popular in the United States.[68] Therefore, it is impossible to apply this rule to a derivative action in China.

In the United States, when the BOD receives the written demand for the plaintiff, it forms a special committee with disinterested persons as members to determine whether the company should assert a claim. If the committee decides not take any action, the decision is respected by the court.

(c) The Derivative Action Shall Not Be Abused

The derivate action may be considered as a useful device to protect the legal interests of minority shareholders. At the same time, the derivative action may itself be abused by minority shareholders and their lawyers bringing so-called "strike" lawsuits for personal gain rather than the correction of management misconduct. Thus, if the purpose of a derivative action is originally to obtain some form of private settlement, defendants would be willing to pay either to avoid the nuisance of the suit or to escape the potentially larger liability of a judgment. The complaining shareholder would be willing to accept a fraction of the alleged damage to the corporation because this personal recovery would have far exceeded the derivative benefit recovered by the corporation. This opportunity, however, has been greatly diminished by the more recent doctrinal development that derivative action settlements must go to the corporation. Thus, at least from the perspective of some authors, these strike suitors are likely to be lawyers who instigate derivative suits hoping for a substantial fee after a judgment or a settlement for the corporation where the net value to the company may be greatly exceeded by the actual or potential costs related to defending the lawsuit (including

67. Ibid.
68. For detailed information about this rule, please see Ding Ding, *Research on the Business Judgment Rule (Shangye Panduan Guize Yanjiu)*, Jilin People's Press (Jilin), 2005.

reputation damages and diversion of management's energy from the normal business activity).[69]

In order to avoid the abuse, plaintiffs must be required to post security that is usually defined in terms of the size of their holdings. One purpose of requiring the security is to deter "strike" suits brought forward in the hope of securing a settlement profitable to the plaintiff shareholders and their attorneys. In China, the SPC followed practices in other jurisdictions and suggested requiring the plaintiff to post security if the defendant were able to prove that the action taken could have been based in bad faith.[70]

(d) Who Should Be Compensated If the Action Is Successful?

Because this is a derivative action and the plaintiff sues the wrongdoers on behalf of the company, it is logical that the company should be compensated. However, debate still exists as to whether both the plaintiff and the company should be entitled to the "mutual benefit". In other words, the plaintiff should be compensated too if he or she wins the case.

It is true that the plaintiff will obtain certain benefits indirectly if the company is properly compensated. However, it cannot be considered as a "mutual benefit" because only the company is compensated directly. The plaintiff may be compensated for necessary expenses, but he or she is not the direct beneficiary.

(4) A Short Summary

Article 151 makes the derivative action possible in China. This provision, however, is far from sophisticated and has no sufficient theoretical foundation. Certainly, one has to admit that it is impossible to establish a perfect system within a short period of time. Thus, it is necessary to accumulate sufficient experience before this provision can be further improved.

---

69. Choper, Coffee, and Morris, supra note 40, pp. 785–901.
70. The SPC circulated a draft of the Provisions on Certain Issues Concerning the Application of the "Company Law of the People's Republic of China" (IV) for public consultation in 2011. Article 53 proposed the requirement of security.

7

Directors and Board of Directors

I. CREATION OF DIRECTORS

1. Definition

The Chinese company law does not define the term "director". This is similar to the situations in the United States and Hong Kong. *The Chinese Encyclopaedia (Law Volume)* defines a director as "a standing organ which carries out businesses and represents a company". Some books describe a director as a member of BOD and the legal standing organ of a company for carrying out business. In fact, Taiwanese scholars originated this kind of definition when they interpreted Japanese company law. In line with the continental legal system that Taiwan belongs to, the term "director" means two things. Firstly, a "directorship" is one of the organs of a company, and a director's act is deemed to be an act of the company. Secondly, a director is a person who has an authorizing relationship (*weiren guanxi*) with the company, i.e., a director carries out business under the authorization of his or her company.

The Hong Kong Companies Ordinance (Cap. 622) does not define the term "director" either. Under Section 2 of Cap. 622, a "director" is defined as including "any person occupying the position of director (by whatever name called)". This seems unhelpful for a legal interpretation and an academic discussion. Actually, directors in Hong Kong may include *de jure*, *de facto*, and shadow directors. A *de jure* director is a person who has been validly appointed as a director, has agreed to be appointed as the director, and is not disqualified from acting as a director. By contrast, a *de facto* director is a person who acts as a director of a company without a valid appointment. Under Section 2 of Cap. 622, a shadow director refers to "a person in accordance with whose directions or instructions (excluding advice given in a professional capacity) the directors, or a majority of the directors, of the body corporate are accustomed to act".[1] Thus, a person shall not be considered a shadow director merely based on the act of delivering advice in a professional capacity. The concepts of the *de facto* director and shadow director are meaningful because persons who are recognized as directors have to observe their duty of loyalty and duty of care and have to be liable if those duties are breached.

One book defines a "director" as a member of the BOD or the business executor according to company law in the absence of BODs during the time when companies emerged. Following the development of company law around the world, the BOD has played a more and more important role than individual directors. In many large-sized companies, the number of directors has increased, and directors are required to form collective decisions rather than a decision in their individual capacity.[2]

In Hong Kong, the most common types of directors within the BOD are:

- Governing directors. It is unusual for public companies to have a governing director. Only some private companies that are formed to operate a family business provide for the nomination of a governing director. However, the creation of governing directors shall be done through the memorandum or the articles of association.
- Managing directors. It is a common practice for the BOD to delegate some of its functions to a managing director. Sometimes, people use the term "chief executive officer" (hereinafter referred to as "CEO") to mean the same thing.
- Chairman of directors. In practice, the chairman is often given special powers, and in large public companies this position carries great

1. However, the concept of the shadow director was criticized by the Review of the Hong Kong Companies Ordinance (consultant report) 1997. This report offered the recommendation that the troublesome and unenforceable concept of the shadow director should be eliminated for the following main reasons: "Where it is considered desirable to impose duties or liabilities on non-directors, rather than deeming a non-director to be a director, consideration should be given to identifying those to whom liability would attach, for example, executive officers or major shareholders. Where personal liability is in issue, it is important that there be reasonable certainty. Measures which are vague or commercially uncertain will inevitably be difficult to enforce, thereby undermining their utility."
2. Liu Ruifu, *Chinese Company Law* (*Zhongguo gongsi fa*), Joint Publishing (Hong Kong), 1998, p. 101.

prestige. Frequently, the managing director of a company also acts as a chairman of the BOD.

- Committees of directors. Companies with relatively large numbers on the board may decide that various management functions shall be delegated to committees of directors.
- Alternate directors. If the director of a company is unable for any time to act as a director, he or she may appoint an alternate or substitute director. According to Section 478 of Cap. 622, an alternate director so appointed is deemed to be the agent of the director who appoints the alternate and the director is vicariously liable for any tort committed by the alternate director while acting in the capacity of alternate director.
- Associate directors. Some companies adopt a practice of appointing their junior executives as associate directors. The purpose of doing so is to increase the status of the person appointed.
- Nominee directors. Sometimes a director is appointed to represent the interests of particular shareholders (such as a holding company) or creditors on the BOD.

These classifications are helpful for the development of the Chinese company law in the area of dealing with the liabilities of directors. In comparison, theory on directors has not been fully developed in China, even though chair directors or managing directors are often seen playing very important roles in companies.

2. Election of a Director

(1) Reasons for Choosing a Director

When shareholders choose their directors, do they ever think about the reasons for choosing them? In the 1970s, an interesting survey[3] was conducted in the United Kingdom in order to find out the reasons for choosing directors. Among the 2,450 answers received, the reasons were organized as follows:

(a) Good at operations (672 answers)
(b) Thoughtful in business operations (519 answers)
(c) Representative of major shareholders (330 answers)
(d) Major shareholders (229 answers)
(e) Legal consultants (168 answers)

3. Unfortunately, the source of this information cannot be recovered.

(f) Financial consultants (148 answers)
(g) Experience and knowledge of business (133 answers)
(h) Retired high-ranking officers (102 answers)
(i) Representative of the banking and financial field (73 answers);
(j) Consultants for buying and selling (51 answers)
(k) Good at labour relations (13 answers)
(l) Representative of customers (12 answers)

From these survey outcomes, one can see that most shareholders choose directors based on their capabilities and skills in business operations, rather than their reputations or formal official positions. This is the tendency around the world, and China should follow this trend.

(2) Number of Directors

Directors are elected by shareholders through the SHM. In China, the number of directors shall not be fewer than three in an LLC (Art. 44) and shall be no fewer than five and no more than nineteen in a JSC (Art. 108).[4] This number requirement is different from that of Hong Kong, where the required number of directors is at least two for both public companies[5] and companies limited by guarantee[6] and just one for private companies.[7] However, in the United States, there is an exception that the number of directors of a corporation may be specified or fixed in accordance with the articles of association or the byelaws. Usually, if the number of directors fails to meet the statutory requirements or there are fewer than two or three directors in number as provided by a company's byelaw, then the BOD shall call a special SHM to elect new directors again.

The Chinese company law has started to deal with the situation where the number of directors does not satisfy the statutory requirement because no re-election is carried out in a timely fashion after the expiration of

4. One interesting development is that in the EU, the European Commission has proposed to require companies listed in EU countries with more than 250 workers to have 40 per cent of women siting on the BOD by 2020. Tomas Jivanda, "Germany Set to Introduce Legal Quota for Women in Boardrooms", retrieved from http://www.independent.co.uk/news/world/europe/germany-to-introduce-legal-quota-for-women-in-boardrooms-8947277.html on 14 October 2015. Apparently, this is too new a topic to Chinese company law.
5. Cap. 622, Section 453.
6. Ibid.
7. Cap. 622, Section 454. In China, one director is allowed in exceptional situations. Article 50 of the Company Law states that "for a limited liability company with a relatively small number of shareholders or for a relatively small limited liability company, it may have an acting director and no board of directors. The acting director may concurrently hold the post of the company's manager."

the term of office of the directors or some directors resign prior to the expiration of their jobs. In this situation, the original directors shall, before the newly elected directors assume their posts, exercise the authorities of the directors pursuant to laws, administrative regulations as well as the articles of association (Art. 45.2)

This provision, however, cannot be justified theoretically. It fails to address the circumstance where a director is either disabled or dead. How should the BOD solve this problem? One suggestion is that in this situation one person should be appointed to be the executive director until the term of vacancy expires or the SHM re-elects new directors. However, another issue arises: whether the *de facto* director is a valid concept in China. Until now, it has been hard to see any formal discussion of this issue, in part due to the short history of Chinese company law. Chinese legislators' reluctant attitudes towards the *de facto* director may be another reason.

Contrarily, the concept of the *de facto* director is popularly recognized in common law jurisdictions. For example, in *Corporate Affairs Commission v. Drysdale* (1978) 141 CLR 236, Drysdale was appointed as a director to fill a casual vacancy on the board. The articles of association provided that such a director could hold the office only until the next annual general meeting, at which he or she was permitted to stand for re-election. Drysdale's retirement or re-election was, however, not considered at the next general meeting. Consequently, under the articles of association, Drysdale was no longer a director of the company. Nevertheless, he continued to participate in the management of the company as if he was a director. The High Court of Australia held that despite the defect in his appointment, he was deemed to be a director.

In the United States, despite the expiration of the term of his or her position, a director continues to hold the office until a successor is "elected and qualified". As a result, the failure to hold an annual meeting does not affect the power of a company to continue its business, since the director presently in office continues in office with the power to act. This director is a so-called "hold-over director". It has been said that the holdover director is particularly important in the situation where the shareholders are deadlocked in their voting power and unable to elect successors to replace the directors whose terms have expired.[8] In this circumstance, both *de facto* directors and holdover directors are seemingly fit for the changing situation. Thus, it is suggested that the concept of a *de facto* director shall be transplanted into China in the near future to deal with any complicated situation.

8. Robert W. Hamilton, *The Law of Corporations*, West Publishing (St. Paul, MN), 1996, p. 259.

(3) Methods of Election

Under the Chinese company law, there are two ways to appoint directors. Firstly, employees of an LLC established by two or more SOEs or State-owned investment entities are empowered to elect employees' representatives sitting on the BOD through a democratic election (Art. 44.2). This is deemed to conform to the Chinese socialist characteristic and tradition. Secondly, the directors in a wholly State-owned company shall be appointed and removed by the State-owned Assets Regulatory Authority (Art. 67.2). For other companies, especially for listed companies, the election of directors is not specified. However, in the situation where the State-owned shares or legal person shares usually represent about 50 per cent of the total shares issued by companies,[9] the appointment of directors becomes a mere formality because candidates are usually nominated by the State as shareholders and will be easily appointed by the SHM.

It is also worth mentioning the means of electing directors in a JSC. So far there are two methods of election around the world. The traditional method is called the "direct election" method, i.e., shareholders vote for their directors based on the principle of "one share, one vote", and directors are elected by majority votes. On the face of it, this method reflects the democratic principle. However, this election method opens the door for majority shareholders to abuse their power, and minority shareholders may not be able to successfully elect their expected representatives. To deal with this situation, a new election method called the "accumulative election" method was created in the United States and adopted by many states.[10] This method has been adopted by Japan, Taiwan and other countries and regions, but was not adopted by the 1993 Company Law.

However, it is important to note the Code of Corporate Governance for Listed Companies (*Shangshi Gongsi Zhili Zhunze*), which was issued by the Chinese Securities Regulatory Committee (hereinafter referred to as the

---

9. By the end of 2012, there were 378 listed companies whose major shares were owned by centrally controlled SOEs and their subsidiary companies. Among those listed companies, the percentage of non-State-owned shares exceeded 53 per cent. See "Most SOEs Will Reduce Their State-owned Shares" (*Guoqi jiang pubian jiangdi guoyougu bili*), retrieved from http://finance.ce.cn/rolling/201312/20/t20131220_1959771.shtml on 8 October 2015.

10. There is, in England, nothing comparable to the system of "accumulative voting" which is optional or compulsory in many states of the United States and which affords shareholders the possibility of board representation proportional to their holding. See Paul L. Davies, *Gower's Principles of Modern Company Law* (6th ed.), Sweet and Maxwell, 1997, p. 181.

"CSRC") on 7 January 2002. This Code marked the beginning of the adoption of accumulative election in China. Article 31 of the Code stated,

> The election of directors shall fully reflect the opinions of minority shareholders. An accumulative voting system shall be earnestly advanced in shareholders' meetings for the election of directors. Listed companies that have more than 30 per cent of its shares owned by controlling shareholders shall adopt an accumulative voting system, and the companies adopting such a system shall stipulate the rules for implementing such accumulative voting system in their articles of association.

This provision indicates two approaches. For listed companies with more than 30 per cent of their shares owned by controlling shareholders, it is compulsory to adopt the accumulative voting system. Other listed companies are encouraged to adopt this voting system, but they can retain the direct voting system. More and more listed companies have adopted the accumulative voting system.[11] However, it is evident that more than 40 per cent of listed companies have controlling shareholders owning shares, representing more than 50 per cent of their companies. In the situation where other shareholders own less than 5 per cent of the shares of their companies, it is difficult to expect the accumulative voting system to work properly.[12] One possible resolution is to further dilute the State-owned shares or to make the accumulative election system compulsory.

Subsequently, the 2005 Company Law admitted this election method. With this method applied, each share equals the number of directors, and a shareholder can cast all of his or her votes for one director or for several shareholders. For example, if three directors need to be elected and there are one hundred shares in total, in the direct election situation the majority shareholders who hold fifty-one shares can control the election because each director is elected by those shareholders by fifty-one votes. However, under the accumulative election system, each share equals three votes, so the total votes of a company shall be three hundred. Among three hundred votes, the majority shareholder holds $51 \times 3 = 153$ votes, and the other shareholders hold $49 \times 3 = 147$ votes. By utilizing this election method, the minority shareholders can elect at least one director to represent their interests. In China, because the biggest shareholder is the State, it is logical

11. Xu Qing, "The Existing Flaws of the Accumulative Voting System for Listed Companies in China" (Woguo shangshi gongsi leiji toupiao zhidu cunzai quexian), retrieved from http://news1.jrj.com.cn/news/2004-09-16/000000901867.html on 8 October 2015.
12. Ibid.

to provide an accumulative election so that minority shareholders have the hope of electing some directors who can represent their interests.

3. Term of Office for Directors

Article 45 of the Company Law requires that the articles of association shall state the term of office of directors and that the term shall not exceed three years. A director may, if re-elected upon the expiration of his or her term of office, serve consecutive terms. Thus, in China, it is very possible for a director to remain in office as long as possible even though it is illegal to provide a life term for a director in the articles of association, because he or she can always manage to be re-elected by using his or her powerful influence. Contrarily, in Hong Kong, the articles of association may allow directors to be appointed for life, for an indefinite term or for a certain prescribed term.[13] However, if a company adopts Table A (Art. 91) and new Model Articles (public companies, Art. 21), retirement from office by rotation is compulsory every year. Apparently, the decision to adopt a particular term is in the hands of shareholders. Thus comparatively, the approach adopted by the Chinese company law is less significant.

4. Qualification for Appointment

Generally, most jurisdictions require positive qualifications (a person must meet these conditions in order to be a director) and passive qualifications (in case something happens, a director shall be dismissed immediately) of a candidate.

(1) Positive Qualifications

(a) Nationality

Very few countries have set out such positive qualifications. Early company law in Switzerland stated that if there was only one director, that director should be a citizen of Switzerland and live in the territory, and if there were several directors, the majority should be citizens of Switzerland and live therein.[14] The Chinese company law does not provide this kind of limitation,

13. K. Arjunan and C. K. Low, *Understanding Company Law in Hong Kong*, the LBC Information Services, 1996, p. 205.
14. However, this requirement has been changed in Switzerland. Today, the law requires that at least one board member or one member of management who is entitled to represent the company be resident in Switzerland. See Rolf Watter and Katja Roth Pellanda,

and it is particularly easy for foreign investors to take the position as directors. Following the trend of globalization, it is foreseeable that nationality as a qualification will be largely ignored.

(b) Requirement of Shareholding Status

Around the world, there are three types of legislation concerning whether directors shall concurrently be the shareholders of a company. Firstly, directors do not have to be shareholders (examples may be seen in Japan, Italy, Australia, and Germany). Secondly, whether a director should concurrently be a shareholder is not required by law, but the byelaw of a company can provide such a limitation (see the example in the United States). Thirdly, shareholders must be shareholders concurrently (examples can be seen in Belgium and France). In Hong Kong, the old Companies Ordinance (Cap. 32) used to state that if a director did not obtain the share qualification within the prescribed period or ceased to hold this qualification, he or she must vacate the office of director (Section 155/3), and he or she was then incapable of being re-appointed as a director until the qualification had been obtained (Section 155/4). Furthermore, a person who purported to act as a director in contravention of Section 155/3 was guilty of an offence (Section 155/5). However, the new Companies Ordinance (Cap. 622) does not contain such provisions. A possible interpretation is that this matter should be dealt with by companies and that the law is no longer making it a crime. The Chinese company law takes the same approach as that of Japan and Germany. Furthermore, it does not require the qualifying shares to be held by directors. At this stage, it is difficult to determine which approach is better. Obviously, the requirement for a director to be a shareholder concurrently is based on a theory that directors closely tie their personal interests with the interests of the company. However, there is no persuasive evidence to show that other approaches are not good.

The next issue is whether, despite the silence of the existing Company Law on the matter of share qualification, companies in China can require directors to be shareholders through their articles of association. There are two arguments to support an affirmative answer. Firstly, in line with Chinese civil law tradition, if a general law does not specifically prohibit one particular conduct, people may act without suffering legal consequences. Secondly, both Articles 25(8) and 81(12) authorize companies to provide in their articles of association any lawful items that shareholders think

---

Executive Risks: A Boardroom Guide 2010/11, Legal Developments for Directors and Officers in Switzerland, retrieved from https://www.amcham.ch/members_interests/p_business_ch.asp?s=2&c=22 on 8 October 2015.

necessary. These two provisions indicate the possibility that the articles of association may require directors to have qualifying shares.

Qualifying shares may serve two purposes. Firstly, it is good to closely associate personal interests of directors with the interests of their company. Secondly, it is a great incentive to push directors to work hard and bring more profits to the company as well as to shareholders. However, there is no evidence to support the view that a compulsory requirement of qualifying shares makes directors effectively carry out their duties and makes directors with no qualifying shares perform badly. It thus suggests that this option should be left to companies to decide rather than be regulated by the Chinese company law. If a company considers that qualifying shares are necessary, it can require them through a special provision of its articles of association.

(c) Legal Person Directors

Different countries may have different regulations dealing with this issue. The Chinese company law does not expressly state that a legal person director is not allowed. The remaining issue is whether it is possible to interpret the existing Company Law in a positive way. In order to do so, we have to carefully examine relevant theories and practice. In fact, there are two opposite positions taken around the world. On the one hand, some jurisdictions are in favour of legal person directors. For example, Article 91 of the French Company Law provides that the powers of legal person directors are exercised by their agents. On the other hand, it is important to note that the idea of legal person directors is subject to heavy criticism. The "Review of the Hong Kong Company Ordinance (Consultant Report) 1997" offered the recommendation that "permitting corporations to be directors cuts directly across current preoccupations of proper exercise of directors' discretion and board accountability. It should not be permitted." The Companies Ordinance (Cap. 622) takes a compromised approach by prohibiting corporate directors from public companies[15] and companies limited by guarantee[16] but allowing most private companies to have corporate directors.[17] In China, the Mandatory Provisions for the Articles of Association of Companies Seeking to Be Listed Outside the PRC, which governs Chinese companies listed outside China, clearly excludes a non-natural person from being a director of a company listed outside China. This legal document clearly indicates

15. Cap. 622, Section 456(1)(a).
16. Cap. 622, Section 456(1)(c).
17. Cap. 622. Section 456(1)(b) prohibits corporate directors only if a private company is a member of a group of companies of which a listed company is a member.

that relevant Chinese authorities have considered this issue and hold a negative position. One could argue, however, that this legal document applies only to companies listed outside China, especially in Hong Kong. It has no direct connection to the Chinese Company Law, which may indirectly allow the existence of legal person directors. Article 15 of the Company Law authorizes a company to invest in other enterprises including companies. Furthermore, one needs to know that in practice, nominee directors (which are equivalent to legal person directors) commonly exist in China. For example, in Sino-foreign joint venture companies, directors are nominated by each party who invests in a company. Obviously, further research is required before taking a proper position on this matter, but legal person directors should be permitted at least for domestic companies.

(d) Age of Directors

The Chinese company law provides no age limitation for a director. But different countries (or regions) may provide different limitations. In general, it is recognized that a director should have civil capacity, and most countries provide that a natural person shall not have civil capacity unless a certain age is reached. For example, the Hong Kong Companies Ordinance requires that a person must have attained eighteen years of age at the date of his or her appointment as director.[18] However, as argued in the previous chapter, a person who has not attained the age of eighteen may nevertheless be permitted to be a director if he or she is properly represented by his or her agent(s). On the other hand, even though most countries (regions) provide no age ceiling for directors, the British Company Law used to provide seventy as a maximum age.[19] However, the Company Act 2006 now provides only the minimum age of a director, which is sixteen.[20]

It seems that the age ceiling for a director may be a sensitive issue that leads to cases of age discrimination. Companies may choose to provide an age ceiling for directors, but they should implement this requirement based on strong justifications.

(2) Passive Qualifications

As mentioned before, passive qualifications refer to situations where a director should be immediately disqualified and dismissed if problems arise. Company laws around the world provide similar requirements. In line with

18. Cap. 622, Section 459(1).
19. Article 185(1) of Company Act 1948.
20. Article 157.

the Chinese Company Law, a person shall not hold a position as a director if the following situations exist (Art. 146):

(a) he or she has no capacity or has restricted capacity for civil acts;
(b) he or she was sentenced to criminal punishment for the crime of embezzlement, bribery, seizure of property or misappropriation of property or for undermining the socioeconomic order, and not more than five years have elapsed since the expiration of the enforcement period; or he or she was deprived of his or her political rights for committing a crime, and not more than five years have elapsed since the expiration of the enforcement period;
(c) he or she was a director, a factory head or a manager personally responsible for the bankruptcy or liquidation of a company or an enterprise due to mismanagement, where not more than three years have elapsed since the date of completion of the bankruptcy or liquidation;
(d) he or she was a legal representative of a company or an enterprise that had its business licence revoked for violating the law, where such a representative therefore bore individual liability and not more than three years have elapsed since the date of revocation of the business licence; or
(e) he or she is a person with a relatively large amount of personal debt that has fallen due but has not been settled.

These requirements clearly indicate that a director should not have problems with capacity, a criminal record, business ability or credibility. One remaining problem is whether a person who has been deprived of his or her political rights can be elected as a director. Although the deprivation of political rights indicates the serious nature of the crime committed, political rights mainly refer to the right to participate in political activities.[21] Nevertheless, it is understandable that the deprivation of political rights is a supplementary punishment and that the main criminal sentence itself has already disqualified the person from being a director.

---

21. According to Article 54 of the Criminal Law, the deprivation of political rights shall refer to the deprivation of (1) the right to vote and to be elected; (2) the right of freedom of speech, press, assembly, association, procession and demonstration; (3) the right to hold a position in a State organ; and (4) the right to hold a leader position in any State-owned company, enterprise, institution or people's organization. Thus, one possible interpretation is that regular companies are not included.

(3) Disqualification

The Chinese Company Law stipulates that directors will be disqualified if situations under Article 146 arise. It should be noted that in cases where these situations happen, the directors should be automatically disqualified without waiting for an action to be taken by the SHM or the BOS. Certainly, how to prove the disqualification can be a serious problem. Without proper procedures stipulated by the Chinese company law or by articles of association, directors can easily be disqualified because there is no legal proceeding to protest against any such action. In comparison, the approach taken in Hong Kong may be better because directors are not be automatically disqualified if they commit a crime. In that case, directors are disqualified by a court order. As pointed out by some scholars, "the disqualification provisions in Part IVA,[22] however, require substantial resources to enforce and regulate and as a result, may ultimately prove to be an expensive and limited device for controlling the actions of company directors".[23] In addition, even though a director is announced to be bankrupt, he or she may apply for a court order to continue his or her position as a director.[24]

(4) Termination

Article 45 states that the term of office of a director shall be stipulated in the articles of association, but each term shall not exceed three years. Unlike the 1993 Company Law, which prohibited an SHM from removing a director from office before the expiration of his or her term of office without any specific reason,[25] the existing Company Law does not contain such particular words. One possible reason is that the lawmakers want to follow the international practice by giving this power to shareholders. In other words, shareholders can, through proper procedures, terminate or replace directors without any reason.

If this is the case, then a director can be removed by the SHM merely for not working hard or being too incompetent to act as director, but without

22. Cap. 32, Part IVA. It has been said that "Part IVA will remain in force even after the commencement of the new Companies Ordinance (Cap. 622)". See Stefan H. C. Lo and Charles Z. Qu, *Law of Companies in Hong Kong*, Sweet & Maxwell, 2013, p. 254.
23. Philip Smart, Katherine Lynch and Anna Tam, *Hong Kong Company Law: Cases, Materials and Comments*, Butterworths Asia (Hong Kong), 1997, p. 221.
24. Huang Jiangwen, *Comparative Research on Legal Principles Concerning Company Directors in Both Hong Kong and the PRC (Zhongguo gongsi dongshi falü guize bijiao yanjiu)*, in Wang Baoshu (ed.), *Commercial Law Review*, Vol. 4, The Law Press (Beijing), 2001, p. 190.
25. The 1993 Company Law, Art. 47(2).

necessarily breaching his or her duties. If this is the case, it is easy to answer the next question, i.e., whether shareholders can remove a director after the company is taken over by another company. After a takeover, the new majority shareholders frequently remove subsisting directors and appoint new directors with the approval of the shareholders' general meeting. This happened in the case of Shenzhen Bao An Co. Ltd. when it took over Shanghai Yan Zhong Co. Ltd., the first Chinese corporate takeover case reported in China.[26]

As discussed before, the SHM is the highest authority of a company, so it must be given the power to terminate a director even within a term of office. To be fair to directors, they may be allowed to recover some economic compensation under contract law. This conclusion is supported by the practice in Hong Kong, where a director cannot prevent the company from exercising its right to remove him or her. However, the termination may nevertheless constitute a breach of contract if it is validly made before the alteration, as in *Southern Foundries v. Shirlaw* (1940) A. C. 701. Furthermore, the members of a company must not exercise the company's power to amend the articles of association unless to do so is "*bona fide* for the benefit of the company as a whole".

(5) Statutory Situations

In addition, death, disability, resignation and so on will also terminate a director's term of office.

II. DUTIES OF DIRECTORS

Directors are under certain duties and are liable if those duties are breached. On the other hand, directors are highly rewarded if they discharge their duties satisfactorily. That is why directors are normally given high remuneration.[27] A survey of 1,000 leading UK companies was conducted in 1994. It was revealed that the average total remuneration for chief executives was £351,000. This was over twenty times the annual salary of the typical

26. Duan Yicai, Lu Gongxia and Wangyimin, *The Board of Directors in Modern Companies* (*Xiandai gongsi dongshihui*), Chinese Society and Science Publishing House (Beijing), 1995, p. 90.
27. According to advocates of board capture theory, directors and especially CEOs are able to "capture" (convince) the BOD to set their own remunerations. On the other hand, advocates of optimal contracting theory believe that BODs are usually able to negotiate the best possible remuneration given that they are able to maximize shareholder value. See Lin Lin, "Regulating Executive Compensation in China: Problems and Solutions", *The Journal of Law and Commerce*, Vol. 32, Issue 2, Spring 2014, pp. 210–11.

rank-and-file worker (approximately £16,500). The same 1994 survey revealed that senior executives who also served as directors received on average a total remuneration package of £186,000 while other executives were paid £128,000.[28] One similar survey was also conducted in 2001 in China. The Shanghai Rongzheng Investment Consulting Limited Liability Company conducted a survey that covered 1,094 listed companies. Among those companies, the chairman of the BOD, Wang Guorui, was given the highest annual salary of ¥1.25 million. Another chairman of the BOD, Zhang Hongwei, held shares worth more than ¥24 million.[29] In 2009, the remuneration was dramatically increased in China. According to the Chinese edition of *Forbes*, each chairman/CEO was given a salary of ¥15.98 million.[30] Following the deep reform of SOEs, CEO salaries will be reduced dramatically. It has been said that CEOs' annual salaries will be controlled below ¥600,000.[31] However, taking into consideration today's economic situation in China, the incomes of chairmen or CEOs may be less attractive. Thus, there is a doubt whether the principle of "high pay with high responsibility" can still be applied to directors in China.[32]

1. The Legal Relationship between a Director and the Company

Both common law jurisdictions and continental law jurisdictions recognize that a director is the agent of a company. Companies are the artificial persons and can only act through their agents. This view is supported by the statement made by Lord Cairns in *Ferguson v. Wilson* (1866) LR 2 Ch 77, 89:

> The company itself cannot act in its own person; it can only act through directors and the case is, as regards those directors, merely the ordinary case of principal and agent.

28. Brian R. Cheffins, *Company Law: Theory, Structure and Operation*, Clarendon Press (1997), pp. 112–13.
29. Cai Xianjie, *A Comprehensive Analysis of Shareholding and Salary of CEO of Listed Companies in China (Zhongguo shangshi gongsi gaoguan chigu ji xinchou zhuangkuang zonghe fenxi)*, Tsingtao Daily News (Hong Kong), 5 June 2001.
30. "The Chairman's Annual Salary Is ¥15.98 million, Which Is the Most Expensive CEO" (*Shenfazhan dongshizhang cheng Zhongguo zuigui CEO, 2008 nian nianxin 1598 wan*), retrieved from http://news.qq.com/a/20090716/000636.htm on 8 October 2015.
31. Wen Haiying, "Reduction of Salaries of CEOs of SOEs and Reform of SOEs", retrieved from http://www.on.cc/cn/bkn/cnt/commentary/20140903/bkncn-20140903000315423-0903_05411_001.html on 8 October 2015.
32. Lin Lin once pointed out that CEOs of SOEs could be "largely compensated by on-duty consumption, grey income and political reward". Lin, supra note 27, p. 207. Under the new policy, it may be too difficult to still enjoy those "benefits".

For this reason, some of a director's rights and duties are similar to those applicable to an agent in the principal-agent relationship. For example, when a director enters into a contract on behalf of the company, the contract binds the company. Similarly, if directors exceed their given authority, they may be personally liable to a third party or even to the principal for breach of the authority. Like other agents, directors must be accountable to their principals for any personal profits made by them from their position.

Directors are sometimes held to have fiduciary relationships with their companies. A fiduciary relationship is a relationship between a person in a position of trust (the fiduciary) and a person for whose benefit the fiduciary acts. A trustee usually holds a legal title in a property while a beneficiary holds only an equitable title in the property. A fiduciary's powers are exercised on behalf of others who are in a dependent position. Fiduciaries also control a property in which others have an interest. There are numerous relationships that can be categorized as fiduciary. The best-known fiduciary relationships are those between trustee and beneficiary and between agent and principal. Promoters and directors of a company are also regarded as fiduciaries with respect to the company.

Many scholars believe that the position of a director is in some respects similar to that of a trustee, but it also differs in other respects.

- One obvious difference is that a director does not possess a proprietary interest in property held by the company, while a trustee holds the legal title of the entrusted property.
- The objectives of a company are usually quite different from that of a trust. Companies are generally formed for the purpose of engaging in business for profit. This inevitably involves some risks, and directors must be given a high degree of freedom in the ways in which they cause the company's funds to be used. In the case of a trust, it is usually of great importance that the property of the trust be preserved for the beneficiaries, often for a long period.
- The rules of equity recognize and require a trustee to preserve the trust property by investing it in relatively safely. Shareholders, on the other hand, are regarded as having some knowledge of business and take up shares based on the understanding that some risk may be involved.
- Beneficiaries of a trust are often incapable of looking after the trust property and are mainly concerned that the property is not dissipated. They are generally in need of a greater degree of protection than shareholders. Consequently, a trustee owes stricter duties of care than a director.[33]

---

33. Arjunan and Low, supra note 8, pp. 217–18.

Fiduciary duty is a concept developed from the British law of equity. Today, it is common sense that directors are the agents of their companies. However, fiduciary duty continues to be one of the duties imposed on directors.

In China, it is popular to apply the principle of agency by mandate in order to explain a director's position in a company. This again indicates that the Chinese company law adopts the traditional civil law approach, which is the same as that of Japan and Taiwan. Article 254(3) of the Japanese Commercial Code specifies that the relationship between a company and its directors should be dealt with in accordance with the provisions regarding mandate in the civil law. The traditional mandate under the civil law system is an agreement whereby parties agree that one party commissions the other to take charge of his or her affairs and the latter agrees to do so. Transporting this process into a company law regime under the civil law tradition, the director is the attorney and the company is the principal, and the object of the mandate is to manage the affairs of the company. The mandatory relationship subsists when a person promises to be a director appointed by promoters at an inaugural or general meeting. It seems that different terms in common law jurisdictions and continental law jurisdictions may not mean different things. However, it is important to point out several major differences:

(1) a mandatory relationship follows a non-profit tradition, i.e., the commissioned person may not take the position for the purpose of fee payment, while an agent relationship can be created under the legal relationship even if no authorization is given (e.g., parents are the legal agents of their children); and
(2) there is no implied agent under the mandatory system. However, Articles 402 and 403 of the Chinese Contract Law may offer some exceptions.[34]

34. Article 402 states, "if the mandatary concludes a contract with a third party in his/her own name and within the scope of authority delegated by the mandatary, and, at the time of concluding the contract, the third party is aware of the agency relationship between the mandatary and the mandatory, the contract directly binds the mandatory and the third party, unless there is conclusive evidence that the said contract binds only the mandatary and the third party." Article 403 states, "where the mandatary concludes a contract with a third party in his own name and, at the time of concluding the contract, the third party is not aware of the agency relationship between the mandatary and the mandatory, if the mandatary fails to perform his obligation toward the mandatory due to reasons attributable to the third party, the mandatary shall disclose the third party to the mandatory and the mandatory may on those grounds exercise the rights of the mandatary against the third party, unless the third party would not have entered into the contract with the mandatary if at the time of its conclusion he had known that the mandatary's principal was the mandatory in question".

Obviously, the drafters of Articles 402 and 403 were influenced by the common law tradition.

On the other hand, one view concerning the mandatory relationship deserves attention. It points out the differences between agent theory (or trust theory) in common law jurisdictions and mandatory theory in continental law jurisdictions. According to this view, mandatory theory is a better theory and can solve the theoretical problems arising out of agent theory (or trust theory). It has been concluded that agent theory cannot fully explain issues concerning the duty of loyalty and conflict of interest, while trust theory cannot answer why a BOD should act on behalf of its company rather than itself. In this regard, the Chinese company law adopts mandatory theory, which can explain both of the following situations, i.e., the relationships between directors and their companies.[35]

Regardless of whether directors are treated as trustees, agents or employees of a company, they are held responsible for the company when they exercise the power of that company.

It has been said that the existing Company Law provides only that a director must be honest in discharging his or her duties (Art. 147). However, it has been pointed out that this duty is different from the fiduciary duty because it is a passive duty, i.e., one needs no volunteer information. He or she is only required to respond truthfully when confronted with questions about conflicts of interest. In contrast, the fiduciary duty is a higher degree of duty because it is a pro-active duty. For example, under the fiduciary duty, the fiduciary should not wait until he or she is confronted by questions of conflict before declaring his or her interests.[36] This view is subject to further argument. One could further argue that even though the existing Company Law does not impose systemic duties on directors, Articles 147 and 148 do outline general duties, which are similar to those of common law jurisdictions. In other words, those duties have a prescription that corresponds to the duty of loyalty in common law jurisdictions.

2. Duty of Loyalty

In common law jurisdictions, the duty of loyalty usually includes the duties to act *bona fide* for the benefit of the company, to exercise directors' powers

35. Xu Xiao and Yang Zhongren, "Duties of Directors and Business Judgment Rules" (*Lun dongshi yiwu yu shangye caipan guize*), *The Law and Social Development* (Jilin University), No. 5, 2001, pp. 38–39.
36. K. L. Alex Lau, *Proposals for Chinese Company Law Reform, "Papers on China 2006–2007"*, Hong Kong Baptist University, pp. 17–18.

for their proper purpose and not to allow any conflict between their duties as directors and their personal interests. The Chinese company law also mentions the "duty of loyalty" (*zhongshi yiwu*) and further lists out conducts that are considered to be violations of that duty:

- to accept bribes or other unlawful incomes, or to misappropriate the property of the company;
- to deposit the company's assets in their own personal accounts or in the personal accounts of other individuals;
- to lend the company's funds to others without authorization;
- to enter into contracts or to conduct transactions with the company without authorization;
- to seek for themselves or others a commercial opportunity that should belong to the company, or to operate for themselves or others the same category of business as that of the company without authorization;
- to accept and possess the commission in the transaction between others and the company;
- to disclose the company's secrets without authorization; and
- to commit other acts in violation of the duty of loyalty to the company.[37]

(1) Duty to Act Bona Fide *for the Benefit of the Company*

In common law jurisdictions, how to perform this duty is quite subjective. The test is whether directors honestly believe that their decisions or actions are for the interest of the company. Courts are generally reluctant to override the business judgments of directors. Also, as a general rule, directors are assumed to have acted *bona fide* for the benefit of their company, and those persons alleging a breach of duty shall bear the burden of proving that this is in fact the case. In China as well as around the world, the duty to act *bona fide* for the benefit of the company should be changed into an objective test by adopting the "reasonable person test", which is very important under tort law theory. If this test were established, the issue of whether directors act *bona fide* for the benefit of their companies could be easily dealt with by looking at the conduct of directors in other companies in the same or similar situations.

37. The Company Law, Article 148.

(2) Duty to Exercise Powers for Proper Purposes

This duty can be interpreted to mean that directors must not take into account irrelevant, extraneous or collateral factors when making their business decisions.

In *Howard Smith v Ampol Petroleum Ltd.* [1974] AC 821, two shareholders holding 55 per cent of the shares in a company announced that they would jointly reject a takeover bid. The BOD then allotted new shares to the intending bidder so that the bidder would command a sufficient majority to approve the bid. The share issue was challenged by one of the minority shareholders. It was held that although the allotment was within the BOD's powers, it had acted based on an improper purpose, and the issue of shares to the bidder should be set aside.

The Chinese Company Law does not mention this specific duty. This duty, however, can certainly be inferred from Article 148(8), which states that directors shall not commit other acts in violation of the duty of loyalty to the company. This would certainly test the wisdom of a judge if he or she were to deal with this particular issue.

(3) Duty to Avoid a Conflict of Interests

A contract in which a director has a personal interest adverse to that of the company is avoidable by the company. Any profits made by the director based on the conflict of interest may be recovered by the company unless such a contract is authorized by the company's articles of association or the conflict of interest is disclosed to the shareholders and the resulting contract is sanctioned by them. Article 148 of the Company Law contains a similar prohibition. However, this provision does not discuss the issue of ratification, nor does it mention the consequence of violating the doctrine of "corporate opportunity". The doctrine of "corporate opportunity" originated from common law jurisdictions. Section 5.05(b) of the American Law Institute's Corporate Governance Project defines a "corporate opportunity" as one business opportunity that (1) the director should reasonably believe was offered to the corporation, (2) the director believes would be of interest to the corporation, or (3) is "closely related" to the business in which the corporation is engaged or expects to be engaged. As a general principle, the corporate opportunity shall belong to the company instead of its directors. Although a business opportunity is in fact offered to a director, he or she shall not take this business opportunity if it is offered to him or her when he or she acts on behalf of his or her company. In an exceptional case, a director is allowed to use the corporate opportunity in a situation where the director has disclosed the obtained corporate opportunity to the company and the latter has voluntarily relinquished it and permitted the director to take advantage of it because it may be unwise to expand the corporation's business or the corporation has no sufficient funds to do so. Even in this circumstance, if engaging in a similar line of business would compete with the corporation's business, the director may take the risk to do so. Many cases have already held a competing director guilty of a breach of the fiduciary duty under several possible theories, including "conflict of interest, misuse of corporate opportunity, misappropriation of trade secrets or customer lists, or wrongful interference with contractual relationships".[38]

3. Duty of Care

Duty of care is basically a tort law concept. Company laws in most jurisdictions also impose this duty on directors, i.e., a director owes a duty to his or her company to exercise proper care in managing the corporation's affairs. For example, the formal test usually quoted is set forth in Section 8.30 of the Model Business Corporation Act (1984):

> Duties must be discharged "(1) in good faith; (2) with the care of an ordinarily prudent person in a like position would exercise under similar circumstances; and (3) in a manner he or she reasonably believes to be in the best interests of the corporation."

Some US states have eliminated the "reasonably believes" standard and substituted a standard of decisions "in accordance with his or her good faith business judgment of the best interests of the corporation" (Va. Code Ann. S13.1-690). Another test that is often quoted includes a degree of diligence, care and skill "which ordinarily prudent men or women would exercise under similar circumstances in their personal business affairs". This language is taken from a leading Pennsylvania case: *Selheimer v Manganess Corp. of American* (1966). In comparison, the latter is better because it is a reasonable person test, which would enable a court to decide relevant cases.

Usually, if the duty of care is breached, the director(s) involved are ordered to pay damages. In *Dorchester Finance Co. Ltd. v Stebbing* (1989) BCLC 498, the company was in the money lending business and had three directors. No board meeting had ever been held. Two of the directors left all of the affairs of the company to a third and signed blank cheques on the company's account. The third director lent the company's money to companies controlled by himself, his clients or his brother, but without complying

38. Hamilton, supra note 4, pp. 409–13.

with the statutory controls on money lending then in force. As a result, all of the loans were unenforceable. The court held that all three directors should be liable to the company for their negligence.

Traditionally in common law jurisdictions, the standard for the duty of care is relatively lower. However, the law in this area has been changed slightly. Given the recent development of the profession of directors, the standard of care expected for a director will be much higher than before. In two recent English cases, Hoffmann J put forward an objective standard for the duty of care. In *Norman v Theodore Goddard* (1992) 10 ACLC 2016, Hoffmann J introduced an objective requirement that a director must possess the skill "that may reasonably be expected from a person undertaking those duties". He gave an example that "a director who undertakes the management of the company's properties is expected to have a reasonable skill in property management, but not offshore tax avoidance". Hoffmann J held the view that the appropriate test of the common law duty to exercise care and skill was set out in s. 214(4) of the UK Insolvency Act 1986. This provision lays down an objective test of standards for directors' duty in the context of wrongful trading. An assessment of what a director would have done or would have known is based on what "a reasonably diligent person having both (a) the general knowledge, skill and experience that may reasonably be expected of a person carrying out the same functions as are carried out by that director in relation to the company and (b) the general knowledge, skill and experience that the director has". The same idea was stated in the case of *Re D'Jan of London Ltd.*, (1993) BCC 646; (1994) 1 BCLC 561. In that case, Mr D'Jan was held to have acted negligently, having regard for only his own knowledge and experience. He was liable for negligence to the company at the common law level for failure to read an insurance policy before signing it. It is very clear that a director may not need to have a high level of skill to satisfy the duty of care. He or she nevertheless needs to have the necessary skill to exercise his or her duty of care. Furthermore, he or she should try to learn as many skills as possible in order to be capable in his or her position as a director.

The Chinese Company Law does not provide this type of duty specifically, even though the term "duty of care" is mentioned in Article 147. However, as a general law, the General Principle of Civil Law could be used to solve the problem in cases where the duty of care is breached. Furthermore, Article 149 provides that directors shall be liable to pay compensation if they violate laws; administrative rules and regulations; or the articles of association in performance of their duties and thus cause damage to the company. It may be inferred from this provision that breach of duty of care is closely related to the rules and articles of association. However, many cases have revealed that when directors violate the rules and articles of association, the imposition of a personal liability is hardly ever seen. A traditional breach of the duty of care is usually subject to administrative or criminal liability in China. For example, Article 63 of the Law of Wholly State-Owned Enterprises states that a leading cadre of an enterprise or a relevant government department who causes relatively heavy losses to the enterprise and the state due to errors in his or her work shall be subject to administrative penalties imposed by the government department in charge of the relevant higher-level organ. The criminal liability of a leading cadre of an enterprise or a relevant government department who, through neglect of duty, causes serious losses to enterprise property and the interests of the state and the people, shall be investigated.

Furthermore, a director may be free from any personal liability for the loss of his or her company caused by his or her negligence, as long as he or she does not breach the duties imposed by the Chinese company law, administrative law and the articles of association. The case of the Jin Hua Department Store Joint Stock Company (hereinafter referred to as "Jin Hua") is a typical example. In that case, the chairman of the BOD, Dan Hua, was sentenced to three years' imprisonment for causing damage in the sum of ¥1,041,000 to Jin Hua. The sentence was due to his responsibility for arbitrarily offering ¥1,416,000 as the guarantee in Jin Hua's name for the debts of other companies or other persons. In that case, the other eleven directors took no responsibility for the loss suffered by Jin Hua and were not asked to pay any compensation for the loss. The two directors who were appointed by the state attended only one meeting of the BOD after Jin Hua was converted into a company in 1995. The other nine directors were appointed by shareholders of Jin Hua. Before the guarantee was offered, the directors did not make any inquiry about the risks of the guarantee and simply followed the opinion of Dan Hua, the most powerful man in the company. However, any ordinary person may be aware that it is a very high risk for a company with ¥1.7 million in registered capital to offer a guarantee in the amount of ¥1,416,000 and will usually oppose this guarantee. Other directors were used to accepting the directions of the chairman and had acted only as passive or sleeping directors. As such, they did not wish to offend the most powerful man in Jin Hua. Thus, this case created the bad precedent for passive or sleeping directors not running the risk of assuming any liability for the loss of a company under the 1993 Company Law.[39] This

39. Citing Huang Jianwen, "The Role of Directors under the Company Law of the PRC in Comparison with Hong Kong Law", Master of Law Thesis (unpublished), August 1998, p. 208.

had clearly been a familiar pattern in a number of similar cases in China in the past. It is reasonable to expect that detailed rules concerning the breach of duty of care should be provided either by the State Council or the SPC, and the preceding case should be dealt with differently if it happens today.

4. Remedies for Breaching Duties

In common law jurisdictions, directors shall be liable for serious consequences caused by breach of their duties. Directors can be either brought to account for their personal gain or asked to compensate the company. The same approach is taken by the Chinese Company Law. Article 149 expressly states that if a director violates the provisions of the Law, statutory regulations or the company's articles of association during the performance of his or her duties and thereby causes damage to the company, the director shall bear the liability to pay compensation for such damage.

In addition, China should learn from the company laws of other jurisdictions and provide a clear distinction between a company's liability and a director's personal liability in order to protect the interests of the company. Although Article 149 of the Company Law provides civil liability in the case where directors cause damage to the company, nowhere does it provide personal liability if directors infringe on the interests of creditors. In order to fill this gap, it is recommended that similar provisions be copied from other jurisdictions. For example, Article 275 of the Hong Kong Company Ordinance (Cap. 32) used to provide that,

> if in the course of the winding up of a company it appears that any business of the company has been carried on with intent to defraud creditors of the company or creditors of any other person or for any fraudulent purpose, the court, on the application of the Official Receiver, or the liquidator or any creditor or contributory of the company, may, if it thinks proper so to do, declare that any persons who were knowingly party to the carrying on of the business in a manner aforesaid shall be personally responsible, without any limitation of liability, for all or any of the debts or other liabilities of the company as the court may direct.

In this situation, the company is disregarded and directors bear civil liability for their misconduct.[40] With this kind of liability in mind, directors are made more responsible for their conduct.

---

40. In Hong Kong, this is another example of "lifting the corporate veil". See Arjunan and Low, supra note 13, pp. 16–17.

5. To Whom Directors Owe Their Duties

Traditional company law theory treats shareholders as members of the company. Thus, the interests of shareholders as a whole are equivalent to the interests of the company. In the United Kingdom, this view was upheld for almost two centuries until the alteration of its company law in 1995.[41] On the other hand, it has been generally recognized in common law jurisdictions that directors owe duties to the company rather than to particular shareholders.[42] In *Percival v Wright* (1902) 2 Ch 421, the directors purchased shares from existing shareholders without disclosing that they were in the process of negotiating a higher price for the shares. The decision of the court was in favour of the directors. The court held that the directors owed no fiduciary duties to the shareholders. However, in very limited circumstances, directors may owe a duty to the shareholders if, for example, they agree to act as agents for the shareholders.

Article 147 of the Company Law provides the similar principle that directors owe duties to the company. In addition to this, many Chinese scholars argue that directors may owe duties to other subjects too.

(1) Directors Owe Duties to the State

The 1993 Company Law marked a new economic change in China. A great number of SOEs were reorganized and converted into companies, and many new companies were set up by the state. Initially, the state shares represented more than 80 per cent of the total shares of Chinese companies.[43] For quite a long period, the state remained the biggest shareholder in most companies. During the conversion process, the state's assets and interests have suffered serious losses and erosion in the corporatization of SOEs due to the under-evaluation of state-owned assets. In this situation, it should be part of a director's duties to take care of the interests of the state. One notable example may explain this duty even though the outcome may not be positive.

---

41. Liu Junhai, "A Comparative Research on Employees Involving in Company's Organs" (*Zhigong canyu gongsi jiguang zhidu de bijiao yanjiu*), in Wang Baoshu (ed.), *The Comparative Law Review*, The Law Press (Beijing), September 1999, p. 59.
42. However, in some cases a duty may be owed directly to the shareholders as a result of some representation or agreement. Smart, Lynch, and Tam, supra note 10, p. 232.
43. Wan Guohua, "On Three Important Issues of the Company System of the PRC", in Gao Ersen (ed.), *Symposium on Chinese Economic Law*, Law Publishing House (Beijing), 1996, p. 9.

The X Company was a profitable company publicly listed on a Chinese stock exchange and the state was its biggest shareholder. Subsequently, directors of the X Company were asked by some officials of the local government to merge the X Company with the Y Company, a wholly state-owned company that was going to be insolvent. The merger would benefit the state in three ways. Firstly, it would relieve the financial burden of the local government. Secondly, it would reduce the rate of unemployment. Thirdly, it would maintain the stability of society. In order not to hamper the good relationship (*guanxi*) the X Company had built up with local officials, directors of the X Company finally decided to take over the Y Company.[44] Obviously in this circumstance the directors considered the interests of the state more than the interests of their own company. Thus, how to strike a balance between the interests of the state and companies is still a big research topic today.

(2) Directors Owe Duties to Shareholders

In China, directors are said to owe duties to their shareholders. This opinion is supported by two factors. Firstly, the appointment and removal of the directors are decided by the SHM. Under the Company Law, the SHM is deemed to be the highest authority of a company and the BOD is an executive organ. Secondly, running Sino-foreign joint venture companies in China has given rise to the concept that directors owe their duties to the shareholders who appoint them. One simple reason is that directors are separately appointed by both the Chinese and foreign parties.

(3) Directors Owe Duties to Employees

In the past forty years or more, Chinese workers have obtained high social positions. They used to be recognized as the masters in China.[45] On the one hand, employees of companies should be allowed to be involved in the management of those companies. In order to reflect this idea, the Chinese Company Law provides that "the board of supervisors shall consist of shareholders' representatives and an appropriate proportion of the employees' representatives" (Art. 51.2). On the other hand, directors should take care of the legitimate interests of employees (Art. 17). This is particularly true in the situation of mergers and acquisitions. While shareholders of the targeting company may welcome selling their shares at a high price, employees of

44. Citing Huang, supra note 23, p. 128.
45. The Constitution of the PRC, Article 2.

the targeting company may worry about losing their jobs. Thus, the logical interpretation of Article 17 is that directors shall strike a balance between shareholders and employees.

(4) Directors Owe Duties to Creditors

The general understanding is that directors do not owe any duty to the company's creditors or to the trustees of those creditors. However, in common law jurisdictions, a special duty may arise by agreement or representation. For example, if a company is insolvent, directors must act in the interest of the company's creditors by telling them the truth. Section 214 of the 1986 UK Insolvency Act also proposes that directors should have a duty to consider the interests of creditors even though there is no such analogous provision under the Chinese Company Law. Under the said British law, the interests of companies have also been extended to include the interests of the employees of those companies by operation of law under Section 309 of the UK Companies Act of 1985, which states, "The directors of a company are to have regard to the performance of their functions including the interests of the company's employees in general, as well as the interests of its members."

Even if directors do not directly owe a duty to creditors, the latter may choose to sue directors under the doctrine of "piercing the corporate veil". It has been recognized that a company is a separate legal entity that can protect its members from taking unlimited liabilities of the company. The first case to consider a company as the "veil" of its members was the leading case *Salomon v Salomon & Co. Ltd.* (1897) 1 AC 22.

Courts consider several factors when deciding whether to pierce the corporate veil. Firstly, in the case of a voluntary creditor, courts are more likely to pierce the veil in a tort case (where the creditor is "involuntary") than in a contract case (where the creditor is "voluntary"). Secondly, veil piercing is more likely to be the case where there has been a grievous fraud or wrong committed by the shareholder (i.e., the sole shareholder siphons out all profits, leaving the corporation without enough money to pay its claims). Thirdly, the court will most likely permit the corporate veil to be pierced if the corporation has been inadequately capitalized.

The United States case of *Sea-Land Services, Inc. v Pepper Source*[46] sets out a two-part test that a court will apply when determining whether the corporate veil should be pierced. Firstly, there must be such a unity of interest

46. 993 F.2d 1309, C.A. 7 (Ill.) (1993).

and ownership that the separate personalities of the corporation and the individual (or other corporation) no longer exist. Secondly, circumstances must be such that adherence to the fiction of separate corporate existence would sanction a fraud or promote injustice.

The Chinese Company Law does not provide this effective device despite several provisions providing administrative sanctions and criminal punishments in cases of fraud and cheating (e.g., Articles 198 and 215). Article 149 provides the civil liabilities of a director only to his or her company. However, whether the creditors of a company can ask a court to disregard the veil of the company and hold responsible directors liable for a committed fraud deserves further research. Creditors may try Article 20(3) of the Company Law, which allows them to pierce the corporate veil and to hold the shareholders (if the directors are also the shareholders) jointly liable for the abuse of the independent status of corporate legal person.

(5) Directors Owe Duties to Their Communities

The new tendency is that directors may have to consider their duties to society. There is an emerging theory called "corporate social responsibility" (hereinafter referred to as "CSR"). This concept was firstly seen in the United States and has developed along several stages. In its very beginning, CSR referred only to charitable donations to the local community, such as to Boy Scouts and hospitals. After World War II, the scope of CSR was extended to support the development of artwork, scholarships and private universities. Thereafter, security and environmental protection has become more and more reliant on CSR.[47] The UK Company Act 2006 sets up a good example to impose a comprehensive list of duties (including the duty to communities) on directors. Article 172(1) states:

> A director of a company must act in the way he considers, in good faith, would be most likely to promote the success of the company for the benefit of its members as a whole, and in doing so have regard (amongst other matters) to—
> (a) the likely consequences of any decision in the long term,
> (b) the interests of the company's employees,
> (c) the need to foster the company's business relationships with suppliers, customers and others,
> (d) the impact of the company's operations on the community and the environment,

47. For detailed information, see Liu Junhai, *Corporate Social Responsibilities* (*Gongsi de shehui zeren*), The Law Press (Beijing), March 1999.

(e) the desirability of the company maintaining a reputation for high standards of business conduct, and
(f) the need to act fairly as between members of the company.

Although the 1993 Company Law did not use the specific term "CSR", in Article 14(1) it stated, "A company engaging in business operations must abide by the law and uphold professional ethics and strengthen the construction of the socialist spiritual enlightenment under the supervision of the government and the public." The 2005 Company Law, for the first time, states clearly that companies shall undertake social responsibility (Art. 5). However, from a theoretical viewpoint, the issue of CSR deserves further debate because governments could use this liability to escape their responsibility to society.

Nevertheless, it is observed that many additional duties may be too burdensome for directors to concentrate on their major duties. This is another issue that deserves further research.

III. RIGHTS OF DIRECTORS

The Chinese company law does not stipulate the rights of directors in a particular way. Maybe the rights are presumed under the Law, and the directors have enough power to protect their interests due to their special positions in their companies. Usually the rights can be divided into two parts: (1) the rights empowered by the SHM to make business decisions and engage in business activities and (2) personal rights, such as the right to obtain rewards or remuneration. However, under the Chinese Company Law, the amount of payment is decided by the SHM (Art. 37.2) rather than by the BOD itself.

IV. THE BOD

1. The Nature of the BOD

The word "board" originally referred to the table around which a council sat and was sometimes used in the nineteenth century to mean a meeting of directors. When directors met, they were said to "hold a board"—hence, the term "boardroom" refers to a room in which directors meet to have meetings and to make decisions. Now, the word "board" has been used as a collective noun for directors, who are said to hold a "board meeting", a term that was once tautological.[48]

48. Mayson, French, and Ryan, *Company Law*, Blackstone Press, 11th ed., 1994, p. 423.

The BOD is an indispensable organ required by almost all company laws to be established within a company. For example, Article 79(7) of the 1993 Company Law requires the articles of association to include the composition, functions and powers, term of office and deliberation rules of the BOD.[49] Presumably, the BOD is a "must" in a JSC situation and a "maybe" in an LLC situation,[50] even though the 2005 Company Law omits the similar language seen in Article 79(9) of the 1993 Company Law. Thus, one would expect to see that the company registry may not approve a registration if the articles of association fail to mention the BOD. As a result, the company may not be successfully established.

According to the Chinese Company Law, the BOD cannot be considered as a standing organ of a company simply because it usually exercises its power through its meetings. In the JSC situation, the BOD shall at least have two meetings within a year (Art. 110), while in the LLC situation, there is no minimum amount of meeting times. Presumably, the BOD of an LLC can hold more meetings due to its limited size. The BOD shall be responsible for the SHM simply because directors are elected by the SHM. In other words, the decisions of the SHM shall have a binding force over the BOD, and the BOD has obligations to perform the decisions of the SHM and to report the result of its performance. In comparison, common law jurisdictions deal with the BOD differently because major management powers are usually given to the BOD. As the court said in *John Shaw & Sons (Salford) Ltd. v Shaw* [1935] 2KB 113:

> A company is an entity distinct from its shareholders and its directors. Some of its powers may, according to its articles of association, be exercised by the directors, and certain other powers may be reserved for the shareholders in general meeting. If powers of management are vested in the directors, they and they alone can exercise these powers. The only way in which the general body of the shareholders can control the exercise of the powers vested by the articles of association in the directors is by altering their articles of association, or, if opportunity arises under the articles of association, by refusing to re-elect the directors of those actions they disapprove. They cannot usurp the powers, which by the articles of association are vested in the directors any more than

49. This is not the same as the situation in LLCs. Article 22 of the 1993 Company Law is silent on the issue of the BOD. By interpretation of the provision, the BOD is not a "must", and this argument is consistent with Article 51 of the 1993 Company Law: "where a limited liability company has a small number of shareholders and is comparatively small in scale, it may have an executive director instead of a board of directors."

50. Article 40(2) of the existing Company Law still gives this option to small-sized LLCs.

the directors can usurp the powers vested by the articles of association in the general body of shareholders.

Since the BOD under the Chinese company law is responsible for the SHM, its functions and powers are limited to the following aspects:

(a) to convene the SHM and to report on its work to the SHM;
(b) to implement resolutions passed at the SHM;
(c) to decide on the business operation plans and investment plans of the company;
(d) to formulate the fiscal financial budgets and final accounts of the company;
(e) to formulate plans for the profit distribution and making up of losses of the company;
(f) to formulate plans for increasing or reducing the registered capital of the company and plans for the issue of company bonds;
(g) to formulate plans for the merger, division and dissolution of the company;
(h) to decide on the establishment of the internal management organs of the company;
(i) to appoint or dismiss the manager and upon recommendation of the manager to appoint or dismiss the deputy manager(s) and responsible persons in charge of the financial affairs of the company and to decide on matters concerning their remuneration;
(j) to formulate the basic management system of the company; and
(k) to exercise other powers authorized by the articles of association.

2. The BOD and the "Business Judgment Rule"

In common law jurisdictions, the BOD is usually protected by the business judgment rule. The phrase "business judgment rule" is a helpful shorthand description of a basic principle that is applicable to business decisions made by the BOD. In most situations, the decisions made by the BOD upon reasonable information (informed decision) and with some rationality do not give rise to the directors' liability, even if the decisions turn out badly or disastrously from the standpoint of the corporation. A variation of this doctrine is sometimes called the "business judgment doctrine", which states that such decisions are valid and bind the corporation and cannot be enjoined, set aside or attacked by shareholders. This rule reflects that courts will not interfere with an informed decision because informed directors are in a good position to make their decisions.

It should be noted that most statements of the business judgment rule provide a further qualification that a decision is not protected if the directors making it have "a disabling conflict of interest" or are involved in self-dealing transactions. This rule thus has its principal application in claims based on alleged mismanagement or misjudgement unaffected by any claim that personal gain was sought.

In a broad sense, the business judgment rule codifies the basic principles that directors are granted certain discretion with respect to the management of the corporation, that the rational exercise of that discretion is generally not subject to any judicial review and that most judges are not businesspeople capable of second-guessing the exercise of that discretion effectively.

It should be further noted that the business judgment rule must involve a decision or a judgment. Doing nothing without more can never be protected by the business judgment rule. However, a positive decision to do nothing about some issues can be protected by the business judgment rule if in fact the directors are informed about the issues and rationally believe that a decision to do nothing is in the best interest of the corporation. In comparison, the latter situation is encouraged because a positive decision to do nothing is based on an informed and rational decision. As a matter of evidence, it is necessary to record this rejection in the minutes of the BOD's meeting.

In the United States, the business judgment rule can also apply to the decisions made by an "independent" committee established by the BOD to discontinue a derivative action brought by minority shareholders seeking recovery in favour of the corporation against one or more officers or directors for alleged misconduct. Typically, the decision whether to seek to discontinue such litigation is delegated to a "litigation committee" composed of outside directors who are not themselves principal defendants or involved in the acts complained of. The recommendation to discontinue a derivative action is made following an investigation by the independent committee into the merits of the derivative action and the advantages and disadvantages to the corporation of pursuing it.

If a decision of a litigation committee is protected by the business judgment rule, the decision to discontinue the derivative litigation will bind the plaintiff shareholder who is prevented from litigating the merits of his or her case because of the impartial directors' business judgment. In this situation, the plaintiff may only litigate issues such as the independence and lack of involvement of the members of the committee recommending discontinuance of the litigation or of the adequacy of the underlying investigation. Furthermore, the court will inquire into the independence and good faith of the committee and the bases supporting the committee's conclusions. The court will also strike a balance between legitimate corporate claims as expressed in a derivative action and a company's best interests as expressed by an independent investigating committee.[51]

In China, the business judgment rule has not yet been formally adopted. This is partly due to the short history of the Chinese company law and partly due to the situation of administrative intervention. In addition, the Chinese company law has provided too many powers to the SHM, which almost controls the daily operations of a company. Thus, in order to adopt the concept of the "business judgment rule", it is necessary to reallocate the powers between the SHM and BOD.

As has been suggested, before determining whether the business judgment rule will improve the Chinese company law one way or another, one should consider a number of different questions. Firstly, what will the rule protect and under what circumstances? Secondly, against whom will the rule provide protection? Thirdly, will the protection provided by the business judgment rule be used in practice? Fourthly, is now the correct time to introduce the business judgment rule into the Chinese company law? Finally, what will be the effect of implementing this rule in foreign invested companies?

The following is an examination of where and how the business judgment rule could be included in the Chinese company law. If Chinese legislators want to include the business judgment rule in the body of the Chinese company law in the near future, this rule would best be included in either the Chinese company law itself or in its implementing regulations. The business judgment rule should not be established through court decisions as done in the United States because the enforcement of company law is based on administrative and criminal processes rather than on derivative civil liability actions brought by shareholders. Within the Chinese Company Law, the business judgment rule would most appropriately be included in Section 2 as a new paragraph within Article 149, which sets out the requirement that directors will bear liability for damages resulting from an action taken in violation of the Chinese company law, statutory regulations or the company's articles of association. The new paragraph may read, "In the event that the director has exercised due care in carrying out the role of director, the director's decisions shall not be subjected to civil liability provided that the director was fully informed and disinterested." Such a

51. Jesse H. Choper, John C. Coffee, and C. Robert Morris, *Cases and Materials on Corporations* (3rd ed.), Little, Brown and Company (Boston), 1989, pp. 808–9.

provision would provide the basis for further development in subsequent regulations and proceedings.

Secondly, to whom and when the business judgment rule would provide protection need to be carefully discussed. As mentioned previously, the business judgment rule protects the decisions made by directors while exercising their corporate responsibilities without incurring civil liability. Therefore, under the Chinese company law, the business judgment rule would protect directors when they perform the duties listed in Article 46 of the Company Law. Specifically, the rule would protect directors' decisions made when formulating business plans concerning budget, accounting, profits and losses, capital, mergers, divisions and management. The rule would also provide directors with protection for decisions made when compiling work reports, implementing shareholder resolutions and establishing the company's internal management. With regard to these specific duties, the disinterested and fully informed directors would be able to invoke the protections if they acted in good faith and in the absence of fraud or self-dealing. Following the US concept of the business judgment rule, protection would be available only to thwart civil liability claims and would not be available as a defence in any criminal or administrative proceedings.

3. The Chairman of the BOD

Theoretically, the BOD is not a standing organ because it is in session only a few times a year. If this is an acceptable conclusion, then the chairman of the BOD, who is usually the legal representative of his or her company,[52] becomes very important in dealing with a company's business on a day-to-day basis.

(1) Introduction

The legal representative system is supposed to be a very important system within Chinese company law. Under the 1993 Company Law, this system was not a perfect governing system for obvious reasons stated as follows.

Chinese leaders used to emphasize the building up of socialism with the Chinese character on various occasions. The purpose of this emphasis was to remind people to work for the modernization of China based on real

52. Unlike the 1993 Company Law, which made the chairman of the BOD the sole legal representative, the 2005 Company Law allows the legal representative to be taken by either the chairman, managing director or manager. Article 13.

Chinese situations, such as high population and insufficient resources.[53] However, the Chinese character was used so broadly that even some unreasonable systems were retained under this umbrella.[54] Because of this reason, many people dared not to challenge some problematic systems. Nevertheless, the existence of some systems may curb the further development of economic reform in China.

In line with the Chinese Civil Law Principles, the legal representative (*fading daibiao ren*) system is one of the systems deemed to have the Chinese character.[55] It could also be named as a legal person representative system.[56] According to Chinese civil law theory, it is the organ of a legal person.[57] Article 38 of the Chinese Civil Law Principles states that the legal representative can be created by either law directly or members of a legal person based on the articles of association. Furthermore, the legal representative is not a group formed by individual persons (such as the representative assembly of work and staff and the BOD),[58] but is an individual natural person.[59] In the past, the legal representative was selected from the following persons: (1) the administrative responsible person of a legal person, such as a previous factory director or a manager; (2) a deputy factory director or a deputy manager in cases where a legal person did not have an administrative responsible person or (3) the person in charge of the legal person in cases where a legal person did not have an administrative responsible person.[60]

In summary, the legal representative in the past was a natural person authorized by either laws or the articles of association of a company to act

53. The Preamble of the PRC Constitution also endorses this theory. See the Constitution of the People's Republic of China (*Zhonghua Renmin Gongheguo Xianfa*) adopted at the Fifth Session of the Fifth NPC and revised by the First Session of the Seventh NPC on 12 April 1988.
54. "Economy Has Its Own Rules, Talk Less about Chinese Characteristics" (*Jingji ziyou guilu, shaotai Zhongguo teshe*), Editorial of *Xinbao* (Hong Kong), 23 September 1997.
55. Robert C. Art and Minkang Gu, *China Incorporated: The First Corporation Law of the People's Republic of China*, *Yale Journal of International Law*, Vol. 20, No. 2. 1995, pp. 273, 294.
56. Yang Zhenshan and Li Jingbing, *Chinese Civil Law Text Book* (*Zhongguo minfa jiaocheng*), Shanxi Economic Press (Shanxi), 1991, p. 99.
57. Tong Rou (ed.), *Study of Chinese Civil Law: The General Introduction* (*Zhongguo minfa xue: Minfa zongze*), Chinese People's Public Security Press (Beijing), 1995, p. 165.
58. Wang Liming, *New Comments on Civil Law* (*Minfa xinlun*), China University of Politics and Law Press (Beijing), 1988, p. 252.
59. The chairman of the BOD must be a director first. The Company Law provides the clear qualifications for a director. See Articles 57–58 of the 1993 Company Law (now Article 157 of the 2013 Company Law).
60. Tong, supra note 54, pp. 165–66.

on behalf of and bind the company.[61] If the legal representative caused big economic losses to an enterprise or to the State, he or she did not need to take any personal liability. In this situation, the relevant government authorities or the administrations in charge would provide an administrative sanction, or the legal representative would be criminally prosecuted if the losses were serious enough.[62]

Based on this historical review, one could see that there was a close relationship between the legal representative system and the planned economy that was implemented before China truly adopted the market economy with socialist characteristics.[63] Furthermore, this kind of relationship was retained when the Chinese government tried to change the State-run enterprises into SOEs.[64] Regardless of what has changed, one thing is clear: the assets of these enterprises were largely owned by the State. The State certainly needed to appoint its own representatives, who could be entrusted to manage those assets. Therefore, factory directors and managers were the ideal candidates and were appointed as the legal representatives by the relevant government authorities.[65] Unfortunately, this kind of practice caused a serious problem: the leaders of the SOEs were not bound by market forces, but by their superiors.[66] For this reason, they had to choose between being responsible for their enterprises or being responsible for their superiors. In order to keep their positions and to protect their gained interests, they tried to keep a good relationship with their superiors. If everything went well, they would not lose their positions even if they had caused damage to their enterprises. In a worse situation, they might have been transferred to another SOE by taking up the same level positions.

61. Chinese Civil Law Code (*Zhonghua Renmin Gongheguo Minfa Tongze*) adopted 12 April 1986 by the Fourth Session of the Sixth NPC, Article 43.
62. The Law of the PRC Enterprises Owned by the Whole People (*Zhonghua Renmin Gongheguo Quanmin Suoyouzhi Gongye Qiyefa*) adopted 13 April 1988 at the First Session of the Seventh NPC, Article 63.
63. Since the state represents the whole people to run all of the SOEs, it needs to find some trusted persons to be its representatives.
64. Under the system of State-run enterprises, the State is responsible for the losses and profits of the enterprises. Under the system of SOEs, the enterprises are authorized to manage or operate the enterprises, and the State is not responsible for the losses and profits.
65. Although the SOE Law allows the representative assembly of workers and staff to elect factory directors or managers, the election should be subject to approval by the relevant government authority. See Article 44 of the SOE Law.
66. He Qinglian, *The Pitfall of Modernization* (*Xiandaihua de xianjing*), Today's China Press (Beijing), 1998, p. 91.

(2) The Legal Representative under the 1993 Company Law

The legal representative system might have provided some advantages. Those advantages, however, were weak compared with its disadvantages. On the one hand, this system might have enabled a third party to have a clear picture about the person with whom he or she was dealing. Therefore, the possibility of people other than the chairman dealing with a third party on behalf of the company could be avoided. Furthermore, the legal representative could make his or her decisions in a timely manner when he or she faced unpredictable market competition or a changeable situation. On the other hand, the 1993 Company Law made it possible for the legal representative to acquire a combination of power to make decisions and power to direct operations.[67] When one person was appointed as a chairman and a manager of the company concurrently, it was especially easy for this person to abuse his or her power.

As the only representative organ of a legal person, the legal representative was usually appropriate for economic organizations that had a relatively simple property relationship.[68] Today, most public companies are large-sized companies with very complicated economic relationships. In this type of company, a one-person representative system would become more and more unsuitable. In addition, it is evident that many legal representatives did not have enough business experience and that it was very difficult for a chairman to serve as the only agent for a company. As a result of this concurrent appointment, "the most important decision-making power will probably fall into the hands of the general managers in most companies".[69]

Interestingly, the 1993 Company Law kept the legal representative system for unclear reasons. Under Articles 45, 68, and 113, a chairman of the BOD (hereinafter referred to as the "chairman") should be a company's legal representative. If a company chose not to have a BOD due to its relevantly small size, an executive director served as the legal representative. One thing that was different from the previous legislation was that the 1993 Company Law stated, "If a director violates the provisions of this Law, other regulations or the company's articles of association during the performance of his or her duties and thereby causes damage to the company, he or she should bear civil liability for compensation to the company."[70] In accordance with those provisions, only the chairman had the right to conduct

67. Jiang Ping (ed.), *Legal Person System* (*Faren zhidu*), Chinese University of Politics and Law Press (Beijing), 1994, p. 294.
68. Ibid.
69. Ibid., at pp. 53–54.
70. The 1993 Company Law, Article 118.

businesses with outsiders on behalf of the company, and he or she should bear civil liability for compensating the company if he or she caused any damage improperly. However, if there was no evidence of impropriety, the chairman would not assume any civil liability despite directly causing the economic losses.

In fact, the legal representative system under the 1993 Company Law was similar to the agent system that is very popular in common law jurisdictions. Every company is an independent legal person after it is legally established. It can then enjoy civil rights and bear civil liabilities in its own name. Since a company is treated as a "person" by the Law, it must exercise its rights and bear its duties through its agent. However, the 1993 Company Law was different from the legislation in other jurisdictions because the agent's power was granted only to one individual (the chairman[71]), while in many other jurisdictions (especially in common law jurisdictions) the agent of a company could be either the BOD or individual directors.[72]

On the face of it, the legal representative in China had very limited powers. In line with the 1993 Company Law, the chairman had only powers to (1) preside over SHMs and convene and preside over the BOD's meetings, (2) examine and implement resolutions of the BOD, and (3) sign the company's share certificates and corporate bonds.[73] However, in practice, the legal representative might have had very wide powers and might have easily abused those powers. The typical example was that a legal representative could practically block a lawsuit filed against him or her by the company because all cases of a company should be filed by the legal representative.[74] Therefore, if a legal representative had committed a wrong against his or her company, the company could not successfully sue him or her. It was common sense that the legal representative would not sue himself or herself.

71. If other responsible persons or personnel of a company have legal relationships with outsiders on behalf of a legal person, they should be authorized by the organ of the legal person or the legal representative. See the Summary of the Research of Chinese Civil Law, Chinese Social Science Press (Beijing), 1990, p. 120.

72. Zhang Kaiping, *Research on Legal System of Company Directors in England and the USA* (*Ying-Mei gongsi dongshi falü zhidu yanjiu*), p. 43, The Law Press, (1998). Strictly, this statement is too vague. Actually, "the directors individually have no power to act as agents of the company, rather it is the board of directors acting collectively which represents the company". However, "board meetings are not usually required for every decision the board makes due to its ability to delegate its decision-making powers either to a managing director or committees of directors". See Smart, Lynch, and Tam, supra note 10, p. 140.

73. The 1993 Company Law, Article 114.

74. Tong, supra note 54, p. 166.

As a result of this practice, the legal representative could simply escape liability.[75]

Due to this problem, the 1993 Company Law could do nothing to punish the legal representative. In this situation, people may suggest the removal of the chairman through a resolution of the BOD. But according to the law, the board meeting should be presided over and convened by the chairman.[76] In other words, if the chairman refused to preside over and convene the board meeting, a motion to remove the chairman would have been futile. Even if a company had a vice-chairman, he or she could not exercise the power to preside over and convene the board meeting, because he or she could only assist the chairman in his or her work.[77] At least, this deadlocked situation meant that the 1993 Company Law contained irrevocable problems regarding the legal representative, or the mechanism for preventing a chairman from abusing his or her power was missing under it.

In this situation, another suggestion was to seek the relevant actions from the BOS. However, the 1993 Company Law only authorized the BOS to (1) urge the chairman to correct his or her wrongs and (2) propose an interim meeting for the purpose of taking relevant actions against the chairman.[78] The request to correct wrongs could simply be ignored and the interim meeting could easily be blocked by the BOD since they wanted to protect their own interests. Therefore, the BOS could not do anything because it was not armed with teeth like the BOS in Germany and France.

Under the German Company Law, the BOS exercises substantial supervising power over the BOD because the BOD of a JSC is established by the BOS.[79] Under the French Company Law, the chairman of a company may have a similar responsibility to lead the whole operation of a company. Furthermore, the chairman represents the company when dealing with a third party. But unlike the 1993 Company Law, the French Company Law provides one important mechanism to prevent a chairman from abusing power: the board of directors has the power to discharge the chairman at any time.[80]

---

75. Wu Xielin, *Research on the Mechanism of Lawsuits of Hong Kong Companies, Comparative Research on Legal Systems in Hong Kong and Mainland China*, Hong Kong Legal Educational Foundation, 1997, p. 188.
76. The 1993 Company Law, Article 114(1).
77. The 1993 Company Law, Article 114(4).
78. For example, Articles 54(4) and 126(4) of the 1993 Company Law stated that a supervisory committee should have the right to propose the convening of interim meetings of shareholders.
79. See Xu Yan, *The Principles of Company Law (Gongsi fa yuanli)*, The Law Press (Beijing), 1997, pp. 297.
80. Xu Yan, ibid. pp. 286–97.

Under the 1993 Company Law, shareholders representing one-quarter of the voting rights of the shareholders, or one-third of the directors or supervisors, might have raised a proposal to convene an interim meeting too.[81] According to this provision, if a chairman decided not to convene a board meeting or an SHM in order to protect his or her own interests, then shareholders, directors or supervisors might have raised a proposal to convene an interim meeting. However, the right to propose a meeting did not equally mean the right to convene the meeting. In a case where the proposal was rejected by the BOD or the chairman himself, the interim meeting could not function at all. Although the 1993 Company Law provided that the SHM should be convened by the BOD,[82] the chairman could refuse to preside over the SHM and no other person could legally preside over the meeting.[83] For the same reason, the chairman could block the board meeting too.[84]

(3) The Legal Representative under the 2005 Company Law

The legal representative under the 1993 Company Law was heavily criticized and many suggestions were made to improve the Law. One suggestion was to learn from the experiences of Hong Kong. Based on the Hong Kong Company Ordinance, a chairman of the meeting may be elected by the members who are present at the meeting, unless the company's articles of association provide otherwise.[85] Furthermore, in case the chairman is absent,

---

81. The 1993 Company Law, Article 43.
82. Ibid., Articles 43 and 105.
83. Article 43 of the 1993 Company Law states that if an LLC establishes a BOD, then the meetings of the board of shareholders shall be convened by the BOD and shall be presided over by the chairman of the BOD. In case the chairman of the BOD is unable to perform his or her duties due to special reasons, the chairman may appoint a vice-chairman of the BOD or another director to preside over the meeting. Article 105 of the 1993 Company Law states that an SHM shall be convened by the BOD in accordance with the provisions of this Law and shall be presided over by the chairman of the board. In case the chairman of the board is unable to perform his or her duties due to special reasons, the chairman of the board shall designate a vice-chairman of the board or another director to preside over the meeting.
84. Article 48 of the 1993 Company Law states that meetings of the BOD shall be convened and presided over by the chairman of the BOD. If the chairman is unable to perform his or her duties due to special reasons, the chairman may appoint a vicechairman or another director to convene and preside over meetings. Article 114(1) of the 1993 Company Law states that the chairman of the BOD shall preside over SHMs and convene and preside over meetings of the BOD.
85. Hong Kong Companies Ordinance (Cap. 32), Article 114A(1)(d). Now, a similar idea can be seen from Model Articles (private companies) Article 13 and Model Articles (public companies) Article 11.

other directors nominated by the board shall preside over the meeting.[86] In a worse situation, another Hong Kong approach could be adopted to confer the BOD's power on the court to call a meeting (either an annual general meeting or an extraordinary general meeting) either on its motion or on the application of any director or any member entitled to vote at the meeting.[87] In that situation, it would be logical to appoint a person to preside over the meeting.

The lawmakers of the 2005 Company Law definitely know the relevant criticisms and have made the following changes.

Firstly, the legal representative is no longer the privilege of the chairman. The managing director or manager can also be the legal representative (Art. 13; no change under the 2013 Amendment).

Secondly, the SHM can be convened by the BOD and presided over by the chairman. But if special circumstances preclude the chairman from performing his or her functions (presiding over the SHM), the meetings shall be presided over by the vice-chairman; if the vice-chairman cannot or fails to perform his or her function, the meeting can be presided over by a director elected by half or more of the directors (Art. 41; now Art. 40 of the 2013 Amendment).

Thirdly, the BOS is given the power to not only urge the chairman to correct his or her wrongs but also convene and preside over the SHM if the BOD fails to do so (Art. 54.4; now Art. 53.4 of the 2013 Amendment).

Fourthly, the BOS is authorized to bring a lawsuit against the chairman if the BOD fails to take necessary action to correct the wrongs (Art. 152; now Art. 151 of the 2013 Amendment).

(4) Suggestions to Cancel the Legal Representative

Although both companies and SOEs have legal person status, they are different in several aspects. (1) The property of an SOE belongs to the State, while the property of a company belongs to the company itself. (2) Legal representatives of SOEs are usually appointed by the government organs in charge,[88] so they are usually responsible to the government organ in charge.

86. Ibid., Article 57 of Table A. Now, a similar idea can be seen in Model Articles (private companies) Article 13(4) and Model Articles (public companies) Article 11(5).
87. Smart, Lynch, and Tam, supra note 10, p. 107. Also, according to Article 114B of the Hong Kong Companies Ordinance, the court may order (1) a meeting to be called, held and conducted in such a manner as the court thinks fit and (2) may give such ancillary directions as it thinks expedient (including a direction that one member present in person or by proxy shall be deemed to constitute the meeting).
88. All of the senior management personnel of the 500 biggest SOEs will be appointed directly by the State Council. See Hong Kong Economic Daily, 12 October 1998, A23.

However, the legal representatives of companies are elected by the BOD, and they should be responsible to the company or sometimes to the shareholders. (3) The legal representative of a SOE has almost absolute power to control the enterprise.[89] However, the legal representative of a company usually does not have such absolute controlling power. (4) The SOEs shall fulfil the mandatory plans[90] while companies shall follow the market rules and take care of their own interests.

Based on these differences, the legal representative may be suitable for SOEs but not for companies. For this reason, it is necessary to examine the legal representative system under the Chinese company law. According to the company laws in Western countries, directors may be divided into managing directors, *de jure* or *de facto* directors, shadow directors and so on.[91] The management power is usually vested in the BOD and not just in one individual director. For example, Article 53 of the Japanese Civil Code provides that directors can represent their companies in conducting any business with a third party. Article 27(b) of Taiwanese Civil Code provides that if there are several directors, all of the directors can represent the legal person to carry out all business with a third party unless the law stipulates otherwise.[92] If there is a special situation, any director or chairman can demand an extraordinary board meeting.[93] All of these legal arrangements enable the BOD to not only handle the business of the company in a timely manner, but also prevent a chairman from abusing his or her powers. Furthermore, when the management of a company becomes more and more sophisticated and professional, it is unreasonable to entrust the management power to just one person. Therefore, the legal representative system is not suitable for developing modern companies in China and should be removed.

4. The Board of Directors' Meeting

In line with the Company Law, BOD meetings shall be held at least twice a year. All directors and supervisors shall be notified of the meeting ten days

89. Article 45 of the SOE Law states that the factory director shall be the legal representative of an enterprise. An enterprise shall establish a production and operational management system headed by the factory director. A factory director shall occupy the central position in an enterprise and shall assume overall responsibility for the material and spiritual development of the enterprise.
90. The SOE Law, Article 35.
91. Zhang, supra note 56, pp. 56–58.
92. Wang Zejian, *Civil Law, Case Study* (*Minfa shili yanxi*), 1991, San Min Book Co. Ltd. (Taipei), pp. 125–26.
93. Liang Huixin, *The General Principles of Civil Law* (*Minfa tongze*), The Law Press (Beijing), 1996, p. 109.

prior to the meeting (Art. 110). This usually refers to an ordinary meeting. Special meetings are held from time to time and are decided by the BOD. Furthermore, the meeting shall be convened only if more than one half of all directors are present. Any resolution of the board must be adopted by the affirmative votes of more than one half of all directors (Art. 111). Usually, the ordinary meeting shall be attended by directors in person. If a director is unable to attend a meeting for certain reasons, he or she may entrust another director in writing to attend the meeting on his or her behalf. In this situation, power of attorney shall define the scope of the authorization. However, Article 112 seemingly fails to address whether a director who is refused the commission can appoint a person other than directors as his or her agent to attend the meeting.

In one case, a director was unable to attend a board meeting and asked another director to be his or her agent but was refused purposefully. The director then appointed his lawyer as his agent to attend the meeting. However, other directors refused the lawyer to vote against a resolution. Eventually, the director brought the case to a people's court. The court dismissed the claim on the basis that Article 118 of the 1993 Company Law (now Article 112 of the Company Law) expressly states that if a director is unable to attend a board meeting, he or she may commission in writing "another director" to act on his or her behalf. Here, the lawyer was not "another director" and thus could not represent the director.

The purpose of Article 112, which requires the commission of "another director", is not clear. One acceptable reason is that "another director" is more competent or skilful than a non-director. However, this interpretation conflicts with the last sentence of Article 112, which states "the letter of proxy shall stipulate the scope of authority". This means that regardless of how competent and skilful "another director" is, his or her action is subject to the scope of authority. In the aforementioned case, the director knew the company well, and he or she could authorize his or her lawyer as his or her agent to vote against the resolution. Thus, a logical interpretation of Article 112 should permit the lawyer to act alternatively.

Decisions on matters discussed at a meeting of the BOD shall be put into the minutes. Such minutes of the meeting shall be signed by the directors and clerks present at the meeting. It is very important to know that directors shall be responsible for resolutions passed by the BOD. If a resolution is in violation of the law, administrative rules and regulations, or the articles of association, and thus causes serious losses to the company, the directors who participated in the adoption of such a resolution shall be liable for compensating the company. In this case, it is clear that the business judgment rule is not applicable in China.

However, there is one way to be exempted from the liability. If a director is proved to have expressed his or her objection to such a resolution and his or her objection was recorded in the minutes of the meeting, he or she may be exempted from such liability (Art. 112.3).

V. MANAGERS

1. Introduction

The manager system has not been well discussed in China. The same situation has arisen in Hong Kong. Many books on Hong Kong company law mainly address the role and function of directors as well as the company secretary. The impression is that one or more directors can be appointed as managing directors to take care of a company's day-today business or that some administrative matters can be handled by a company's secretary because he or she will be recognised as an officer of the company.[94]

In the United States, the title of "chairman" or "president" refers only to the person who presides over the meetings, while the CEO is called the "general manager". When these functions and powers are united in the same person, he or she is usually called a president/CEO. That is why one person wearing two hats is a common phenomenon in the United States.[95]

In China, a manager is only an assistant organ for the BOD and so is not regarded as an important organ, despite the fact that in reality a manager plays a very important role in managing day-to-day operations. As discussed before, the chairman of the BOD is usually a legal representative of a company. If a legal representative wants a manager to engage in business with an outsider, authorization must be given. Thus, a manager may not be regarded as an agent of a company, but only an agent of a legal representative if such authorization is given. Although a manager may not be regarded as an agent of his or her company, he or she still bears duties, which are similar to that of a director due to his or her important position in the company.

On the other hand, such authorization can be implied even though express authorization is not given, because Article 49 of the Company Law clearly provides the powers and functions of a manager. The exercise of those powers and functions must enable a manager to deal with outsiders.

94. "Being an officer of the company, the company secretary owes fiduciary duties and a duty of care and skill to the company." Vanessa Stott, *Hong Kong Company Law* (12th ed.), Pearson, 2008, p. 268.
95. Choper, Coffee, and Morris, supra note 35, p. 206.

Furthermore, those powers and functions can be specified by a company's articles of association or the decisions of the SHM.

2. Powers and Functions of Managers

The Chinese company law provides that a manager is appointed or dismissed by the BOD. He or she shall be responsible to the BOD. Managers have the following functions and powers:[96]

(a) to be in charge of the production, operation and management of the company and to organize the implementation of resolutions of the BOD;
(b) to organize the implementation of the annual business plans and investment plans of the company;
(c) to draft plans for the establishment of internal management organs of the company;
(d) to draft the basic management system of the company;
(e) to formulate specific rules and regulations of the company;
(f) to propose the appointment or dismissal of deputy managers and responsible persons in charge of the financial affairs of the company;
(g) to appoint or dismiss management personnel except those who shall be appointed or dismissed by the BOD; and
(h) to exercise other functions and powers authorized by the articles of association and BOD.

Based on these powers and functions, a manager must be considered a key operator of a company. That is why the Chinese company law imposes the same obligations and duties on managers. In practice, the role of a manager and a director may be mixed and thus the checks-and-balances system between the two positions is problematic. This may be partly due to the system of concurrent appointments.

3. Concurrent Positions as a Chairman and a General Manager

The BOD may decide that one of its members shall concurrently serve as the manager of the company (Art. 114). In other words, it is possible for a director and especially the chairman to take the position of manager concurrently. Before commenting on these concurrent positions, the reality around the world needs to be examined. It was reported that a chairman

96. The Company Law, Art. 49.

taking a manager's position concurrently was a common phenomenon in common law jurisdictions. For example, in the United Kingdom in 1995, 20 per cent of public companies adopted this practice, i.e., one person took both positions as chairman and manager concurrently. In the United State in 1995, 65 per cent of public companies adopted the same practice. In China, in 1998, about 20 per cent of the listed companies adopted the same practice.[97] On the one hand, one person taking both positions of chairman and manager may be efficient at operating a business. On the other hand, this situation could easily destroy the checks-and-balances relationship between the BOD and a manager. The BOD may, in accordance with its needs, authorize its chairman to exercise part of the powers of office of the BOD during periods when meetings of the board are not in session. Furthermore, the manager shall be responsible to the BOD. In this situation, the chairman would not be able to effectively supervise himself or herself as a manager. The powers of both positions could be easily abused.

Despite the fact that in many common law jurisdictions one person holds two positions concurrently, in Germany and Holland the positions of chairman director and general manager (or CEO) are taken by two independent persons. Japan also takes this approach. India adopts the same approach as that of common law jurisdictions but adds a new requirement, i.e., the BOD must include certain independent directors.

On balance, future Chinese company law should provide clearly that (a) in general, the positions of a chairman director and a general manager should not be held by one person concurrently and (b) when these two positions are held by one person concurrently in a company, that company shall include independent directors in the BOD. These two approaches could hopefully help to avoid conflicts of interest and the abuse of power.

4. Managers' Powers Shall Be Subject to Effective Control

In a survey conducted by China's Confederation of Enterprises concerning the appointment of managers, approximately 81 per cent of the respondent managers said that they were appointed by government agencies, 46 per cent of the respondent managers replied that they preferred to be selected by the BOD and only 7 per cent said that they would prefer to be selected

97. Lin Ling and Dong Hong, *Corporate Governance of Legal Persons and Operational Performance, Practical Analysis from Listed Companies Engaging In High Technologies (Faren zhili jiegou yu jingying jixiao: Laizi gaokeji shangshi gongsi de shizheng fenxi)*, in Guo Feng and Wang Jian (eds.), *Intensive Discussion on Amendment of Company Law (Gongsi fa xiugai zhongheng tan)*, The Law Press (Beijing), 2000, pp. 218–19.

by government agencies. A survey in early 1999 also revealed that "of the enterprises which are undergoing the reform of establishing a modern enterprise system, officials are still nominated by government departments instead of by the board of directors".[98]

Even if the BOD does exist, some listed companies do not convene regular board meetings. The figure shows that there are only on average 4.2 board meetings per year in China compared with their counterparts in other jurisdictions such as companies in the United States, which have an average of 7.2 meetings per year.[99] As a result, there is little check performed on the managerial power of managers.[100] There are also some directors who do not take the resolutions of board meetings seriously.[101]

5. From Manager Capitalism to Investor Capitalism

Before the end of the 1990s, corporate governance emphasized manager capitalism, i.e., granting managers full power to operate a business without any supervision or interference. This situation was changed by investor capitalism after the end of the twentieth century. This change became possible due to the fundamental structural change of the American capital market, i.e., the percentage of institutional investors increased remarkably from 6.1 per cent in 1950 to 48.8 per cent in 1996. These institutional investors did not simply use their feet to vote when a company was not well operated. Rather, they actively became involved in the strategic management of their companies.[102]

Although most SOEs were converted into companies after 1993, the idea of SOEs still remains. For example, in most wholly State-owned companies, directors and managers are normally appointed by CPC organizations.[103] There existed the wrong concept that managers were the centre of

98. "Enterprises Need Management Freedom", *China Daily* (Beijing), 16 January 1999, p. 4.
99. Stoyan Tenev and Chunlin Zhang, *Corporate Governance and Enterprises Reform in China* (2002), World Bank and the International Finance Corporation, p. 93.
100. Wang Yanchun, Che Haigang and Zhao Ming, "Listed Corporations Walking on the Old Way in New Shoes", *The China Economic Times* (*Zhongguo jingji shibao*), 20 January 2000, p. 1.
101. Chen Qingtai, "The Chair is Not the Number One Leader in the Corporation", The People's Daily (*Renming ribao*), 10 January 2000, p. 2.
102. Liang Neng, Guanyu Gongsi Zhili Jiegou de Ruogan Wenti, ("Issues concerning the Structure of Corporate Goveranance"), retrieved from http://old.ccer.edu.cn/workingpaper/paper/c2000009.pdf on 20 September 2009.
103. Zhang Chunling, "Push Forward to Corporate Governance of SOEs" (*Tuijin guoqi gongsi zhili*), retrieved from http://www.china.com.cn/chinese/OP-c/379356.htm on 13 October 2015.

management power, which was based on the belief that former managers (or factory directors) were responsible for the whole production operation and management was regarded as the highest body of the SOE. This wrong concept caused the powers of the BOD and managers to be misplaced in practice, and managers in fact enjoyed the independent execution of business.[104] In comparison with the powers and functions of managers (or factory directors) of the SOEs and managers of companies, there are strong similarities. Article 45 of the 1988 Law of the PRC on Industrial Enterprises Owned by the Whole People states:

> The factory director shall be the legal representative of an enterprise. An enterprise shall establish a production and operational management system headed by the factory director. A factory director shall occupy the central position in an enterprise and shall assume overall responsibility for the material and spiritual development of the enterprise. A factory director shall exercise leadership in the production and operational management of an enterprise through the following functions and powers: (1) determining or submitting for examination and approval the various plans of the enterprise, in accordance with the law and State Council regulations; (2) determining the administrative structure of the enterprise; (3) submitting to the government department in charge requests for the appointment or removal or employment or dismissal of leading administrative cadres at the level of deputy factory director, unless the law and State Council regulations prescribe otherwise; (4) appointing or removing or employing or dismissing middle-level administrative cadres, unless the law prescribes otherwise; (5) proposing wage adjustment and bonus distribution plans and important rules and regulations to the representative assembly of staff and workers for examination and approval and proposing welfare benefit fund usage plans and other proposals important to the well-being of staff and workers to the representative assembly of staff and workers for consideration and resolution; and (6) rewarding or penalizing staff and workers in accordance with the law and submitting to the government department in charge proposals for rewarding or penalizing leading administrative cadres at the level of deputy factory director.

The consequence of this misconception provided managers with power without effective control by the BOD.

There is a good indication that such a situation will change, as it did in the United States. Since 1998, institutional investors have substantially increased. In November 2002, the CSRC and the People's Bank of China

104. Xu, supra note 63, p. 292.

jointly issued a document that permitted "Qualified Foreign Investment Institutions (QFII)" to invest in China's A-share market.[105] Institutional investors will pay attention to the corporate governance in their companies and managers will be under close supervision.

6. Managers Should Be Professionals

Managers are selected on the basis of their professional skills or strong working experience. In every jurisdiction, managers are paid very high salaries because they are expected to use their professional skills or good experience to lead their companies towards success. So far, there exists no unified standard of professionalism in China. Presumably, this matter should be carefully dealt with by the BOD itself.

VI. A NEW ISSUE: SEPARATION OF A COMPANY AND ITS MANAGEMENT POWER

The traditional view is to regard a company as an independent person largely due to its internal management team, especially its BOD and managers. However, a recently created device, the so-called variable interest entity structure (hereinafter referred to as the "VIE structure"), has almost destroyed this traditional view. In China, not all industries (such as the Internet and telecommunications) will be opened to foreign direct investment. Thus, the VIE structure was created with a purpose to circumvent certain legal restrictions. The VIE structure is usually achieved through a series of contracts. To illustrate this point, foreign investors and PRC individuals will firstly establish one special-purpose vehicle in a place such as Cayman. The first special-purpose vehicle then sets up a wholly owned second special-purpose vehicle in a place such as Hong Kong. The second special-purpose vehicle further establishes a wholly foreign-owned enterprise (hereinafter referred to as a "WFOE") in China. Together with Chinese individuals, the WFOE acquires 100 per cent equity interests in a Chinese domestic company (hereinafter referred to as the "C Company") that owns licenses or approvals for particular business.[106] By doing so, the C Company gives away all of its management powers to the WFOE. In other words,

105. "Summary of 2003 China's Listed Companies Corporate Governance Report" (*Zhongguo gongsi zhili baogao (2003) zhaiyao*), retrieved from http://www.chinaacc.com/new/287/294/352/2006/1/dr72414162419160021 26-0.htm on 13 October 2015.

106. For a detailed introduction, see Zeng Xianwu and others, "Variable Interest Entity Structure in China", retrieved from http://www.chinalawinsight.com/2012/02/articles/corporate/foreign-investment/variable-interest-entity-structure-in-china/ on 30 November 2015.

the C Company itself can no longer be qualified as an independent legal person because it cannot make any independent decision, or it becomes a person with no capacity for civil conduct. If this structure is allowed, it will definitely change current company law theory concerning an independent legal person. On the other hand, the VIE structure will have to face a situation regulated by Article 32 of the Company Law, which states, "the shareholder who is recorded in the shareholder's list may claim to and exercise the shareholder's rights. A company shall register each shareholder's name in the company registry. Where any of the registered items is changed, the company shall modify the registration. If the company fails to do so, it shall not, on the basis of the unregistered or un-modified registration item, stand up to any third party." Certainly, people may argue that this provision does not affect the relationship between the actual contributor (the WFOE) and the nominal contributor (the C Company). According to the SPC's Judicial Interpretations of Company Law (III), which was implemented from 16 February 2011, "where the actual contributor enters into an agreement with a nominal contributor of a limited liability company, which stipulates that the actual contributor shall make capital contributions and enjoy the investment rights and interests, and the nominal contributor shall be the nominal shareholder, and there arises any dispute between the actual contributor and the nominal shareholder over the validity of the contract, if it does not fall into any of the circumstances as prescribed in Article 52 of the Contract Law, the people's court shall determine the contract valid" (Art. 24). However, under Article 52 of the Contract Law, an illegal contract will not be protected.[107] How will this situation be dealt with in the near future? The answer depends on the proposed foreign investment law. According to the relevant report, the draft law will adopt a new approach to determine a company in a restricted industry by focusing on the identity of the actual controller of the company.[108] On the other hand, the question remains as to whether a company can be regarded as an independent legal person after it has been converted into a person with no capacity for civil conduct.

107. Article 52 of the Contract Law states, "A contract is invalid under any of the following circumstances: (1) either party enters into the contract by means of fraud or coercion and impairs the State's interests; (2) there is malicious conspiracy causing damage to the interests of the State, of the collective or of a third party; (3) there is an attempt to conceal illegal goals under the disguise of legitimate forms; (4) harm is done to social and public interests; or (5) mandatory provisions of laws and administrative regulations are violated."

108. Gillian Wong and Juro Osawa, "How China's New Foreign Investment Rules Might Play Out", retrieved from http://blogs.wsj.com/digits/2015/01/22/how-chinas-new-vie-rules-might-play-out/ on 30 November 2015.

8

Board of Supervisors

I. LEGAL STATUS AND POWERS

Why is a Board of Supervisors (BOS) needed? In common law jurisdictions, the function and power of the BOS are usually exercised by the Board of Directors (BOD). The duty of care ensures that the BOD shall perform its duties properly and effectively. In the case where the relevant directors have breached their duties, they should be sued and are liable for the consequence. In common law jurisdictions, the activities of directors are supervised by external directors who are independent. The financial activities are usually controlled by independent audit firms.

On the other hand, the BOS is a tradition of continental law jurisdictions. France is recognized as the first country to adopt company legislation. In 1673, the French Commercial Regulations absorbed the experiences of Germany and added the BOS. Under the Regulations, the BOS should have the power to receive a report from the BOD once every three months, which means that the BOD is under close supervision by the BOS.

In this world, the BOS has been divided into two different models. In the first model (the French model), the SHM creates both a BOS and a BOD, both of which have equal status. The company laws in Japan and China have adopted the French approach with some variations. In China, the BOS is an important organ inside a company. It shall be composed of shareholders' representatives and an appropriate proportion of representatives of employees. The specific proportion of representatives of employees shall be provided for by the articles of association.

In the second model (the German model), both the BOS and BOD are under the SHM, but the BOS is in charge of the BOD; it supervises the company's business and financial situation as well as the activities of the BOD. A typical example can be seen in German company law. In Germany, establishing the BOS is a mandatory requirement for JSCs under the German Stock Corporation Act. The BOS is elected by the SHM and has broad powers. It then elects or dismisses the members of the BOD. In other words, the BOD is somewhat responsible to the BOS.

At this stage, it is difficult to say which model is better. However, the 1993 Company Law followed the French model but failed to give sufficient powers to the BOS. Fortunately, the 2005 Company Law and the 2013 Amendment largely resolved this problem.

Under the existing Company Law, the BOS shall exercise the following functions and powers:[1]

(1) to examine the financial affairs of the company;
(2) to supervise whether the acts of directors and managers violate the laws, to supervise the administrative rules and regulations or the articles of association of the company during the performance of their functions and to propose the dismissal of relevant directors;
(3) to demand that directors or managers make corrections if any of their acts are found to have damaged the interests of the company;
(4) to propose the convening of interim shareholders' general meetings and to convene and preside over the meetings if the BOD fails to do so;
(5) to put forward proposals to the meetings;
(6) to sue the directors or senior officers in accordance with Article 151; and
(7) to exercise other functions and powers provided for in the articles of association.

In comparison with the 1993 Company Law, the current Company Law gives several important powers to the BOS. One is the power to propose the convening of interim shareholders' general meetings and to convene and preside over the meetings if the BOD fails to do so (Art. 53.4). This power is important because it gives shareholders a chance to reconsider whether relevant directors should be replaced. Another one is the power to sue relevant directors and senior officers if the relevant directors or senior officers have breached their duties and the BOD is not going to take legal action against them (Art. 53.6). The third one is the power to conduct an investigation if

1. The Company Law, Article 117(5).

in its view the business situation of the company is abnormal. Furthermore, if necessary, the BOS can engage any accountant's firm to assist its work at the expense of the company (Art. 54.2). The fourth power allows supervisors to bring enquiries and suggestions to the matters decided by the BOD even though they can only attend BOD meetings as non-voting participants (Art. 54.1). Armed with those necessary teeth, one may believe that the main purpose of checks and balances between the BOS and the BOD can be largely achieved.

II. ESTABLISHMENT OF THE BOS

1. Number of Members and Their Term

The number is usually stated in the articles of association. In JSCs, the BOS must have no fewer than three members, while in LLCs the BOS may not be required and only one or two supervisors are required (Art. 51). The Chinese company law does not state the maximum number of supervisors for the BOS. Usually this is done according to the capital size of a company. In Germany, nine supervisors are allowed if the capital is less than €1.5 million, fifteen supervisors are allowed if the capital is over €1.5 million and twenty-one supervisors are allowed if the capital is over €10 million.[2] The term of a supervisor is usually three years. In some jurisdictions, a supervisor cannot be re-elected. In China, however, re-election is not a problem.

2. The Qualifications and Duties of a Supervisor

Generally, the qualifications of a supervisor are similar to that of a director. Interestingly, supervisors are assumed to be good people when directors and senior management personnel are not allowed to commit the acts listed in Article 148.

Chapter 6 of the Company Law provides conditions for disqualification. Furthermore, directors, managers, and responsible persons in charge of the financial affairs of the company shall not serve concurrently as supervisors (Art. 51.4). However, the existing Company Law may still contain one problem: Article 51 states that supervisors shall be the representatives of shareholders or a certain percentage of employees of the company. This

2. Jean J. du Plessis, Bernhard Großfeld, Claus Luttermann, Ingo Saenger, Otto Sandrock, and Matthias Caspe, *German Corporate Governance in International and European Context* (2nd ed.), Springer (Berlin), 2012, p. 217.

does not necessarily mean that the representatives themselves must be shareholders or employees of the company. One reasonable interpretation is that the representatives must be elected by shareholders or employees. Since Article 51 does not specify who can serve as a representative, it is possible to say that shareholders or employees may be allowed to authorize their agents, who are professional in handling corporate businesses to represent them. People can still discuss whether this proposal is good.

As discussed in the previous chapter, supervisors, like directors or managers, owe fiduciary duties and duty of care and skill to their companies.

III. REMAINING PROBLEM: SUPERVISORS VERSUS INDEPENDENT DIRECTORS

1. Introduction

The concept of the "independent director" is now becoming popular in China. Pursuant to certain rules and regulations, all Chinese-listed companies must establish a special governing organ, i.e., the independent director system. Many people hope that this new system will effectively improve the corporate governance of listed companies despite the lack of sufficient practice and theoretical basis. Actually, this concept originated in Western countries, in particular from the common law jurisdictions. (The United States and United Kingdom are two representative countries.) In Western countries, the concept of the "independent director" is similar to the concepts of the "outside director" or "non-executive director".[3] As the data indicate, independent directors are seen as playing more and more important roles in corporate governance throughout the world. Statistics show that in 1999, the percentage of independent directors on the BOD increased: in the United States, the United Kingdom, and France, independent directors amounted to 62 per cent, 34 per cent, and 29 per cent, respectively.[4] A conclusion based on these statistics is that independent directors are much

3. Gao Jinkang and Tang Huojian, "Several Thoughts about the Transplant of the Independent Director System", an unpublished paper presented to the First National Conference on Commercial Law Theory at the East China University of Politics and Law, November 2001.

4. These numbers were released by the UN Organization for Economic Cooperation and Development. See Zhang Xuedong, "Why Should Listed Companies Adopt the Independent Director System?" (*Shangshi Gongsi Weishime Yao Jianli Duli Dongshi Zhidu*), retrieved from http://www.people.com.cn/GB/jinji/222/5971/5973/20010531/478473.html on 13 October 2013.

more popular in common law jurisdictions than in continental law (or civil law) jurisdictions. (Germany and France are two representative countries.)

On 6 August 2001, the CSRC issued an important legal document: the Guideline Opinions on the Establishment of Independent Directors Within Listed Companies (hereinafter referred to as the "Guideline Opinions").[5] Before this legal document was published, provisions concerning independent directors were scattered amongst various rules and regulations. For instance, on 16 December 1997, the CSRC, for the first time, introduced the concept of the independent director, which was highlighted in the CSRC's Guidelines Concerning Articles of Association of Listed Companies.[6] The existing Company Law expressly requires listed companies to have independent directors. The rationale behind the establishment of an independent director system was quite different from that of Western countries. The purpose of creating this governing organ in China was (and still is) attempting to resolve one of the big problems of listed companies, i.e., the State continuing to be the largest shareholder of most listed companies.[7] It was evident that State-owned shares still amounted to 79 per cent in almost all listed companies despite a tendency for State-owned shares to be diluted or transferred to private interests.[8] Thus, the "insider controller" of listed companies in China is different from that of listed companies in Western countries. In China, as the true owner, the State fails to effectively supervise the operation of listed companies. However, in Western countries, no shareholder can effectively control listed companies because shares are scattered everywhere and managers can do almost everything they want.

---

5. *Guanyu zai shangshi gongsi jianli duli dongshi zhidu de zhidao yijian*. On 28 July 2010, the Notice of the Shenzhen Stock Exchange on Issuing the Guidelines of the Shenzhen Stock Exchange for Standardized Operation of Companies Listed on the Main Board and the Guidelines of the Shenzhen Stock Exchange for Standardized Operation of Companies Listed on the Small and Medium-Sized Enterprise Board was issued. Section 5 deals with the special code of conduct for independent directors, which are similar to that of the Guideline Opinions.
6. Article 112 of which states that a company may establish independent director(s) if it is necessary. Furthermore, it states that this provision is optional.
7. Shi Meilun, Vice-Chairman of the CSRA, pointed out that due to the reason of unperfected corporate governance the State becomes the biggest shareholder of most listed companies. In addition, there was a problem of insider control. In this situation, it was urgent to perfect the corporate governance of listed companies and it was regarded as an important measure to adopt an independent director system. See Shi Meilun, "The Independent Director System Could Improve the Corporate Governance of Listed Companies" (*She duli dongshi neng gaishan shangshi gongsi zhili jiegou*), retrieved from http://stock.hexun.com/2008-11-29/111803358.html on 13 October 2015.
8. Le Jiachun, "There Will Be a High Tide of Reorganizing State-Owned Shares in China" (*Zhongguo guoqigu chongzu jiang zai xian gaochao*), *Shanghai Securities Newspaper* (Shanghai), 15 January 2003.

Against this background, it is reasonable to conclude that the independent director system was established to help the State supervise the operation of listed companies by internal directors. It has been closely associated with the further reform of corporate governance of listed companies in China.

The Company Law mentions that the specific measures for regulating the independent directors shall be stipulated by the State Council and no relevant regulations have yet been published by the State Council (Art. 122). The Guideline Opinions can still serve as important administrative rules in this area.

The Guideline Opinions define what constitutes an independent director. It refers to a person who takes a job only as a director in a listed company. He or she exercises independent judgment and should not be interfered with by either his or her company or large shareholders in the company.[9] The independent director system has a short history in China, whereas in many Western countries and regions, especially in the United States and United Kingdom, this system has a long history because of their unique theories and practices of corporate governance.

The concept of independent directors initially emerged in the United States in the early twentieth century. It was derived from concepts of the external director and non-executive director.[10] Independent directors have been welcome (or well received) in the United States and United Kingdom because the corporate governance has been implemented in accordance with the relationship between the legislative bodies and executive branches. In common law jurisdictions, the SHM is regarded as the highest authority within a company. It has the power to make the company's constitution, i.e., the memorandum of association and/or articles of association. It has the power to appoint directors and to decide other important matters of the company.[11] The BOD is regarded as the executive branch of the company. It decides the daily operation of the company, and the SHM cannot interfere with these management powers. If shareholders dislike the performance of directors, they have to wait until there is an opportunity for

9. Article 1 of the Guideline Opinions.
10. Gao and Tang, supra note 1, p. 1.
11. Taking the Hong Kong Companies Ordinance (Cap. 32) as one example, the powers of an SHM are listed by law, such as altering objects, articles, and names [8, 13, 33]; buying back own shares [49BA, E, D I]; issuing discount shares [50]; altering capital [53–55]; altering directors' power to allot shares [57B]; reducing capital [58–63]; varying class rights [63A]; arrangements and reconstructions [166–67]; appointing/removing auditors [131]; altering directors' power to dispose of assets [155A]; removal of directors [157B]; approving payments to directors [163–64]; court-ordered winding up [177(1)(A)]; and voluntary winding up [228].

re-election,[12] or they can simply vote by their feet, i.e., sell their shares and leave the company. Thus, it is important to take note of the fact that in most common law countries or regions the structure of corporate governance does not contain a supervisory board. Shareholders, especially shareholders of public companies, do not have sufficient powers to oversee the activities of directors. In this circumstance, independent directors have been selected to supervise and control the corporate operations. Independent directors are usually management professionals but are not just limited to professionals. As pointed out by Tom Hadden:

> [I]t is accepted practice in many large British companies for the board of directors to operate in a largely supervisory capacity. This is achieved by making a clear distinction between executive management, which controls the day-to-day operation of the company, and non-executive directors who may be recruited from any source outside the company, but will typically include prominent industrialists and city personalities and perhaps politicians.[13]

Unlike the corporate governance in common law countries (or regions), countries (or regions) with civil law traditions have developed a supervisory board system within the corporate governance structure. Thus, corporate governance is similar to the concept of the separation of powers. As in the relationship between the legislature, executive, and judiciary, there exists a checks-and-balances mechanism within the SHM, BOD, and BOS. Taking Germany as one example, the theory and practice of corporate governance of JSCs is quite unique: the highest authority is the SHM. The SHM elects members of the BOS, and the BOS has the power to appoint and discharge directors. Under this unique structure, even though directors control the daily operations of the company, they are subject to the supervision of the supervisors.[14] Armed with the special powers of appointing and discharging directors, BOSs can function very well.

---

12. The division is clearly stated by Greer LJ in *John Shaw and Sons (Salford) Ltd. v Shaw* (1935), UK: "A company is an entity distinct from its shareholders and its directors. Some of its powers may, according to its articles, be exercised by the directors; certain other powers may be reserved for the shareholders in general meeting. If the powers of management are vested in the directors they and they alone can exercise those powers. The only way in which the general body of the shareholders can control the exercise of the powers vested by the articles in the directors is by altering the articles, or, if the opportunity arises under the articles, by refusing to re-elect the directors of whose actions they disapprove." See Vanessa Stott, *Hong Kong Company Law* (9th ed.), Financial Times and Prentice Hall (Hong Kong), 2000, p. 151.
13. Tom Hadden, *Company Law and Capitalism* (2nd ed.), Weidenfeld and Nicolson (London), 1977, p. 321.
14. Xu Yan, *The Principles of Company Law (Gongsi fa yuanli)*, The Law Press (Beijing), 1997, pp. 237–39.

The Chinese company law also provides a corporate governance structure that is similar to that of most continental law countries or regions, i.e., it requires most companies (regardless of whether they are LLCs or JSCs) to establish an SHM, a BOD, and a BOS.[15] This type of corporate governance is, however, either in theory or in practice, quite different from that of Germany or France. The Chinese company law firstly emphasizes that the SHM is the highest authority of a company. This is a generally acceptable provision. The problem is that the powers and functions of SHMs are more extensive and more detailed in China than in Western countries. For example, the SHM has the power to decide matters of mergers, divisions, dissolutions, and liquidations; the amendment of articles of association; the appointment and dismissal of directors; operational policies and investment plans; annual reports and budgets; and so on.[16] Of those powers, some should be exercised by directors in common law jurisdictions.[17] China started to operate securities markets in Shanghai and Shenzhen in 1992. The fundamental motivation was to promote the reorganization of SOEs.[18] Now, most listed companies are former SOEs, and State-owned shares represent a predominant percentage of listed companies. It is also evident that the 1993 Company Law was trying to protect State-owned assets in two unusual ways. Firstly, it permitted a "one-person company" to be established in China, which is known as a wholly State-owned company.[19] Secondly, it emphasized that State-owned assets should reside in the State where those assets were invested in companies.[20] Based on these two methods, the State was/is secured to be the biggest shareholder in listed companies.

Under the 1993 Company Law, the BOS could not function properly because it did not have any substantial power to deal with directors as mentioned before.[21] For example, when directors or managers did something that was not in their companies' interest, supervisors could only demand that they correct their wrongs. If this demand did not work, supervisors

15. A small-sized limited liability company may only need supervisors instead of a BOS.
16. For detailed information, see Article 37 of the Company Law.
17. In Hong Kong, the BOD usually exercises the power of deciding investment plans.
18. For detailed information, see Gu Minkang and Robert Art, "Securitization of State-Owned Enterprises", *Michigan Journal of International Law*, Vol. 18, No. 1, 1996.
19. The wholly State-owned company refers to a limited company established solely by a State-authorized investment institution or department. See Article 64 of the 1993 Company Law and Article 64(2) of the existing Company Law.
20. Article 4 of the 1993 Company Law provided that the State assets of a company belonged to the State. However, the 2005 Company Law deleted this provision.
21. Articles 54 and 126 of the 1993 Company Law provide BOSs with only ineffective powers.

could propose the holding of an interim SHM and report the misconduct to shareholders. The proposal to hold an interim SHM could, however, be rejected because the power to convene an interim SHM was vested in the BOD. Chinese BOSs did not have the power to dismiss directors, as could be done in Germany. They did not have the right to sue either.[22]

Before the 2005 Company Law, there were many good suggestions for improving the existing company law. It was suggested to learn from the experiences of foreign jurisdictions. Under the French Company Law, the chairman of a company has the responsibility of leading the entire operation of the company. Furthermore, the chairman represents his or her company in dealing with third parties. However, unlike the 1993 Company Law, the French Company Law provides one important mechanism for preventing a chairman from abusing power: the BOD has the power to discharge the chairman at any time.[23] Under the Hong Kong Companies Ordinance, a chairman may be elected by the members who are present at the meeting, unless the company's articles of association provide otherwise.[24] Furthermore, where the chairman is absent, some other directors nominated by the board may preside over the meeting.[25] In addition, Hong Kong courts have a broad power to call an annual general meeting or an extraordinary general meeting, either on its own motion or on an application by any director or any member entitled to vote at the meeting.[26] In that situation, it would also be logical to appoint a person to preside over the meeting. Therefore, improving the power of the BOS is the key to the success of corporate governance.

Fortunately, the powers of the BOS have been substantially increased by the 2005 Company Law, even though the relevant suggestions have not been fully adopted. From now on, it is expected that the BOS be given teeth to effectively supervise the activities of directors and senior management personnel.

Despite the new changes made by the 2005 Company, people still pay attention to the newly created independent director system and treat

---

22. The supervisors could not rely on Article 111 of the 1993 Company Law to sue because the article gave the right to sue only to shareholders.
23. Xu, supra note 13, pp. 286–87.
24. Model Articles (private companies), Art. 13; Model Article (public companies), Art. 11.
25. Model Articles (private companies), Art. 13(4); Model Article (public companies), Art. 11(5).
26. Philip Smart et al., *Hong Kong Company Law*, Butterworths Asia (Hong Kong), 1997, p. 107. Also, according to Section 114B of the Hong Kong Companies Ordinance (Cap. 32), the court (1) may order a meeting to be called, held and conducted in such manner as the court thinks fits and (2) may give such ancillary directions as it thinks expedient (including a direction that one member present in person or by proxy shall be deemed to constitute the meeting). Section 570 of Cap. 622 reflects the similar ideas.

this new system as a panacea to cure the problem of corporate supervision. Thus, the greater importance of BOSs is related to the independent director system.

In the following section, it is necessary to examine the rules concerning independent directors and outline the effectiveness of independent directors in China.

2. The Contents of the Guideline Opinions

(1) Qualifications for an Independent Director

It is true that the qualifications for becoming an independent director are more concrete and restrictive than those for a supervisor.[27] Article 2 of the Guideline Opinions provides the following requirements:

- He or she shall possess the qualifications of being a director of listed companies in line with the relevant provisions of laws and administrative rules.
- He or she shall be independent, which is required by the Guideline Opinions.
- He or she shall be equipped with basic knowledge of the operations of listed companies and shall be familiar with relevant laws, administrative rules, and other rules and regulations.
- He or she shall have working experience with addressing legal or economic issues, as well as working experience with exercising powers and functions as an independent director.
- He or she shall satisfy other conditions that are stipulated by corporate articles of association.

In addition, Article 3 of the Guideline Opinions prohibits the following persons from being independent directors:

- Those who have already taken job positions in listed companies or subordinate enterprises of listed companies, or those persons' direct relatives or main social relationships.[28]

27. Although the Chinese company law does not mention the qualifications for being a supervisor, those qualifications can be found elsewhere. For example, 1996 Shenzhen's Interim Rules on Corporate Supervisory Boards provide that a supervisor should be able (1) to protect the owner's rights and interests; (2) to adhere to principles, to be honest and upright, to be fair and just; and (3) to have relevant working experience, which is compatible with the position of a supervisor (Article 14). In comparison, the Guideline Opinions provide detailed qualification requirements.
28. "Direct relatives" refer to spouses, parents, and children, while the main social relationships

- Those who hold 1 per cent of the outstanding shares of listed companies directly or indirectly or are natural person shareholders who are within the top ten shareholders of listed companies or their direct relatives.
- Those who have taken job positions with legal person shareholders that have already obtained 5 per cent of the outstanding shares of a listed company or with legal person shareholders who are within the top five legal person shareholders or their direct relatives.
- Those who have been in the preceding situations within one year.
- Those who provide financial, legal or consultant services to listed companies or their subordinate enterprises.
- Other persons who have been listed by the corporate articles of association.
- Other persons who have been identified by the CSRC.

Clearly, these provisions intend to create true independent directors who have no conflicts of interest and are not subject to improper influence when carrying out their supervisory functions.

(2) Rights and Obligations of an Independent Director

The Guideline Opinions assign more rights to independent directors. It is said that in order to fully play their roles, independent directors are given not only rights and powers of regular directors in line with the Chinese company law and other relevant laws and regulations, but also the following special rights as independent directors:

(a) to approve a major associated trade, i.e., the associated trade conducted between a listed company and its associated partner in an amount higher than ¥3 million or more than 5 per cent of a listed company's nearest audited net asset value, before submitting it to the BOD for further discussion. In order to make such a decision on whether to give their approval, independent directors may hire intermediate institutions to draft an independent financial consultant report for their consideration;
(b) to propose to hire or dismiss accountant firms;
(c) to request that the BOD hold an interim SHM;
(d) to propose to hold a meeting of the BOD;
(e) to hire external audit and consultant institutions independently; and
(f) to publicly collect shareholders' voting proxies before a formal SHM.[29]

---

refer to brothers and sisters, parents-in-law, sons or daughters-in-law, spouses of brothers and sisters, or spouses' brothers and sisters.

29. The assumption is that this right is to help minority shareholders.

Furthermore, independent directors shall express their independent opinions to the BOD or SHM concerning the following matters:

(a) nomination, appointment, and dismissal of directors;
(b) appointment and dismissal of senior management personnel;
(c) salaries of directors and senior management personnel;
(d) existing and new loans or other financial relationships between listed companies and their shareholders, actual controllers, and associated enterprises in an amount higher than ¥3 million or higher than 5 per cent of the nearest audited net asset value. This includes whether the relevant listed companies have taken effective measures to pay back outstanding loans;
(e) any matter that, in the view of independent directors, will harm the rights and interests of shareholders; and
(f) other matters that are stipulated by the corporate articles of association.[30]

As a general principle, rights and duties should be equivalent. The Guideline Opinions have one general provision outlining the duties of independent directors, i.e., independent directors owe the duty of loyalty and care to their listed companies.[31]

In addition, independent directors should seriously perform their duties in order to wholly protect the interests of a listed company, especially the legitimate interests of medium and small shareholders. With respect to the duty of care, the Guideline Opinions state that if any independent director fails to attend board meetings in person on three consecutive occasions, the board shall make a proposal to dismiss that independent director at the SHM.[32] In practice, one judgment has revealed that if an independent director fails to take action without justification, he or she will be liable for his or her omission. Lu Jiahao, an independent director of Zeng Baiwen, failed to take any action when the company submitted a false accounting report.

30. The Guideline Opinions, Article 6(1). The CSRC issued "Several Rules to Strengthen the Legal Rights and Interests of Individual Shareholders" (*Guanyu jiaqiang shehui gongzhonggu gudong hefa quanyi baohu de ruogan guiding*) in 2004. The Rules give further power to independent directors: "When there are proposals concerning the major related party transactions, or employment or dismissal of relevant accountant firms, the proposals should be agreed by more than half of the independent directors before they could be discussed by the BOD. If agreed by all independent directors, independent directors could hire external audit institutions or consultation institutions to provide detailed auditing and consultation and the relevant expenses should be borne by the company."
31. The Guideline Opinions, Article 1(2).
32. Ibid., Article 4(5).

Consequently, Lu was fined ¥100,000 by the CSRC. Lu subsequently sued the CSRC for this decision, but the Intermediate People's Court of Beijing rejected the lawsuit. Lu was the first independent director to be punished in China. This was a lesson for Lu and set a good example for those acting as or preparing to act as independent directors of listed companies to perform their duties properly.[33] Based on the No. 14 documentation, the CSRC unequivocally requires that independent directors shall express their views when a listed company decides to issue new shares. Their views should be stated on the application form. Otherwise, the application will not be accepted. Thus, some authors believe that independent directors will play increasingly important roles due to additional new regulations requiring them to express their views. On the other hand, it must be realized that more powers may mean more risks and more responsibilities. It is a "double-edged knife".[34] According to a report, many independent directors have resigned from listed companies. One university professor who had just resigned from his post as an independent director told a reporter his story. In his opinion, it was not a good idea to be an independent director because there were high risks and it was easy to be blamed by regular directors. Firstly, if an independent director wanted to seriously perform his or her duties, he or she must examine and investigate every item in detail. It is, however, impossible to do so in a real situation because the examination and investigation may indicate distrust of other regular directors. On the other hand, independent directors are paid by listed companies and they may feel too embarrassed to point out company weaknesses. Secondly, if independent directors pay too much attention to "face" (*mianzi*) and choose not to say anything, they have to take risks: the consequence of their blinded actions will either destroy their reputation, or in a serious situation they will be sued by investors.[35] In fact, this is just the tip of the iceberg. In the next section, existing problems involving independent directors are discussed.

33. Liu Yan, "Independent Directors Are Not Just Vases" (*Duli dongshi buneng shi huaping*), retrieved from http://big5.xinhuanet.com/gate/big5/news.xinhuanet.com/zonghe/2002-08/26/content_537691.htm on 13 October 2015 (hereinafter referred to as "Liu Yan").

34. Zhang Wei, "Will Independent Directors Become Short-lived Career?" (*Duli dongshi cheng "duanming zhiye"?*), retrieved from http://business.sohu.com/06/85/article203138506.shtml on 13 October 2015.

35. Ai Jun, "Why Independent Directors Quit Their Jobs" (*Duli dongshi yuanhe fenfen chizhi*), retrieved from http://past.people.com.cn/GB/news/8410/20020930/835056.html on 13 October 2015.

(3) The Deficiencies of Independent Directors

Today, independent directors are giving a more negative voice in corporate governance.[36] This was usually unheard of in the past. However, it is not a common phenomenon in China today. There are many existing problems, even though many people are in favour of this newly created system. Data revealed that the independent director system was not ideal because of the problems of qualification, true independence and insufficient time to participate in corporate governance.

(a) Independent Directorships Are Seen as an Honour

Professor Li Yining pointed out clearly that independent directors are usually selected by big shareholders. Most of them are well-known scholars and entrepreneurs. It is difficult for them to have enough energy and sufficient time to participate in various directors' meetings. At the same time, because of the short history of the independent director system, it is impossible for listed companies to find as many as possible qualified and responsible candidates to be appointed as independent directors.[37] Today, qualification may not be a problem, but true responsibility may continue to be a problem. Jamie Allen, the General Secretary of the Asian Corporate Governance Association, raised a very interesting issue. On the one hand, he indicated that the role of independent directors has been recognized widely because regulatory authorities in many countries and regions in Southeast Asia have required listed companies to establish independent directors or suggested they do so. On the other hand, he has to acknowledge that corporate internal reforms have mainly been done by management personnel and shareholders who directly push forward those reforms. It is difficult to find a case where corporate reforms have been initiated by independent directors.[38]

Furthermore, one author sharply pointed out that today's independent directors are selected from two categories of person. The first category includes public figures, such as economists, government officials (most of them retired officials) and stars. They are selected for the sole purpose of increasing the reputation of enterprises. The second category includes

---

36. Li Mingliang, "Independent Directors Want to Say No" (*Wo shi duli dongshi, wo yao shuo "bu"*), retrieved from http://finance.sina.com.cn/roll/20040529/1634785654.shtml on 9 December 2015.
37. Li Yining, "Independent Directors of Listed Companies Could Not Play Effective Role Yet" (*Shangshi gongsi duli dongshi shang nan fahui zuoyong*), retrieved from http://www.chinanews.com/2001-06-12/26/97419.html on 14 October 2015.
38. "The Independent Director System Is Still Facing Three Big Challenges" (*Duli dongshi zhidu reng mianlin san da tiaozhan*), retrieved from http://mil.eastday.com/epublish/gb/paper92/20010913/class009200001/hwz404779.htm on 14 October 2015.

professionals, i.e., academics and principals of research teams in universities. They are selected for the purpose of providing technological consultation to enterprises. Regardless of which category the individuals belong to, they are all selected to work for listed companies.[39] In fact, to be an independent director is not just an honour; he or she must have management skills and work for the appointing company as a supervisor instead of just increasing his or her reputation or offering technological advice.

(b) Independent Directors Are Not Always Independent

It has been revealed that independent directors are not always independent and are often afraid of speaking out because of their close relationship with the BOD that created them. It was observed that the CSRC initially wanted to create the independent director system because it sought to provide medium and small shareholders with a voice. In order to represent the interests of medium and small shareholders, independent directors were put in place to fairly supervise the BOD, which is usually formed by big shareholders, as well as the operations of the company. However, when this system was imported into China, it quickly became advantageous to build up a "friendship" between big shareholders of listed companies and various well-known persons. Once independent directors become "good friends" of big shareholders, it became very difficult for them to speak out. In this situation, the directors' supervisory functions could not be properly exercised, nor could the directors speak on behalf of medium and small shareholders. Mr Zhong Pengrong, an independent director for several listed companies, shared his own experience. According to him, it was a normal practice that independent directors would, just before meetings, only take time to briefly read the background materials given by listed companies before rushing off to meetings. Following the meetings, they would often leave in a hurry. Mr Zhong said that no one ever carried out any kind of investigation or did in-depth research for more than three days. In his view, at the very least, directors needed to take the time to reading through all of the materials before going to meetings. Sometimes, independent directors had no time to read the prepared materials or were unable to attend the meetings. Mr Zhong concluded that those were not rare cases. If an independent director was too busy to participate in a company's meetings or did not spend time seriously considering a company's actual situation, he or she could not effectively supervise or offer any help to improve the

39. Ji Wenhai, "Four Questions for Independent Directors" (*Si wen duli dongshi*), retrieved from http://www.people.com.cn/GB/jinji/20010618/491092.html on 14 October 2015.

decision-making skills of the BOD.[40] According to the 2012 Report of Evaluating Protection of Investors in Listed Companies, close to 40 per cent of companies' independent directors failed to attend meetings.[41] How could they effectively supervise the activities of the BOD?

Independent directors are the agents of their companies and should act on behalf of their principals. In theory, independent directors are appointed by listed companies and therefore they should work hard or diligently for the interests of those companies. But in reality they are appointed by big shareholders who also decide their salaries. Thus, they naturally may tend to side with the big shareholders. There are only a few people who act like Bao Qingtian, who was upright and honest in performing his official duties during the Song Dynasty. Nevertheless, people who act like Bao Qingtian do so not because of this system, but because of their own individual personalities and moral standards. Thus, a system cannot be built based on a few individuals' personalities and consciousness, but should be built based on well-established theory and practice.[42] Since there is no basis of trust between independent directors and minority shareholders, their nature of independence is quite suspicious. As one author concluded, this may be one important drawback of this system.[43]

3. Independent Directors versus Supervisors

Broadly speaking, a director will perform one or more of these three functions: execution, instrumentation, and control. Independent directors are supposed to be external directors, and their function is mainly to supervise internal directors. The independent director system is the legacy of common law jurisdictions, where companies are usually controlled by the BOD. The main purpose of importing this system is to improve supervision over the BOD and to prevent a company from being controlled by improper insiders.

---

40. Zhong Pengrong, "Independent Directors Could Not Be Seen as Bao Qingtian" (*Duli dongshi dangbuliao "Bao Qingtian"*), retrieved from http://news.xinhuanet.com/fortune/2002-09/03/content_548268.htm on 14 October 2015.
41. Hou Jiening, "About 40 Per Cent of Listed Companies' Independent Directors Failed to Attend Meetings" (*Jin sicheng gongsi duli dongshi butong chengdu quexi huiyi*), retrieved from http://finance.people.com.cn/stock/n/2013/0911/c67815-22879282.html on 14 October 2015.
42. Zhong Pengrong, "Independent Directors Should Not Be Seen as Bao Qingtian" (*Duli dongshi dangbuliao "Bao Qingtian"*), retrieved from http://news.xinhuanet.com/fortune/2002-09/03/content_548268.htm on 14 October 2015.
43. Xu Lingang, "Shortcomings of the Independent Director System" (*Duli dongshi de zhidu quexian*), retrieved from http://business.sohu.com/26/08/article201970826.shtml on 14 October 2015.

However, China adopts a similar model of continental law jurisdictions where the BOD is under supervision by the BOS. Under existing company law, emphasis should be placed on how to strengthen the supervisory function of the BOS, rather than to place all hope on the system of independent directors.

In China, the BOS cannot function well due to the drawbacks of the system discussed previously. Now, the power of the BOS has been increased, and it may not be ideal to import independent directors to act effectively. Since both the BOS and independent directors are expected to serve as "supervisors" of a company, their roles and functions may overlap and thus increase the cost of corporate operation. Independent directors are also questioned for their capacity to supervise every important matter. Taking investment decision making as one example, most independent directors are "part-time directors". Furthermore, they are often academics or well-known persons who do not necessarily possess degrees or expertise in business management and may be less susceptible to market changes. Because of their limited knowledge and time, they are barely able to evaluate the reasonableness of decision-making procedures.[44]

Most importantly, there is no direct relationship between the establishment of an independent director system and the role played by this system. In the United States, the independent director system is well established and quite developed. Nevertheless, independent directors, from time to time, cannot play their roles very well, and some even go so far as to breach their duties. For example, the famous Enron Company had seventeen directors. Among them, fifteen were independent directors. For many years, independent directors acted just like the vases that serve a decoration purpose. In this situation, the existence of these "vase" directors created a false image of the company and defrauded small and medium investors.[45]

Thus, there is a need to carefully examine the importance of the independent director system in China and especially its relationship with the supervisory board system. So far, there is a perception that the establishment of an independent director system is a major action to improve the corporate government of listed companies. This system involves the creation of

44. Ibid.

45. Liu, supra note 33. Interestingly, in China, some people suggested that because of the Enron incident the issue of corporate governance had become more critical. Thus, one of the resolutions was to increase the percentage of independent directors in listed companies. See Jiang Dezeng, "Worldwide Corporate Governance Facing New Situation after the Enron Incident: Percentage of Independent Directors Should Be Dramatically Increased" (*Enran shijian hou quanqiu gongsi zhili suo mianling de zin zingshi—duli dongshi bizhong ke wang dafu zengjia*), *The Securities Daily* (Beijing), 26 January 2003.

an external supervision mechanism and will change the managing structure of the BOD. In conclusion, both independent directors and supervisors will be introduced to improve internal and external supervisory systems of listed companies in order to prevent those companies from taking any risks.[46] This view is too optimistic. It fails to explain why the existing BOS system cannot play an effective role in corporate governance and whether the independent director system will face the same or similar problems in the near future. Furthermore, if there is too much emphasis placed on the independent director system, people will be misled and have a false image that the independent director system alone can bring about perfect corporate governance for listed companies.

Another view is that the independent director system should be abolished in China because it does not fit into the Chinese soil. In common law jurisdictions such as the United States and United Kingdom, there are diversified shareholdings and external supervision works very well. In continental law jurisdictions such as Germany and Japan, the shareholders are many big banks and there exists asymmetric information. Thus, internal supervision works very well.[47] In order to consider whether the independent director system is suitable for China, it is important to consider the shareholding structure of listed companies and to conclude that the BOS is a more effective system in China.

In fact, the most urgent way to improve corporate governance is to consider how the BOS system may function perfectly in order to effectively control directors. For example, it was suggested that one of the effective ways to protect the interests of minority shareholders is to give them veto power on the BOS. Under the Company Law, members of the BOS are formed by both shareholders' representatives and employees' representatives.[48] The important thing is to allocate proper votes to minority shareholders so that they can utilize the forum of the BOS to check and supervise the activities of the BOD.

Since the Company Law now clearly stipulates the powers and functions of the BOS, the next logical thing is to provide supplemental or detailed rules to exercise those powers. For example, the BOS is given the power to hire accountants from outside or to appoint external supervisors at the expense of the company. The BOS should change its "non-existence"

46. Su Min, "Will Independent Directors Replace the Supervisory Board?" (*Duli dongshihui qudai jianshihui*), *The International Financial News* (Beijing), 21 June 2002, p.4.
47. "What Would Have Happened if the Independent Director System Had Not Been Established?" (*Zhenqiangwu, duli dongshi yi zhi bushe you ruhe*), retrieved from http://blog.sina.com.cn/s/blog_539a287001014h8e.html on 14 October 2015.
48. The Company Law, Article 51(2).

status. It should function as an audit committee, which is usually the ancillary committee of the BOD. On the other hand, independent directors could focus on controlling the remuneration of internal directors and managers or on appointing internal directors. In addition, they could cooperate with supervisors to take a joint action.

Thus, this leads to the next issue, i.e., what is the legal position of independent directors? This book holds the view that a relevant legal position for independent directors should not be given, and company law should not be amended in order to redefine their function, role, responsibilities, duties, qualifications, appointing procedures, and relationship with supervisors. Furthermore, it is very fortunate that the 2005 Company Law requires only that the independent director system be adopted by listed companies. Thus, within a listed company, the internal structure includes members' general meetings, a BOD, a BOS, and independent directors. For other regular companies, the matter of the independent director system is left for them to consider through their articles of association. Thus, it seems that the independent director system should be considered only as a supplemental system to the BOS system. In order to realize this structure, the BOS should be given decision-making powers that are similar to those of Germany. Only in this situation can the additional independent director system function like "adding wings to a tiger" and corporate governance be substantially perfected.

9

Other Organs

I. WORKERS' ROLES IN CORPORATE GOVERNANCE

In China, even though workers are considered masters of the state and have been given very high political status, it has never been made clear how that important political and legal status is guaranteed in practice, especially in the employment relationship. Under the previous system of a planned economy, most enterprises were owned by the state and all jobs were allocated by the governments at various levels. The workers were regarded as the masters of the enterprises (mostly SOEs) in which they were working. The enterprises did not have the autonomy to dismiss any worker. Thus, even though workers might not have been able to get a high salary, they were almost guaranteed to work until retirement age.[1] However, since China moved from the planned economy to the market-oriented economy, market competition has been increasing and workers' rights to employment are no longer secured. As their employment mainly depends on employment contracts, workers are virtually the employees of companies, and they may not have a sufficient voice in the management of companies. In other words, they have to rely on the relevant laws or policies to protect their legal interests.

The right of workers to participate in corporate decision making is codified by the Chinese company law. That right does not include voting and, at least by the terms expressed by the Chinese company law, appear far more limited than the rights provided under earlier legislation. Previous

1. This is the so-called "iron rice bowl" (*tie fanwan*).

law, for example, accorded workers the right to remove a director from an enterprise (subject to government approval) and to decide matters directly affecting the workers.[2] Comparatively, the rights of workers involving corporate governance under the Chinese company law are much more limited.

Under the 1993 Company Law, a company must solicit in advance the opinions of the trade union (or labour union) and the employees of the company when studying and deciding on issues involving the personal interests of its staff and workers such as their salaries, welfare, and safety in the realm of production and labour insurance. The representatives of trade unions staff and workers should be invited to attend relevant meetings as non-voting participants (Art. 55). However, under the 2005 Company Law, this will be done if a company considers changing its system or major issues of operation (Art. 18.3). Although the 1993 Company Law further conferred additional powers on workers in certain situations, a detailed guideline was lacking. For instance, corporations formed by more than two State-owned investing bodies had to include democratically elected representatives of the workers on the BOD. The statute was silent, however, as to the number or percentage of worker directors because the Law stated only that the worker representatives should be in "the proper ratio". The 2005 Company Law extended the worker director to other companies[3] but still failed to mention the number (Art. 44.2). One possible suggestion is to follow Article 51(2) of the Company Law, i.e., one third of directors should be worker representatives.

The aggregate of explicit powers accorded to workers by these various provisions is not extensive. Workers in Chinese corporations appear to have less power than their peers in Germany. For example, the relevant law provides a mandatory requirement that nearly equal representation of workers and shareholders on the BOS shall be provided. The experience of most European countries indicates that workers must be permitted to participate in corporate governance. In the United Kingdom, since the amendment of its company law in 1985, the interests of workers have been treated the same as the interests of shareholders and all such interests have been treated as an

2. For example, Article 44 of the SOE Law of the PRC (1988) provides that the opinions of the representative assembly of staff and workers shall be sought if the person selected as factory director is to be appointed by the government department in charge or selected from applications. If a factory director is to be elected by the representative assembly of staff and workers of an enterprise, the matter shall be reported to the government department in charge for approval.
3. Bear in mind that Article 44(2) uses the word "may" only for other companies, which means an optional choice for other companies.

important component of the interests of companies.[4] In Norway, the Joint Stock Law provides clearly that a company must form a corporate assembly if the company has more than 200 workers for three continuous accounting years. One-third or a half of the seats should be taken by worker representatives. Furthermore, the corporate assembly shall have the following powers:

(1) to elect directors and the chairman of the BOD;
(2) to supervise the operation of the company;
(3) to provide opinions to the SHM;
(4) to vote on important matters such as large investments and changes in operational policies; and
(5) to provide suggestions to the BOD.[5]

China is still a socialist country and the Constitution recognizes the leading role of workers. Thus, Chinese lawmakers should pay more attention to this matter when the Chinese company law is further amended in the near future. Nevertheless, in practice, Chinese workers may well wield great influence because of the extensive power of the CPC. Within enterprises, the party organization will continue to play its role as the political nucleus, and workers and staff will participate in democratic management. Following the past practice in selecting their leaders, workers will probably elect Party members to be their representatives sitting on the BOS. Because the "leading role" of the Party is enshrined in the Constitution and pervades the economy, the presence of Party members on the BOS will result in a substantial influence on corporate operations, where the State maintains majority ownership. The Party's influence does not depend on whether its members have extensive formal voting powers on the BOD. However, from a legal viewpoint, it is suggested that workers' roles in corporate governance should be fixed by the Chinese company law rather than through indirect influence.

Workers can participate in corporate governance through both trade unions (*gonghui*)[6] and workers' assemblies for employees and staff. One remaining issue is how to draw a line between these two institutions.

The task of trade unions is to safeguard the lawful rights and interests of staff members and employees pursuant to relevant Chinese laws and

4. Liu Junhai, *A Comparative Research on Employees Involved in a Company's Organs* (*Zhigong Canyu gongsi Jiguang Zhidu de Bijiao Yanjiu*), in Wang Baoshu (ed.), *The Comparative Law Review*, The Law Press (Beijing), September 1999, p. 59.

5. Ibid., pp. 71–74.

6. Article 16 states that the employees of a company shall, in accordance with the Law, organize a trade union to conduct union activities and to safeguard their legal rights and interests. A company shall provide the necessary facilities for the conduct of union activities.

regulations. They assist the enterprise in the arrangement and use of welfare and bonus funds for staff and employees and organize political study, professional knowledge, and cultural and sports activities.

In foreign-invested companies, trade unions have the right to participate as non-voting members in board meetings when companies discuss matters of staff discipline, labour protection, labour insurance, and production activities. Article 33 of the Chinese Labour Union Law provides that "Sino-foreign equity joint ventures and Sino-foreign cooperative joint ventures, while making studies into and decisions in relation to issues of wages, welfare, health and safety, labour protection and labour insurance which affect the vital interests of workers, shall listen to opinions of the trade unions." When an employee is dismissed or disciplined or there is a large-scale reduction in employees planned, the trade union can intervene if it believes that the company is acting improperly or violating employee rights in so doing.

Another problem is that trade unions in foreign-invested companies have played a relatively muted role, limited to advising on matters affecting employees' interests such as the implementation of applicable laws and regulations. This matter, however, is certainly beyond the scope of this book.

II. ROLE OF THE COMMUNIST PARTY OF CHINA

As discussed, the BOD is an indispensable organ of a company. However, due to the existing personnel system, members of the BOD have a close relationship with the CPC. On 29 June 1999, the Office of the CPC Central Committee and the State Council issued the Notice regarding Audition of Economic Responsibility of Legal Representatives. This is a strong indication that the CPC still retains the power to control legal representatives who are the major officials of large-sized companies.

The existing Company Law states that activities conducted by the primary organizations of the CPC through companies shall be handled in accordance with the CPC Constitution (Art. 19). One author points out, arguably, that this provision gives the exclusive application of the Party's Constitution in the company and in effect precludes the application of the Chinese company law to the Party Committee and gives the Party's Constitution implicit statutory authority to supplement the Chinese company law.[7]

7. For detailed information, please see Chao Xi, *Corporate Governance and Legal Reform in China*, Wildy, Simmonds and Hill Publishing (London), 2009, pp. 31–34.

Regarding the function and power of the CPC in companies, the suggestions are never unified. One view is that the CPC shall be deemed as one organ of a company. Furthermore, the leadership of the CPC in companies shall be strengthened. Another view is that Chinese shareholding companies shall have Chinese characteristics. The leadership of the CPC is one of those characteristics. There is a need to modify the style of leadership in companies. The last view is that the CPC is a political organ and shall not be treated as an organ of a company, especially in foreign-invested companies.

So far, the CPC may involve itself in the major decisions of companies through four channels:

(1) Through the CPC's important decisions
(2) Through the BOD meetings if the majority of directors are CPC members
(3) Through the CPC directors trying to persuade non-CPC directors to accept the CPC's decisions; or
(4) Through joint meetings held by the CPC and BOD to discuss the major issues of companies.

It is necessary to conduct further research on the "major decisions" of companies. Those major decisions shall refer to the lawfulness of business operations, the legal rights and interests of employees, and other important political issues. Other important business decisions shall be given to the SHM or the BOD in order to avoid the CPC's intervention in detailed business activities.

III. COMPANY SECRETARIES

In Hong Kong, a company's secretary is an officer of the company. It is required that every company shall have a company secretary. Certainly, company secretaries of listed companies shall meet certain qualifications. They are usually accountants, lawyers or charted secretaries. Furthermore, because the company secretaries are deemed to be the chief administration officers of a company, they owe fiduciary duties and the duty of care and skill to the company as well.[8]

The company secretary system was not established under the 1993 Company Law. However, it is possible to see this system from relevant administrative regulations on either the national or local level. This system was firstly seen in Shenzhen when the Regulations on the Joint Stock Company of the Shenzhen Special Economic Zone (*Shenzhen Jingji Tequ Gufeng*

8. Vanessa Stott, *Hong Kong Company Law*, 9th ed., Prentice Hall (Hong Kong), 2000, pp. 235–37.

Youxian Gongsi Tiaoli) were issued in 1993. According to these Regulations, the company secretaries were appointed by and made responsible for the BOD. In 1994, the State Council issued the Special Rules Concerning Joint Stock Companies Offering Shares or to Be Listed Outside China (*Guanyu Gufeng Youxian Gongsi Jingwai Muji Gufeng ji Shangshi de Tebie Guiding*) and the Compulsory Items of the Articles of Association of Companies to Be Listed Outside China (*Dao Jingwai Shangshi Gongsi Zhangcheng Bibei Tiaokuan*). According to these two Rules, the company secretaries were considered senior management personnel and would be appointed by the BOD. Their duties were (1) to keep documents, (2) to send documents to relevant government authorities, (3) to keep the name list of shareholders, and (4) to make sure that the relevant persons would receive the relevant minutes and documents. Although those duties are not comprehensive enough, it is important to know that company secretaries are recognized as senior management personnel and that their duties and responsibilities are specified.

On the other hand, the CSRC issued the Working Guide for BOD Secretaries of Companies Listed Abroad (*Jingwai Shangshi Gongsi Dongshihui Mishu Gongzuo Zhiyin*) (hereinafter referred to as the "Working Guide") in 1999. The Working Guide indicates clearly that company secretaries of listed companies are senior management personnel (Art. 1) and that their duties are as follows:

(1) to assist the BOD to handle daily work;
(2) to provide directors with relevant policies and rules concerning a company's operations as issued by supervisory authorities abroad;
(3) to prepare relevant documents for the BOD's meetings or the SHMs and to write relevant minutes;
(4) to assist in the matter of disclosing information and to enhance the relationship with investors;[9] and
(5) to handle public relationships.

The Working Guide also requires that company secretaries of listed companies obtain at least associate degrees and have more than 3 years of experience in handling financial or accounting related work. Most importantly, they must receive qualification training organized by relevant supervisory authorities and pass the relevant examinations.[10] Usually, a company secretary shall have reached the age of twenty-five.[11]

9. The Working Guide, Article 2.
10. Ibid., Article 4.
11. The Interim Measures for Governing the BOD's Secretaries of Listed Companies (*Shangshi Gongsi Dongsihui Mishu Guanli Zanxing Banfa*), issued by the Shenzhen Stock Exchange on 10 May 1996.

Furthermore, due to the important role of a company secretary, a company shall make a public announcement if the secretary decides to resign his or her position as the company secretary.[12]

In some listed companies, secretaries may be further divided into three categories, i.e., secretaries at the initial level, secretaries at the middle level, and senior secretaries. Presumably, only the senior secretaries are deemed to be senior management personnel if a company maintains different categories of secretaries.

Because company secretaries of listed companies are senior management personnel, they owe their companies a duty of loyalty and a duty of care.[13] In other words, they will be treated as directors and imposed same duties. Thus, in the following situations, a company secretary will be dismissed.

(1) He or she fails to perform his or her duties and causes gross losses to the company.
(2) He or she violates laws, regulations, and the company's articles of association when discharging his or her duties and causes serious consequences or creates a worse impact.
(3) He or she leaks confidential information of the company, thus causing serious consequences or creating a worse impact.
(4) Relevant supervisory authorities hold that he or she no longer qualifies for the position.
(5) Other situations as decided by the BOD.[14]

Based on those previous regulations and practice, the 2005 Company Law officially announced that company secretaries were senior management personnel. However, based on Article 216(1) of the Company Law, one may understand that only company secretaries of listed companies are treated as senior management personnel. In other words, secretaries of other companies may not be regarded as holding an important position and are instead just ordinary employees. As such, the fiduciary duty and duty of care cannot be imposed on them.

---

12. For example, the Announcement of Zhongwaijian Development Joint Stock Company (*Zhongwaijian Fazhan Gufen Youxian Gongsi Guanyu Ben Gongsi Dongshihui Mishu Chizhi de Gonggao*) states, "This company and all members of the BOD shall ensure that the content of this announcement is true, accurate and complete and shall be jointly liable if this announcement is discovered to be false, misleading or to have a gross omission. Due to the reason of relocation, Mr Feng Xiaoyu, the secretary of the BOD, has resigned his job. The relevant work shall be handled by Mr Sheng Zhibin." *The Shanghai Securities News* (Shanghai), 22 September 2003.
13. The Working Guide, Article 16.
14. Ibid., Article 17.

Article 123 of the Company Law further outlines the duties and responsibilities of company secretaries, which are quite different from those of the previous administrative regulations:

- to be in charge of the preparatory work of SHMs and the meetings of the BOD;
- to keep relevant documents;
- to keep relevant information about shareholders; and
- to handle the relevant information disclosure.

Given the nature of these duties, it is logical to state that the minutes and resolutions of the SHM and the BOD under both Articles 41(2) and 48(2) should be taken care of by the company secretaries. Furthermore, the Working Guide has not been formally abolished, and it is followed in situations where detailed rules have not been issued.

From time to time, company secretaries are sanctioned due to illegal conduct. The situation was worse in the past than it is today simply because corporate governance is now more emphasized.[15] Since company secretaries are deemed to be the senior officers of companies, a high level of responsibility is imposed upon them. Thus, in a worst-case scenario, they are subjected to not only administrative sanctions from relevant authorities but also civil actions by their companies.

Although company secretaries of listed companies are regarded as senior management personnel, they have not functioned well in practice. Their legal positions and remunerations are similar to those of regular management personnel, so they are unable to handle business such as information disclosures. This situation must be improved. One important improvement would be to differentiate company secretaries from other senior management personnel.[16]

Firstly, they must be appointed by the BOD after the nomination is made by the board chairman. Other senior management personnel are usually nominated by the general managers.

Secondly, they shall be responsible for the relevant jobs of the BOD when it is not in session. To some extent, the company secretaries could serve as additional agents of the BOD, while other senior management personnel refrain from performing those duties.

15. Wang Ren, "Preliminary Research on Company Secretaries of Listed Companies and Their Roles in Corporate Governance" (*Qianxi shangshi gongsi dongshihui mishu zai gongsi guifan zhili zhong qidao de zuoyong*), retrieved from http://www.csrc.gov.cn/pub/newsite/flb/lfzl/jnlfssyzn/yjyd/200701/t20070108_77322.html on 15 October 2015.
16. Ibid.

Thirdly, the appointment of company secretaries should go through a qualifications check. Whenever there is a dismissal, the party concerned could be allowed to appeal the decision.

The research on company secretaries is just beginning. It is hoped that this introduction will invite more valuable discussion.

10

Corporate Finance

I. DEFINITION OF CAPITAL

Under the Chinese company law, capital has been given a special meaning, i.e., stock capital. Stock capital is the total amount of capital, usually stipulated in the articles of association, that should or will be contributed by shareholders. So far, different jurisdictions provide different systems concerning capital.

1. Authorized Capital

Authorized capital can also be called stated capital or nominal capital, which is normally seen in common law jurisdictions. It usually refers to the total amount of capital provided by the articles of association, and a company may not need to issue all of its shares to shareholders or to the public. This type of capital is created largely for the purpose of satisfying the formality of registration.

2. Issued Capital

Issued capital usually refers to capital that has been subscribed by the shareholders. However, the subscription may not necessarily mean actual payment. In some jurisdictions, the subscription may be realized by way of paying instalments. Certainly, this gives contributors the flexibility to arrange their capital contributions. The shareholders shall always be liable for the total subscription not yet actually paid.

3. Paid-up Capital

Paid-up capital usually refers to the total amount of capital that has been actually paid up by the shareholders of a company. The minimum amount of capital is required by relevant law. As such, it is also called statutory capital.

The 1993 Company Law adopted the system of statutory capital (also known as statutory paid-up capital). This means that in most situations shareholders shall actually pay for all of their subscriptions before a company can be established. Because of this situation, statutory capital is sometimes called statutory registered capital or paid-up capital. On the other hand, because domestic companies and foreign-invested companies are handled by different Chinese laws and regulations, the requirements for capital contributions were different. However, the 2005 Company Law significantly changed this unequal treatment. The 2013 Amendment made a revolutionary change, which is introduced next.

4. Capital of Domestic Companies

As mentioned before, the 1993 Company Law requires that the total amount of capital provided by the articles of association be issued to and fully paid up by shareholders. If this condition is satisfied, the total amount of capital shall be examined by the relevant authorities. Among other items, the certificate of actual paid-in capital will be issued for the purpose of company registration.

5. Capital of Foreign-Invested Companies

Foreign-invested companies have been treated differently in China. One major difference is that the registered capital should be the total amount of capital subscribed by shareholders, but it needs not be fully paid right away. In practice, the Chinese government allows foreign investors to pay their capital contributions by way of instalment. The instalment payment is made subject to several limitations. For example, Article 4 of the Certain Regulations on the Subscription of Capital by the Parties to Sino-foreign Joint Equity Enterprises[1] states, "if the joint equity venture stipulates that capital is to be fully subscribed in one payment only, the respective joint

1. *Zhongwai Hezi Jingyin Qiye Heying Shuangfang Chuzi de Ruogan Guiding*, which was issued jointly by the Ministry of Foreign Economic Relations and Trade (now the Ministry of Commerce of the People's Republic of China) and the State Administration for Industry and Commerce on 1 January 1988.

venture parties shall settle their contributions in full within six months of the day of issue of the Business Licence. If the joint venture contract stipulates that capital is to be paid up in instalments, the first payment by the respective joint venture parties shall be no less than 15 per cent of the respective capital contribution of each party and shall be paid within three months of the day of issue of the Business Licence." This different treatment should be removed because different treatments have been applied to foreign and domestic investors. In comparison, the limited instalment system is better than the paid-up capital system because the former is more flexible and practicable.

Furthermore, in the case of a foreign-invested enterprise, the total amount of investment is a special term that refers to the capital necessary for a project. If the contribution by each partner cannot reach the total amount of investment, then more money may need to be borrowed. Therefore, the total amount of investment capital may include the registered capital plus debts. The more debts a company incurs, the higher the risk the creditors take. In order to avoid this situation, the Chinese government issued the Interim Regulations on the Ratio between the Registered Capital and the Total Amount of Investment for an Equity Joint Venture in 1987 via the National Administration of Industry and Commerce.[2]

---

2. Article 3 of the Provisional Regulations of the State Administration for Industry and Commerce on the Ratio between the Registered Capital and Total Investment of Sino-Foreign Joint Equity Enterprises states the following:

> The ratio between a Sino-foreign joint equity enterprise 's registered capital and its total investment shall comply with the following provisions:
>
> (1) Where the total investment of a Sino-foreign joint equity enterprise is US$3 million or less, its registered capital shall be at least 70 per cent of its total investment.
>
> (2) Where the total investment of a Sino-foreign joint equity enterprise is between US$3 million and US$10 million (US$10 million inclusive), its registered capital shall be at least half of its total investment. Where the total investment of such an enterprise is less than US$4.2 million, its registered capital may not be less than US$2.1 million.
>
> (3) Where the total investment of a Sino-foreign joint equity enterprise is between US$10 million and US$30 million (US$30 million inclusive), its registered capital shall be at least 40 per cent of its total investment. Where the total investment of such an enterprise is less than US$12.5 million, its registered capital may not be less than US$5 million.

Where the total investment of s Sino-foreign joint equity enterprise is more than US$30 million, its registered capital shall be at least one-third of its total investment. Where the total investment of such an enterprise is less than US$36 million, its registered capital may not be less than US$12 million.

6. Capital under the 2005 Company Law

Under the 2005 Company Law, the different treatment between domestic companies and foreign-investment companies has been abolished. Domestic companies could pay the capital contribution by way of instalment and the first down payment is allowed to be 20 per cent of the total registered capital.[3] This change is significant because shareholders are given the choice of paying less capital contributions and using their other money to make other investments. One may argue that allowing the payment in instalments substantially lowers the threshold of capital contribution.

7. Capital under the 2013 Company Law

The 2013 Company Law replaces instalment capital with the "subscribed capital system" (*renjiao ziben zhidu*). In other words, the amount of capital contribution is initially decided by a company to be established and all shareholders promise to subscribe a certain amount of capital contribution (in the situation of an LLC) or a certain amount of shares (in the situation of a JSC). The important thing is that a promise of subscription does not mean actual payment and the due date of payment is usually decided through relevant agreements. Thus, literally, a company could be registered with "zero capital", which is absolutely different from the authorized capital system.

II. LEGAL MEANINGS OF CORPORATE CAPITAL

It is commonly recognized that legal capital shall mean the following things.

Firstly, corporate capital is the physical basis of a business operation. Every company must possess a certain amount of capital in order to run its business. The more capital a company has, the more competitive power the company will acquire. For example, Walmart was once the number one commercial enterprise in the world. In 1996, it decided to have a foot in China by establishing its first supermarket in Shenzhen. In order to enter the Chinese market successfully, Walmart decided that it could give up all profits during the first three years. This is a typical idea of "first survival, then development, and then profits".[4] If Walmart did not have a strong capital capacity, it never could have thought about this plan at all.

3. The 2005 Company Law, Articles 26 and 81.
4. Li Derong, *The China Road of Transnational Corporation* (*Kuaguo gongsi de Zhongguo zhi lu*), The Jiuzhou Press (Beijing), 2002, p. 183.

Secondly, capital shows the creditability of a company. The continental law tradition is to emphasize secured transactions. Capital is the symbol of the financial capacity of a company. A company that has no substantial capital and no operational site is usually called a "briefcase company" (*pibao gongsi*). People are afraid of dealing with briefcase companies because there is a potential risk that these companies will be unable to fulfil their obligations and sometimes disappear with the money paid as a deposit.[5]

Thirdly, corporate capital is the legal limit of shareholders' liability. While the liability of a company is unlimited, the liability of its shareholders is limited to the amount of their capital contributions. Thus, the total amount of capital indicates the total liability of shareholders.

Fourthly, corporate capital is the basis for a company to pay its contractual obligations.[6] Thus, the company that cannot satisfy its contractual obligations will not only injure the legal interests of contractual parties but also face the danger of being bankrupted.

III. BASIC PRINCIPLES OF CORPORATE CAPITAL

1. The Principles of Identified Capital and Authorized Capital

(1) The Principle of Identified Capital

The same term is called the "principle of statutory capital". It refers to the situation where before the establishment of a company, the total amount of capital must be stipulated by the articles of association and must be fully paid by shareholders. Otherwise, the company cannot be established. Therefore, if a company wants to issue more shares, the articles of association must be amended in order to increase the amount of shares. In order to do so, special procedures must be followed. In most cases, a super majority of votes are required by relevant law in order to amend the articles of association.

The principle of identified capital has been established in continental law jurisdictions, where the emphasis is on secured transactions. According to this principle, corporate capital must be identified to a true and reliable

5. On the one hand, a briefcase company generates a negative image because it may have insufficient capital to deal in business with third parties and the third parties are likely to be cheated. On the other hand, the briefcase company is permitted in common law jurisdictions because third parties can effectively avoid being cheated by requiring the briefcase company to provide security for its business transactions.
6. In reality, the capital is usually part of a company's assets, as the assets include paid-up shares and debts (e.g., borrowed money).

extent in order to prevent any fraud during the establishment of a company or even to protect the *bona fide* third parties who deal with the company. However, this principle may create some difficulties in the establishment of a company. If the minimum amount of capital is too high, promoters may not be able to obtain immediate and sufficient money to establish a company. On the other hand, the high amount of capital may increase the promoters' responsibilities. The most important thing is that all of the contributions collected may not be fully used at the beginning of corporate operation. If the extra capital has to be stored without its effective use, it may be equivalent to a waste of money. According to the 1993 Company Law, however, regardless of what type of domestic company is chosen, the principle of identified capital was adopted and strictly enforced.[7] That is why this principle was heavily criticized and the 2005 Company Law adopted a compromised approach.

(2) The Principle of Authorized Capital

During the process of establishing a company, promoters shall write down in the articles of association the total amount of share capital. However, shareholders may need only to subscribe a certain amount of shares. The rest of the shares can be issued from time to time, based on the need for capital or the market. This principle is often seen in common law jurisdictions, especially in the United States and United Kingdom. Comparatively, this principle does not require shareholders to subscribe the whole amount of shares provided in the articles of association. Therefore, under this principle, people feel that it is much easier to establish a company and the BOD is allowed to issue shares from time to time based on the actual need. In fact, this avoids a situation where all of the capital should be stored in a company's account from the very beginning. Furthermore, since the articles of association have already authorized the total amount of shares, newly issued shares will not need to be approved by the SHM as long as the newly issued shares are within the total amount of shares originally stated in the articles of association. However, there is a downside to this principle. At the time of operation, the actual capital of a company may not meet the real operational situation, so there is a possibility of fraud and the legal interests of *bona fide* third parties may be seriously affected.

---

7. For detailed information, see Articles 23(1) and 78(1) of the 1993 Company Law.

(3) A Compromised Approach

Because of the downsides of both identified capital and authorized capital, more and more countries like Germany, France and Japan have started to adopt some new principles, i.e., the principle of recognized capital or the principle of compromised authorized capital. Firstly, according to the principle of compromised authorized capital, shareholders shall subscribe the total amount of shares issued by the company as a first issuance. A company is allowed to be established if this condition is satisfied. The first issuance of shares shall exceed a certain percentage of the total capital. For example, Article 166(3) of the Japanese Commercial Law provides that the first issuance of shares shall be no less than one quarter of the total capital. Secondly, according to the principle of recognized capital, the total capital must be provided by the articles of association and the shareholders must subscribe the total amount of shares. However, within a certain period of time after the company is formed, the BOD has the right to issue new shares within a certain range and no special resolution is required. For example, Articles 202–206 of the German Shareholding Law provide that within five years after the formation of a company, new shares that are within the limit of one half of the total capital can be issued, provided that the consent of the BOS is required. Obviously, these principles intend to avoid inflexibility on the one hand, yet ensure secured transactions on the other. The 2005 Company Law has adopted this compromised approach. It is obvious that Chinese legislators are not prepared to fully accept authorized capital.

(4) Zero Capital Approach

Chinese legislators have not in fact accepted authorized capital. One possible reason is that they are not prepared to give more power to the BOD and at the same time to give more flexibility to established companies. Under the 2013 Company Law, minimum capital is no longer stipulated and different companies may stipulate different capital through their articles of association. Thus, the Principle of Identified Capital is no longer crucial even though it may not be proper to say "being abolished".

2. Principle of Unchanging Capital

This principle usually prohibits companies from changing the total capital unless the articles of association have been modified in accordance with legal procedures.[8] However, after the zero capital system is adopted, this principle becomes less and less meaningful. Furthermore, this principle could be absorbed by the Principle of Maintaining Capital, which is discussed as follows.

3. Principle of Maintaining Capital

This principle refers to the situation where a company shall maintain assets similar to the capital in order to maintain the ability to pay its debts and protect the interests of creditors. This principle has been adopted by almost every country (or region) regardless of whether they are common law or continental law jurisdictions. In detail, this principle addresses three aspects.

(1) Prevention of Reducing Capital

National company law usually prohibits activities such as withdrawal of investments made by shareholders, purchase back of shares issued by the company and shares issued below their par value.[9] Many of these requirements under the Chinese company law have been subject to heavy criticism and are discussed in detail subsequently.

(2) Prevention of Distributing Profits in an Abusive Manner

As a general practice, every company shall establish a common reserve fund to expend on the development of the company or make up the losses of previous years. Also, many company laws require that companies cannot owe money over a certain amount. Many provisions of the Chinese Company Law reflect the spirit of this principle.[10]

(3) Impact of this Principle

In fact, this principle becomes more crucial when the zero capital system is adopted in China. Capital contribution subscription does not mean that the

---

8. Jiang Ping (ed.), *New Company Law Textbook* (*Xinbian gongsi fa jiaocheng*), The Law Press (Beijing), 1997, p. 73.
9. The Hong Kong Companies Ordinance (Cap. 622) officially abolishes the par value for two reasons: (1) it does not necessarily indicate the real value of the shares, and (2) it gives companies more flexibility to decide their share capital. See Companies Registry, "New Companies Ordinance: Frequently Asked Questions", retrieved from http://www.cr.gov.hk/en/companies_ordinance/faq_nopar.htm#01 on 15 October 2015.
10. For example, see the Company Law, Articles 35, 91, 127, 142, and 166.

shareholders' obligation to make real contributions is waived. The possible existence of false capital contributions, withdrawal of capital contributions and failure to make capital contributions will render the undercapitalization of a company. In order to protect the legitimate interests of creditors, the Principle of Maintaining Capital should be emphasized more. In the United States, piercing the corporate veil is a popular way to prevent undercapitalization. One investigation reveals that among 120 undercapitalization cases, 88 were allowed to pierce the corporate veil.[11] Thus, "undercapitalization is a factor frequently cited by commentators as part of a normative standard in piercing cases".[12] The practice in the United States reveals four things: (1) even under the authorized capital system, both shareholders and management personnel have the obligation to maintain the stability of capital; (2) in case of an undercapitalization situation, both shareholders and management personnel should disclose it in due course, otherwise piercing the corporate veil and imposing personal liability will be an effective resolution; (3) China should conduct further research on reasonable standards to measure undercapitalization; and (4) China should further consider whether to build the avoidance of undercapitalization into the director's duty of care.

IV. FORMATION OF CORPORATE CAPITAL

1. LLCs: Amount of Capital Contribution (*Chu zi er*)

In an LLC situation, the total amount of capital is formed by the total amount of capital contribution subscribed by shareholders. Different countries or regions may adopt different methods to divide the amount of capital contribution. It is possible to summarize them into three methods.[13]

(1) Each Shareholder Could Hold a Different Amount of Capital Contribution

In this approach, each shareholder can subscribe a specific amount of contribution, and the capital contribution is calculated on a percentage basis. In China, both company law and the equity joint venture law adopt this method. This method allows shareholders to subscribe their contributions

11. Robert B. Thompson, "Piercing the Corporate Veil: An Empirical Study", *Cornell Law Review*, Vol., 76. 1991, pp. 1036, 1063.
12. Ibid., p. 1065.
13. Xu Yan, *The Principle of Company Law (Gongsi fa yuanli)*, The Law Press (Beijing), 1997, pp. 318–19.

based on their economic conditions. However, the shortcoming of this method is that it is a bit difficult to calculate the votes.

(2) Each Shareholder Could Hold More Than One Equal Amount of Capital Contribution

In this approach, the capital contribution is divided into equal amounts, and each shareholder can subscribe one or several amounts of capital contribution. For example, Article 10 of the Japanese LLC Law provides that the capital contribution shall be divided into equal amounts for no less than 50,000 Japanese yen. In comparison with shareholders in a JSC situation, the shareholders of an LLC can only hold the certificate indicating their rights, but not the free transferable stocks. The compensatory advantage is that it is easy to count the votes.

(3) Each Shareholder Should Hold the Multiple of a Fixed Amount of Capital Contribution

In this approach, each amount of capital contribution must be the multiple amount of a basic figure. Each shareholder can subscribe only one multiple amount. For example, Article 5 of the German LLC Law states that each shareholder can subscribe only one amount; each amount may not be equal, but must be a multiple of 100 (Deutsche Mark). It is easy to count the votes, but the approach is different from that of a JSC.

It seems that the different amounts of capital contribution are a special feature of an LLC. Thus, the German model can be regarded as the best. Because Chinese company law is silent on which method can be used, it would be logical to state that this matter should be decided by companies through their articles of association.

2. JSCs: Stocks or Shares (*Gufen*)

The capital of a JSC is formed by the stocks (or shares). Each stock (or share) usually refers to the equal amounts of capital contribution. Most countries try to avoid the confusion by using stocks (or shares) in a JSC situation, but "amounts of capital contribution" in an LLC situation.

Under the Chinese Company Law, the term "share" (*gufen*) is used for JSCs only,[14] even though in practice people may use "*gufen*" in both LLC and

14. The Company Law, Article 3(2).

JSC situations. Furthermore, a stock takes the form of a valuable and transferable certificate (*gupiao*) held by shareholders. As such, shares are not necessarily equal to a company's capital, because in an authorized capital situation the first issuance may not represent all of the shares authorized by the articles of association. In any event, the stock is the symbol of a shareholder's legal status. Shareholders will exercise their rights or bear liabilities based on the amount of shares they control, such as votes, interests of shares and the distribution of any surplus.

V. ISSUANCE AND CLASSIFICATION OF SHARES

1. The Classification of Shares

(1) Common Shares and Preferred Shares

Shares can be divided into common and preferred shares based on different shareholders' rights. Common shares are the most popular or basic shares. Almost all jurisdictions give the holders of common shares the right to vote and furthermore prohibit the deprivation of such rights through the articles of association or the SHM. Therefore, the amount of common shares determines the amount of voting powers. Generally, holders of common shares have the following rights:

- unlimited voting rights;
- unlimited dividend possibilities; and
- unlimited rights on liquidation.

As for preferred shares, the shareholders' rights are usually provided by the articles of association. Furthermore, preferred shares can be divided into voting preferred shares, dividend preferred shares and surplus preferred shares.

Dividend preferred shares can be further divided into the following shares.

(a) Participating Preferred Shares and Non-participating Preferred Shares

Participating preferred shares are issued when shareholders participate in the surplus distributions with holders of common shares after they are paid as preferred shareholders and after the common shareholders have been paid dividends. Non-participating preferred shareholders only get dividends based on the amount of their preferred shares.

(b) Accumulative Preferred Shares and Non-accumulative Preferred Shares

The former occurs when a company cannot offer prearranged dividends to the preferred shareholders and thus the relevant portion of dividends should be paid off within the following year before the dividends are given to the holders of common shares. The latter occurs when a company makes no profits in the existing year, such that the holders of preferred shares are not paid. In the following year, this portion of dividends will not be made up to them.

The 2005 Company Law contains no special provision dealing with preferred shares. However, Article 131 states that the State Council may formulate separate regulations on the issue of other classes of share that are not provided for in this law. Fortunately, after a long wait, the State Council issued the Guiding Opinion Concerning the Pilot Implementation of Preferred Shares (hereinafter referred to as the "2013 Guiding Opinion") on 30 November 2013. Following the 2013 Guiding Opinion, the Administrative Rules on Pilot of Preferred Shares was released for public consultation. In practice, many companies have started issuing preferred shares. For example, the Bank of China announced on 31 August 2015 that preferred shares were issued.[15]

(2) Registered Shares and Bearer Shares

Registered shares are usually stock certificates that record the names of shareholders. Because of this, only the named shareholders can enjoy certain rights. According to the 2005 Company Law, if registered shares are issued, the company shall prepare a roster of the shareholders, in which the following items shall be recorded (Art. 131):

(a) the names, titles and domiciles of the shareholders;
(b) the number of shares held by each shareholder;
(c) the serial numbers of the share certificates held by each shareholder; and
(d) the date on which each shareholder obtained his or her shares.

15. The Bank of China announced that "with the approval of the CBRC (Yinjianfu [2014] No. 563) and CSRC (Zhengjianxuke [2014] No. 938), the Bank non-publicly issued RMB39.94 billion of offshore preference shares ('Offshore Preference Shares') on 23 October 2014. With the approval of the Hong Kong Stock Exchange, such Offshore Preference Shares have been listed on the Hong Kong Stock Exchange since 24 October 2014" [Preference Shares]. Retrieved from http://www.bankofchina.com/en/investor/ir4/201501/t20150114_4462474.html?keywords=prefered+shares on 15 October 2015.

Bearer shares, on the other hand, are certificates that do not record the names of the shareholders. Therefore, anyone holding bearer shares shall be able to enjoy certain provided rights. The important distinction between registered shares and bearer shares is that the transfer of bearer shares shall become effective immediately after a shareholder delivers the share certificate to a transferee.

Chinese company law provides both registered shares and bearer shares. It further provides that shares issued by a company to promoters or legal persons shall take the form of registered shares that shall state the names of the promoters or legal persons. Such shares may not be registered in other names or in the names of their representatives.[16] In case registered share certificates are stolen, lost or destroyed, the shareholder concerned may, in accordance with the procedure for publicizing a public notice for assertion of claims provided for under the Civil Procedure Law of the PRC, request a people's court to declare such share certificates void. After the nullification has been declared by the people's court in accordance with the aforesaid procedure, the shareholder concerned may apply to the company for a replacement of the share certificates (Art. 143).

Unlike the 1993 Company Law, which required the transfer of bearer shares to be executed at an established stock exchange (Art. 146), the existing company law is silent on this matter (Art. 140). It is understandable that this matter should be dealt with by the Chinese Securities Law, which states that shares, corporate bonds and other securities that have been lawfully approved for trading shall be quoted and traded on stock exchanges or other trading places approved by the State Council (Art. 39). This is to ensure that the transfer of shares is done fairly. Although the provisions do not specifically mention the term "over-the-counter", which is a popular method of trade in other jurisdictions, this type of trade has been authorized since 1987, when the Provisional Rules on Trade of Securities Over the Counter (*Zhengquan Guitai Jiaoyi Zanxing Guiding*) was issued by the Shanghai Branch Bank of the Bank of China. This is consistent with the term "other trading places" under the Securities Law.

(3) Shares with Par Value and Shares without Par Value

Shares with par value are easily understood. In this case, a stock certificate states a certain amount of money value. Shares without par value are also called "percentage shares", which means that the stock certificate does not

16. The Company Law, Article 129(2).

state the amount of money but indicates the percentage of the total company capital. Company law recognizes only shares with par value (Art. 127). However, the law does not state the minimum monetary amount for each stock certificate. The minimum monetary amount for stock certificates in Germany is about €25, while in France it is about €15. One may argue that Chinese company law is not yet sophisticated enough to consider this issue. However, one may also argue that this gives an issuer more flexibility to decide the minimum monetary amount. As will be mentioned, it is very easy to defeat the purpose of par value and there is a trend toward par value being abolished (for example, Hong Kong's new company law has abolished the par value concept).

(4) Shares with Voting Power and Shares without Voting Power

Shares with voting power can be further divided into common voting shares (i.e., one share has one vote), multiple voting shares (i.e., one share may have more than two votes; usually this type of share is given to special shareholders such as directors) and limited voting shares (i.e., the voting power of the shares may be limited). Shares without voting power, such as non-outstanding shares held by the company, mean that the shareholders have no voting power.

Currently, even though Chinese company law provides only the principle of "one share, one vote", this does not mean that other types of shares will not be created in accordance with Article 131. Apparently, China needs time to develop other special types of shares or possibly give this freedom to companies.

(5) Convertible or Non-convertible Shares

So far, the Chinese company law provides only that company bonds may be converted into shares. However, it does not provide that shares can be converted into company bonds. Practically, it makes no sense to have shares converted into company bonds. In addition, it may be too complicated to do so.

(6) Special Classification of Shares in China

(a) A Shares, B Shares, H Shares, and N Shares

In China, the classification of shares does not follow the international practice due to special considerations, which are discussed as follows. In general, shares in China can be divided into A shares, B shares, H shares, N shares, and so on.

Originally, A shares were available for Chinese citizens only, B shares were subscribed by foreigners, H shares were traded over the Hong Kong Stock Exchange, N shares were traded over the New York Stock Exchange, S shares were listed on the Singapore Stock Exchange, and T shares were listed on the Tokyo Stock Exchange.

Initially, foreign investors who purchased B shares might have also been able to gain control over the target company. An example was the purchase of B shares offered by the Jiangling Motor Corporation Ltd by the American Ford Motor Company and the acquisition of the Beijing Light Bus Company by an alliance between Isuzu and Itochu in 1995. In the former case, about 80 per cent B shares were purchased, which amounted to 25 per cent of the total shares.

From the beginning, B shares were regarded as a temporary measure.[17] The combination of A and B shares is just a timing issue. This conclusion is supported by subsequent developments. On 4 June 2002, additional rules were published by the CSRC, including Rules on Establishing Foreign Involved Securities Companies (*Waizi Cangu Zhengquan Gongsi Sheli Guize*) and Rules on Establishing Foreign Involved Funds Management Companies (*Waizi Cangu Jijin Guanli Gongsi Sheli Guize*). This indicated that there was an irrevocable trend towards opening the financial industry to foreign investors. In October 2002, the CSRC published the Measures of Governing Takeover of Listed Companies (*Shangshi Gongsi Shougou Guanli Banfa*). According to this law, there is no limitation as to the subject of takeovers of listed companies. Foreign investors are permitted to take over A-share listed companies and purchase State shares and legal person shares of non-listed companies. Recently, many listed companies have started to purchase back their B shares.[18] Apparently, the reform direction is seeking to phase out B shares.[19]

17. Gu Gongyun, *Research on Legal Issues of the Newly Emerged Market Economy* (*Xinxing shichang zhong de falü wenti yanjiu*), The World Book Press (Shanghai), 1997, p. 142.
18. "Two Ways to Solve the Problem of the B Shares Market" (*Jiejue B gu shichang wenti de liang da tujing*), retrieved from http://news.xinhuanet.com/fortune/2009-06/26/content_11603304.htm on 16 October 2015.
19. "The Existing Situation of B Shares and Reforming Suggestions" (*Woguo B gu shichang xianzhuang he gaige jianyi*), retrieved from http://company.cnstock.com/company/scp_dsy/tcsy_rdgs/201401/2866849.htm on 16 October 2015.

(b) State Shares (*Guojia gu*), Legal Person Shares (*Faren gu*), Individual Shares (*Geren gu*), and Foreign Capital Shares (*Waizi gu*)

State shares are issued and held by the government. When an SOE issues shares, a portion of the shares must be held by either a government organization or by a holding company authorized by the government.

Legal person shares may be further divided into five different shares: (1) State-owned legal person shares are not owned by the state directly, but rather by an entity that is itself owned by the state, and are labelled "state-owned legal person shares". For example, trust and investment companies and securities companies own this type of share. The only difference between state shares and state-owned legal person shares is that the holder of state shares must be a government organization or a company with governmental functions, and the holder of state-owned legal person shares may not be a governmental organ. (2) Collective enterprise legal person shares are a class of share held by collective enterprises, of which there are three types. One type of collective enterprise is owned by local governments. A second type has assets derived from the state but, for policy reasons, is deemed not to be owned by the state. Collective enterprises of the third type use capital invested by individuals but attach themselves to a supervisory administrative department for purposes such as gaining tax benefits, licences or other benefits available only to public enterprises. (3) Private enterprise legal person shares include LLCs financed entirely by private individuals. (4) Foreign-invested enterprise legal person shares are available to foreign-invested enterprises that have received legal person status. Currently, three types of shares are authorized under special foreign investment laws such as the Sino-foreign Equity Joint Venture Law, the Sino-foreign Joint Co-operation Law, and the Wholly Foreign Owned Enterprises Law. (5) Institutional legal person shares are owned by institutions with legal person status that have raised funds from individuals. Examples include trade unions, the Communist Youth League, and the Women's Federation.

Individual shares are held by Chinese citizens. They are further divided into "internal employee shares" (*neibu zhigong gu*), which are available to the employees of the issuing company, or "public individual shares" (*shehui geren gu*), which are offered to the general public. It is important to note that internal employee shares were once banned. One author explained the reasons for this as follows:

> In the late 1980s and early 1990s hundreds of restructuring firms issued shares to their employees. These were either sold or distributed in lieu of wages. Some of these 'employee shares' found their way onto the open market—others were allocated to senior management

> and sold on to the market for personal profit. This leakage created a problem since the companies involved usually had not obtained any approval from the regulatory authorities for a public share issue. When the two stock exchanges were established in December 1990 none of these shares could therefore be legally registered to trade there. During the 1990s the CSRC oversaw the formal restructuring of many of the firms involved and they have all now either made a standardized public share issue or have bought back their shares. Issuance of employee shares was banned by the State Council in June 1994 (a ban that was mostly effective), and the category is now dying out.[20]

However, evidence shows that employee shares do have certain advantages and are commonly seen in other jurisdictions. The 2005 Company Law also allows share buybacks for the purpose of awarding employees (Art. 143.3, now Art. 142.3 of the 2013 Amendment). That is why employee shares are still seen today in many enterprises[21] and should become a good research topic.

2. The Problems of Classification

The establishment of multiple classes of stock within a single corporation raises certain questions about corporate governance that are important yet poorly answered. Information and regulations explaining the relative rights of different classes are sparse.

(1) The Convertibility of Different Shares

China's security law and regulations do not have clear provisions explaining whether shares of one class can be converted into shares of a different class, either by the corporation or by the holders of the securities. Companies that are controlled by the State cannot freely convert legal person shares into individual shares, because doing so is considered as a special privilege (although some companies apparently have converted shares surreptitiously). No evidence indicates that conversion in the opposite direction, from individual shares into legal person shares is allowed, nor is it likely that shares held by foreign investors can be converted into legal person

20. Stephen Green, "The Privatization is Two-Step at China's Listed Firms", retrieved from http://papers.ssrn.com/sol3/papers.cfm?abstract_id=598277 on 16 October 2015.
21. Xie Lian, "Banks in Hangzhou Secretly Sell Employees' Shares for the Purpose of Listing Their A Shares" (*Hangzhou yinhang qiaoqiao paoshou zhigonggu wei A gu shangshi saoqing zhang'ai*), retrieved from http://finance.sina.com.cn/stock/s/20080812/08555190249.shtml on 16 October 2015.

shares or State shares. Hopefully, this situation will change following the further reform of B shares.

(2) Voting Powers or Rights of Different Shares

Unfortunately, Chinese company law does not indicate how the holders of A, B and H shares and other stock classes may exercise their rights. In regards to voting rights, the United States corporate practice is that each class votes separately, and a majority of each class is necessary to approve major or important decisions. China may follow the United States model or instead treat all shares, regardless of class, as one large constituency.

3. Comments on Classification of Shares

China's system of classifying shares is understandable in light of the government's intention to avoid full privatization, but leaves the owners of many classes of shares in an uncertain and problematic situation. The issues involved control the internal operation of a corporation and the relationship between each class. Interestingly, Li Yining, an economics expert at Beijing University, once proposed that the trading of the three classes of share should be executed in three separate securities markets, defined by the characteristics of the investors. Legal person shares, for example, would be traded only between legal persons. This view is no longer valid because there have been some new developments.

Trading only within each class, however, would eventually destroy the incentive of individuals and foreign investors to invest more money in the securities markets. Those investors would be unable to foresee how the majority shareholders would treat them as minority shareholders, and would recognize that they have neither protection nor a voice in the decision-making process.

4. Issuance of Shares

(1) Characteristics of Shares

To have any rights, shares must be: (a) authorized (permitted by the articles of association); (b) issued (sold by the corporation to anyone else); and (c) outstanding (still held by someone other than the corporation). Similar principles are implemented in China. Obviously, authorization alone may not be sufficient because the issuance of shares is subject to close regulation by the CSRC.

(2) *Consideration for Shares*

(a) Traditional Rules in the United States

The forms of consideration can be money, property (either tangible or intangible property), and services previously performed for the corporation. Services prior to incorporation or promissory notes or contracts for future services are not good consideration.

(b) Modern Trends in the United States

The Revised Model Business Corporation Act imposes no formal restrictions on the form or amount of consideration. The evaluation of a consideration is done by the BOD. In order to do so, directors are subject to the normal fiduciary duties.

In China, as mentioned before, the consideration for shares is limited to currency, goods, intellectual property rights, land use rights, and so on. The precondition is that those non-cash properties could be evaluated and legally transferable.[22]

Other problems concerning the amount of consideration for shares arise from the use of tangible and intangible property. Directors may assign an excessively high value to certain property received in exchange for shares. This may dilute the value of other public investors' shares, which they have purchased at full value. Because foreigners often have the assets that Chinese companies need, they are particularly well placed to take advantage of a corporation by demanding excessively high valuations for property contributed in exchange for shares.

Conversely, the state worries that the value assigned to its contribution will be too low and will unfairly transfer some of the nation's wealth to a private or foreign entity. Private entities, and even local governments, have reaped windfalls as state-owned assets are sold.

The United States and China have chosen contrasting solutions to this problem. In the United States, a corporation's BOD assigns values to assets, subject to a judicial review only in the case of fraud. China has opted for greater regulation. Companies may issue shares for non-cash considerations, including goods, intellectual property rights, land-use rights, and so on, but they must appraise all such considerations in accordance with laws and regulations. Pursuant to these regulations, only specialized institutions and their certified public valuers are assigned to perform the appraisal. The BOD does not have such power. Under the 1993 Company Law, contributions in the forms of intellectual propriety rights and land-use rights cannot exceed

22. The Company Law, Article 27.

20 per cent of the total registered capital (Art. 24). The 2005 Company Law changed this limitation by allowing non-cash considerations to close to 70 per cent of the registered capital (Art. 27.3). Finally, under the 2013 Company Law, such as limitation has been totally abolished.

5. Par Value

The financial provisions of the Chinese company law also apply the concept of par, or face value, for stock. Furthermore, Chinese corporations cannot issue shares for less than par value (Art. 127). This provision ensures that all investors pay the same amount per share and hence affects an element of equity. In fact, a simple and age-old device called "low par" can readily and routinely defeat this approach. A stock is called "low par" when the par value is lower than the price received. To illustrate, a corporation may set par at $1, or even 1 cent, and then sell the shares to the public at $20 per share, their fair market value. The corporation then sells additional shares of the same class to certain favoured insiders at only $5 per share. Because both sales generate at least par value, the company has fulfilled the statutory requirement and fully circumvented the law's intent to ensure that all shareholders are treated equally. In China, low par used to be one possible choice because the 1993 Company Law originally required that shares issued above par should be subject to the approval of the relevant authority (Art. 131).[23]

It must be noted that the concept of par should be reconsidered. The Anglo-American Corporation Law traditionally recognized par as a way to protect both the investors in and creditors of a company. The modern trend in American company law, however, has been to abandon the concept of par and all of its elaborate restrictions in recognition of serious conceptual flaws in its structure. For example, the Revised Model Business Corporation Act now adopted throughout the United States does not assign any legal significance whatsoever to par.[24] Hong Kong again abolished par value recently.

23. It must be noted that on 28 August 2004, the Eleventh Session of the Tenth NPCSC amended Article 28 of the 1998 Securities Law and Article 131(2) of the 1993 Company Law, which excuse the approval requirement when shares are issued above par.
24. Robert C. Art, "Corporate Shares and Distributions in a System Beyond Par: Financial Provisions of Oregon's New Corporation Act", *Willamette Law Review*, Vol. 24, 1998, p. 204.

6. Procedures for Issuing Shares (Public Offer)

(1) The Governing Law and Regulations in China

Prior to 28 December 1998, when the National People's Congress Standing Committee adopted the Chinese Securities Law, securities markets were controlled by various rules (*fagui*), regulations (*guiding*), measures (*banfa*), notices (*tongzhi*), guidelines (*zhiyin*), and so on. The most important of these legal documents was the Interim Rules Regarding Management of Stock Issuance and Exchange (*Gupiao Faxing yu Jiaoyi Guanli Zanxing Guiding*—The Interim Rules) issued by the State Council on 22 April 1993. It was said that the relationship of the Securities Law[25] with the extensive body of securities market rules and regulations, which emerged over the last decade, is not perfectly clear.[26] Article 5 of the Securities Law provides that the issuance and trading activities of securities shall comply with relevant laws and administrative regulations. Presumably, the existing rules and regulations are invalid if they contradict the provisions of the existing Securities Law. At this stage, it is safe to say that some provisions of various rules may still be applicable.

(2) Procedures for Public Offer

The Securities Law not only defines what a "Public Offer (*Gongkai faxing*)" is,[27] but also outlines the preconditions for issuing new shares:

(a) the company has a structural organization in sound conditions and good operation;
(b) the company is capable of continuous profit making and in good financial standing;
(c) the company is not found to have false records in its financial and accounting documents and has committed no seriously illegal acts in the last three years; and

25. The 1998 Securities Law was further amended in 2005, 2013, and 2014, respectively. For the purpose of convenience, the collective term "the Securities Law" is used in this book.
26. Roman Tomasic and Jian Fu, "The Securities Law of the PRC: An Overview" (Draft), p. 1.
27. In order to qualify a public offer, three conditions must be satisfied: (1) securities are offered to unspecific targets, (2) securities are offered to more than 200 specific targets accumulatively, and (3) other offers allowed by the law and administrative regulations. See Article 10 of the Securities Law.

(d) the company satisfies other conditions as stipulated by the securities regulatory authority under the State Council and approved by the State Council.[28]

The Securities Law is silent on what conditions should be satisfied if an enterprise (normally an SOE) wants to convert into a JSC for the purpose of going public. This may indicate that a large-scale conversion has been completed, and most SOEs have been restructured one way or other.

The Securities Law states that after making a decision to ratify or examine and approve the issuance of securities, the relevant authorities can reverse the decision if they subsequently determine that the issuance is not in conformity with law or administrative regulations.[29] In China, the CSRC went unchallenged for its decisions not to approve applications for share issuing until 2000. A substantial step was taken to allow a judicial review of the CSRC's administrative decisions.[30] This was a significant development after China's accession to the World Trade Organization.

The Hainan Kaili Central Development Joint Stock Company (hereinafter referred to as the "Kaili Company") applied to issue A shares. The application, however, was denied by the CSRC on the basis of "making false accounting data". The Kaili Company did not accept the decision and believed that the CSRC violated the procedures for approval and examination. On 29 April 2000, the Beijing Intermediate People's Court accepted the complaint. On 18 December 2000, the Court made its judgment and ruled that the CSRC violated the relevant law by returning the A share application materials submitted by the Kaili Company. The CSRC was ordered to restore the procedures for approval and examination of the Kaili Company's A share application. In January 2001, the CSRC appealed the judgment. In the CSRC's view, it was in charge of national securities and futures markets. It was authorized to decide the procedures for share issuing in accordance with the relevant laws and to interpret those procedures. It further argued that the judgment to restore the approval and examination procedures for the Kaili Company's application was "not realistic and could

28. The Securities Law, Article 13.
29. Ibid., Article 26. However, it is important to know that the Decision of the Standing Committee of the National People's Congress on Authorizing the State Council to Adjust the Relevant Applicable Provisions of the Securities Law of the People's Republic of China in the Implementation of Stock Issuance Registration System Reform was issued on 27 December 2015 and implemented on 1 March 2016. It is foreseen that under the registration system companies will be given more freedom to make issuances to the public, but the relevant authority will conduct post-supervision seriously. In any event, it is too early to evaluate this new system.
30. Ibid., Article 235.

not be implemented". On 5 July 2001, the Beijing Higher People's Court ruled that the judgment was upheld. Thus, the CSRC had to face an embarrassing situation: according to the judgment, the CSRC had to re-examine the listing application made by the Kaili Company and make the relevant decision within sixty days. It was the first time that the CSRC had been challenged and ordered to examine the application in accordance with the relevant laws.[31]

(3) Public Offering Methods

If an issuer wants to issue shares to unspecific targets, the shares should be underwritten by securities companies. Generally, there are two methods by which public offerings can be made: "best effort underwriting" and "firm commitment underwriting". In the case of "best effort underwriting", the securities company sells securities as the agent of the issuer and, at the end of the underwriting period, returns to the issuer all of the securities that remain unsold. "Firm commitment underwriting" occurs when the securities company purchases, pursuant to an agreement, all of the securities to be issued by the issuer or whereby it purchases at the end of the underwriting period all of the securities that remain after sale.[32]

7. Trade of Shares

As discussed before, trade of shares shall normally be carried out within the stock exchanges or other places approved by the State Council.[33] Those shares should be traded in the form of open, centralized, competitive bidding. Furthermore, securities shall be traded in the form of spot securities.

8. Disclosure of Relevant Information

(1) Disclosure When Issuing Shares

All of the issuers, promoters and directors must ensure that all of the released information is authentic, accurate, and complete, and it may not contain any false record, misleading statement or major omission. Securities institutions shall also guarantee the same matters. With regard to information

---

31. Wang Chuanhui, *New Textbook on Commercial Law* (*Xinbian shangfa jiaocheng*), Tsinghua University Press (Beijing), 2005, p. 71.
32. The Securities Law, Article 28.
33. Ibid., Article 39.

involving accounting, legal evaluation or asset evaluation, all of the relevant professionals should ensure that their documents are accurate and not misleading. According to Chinese regulations, lawyers who offer assistance to the issuing of shares must be specialized in securities and permitted to practise securities laws. The relevant securities authorities will examine all of the documents to be released and allow those documents to be published in appointed publications.

Three types of information shall be disclosed: economic information (financial reports or auditing reports), non-economic information (name, age, gender, position, term of position, specialties, remuneration, bonus, welfare and benefits, securities amounts of all of the current directors, supervisors, and senior officers), and soft information (such as the operation of funds, foreseeable profits, the nearest development plan of the company, and so on).

(2) Continued Disclosure of Information

The purpose of continued disclosure is to ensure that all investors have full knowledge of the listed companies to make good investment choices. Usually, the relevant information should be submitted to the relevant securities authorities and to certain appointed media. The disclosure is usually done by way of midterm reports, annual reports, and publication of major events.

Within two months counted from the ending date of the first half of each fiscal year, the listed companies shall submit a midterm report. Five items are required:

(a) the financial statement and operational situation of the company;
(b) major lawsuits concerning the company;
(c) changes in the shares and corporate bonds already issued;
(d) major issues submitted to the general meeting of shareholders for examination and review; and
(e) other matters defined by the securities regulatory authority.[34]

Within four months counted from the ending date of each fiscal year, the listed companies shall submit an annual report to the relevant securities authorities. The annual report is usually audited by a registered accountant. Five items are also required:

34. Ibid., Article 65.

(a) the general situation of the company;
(b) the financial statement and operational situation of the company;
(c) a brief introduction of the directors, supervisors, managers, and senior executives of the company and information on their holding of shares;
(d) information on the situation of the stocks or corporate bonds already issued, including a list of the top ten shareholders holding the largest proportions of shares of the company and the quantities of shares held by them;
(e) the actual controllers of the company; and
(f) other matters defined by the securities regulatory authority.[35]

Major events refer to all of the events that will affect the market price of shares issued. As the 2005 Securities Law requires, if there occurs a major event that may have relatively great impacts on the trading price of shares of a listed company but has not been known by investors, the listed company concerned shall immediately submit an interim report of information relevant to the major event to the securities regulatory authority and the securities exchange and shall proclaim the report as well. According to Article 67 of the Securities Law, major events usually include the following items:

(a) a major change in the company's business guidelines or scope of business;
(b) a decision made by the company concerning a major investment or major asset purchase;
(c) conclusion by the company of an important contract that may have an important effect on the company's assets, liabilities, rights, interests or business results;
(d) incurrence by the company of a major debt or default on an overdue major debt;
(e) incurrence by the company of a major deficit or incurrence of a major loss;
(f) a major change in the external conditions of the company's production or operation;
(g) a change in any director, not less than one third of supervisors or the manager of the company;
(h) a considerable change in the shares of the shareholders holding not less than 5 per cent of the company's shares or any of the company's actual controllers, or a considerable change in the situation that they control the company;

35. Ibid., Article 66.

(i) a decision made by the company to reduce its capital, merge, divide, dissolve or apply for bankruptcy;
(j) major litigation involving the company, or lawful cancellation by a court of a resolution adopted by the shareholders' general meeting or the BOD;
(k) investigation of the company for suspected crimes or compulsory measures imposed on the directors, supervisors, and senior management personnel due to their suspected crimes; or
(l) other events specified in laws or administrative regulations.

The Interim Rules provide that directors, supervisors, and senior management personnel of a listed company who hold common shares in the company shall report to the securities regulatory authority and the stock exchange and their own company concerning the shares they hold. If there are any changes in the shares they hold, the report should be made within ten days of the date of the change. All of the persons concerned have a duty to report to the relevant authorities within six months after quitting or leaving their jobs.[36]

Furthermore, an issuer has an affirmative duty to clear up irrelevant rumours. When there is misleading information that possibly affects the price of stocks, a company shall take affirmative steps to clarify the facts.

The Securities Law provides legal liabilities to those who fail to disclose information. The legal liabilities include not only administrative (Art. 193) and criminal liabilities (Art. 231), but also civil liabilities. If there is a false record, misleading statement or major omission that causes losses to investors in the course of securities trading, the issuer or the listed company shall bear civil liability for the losses. Joint liability is applied to the directors, supervisors, senior executives, and other personnel if they are directly responsible for the false record, misleading statement or major omission (Art. 69).

Certainly, there is room for further improvement. The Securities Law should be improved in the near future in three aspects. The first aspect would be to broaden the liability bearers to directors, managers, and other important personnel, as well as accountants, lawyers, and technical personnel who can gain the relevant information. The second aspect would be to impose strict liability on issuing companies or promoters, but keep the burden of proof on the victims if they want to lodge claims against other personnel. The final aspect would be to allow victims to either rescind the contract and to obtain remedies or to obtain the remedies even if they do

36. The Interim Rules, Article 62.

not want to rescind the contract. As for the remedies, they shall usually be limited to actual losses.

VI. COMPANY BONDS

The term "company bonds" shall mean valuable securities issued by a company in accordance with statutory procedures. The bonds usually have the following characteristics:

- they are valuable securities;
- the holder of the valuable securities is a creditor of the company;
- they are issued in accordance with statutory procedures; and
- they should be repaid together with interest within a definite time limit.

1. Conditions for Issuing Bonds

(1) Every Company Can Issue Bonds Now

Under the 1993 Company Law, only JSCs, WSCs, and LLCs invested in and established by two or more SOEs or two or more other State-owned investment entities could issue company bonds (Art. 159). In accordance with this provision, other LLCs were excluded from issuing bonds. On the one hand, the issuance of bonds may require companies to have sound economic health because investors need to be ensured of their capacity to make repayment. On the other hand, if this approach is taken, small-sized LLCs are deprived of the opportunity to invite capital contributions from potential investors. The existing Company Law seems to resolve this problem by allowing all companies to issue bonds if they meet the conditions.

(2) Preconditions for Issuing Bonds

The Company Law simply leaves this matter to be regulated by the Securities Law, which outlines several preconditions for issuing bonds (Art. 16):

(a) in the case of a JSC, net assets shall be no less than ¥30 million, and in the case of an LLC, net assets shall be no less than ¥60 million;
(b) the aggregate total amount of the bonds cannot exceed 40 per cent of the company's net assets;
(c) the average distributable profits for the last three years must be sufficient to pay one year of interest on the company bonds;
(d) the funds to be raised must be invested in accordance with State industrial policy;

(e) the bond interest rate must not exceed the level determined by the State Council; and
(f) other conditions specified by the State Council

However, a company shall not make another issue of corporate bonds if (1) the corporate bonds of the previous issue have not been fully subscribed for; (2) it is a fact that the company has defaulted on, or deferred repayment of, the principal and the payment of interest of its previously issued corporate bonds or its debts, and such a default or deferment persists; or (3) the company, in violation of the provisions of this law, changes the purpose of the funds raised through the public issue of corporate bonds.[37]

2. Procedure for Issuing Bonds

Usually, if a JSC or an LLC wishes to issue company bonds, its BOD shall formulate a proposal to issue such bonds, and a pertinent resolution shall be adopted by the SHM. If a WSC wishes to issue company bonds, a decision to that effect shall be made by the organization authorized by the State to make investments or the department authorized by the State. Finally, the application for issuing bonds must be approved before the issuance of bonds.[38]

3. Conflict of Law and Regulations

Currently in China, laws and regulations on the same subject may conflict with each other due to the obvious reason that regulations are usually made by various authorities with different interests. For example, Article 161(2) of the 1993 Company Law stated clearly that the total accumulated amount of a company's bonds should not exceed 40 per cent of its net assets. On 25 March 1997, the Securities Committee of the State Council published the Interim Methods Governing Convertible Company Bonds. Article 9 provided that at the time when a company issued convertible company bonds, the total accumulated amount of company bonds, including the bonds to be issued, should not exceed 40 per cent of the net assets at that time, and the total accumulated amount of bonds issued should not exceed 40 per cent of the company's expected net assets. However, on 25 December 2001, the CSRC issued the Notice on Improving Task of Issuing Convertible Company Bonds by Listed Companies, which provides a different version. Article 1(2) states, "before a listed company issues convertible company

37. The Securities Law, Article 18.
38. Ibid., Article 10.

bonds, the total accumulated amount of company bonds shall not exceed 40 per cent of the company's net assets; after this issue, the total accumulated amount of company bonds shall not exceed 80 per cent of the company's net assets. The company's net assets shall mean the data reflected in the last year's annual report which was audited."

In October 2003, the Merchant's Bank decided to issue ¥10 billion in convertible company bonds. This decision was made by the SHM. According to the annual report of the Merchant's Bank in 2002, its net assets were ¥16 billion. This means that the Merchant's Bank could only issue ¥6.4 billion in accordance with the 1993 Company Law and the Interim Methods Governing Convertible Company Bonds. The issue of ¥10 billion in bonds constituted a violation. On the other hand, in line with the Notice on Improving Task of Issuing Convertible Company Bonds by Listed Companies, the Merchant's Bank could issue ¥12.8 billion.[39]

The underlying problem was whether the "total accumulated amount of company bonds" included the total amount of the issue.

Before answering this question, it is important to note that in China the 1993 Company Law was a high-level law, which was regarded as a general law over the relevant regulations, such as the Interim Methods Governing Convertible Company Bonds and the Notice on Improving Task of Issuing Convertible Company Bonds by Listed Companies. The plain language of Article 161(2) indicates clearly that the "total accumulated amount of company bonds" shall include the total amount of this issue. The purpose of the 40 per cent rule is to prevent an issuing company from taking risks that are too high, and this is consistent with the spirit of secured transactions. Contrarily, the 80 per cent rule would create an apparent and imminent danger to the issuing company. It is unbelievable that such a legal conflict would be created today despite China announcing its intention to build up the country with the rule of law. Finally, even though the 2005 Company Law was amended and relevant provisions were moved to the 2005 Securities Law, those provisions are basically the same as those of the 1993 Company Law, and the conflicting problem remains unsolved.

VII. DISTRIBUTION OF PROFITS

Profits are the net income of a company. Before profits can be distributed to shareholders, there is a need to use the profits to cover losses of the

39. "48 Shareholders Say They Have the Right to Sue the Merchant Bank", retrieved from http://old.jfdaily.com/gb/node2/node17/node33/node20724/node20730/userobject1ai302455.html on 27 November 2015.

preceding year and to fill the common reserve (*gongjijin*) in order to maintain the healthy financial condition of the company. The system of keeping a common reserve is believed to have been created in France in the nineteenth century and has been adopted worldwide. It must be noted that in continental law jurisdictions it is mandatory to allocate a certain percentage of profit to the common reserve. For example, in Germany and France, companies are required to allocate 5 per cent of their profit to the statutory common reserve. On the other hand, allocation of a certain percentage of profits to the common reserve is discretionary, i.e., the allocation is not directly required by company law and rather it is the decision of the BOD based on operational conditions. Thus, in common law jurisdictions, there is no difference between the mandatory common reserve and discretionary common reserve.[40]

In order to guide the distribution of earned profits, the 2005 Company Law takes a similar approach to the company laws of Japan or Taiwan and requires the following steps to be taken.

(1) If a company has losses from the preceding year, such losses shall be made up from the profit of the current year.
(2) After the losses have been recovered, the company is obliged to pay income tax.
(3) The company must then allocate profit to the mandatory common reserve (*fading gongjijin*), i.e., 10 per cent of the profit must be allocated. However, a company shall no longer be required to make allocations to their mandatory common reserve once the aggregate amount of such a reserve exceeds 50 per cent of the registered capital (Art. 166).
(4) In addition, the company can allocate profit to the discretionary common reserve (*renyi gongjijin*). However, since this allocation is discretionary and will affect the interests of shareholders, the approval of the SHM must be sought.
(5) When all of the preceding requirements are satisfied, the company is permitted to distribute profits by adopting two methods. In the case of an LLC, the distribution shall be made in proportion to the shareholders based on their capital contributions. In the case of a JSC, the distribution shall be made in proportion to the shareholders based on their shareholdings (Art. 166).

40. Tang Dehua (ed.), *Legal Practice Concerning the Establishment and Internal Operations of Joint Stock Companies* (*Gufen youxian gongsi sheli yu neibu yunzuo falü shiwu*) (*Part Three*), The People's Court Press (Beijing), December 1998, pp. 817–18.

Under the 2005 Company Law, the mandatory common reserve is established for two main purposes. Firstly, the mandatory common reserve makes up the losses because the relevant tax law allows a company to make up losses suffered in the preceding year before paying income tax; if the losses are more than the profits before paying tax, they can be made up using the mandatory common reserve fund. Secondly, the mandatory common reserve increases the capital because after profit is allocated to the mandatory common reserve and discretionary common reserve (usually only for special purposes), part of the money from the mandatory common reserve can be converted into capital; the funds, however, remaining in such a reserve shall amount to not less than 25 per cent of the registered capital (Art. 168).

The 1993 Company Law further required that 5 per cent to 10 per cent of the profit should be allocated to the mandatory provident fund (*fading gongjijin*). Normally, the mandatory provident fund is available for the use of the collective welfare of the companies' staff and workers, such as dormitories, children's gardens, and so on.[41] People believe that this mandatory provident fund was a special character of the 1993 Company Law because it was impossible to see this fund in other common law jurisdictions or continental law jurisdictions. In reality, only a few scholars voted for this type of fund based on the reason that China is a socialist country and the welfare of companies' staff and workers should be improved if the economic situation of the companies is improved. However, most scholars voted against this fund because they believed that it would be likely to jeopardize the shareholders' expected economic interest. One representative view is that the regulation of profit allocation is but a pale reflection of the traditional role Chinese enterprises played in providing lifetime employment, housing, medical care, retirement, and other social services to its workers. Requirements for "welfare funds" and regulation of the use of "common reserve funds" appear to be oriented towards maintaining the traditional social functions and responsibilities of enterprises for their workers. The profit allocation requirements are not onerous, but to date there is no evidence that the State is substituting such requirements for the more encompassing, traditional obligation of State enterprises to provide social services to their work units. If Chinese corporations are to develop into independent, profit-maximizing economic entities based on the international model, they must be relieved of their social welfare burdens.[42]

41. The 1993 Company Law, Article 180.
42. Robert C. Art and Minkang Gu, "China Incorporated: The First Corporation Law of the PRC", *The Yale Journal of International Law*, Vol. 20, No. 2, 1995, p. 306.

Fortunately enough, the 2005 Company Law addresses the concerns of majority scholars and has abolished the mandatory provident fund.

The remaining problem is that the mandatory common reserve or, if necessary, discretionary common reserve is derived mainly from the premiums gained when a company issues shares for more than their face value (Art. 167). However, there is no specific language dealing with the order of using these funds in case a company needs to make up losses. In continental law jurisdictions, the common practice is to use the following order: the discretional common reserve is used firstly and the mandatory common reserve is used subsequently. It is obvious that the 2005 Company Law (as well as the 2013 Amendment) fail to follow this approach.

VIII. REMAINING ISSUES

1. Share Repurchase

Under Article 142 of the Company Law, a company cannot repurchase its shares issued unless the repurchase is made for special purposes. The first reason is to reduce capital. The second reason is that A Company may merge with B Company, which holds shares in A Company. The third reason is to award the employees of the company with shares. However, in this situation, the shares purchased shall not exceed 5 per cent of the total shares already issued by the company. Furthermore, the funds used to make the purchase are the after-tax profits and the shares purchased by the company shall be transferred to the employees within one year. The fourth reason is that the shares of the shareholders who raise their objections to the company's resolution on a merger or a division made by the SHM are required to be purchased.

If a company needs to purchase back its own shares based on the preceding reasons, the company must seek approval from the SHM. After a company has repurchased its own shares for the purpose of reducing capital, that portion of shares must be cancelled within ten days. But after a company has repurchased its own shares for the purpose of a merger or awarding employees or a compulsory buyback from dissenting shareholders, that portion of shares must be cancelled within six months. In any event, it is a general practice that the amendments to a company's registration shall be carried out and a public announcement shall be made accordingly.

It is understandable that a share repurchase is against the basic principles endorsed by the Chinese company law (as mentioned previously, the principle of maintaining capital). If a company is allowed to repurchase its issued shares and to hold those shares, the company becomes a shareholder itself. Therefore, the rights and duties of a company become mixed and confused. It is also said that a repurchase will reduce capital, and that this is equivalent to the withdrawal of shares by shareholders. Therefore, to do so harms the legitimate interests of creditors. Finally, the repurchase will have a great impact on the securities markets because it will allow companies to control share prices and eventually mislead securities investors.

It should be noted that the tendency around the world is to move from an absolute prohibition of share repurchasing to a limited permission of share repurchasing. For example, the company laws in France, Germany, Italy, and Switzerland adopt this approach, i.e., in principle, share repurchasing is not allowed, but is allowed in exceptional situations. This approach is similar to that provided by company law.

Perhaps a more flexible approach could be taken by Chinese company law. During the Asian financial crisis, some people suggested that Hong Kong should learn from the practices in the United States and adopt the system of treasury shares, which allow a company to repurchase its issued shares and when the situation improves to sell those shares again. The main reason for doing so is to allow companies to adjust their capital shares flexibly.

If China wants to take a flexible approach to the permission of share repurchasing in the near future, it should consider effective procedures for share repurchasing. In this regard, the Hong Kong Companies Ordinance provides a good example.[43]

2. Limitations on Share Transfers in the JSC Situation

Generally, shareholders in JSCs can freely transfer their shares. The 1993 Company Law only provided two controversial limitations: (1) shares held by promoters shall not be transferred within three years from the date of establishment of the company, and (2) directors, supervisors, and managers shall not transfer their shares during their terms of office.[44] There are two reasons behind these limitations. Firstly, promoters are limited in transferring their shares in order to prevent them from improperly shifting their investment risks and to strengthen their responsibilities towards the company. Secondly, directors, supervisors, and managers are limited in transferring their shares in order to prevent them from engaging in insider trading.[45]

43. See Section 257 of the Companies Ordinance (Cap. 622).
44. The 1993 Company Law, Article 147.
45. Xu, supra note 8, p. 348.

Both reasons are arguable. Consider how the Taiwanese Company Law deals with them. Under the Taiwanese Company Law, there is one limitation placed on share transfers, i.e., shares shall not be transferred before the company is formally established (Art. 163). There is no limitation on the qualifying status of the holders of shares. Promoters are responsible for incorporation. If they are not permitted to transfer their shares within three years, promoters who have a strong capital capacity may only subscribe the minimum required shares by saving the money for other purposes. In other words, promoters who have a strong capital capacity cannot fully realize their capital contributions because of the limitation placed on share transfers. Furthermore, it is believed that after a company is formally established, it will be managed and supervised by directors and managers, so it is unreasonable to limit share transfers by promoters. On balance, a compromised approach should be taken here, i.e., promoters should not be allowed to transfer their shares within one year after the company is fully established. This approach is further supported by the CSRC's proposal that the promoters of companies listed on the growth enterprise market should be permitted to transfer their shares after one year.

Directors, supervisors, and managers should also be permitted to transfer their shares during their terms of office if effective measures have been taken. Insider dealing could be effectively eliminated under an effective monitoring system, e.g., if there is transparent information of daily share transfers by directors, supervisors, and managers.

All of the preceding concerns are resolved by the 2005 Company Law. Firstly, the Law allows promoters to transfer their shares after one year of incorporation. Secondly, directors, supervisors, and senior managers can transfer their shares after one year of incorporation. Thereafter, they are allowed, during their terms, to transfer 25 per cent of their shares held each year so long as a proper declaration is made. But the transfer of shares is not allowed within a half year after they are removed from their posts. Certainly, in order to ensure that directors, supervisors, and senior managers fulfil their duties, companies are free to restrict their share transfers through the articles of association.[46] For example, during their term, a blackout period, which is popular in Hong Kong, should be introduced so that directors, supervisors, and managers are absolutely prohibited from making transactions on the shares concerned 1 month (or two months)

46. The Company Law, Article 141.

before announcement or one month (or two months) before the date of the announcement deadline.[47]

3. Civil Liabilities for Shareholders' Defective Capital Contribution

Under the Chinese Company Law, shareholders' defective capital contributions usually include three forms: (a) a false evaluation of the capital contribution (other than cash), (b) a false capital contribution, and (c) a withdrawal of the capital contribution. In addition to criminal liabilities, civil liabilities can be imposed as well.

(1) Civil Liability under Article 28

If a shareholder fails to make a capital contribution properly, the shareholder shall be responsible for the breach of contract in relation to the other shareholders who have already contributed their capital in full. This is a similar approach to that of common law jurisdictions, which believe that the articles of association are a contract between shareholders themselves and between shareholders and the company. Although the 2013 Company Law adopts a system of capital contribution subscription, the duty to pay in a capital contribution remains, and it is understandable that a shareholder who fails to make a capital contribution breaches the contract between him or her and other shareholders who have made full capital contributions. On the other hand, common law jurisdictions adopt the system of authorized capital and permit shareholders to guarantee their capital contributions. Thus, a shareholder who fails to make a capital contribution is responsible for the breach of the contract between him or her and the company.

Although Article 28 of the Company Law does not mention the remedy for the breach, it is an acceptable practice that the breaching party shall pay the promised amount of capital contribution plus bank interest and compensate the non-breaching party if any loss is suffered.

---

47. According to the new amendment, which took effect on 1 January 2009, the current blackout period will be extended to commence from the listed issuer's financial period end date to the date on which the listed issuer published the relevant results announcement. See "Director's Blackout Period in Hong Kong Extended to 60 Days for Annual Results", retrieved from http://asria.org/directors-blackout-period-in-hong-kong-extended-to-60-days-for-annual-results/ on 16 October 2015.

For example, the plaintiff, the A Company, was incorporated jointly by the B Company and Mr Wang. On 4 April 1996, the B Company and Mr Wang signed the articles of association under which the B Company should have made a capital contribution in the form of cash for ¥668,300, which was 51 per cent of the total registered capital. Mr Wang should have made a capital contribution in the form of goods and non-patent technology for ¥631,729, which was 49 per cent of the total registered capital. Thereafter, the B Company actually contributed ¥308,300 and owed ¥360,000 while Mr Wang made his full contribution. Nevertheless, on 3 June 1996, the A Company managed to obtain a business licence. On 11 April 1998, the B Company asked Mr Wang to transfer his capital contribution but was refused. Then, the A Company was in fact managed solely by Mr Wang. Because the A Company lacked capital and could not operate normally, Mr Wang called for a BOD meeting several times in the name of the deputy chairman and asked the B Company to make its full capital contribution. The B Company refused. On 28 May 1998, Mr Wang sued the B Company on behalf of the A Company and demanded that the B Company contribute ¥360,000 plus bank interest and bear the litigation fees. The defendant, the B Company, argued that the plaintiff, the A Company, did not have legal standing as the plaintiff and that it should not be liable for breach of contract.

The court of first instance held that the relationship between the A Company and the B Company was that between company and shareholder. It was true that the B Company failed to make its capital contribution in full and thus violated Article 25(2) of the 1993 Company Law. However, in line with Article 25(2), only Mr Wang, who contributed capital in full, had the right to sue the B Company. And because the A Company did not have the legal standing to sue the B Company, the case should have been denied. On 25 June 1998, the Court ruled to dismiss the case.

The A Company was dissatisfied with the judgment and decided to appeal and ask that the judgment of the court of first instance be revised. On 2 September 1998, the Intermediate People's Court decided to maintain the judgment of the court of first instance for the same reason.[48]

In this case, there are two arguable issues. Firstly, was the A Company lawfully established, and thus did it obtain legal person status? It is clear that the A Company was improperly established because there was a violation of Article 19(2) of the 1993 Company Law, i.e., the minimum registered

48. Citing from Jiang Daxing, *Intensive Studies on Company Law* (*Gongsi fa de zhankai yu pingpan*), The Law Press (Beijing), 2001, pp. 148–49.

capital was not fully satisfied.[49] Secondly, should the A Company have been treated as a *de facto* company if it was improperly established? A *de facto* company is a concept often seen in the United States. While most common law jurisdictions generally treat a company as legally established if it has been granted a certificate of incorporation (such as the United Kingdom, Canada, Australia, and Hong Kong), in the United States, a company is treated as legally established if it is a *de facto* company or a corporation by estoppel. On the other hand, most continental law jurisdictions support China's approach that a company is not legally established if it fails to satisfy the legal requirements. In this case, both courts held that the B Company violated Article 25(2) of the 1993 Company Law, but did not address the legal status of the A Company. Obviously, both courts might have held the view that the A Company did not have legal status. Otherwise, it would be difficult to explain why the A Company could not sue the B Company for breach of contract.

The second issue is whether Mr Wang could have sued the B Company on behalf of the A Company. If it is assumed that the A Company was a *de facto* company, then Mr Wang, as the deputy chairman, should have been allowed to sue the B Company on behalf of the A Company. What if Mr Wang was not the deputy chairman and held only a 49 per cent capital contribution? Could he have acted as a minority shareholder and brought a derivative action on behalf of the A Company? As discussed before, the 1993 Company Law did not provide the derivative action, and Mr Wang could only be advised to rely on Article 25(2) of the 1993 Company Law. However, if this case had been tried under existing company law, Mr Wang could have taken a derivative action in accordance with Article 151, and his rights would have been better protected.

(2) Civil Liability under Article 30

Article 30 of the Chinese Company Law deals with a shareholder's non-cash contribution. Sometimes, it is discovered that the actual value of contributed goods, intellectual property rights, or land-use rights are lower than their value as fixed in the company's articles of association, and the shareholders concerned shall make up the difference. In this situation, there is no doubt that the company established is deemed to have a valid legal status and can bring legal action against the shareholders concerned. Again, one

49. Certainly, if the case were to happen today, the company could be considered as established even though a full contribution has not been made by B Company.

obvious reason behind this provision is to emphasize secured transactions. Because of this reason, other shareholders who exist when establishing the company shall bear joint liability. Thus, other shareholders will feel obliged to urge the shareholders concerned to make up the difference and help the company to maintain the proper capital amount.

(3) Civil Liability for Withdrawing Capital Contribution

In the previous chapter, it is mentioned that after a company is registered, shareholders shall not be permitted to withdraw capital (Art. 35); otherwise, administrative or criminal liabilities will be imposed. However, the Chinese Company Law does not expressly address the civil liability for withdrawal of capital contribution (Art. 200). Maybe it is reasonable to infer from Article 200, which states that the party concerned "shall be ordered to rectify the situation". In other words, the party concerned shall return the capital contribution that has been withdrawn plus necessary bank interest.

11

Mergers and Acquisitions

I. INTRODUCTION

People often see mergers and acquisitions as parts of corporate finance. This is simply because mergers and acquisitions may enable one company to obtain controlling power of another company by acquiring all or a certain percentage of the shares or assets of that company.[1] In this way, a company increases its capital and size of operation.

A merger is different from an acquisition. A merger refers to a situation where, by agreement, two or more companies are combined into one company in accordance with legal procedures. An acquisition, on the other hand, refers to a situation where one company acquires substantial control over another company, and two independent economic entities still remain. Detailed differences between mergers and acquisitions are illustrated as follows.

- A merger is a form of cooperation between two companies, while an acquisition is a commercial transaction between a bidder and the shareholders of a targeting company.
- A merger is usually accomplished through a negotiation or an agreement, but not through any force, threat or cheating, while an acquisition can be executed through an agreement or an unfriendly takeover. Thus, a merger involves friendly cooperation while an acquisition may involve hostile resistance.

1. Guan Yide, *Legal Perspective of Takeover of Listed Companies* (*Shangshi gongsi shougou de falü toushi*), People's Court Press (Beijing), 1999, p. 1.

- A merger is executed through an agreement while an acquisition is executed through biddings.
- A merger results in the whole transfer of property or shares, while an acquisition could be a partial or completed takeover.
- After a merger, there is only one economic entity, while after a takeover there are still two economic entities.
- A merger is usually conducted under company law, while an acquisition is usually conducted under a securities law.[2]

Despite these differences, if the term "merger" is interpreted broadly, an acquisition may be treated as one kind of merger. In practice, mergers and acquisitions are usually termed together as "M&As". However, this can be misleading in China, where people may use mergers for other purposes.

For example, there was a piece of news reporting the first merger case at the provincial level. It was reported that the Shanghai Tire Company merged with the Haikou Tire Company. The latter had total assets in the amount of ¥180 million and total debt in the amount of ¥250 million. The former paid only ¥14.63 million in order to merge with the latter, which did not need to pay off any debt. By looking at the news, this situation is not understandable: why did the Shanghai Tire Company merge with the Haikou Tire Company without paying off any debt? In fact, the Shanghai Tire Company bought the Haikou Tire Company in a bankruptcy auction.[3] A merger and a bankruptcy auction are entirely different things and should not be mixed.

The merger itself has a very important meaning to the economic development of the world. On the one hand, a merger enables a new company to expand the size of its production or operations, to adjust its organizational and product structures and to survive competition. In addition to that, a merger itself does not require the procedure of liquidation; all of the original legal duties or obligations can be retained, the original shareholders can maintain their shareholder status in a new company and a large number of workers may not be dismissed. On the other hand, a merger can help to realize a fair allocation of social resources and maintain the stability of the social economy.

Around the world, most past cases of M&As have happened in the United States.[4] Following economic globalization, the cross-border M&A

2. Liu Chengqing, *Legal Practice for M&A (Gongsi binggou falü shiwu)*, The Law Press (Beijing), 1998, pp. 2–3.
3. Jian Danlin, "Legal Analysis of a Company's M&A" (*Gongsi jianbing shougou hebing he binggou falü bianxi*), *Research on Financial and Economic Issues*, No. 2, 2001, p. 77.
4. In the United States, there were two high tides for M&As. The first one happened between 1879 and 1893. This tide ended when the US Sherman Act was adopted. The second tide

has become a major form of international investment. Although 2002 was a tough year for M&As in the Asia-Pacific region owing to the impact of the previous Asian financial crisis, the number of transactions was still impressive. It was reported that Australia generated the most amount of M&A business in 2002, accounting for 112 deal announcements valued at US$24.27 billion. China leapfrogged a number of its neighbours to become the second busiest jurisdiction, accounting for 74 deal announcements valued at US$22.39 billion. Korea was third with 74 deals valued at US$21.83 billion.[5] Furthermore, according to the World Investment Report 2015, even though global foreign direct investment (hereinafter referred to as "FDI") inflows declined in 2014, "cross-border M&As rebounded strongly to $399 billion and the number of multinational enterprises (MNE) deals with values larger than $1 billion increased to 223—the highest number since 2008—from 168 in 2013".[6]

From these data, one must agree that it is important to study the rules and regulations of M&As in China because it will facilitate successful transactions. After China's accession to the WTO, foreign involved M&As will become more realistic and smooth. However, there are still many legal issues that require further consideration and resolutions. So far, the PRC Foreign Investment Law (Consultation Paper) has been released to solicit public views. One thing is for sure: foreign involved M&As will be subjected to not only antitrust reviews, but also national security reviews.[7] The Chinese company law cannot avoid those issues when it deals with M&As. Thus, the focus will be on discussing problems rather than giving a general description of M&As.

II. THE POSSIBILITY OF M&AS IN CHINA

Originally, certain transactions that were routine processes in Western economies and that contributed to the vigour and efficiency of the economy

was caused by the beginning of World War II. For detailed information, see Wang Guiguo, *The International Investment Law (Guoji touzi fa)*, Beijing University Press (Beijing), 2001, pp. 308–9.

5. "Legislation Paves Way for M&As", *Asian Legal Business*, June 2003, p. 42.
6. UNCTAD, *World Investment Report 2015*, retrieved from http://unctad.org/en/PublicationsLibrary/wir2015_en.pdf on 16 October 2015.
7. Article 31 of the PRC Anti-monopoly Law states that "where a foreign investor participates in the concentration of business operators by merging or acquiring a domestic enterprise or by any other means and the national security is involved, besides the examination on the concentration of business operators according to this Law, the examination on the national security shall also be conducted according to the relevant provisions of the State".

were all but impossible under Chinese conditions. Although it has been recognized that M&As can improve the management of enterprises, the transactions are largely dependent on an alienability of ownership in enterprises. In China, State shares and legal person shares, which comprise the preponderance of all outstanding stock, are critical impediments to alienability. Although one enterprise may buy some of the outstanding shares of another on the securities markets, it cannot possibly buy enough to acquire the controlling power.

The difficulty with freely permitting the acquisition of Chinese firms is ideological: there is a danger of undercutting the Marxist-Leninist principle of ownership of the means of production by the people, as represented by the State. As stated in Article 6 of the Chinese Constitution, "The basis of the socialist economic system of the People's Republic of China is socialist public ownership of the means of production, namely, ownership by the whole people and collective ownership by the working people". Unless the Chinese central government is willing to drop this key ideological tenet, Western-type M&As or takeovers will be more restrictive if not problematic in China.

When an SOE cannot succeed on its own in China, there are two alternatives. One is to further develop joint ventures, which has been termed the "Chinese approach to M&A". Under this approach, Chinese partners contribute the SOEs while foreign partners contribute money and technology. Although the foreign partners may not be able to acquire the controlling shares, they can still influence the operation of the enterprises because their technology and management experiences are attractive to the Chinese partners. The other alternative is allowing investors to acquire small SOEs.

However, as predicted by many people, a large number of the SOEs have disappeared as a result of conversion, acquisitions, mergers, and bankruptcies. As such, the relevant laws and rules should be further developed in order to reflect this situation. As recently as a few years ago, the word "privatization" was taboo in China: "Now, with more and more Chinese companies already listed over international stock exchanges, or authorized to be listed, with two official domestic stock markets plus other many informal ones scattered across the country, the adoption of privatization in practice is all but a matter of vocabulary."[8] Nowadays, people are quite familiar with the term.

Initially, foreign investors tried to gain controlling power of domestic companies through the purchase of B shares. The purchase of B shares

8. Colleen Lau, "New Company Law Paves the Way for M&A", *China Law & Practice*, April 1996, p. 16.

offered by Jiangling Motors Corporation Ltd. via the American Ford Motor Company and the acquisition of the Beijing Light Bus Company by an alliance between Isuzu and Itochu are two traditional examples of the old type of M&A transactions made in 1995.

Jiangling was permitted to offer B shares on the Shenzhen Stock Exchange in September 1995. This involved the offer and sale of approximately 25 per cent of the enlarged share capital of the light truck manufacturer based in Jiangxi. The uniqueness of this transaction was the acquisition of 80 per cent of the entire 25 per cent enlarged capital by one single foreign investor, the Ford Motor Company, at a price of 13.9 times its historical earnings. It was clear that Ford had turned itself into a strategic investor by entering into this investment. This transaction combined a number of distinct M&A features, including issues of control and board of directors' representation, while at the same time being a standard B share offering.

Another notable transaction involved the acquisition of a 25 per cent stake, or US$42.05 million, of legal person shares in the Beijing Light Bus Company by two Japanese companies: Isuzu Motors Corporation and Itochu Trading Company Limited. The significance of this transaction was that the shares traded were not newly issued shares of the type to be held by non-PRC entities, but legal person shares held by governmental entities. Relevant government approvals for the conversion of legal person shares to B shares were obtained from central authorities to facilitate the completion of the transaction. Isuzu and Itochu's acquisition can be seen as similar to the conversion of an SOE or collectively owned enterprise into a foreign-invested JSC. In this case, the business vehicle was governed in accordance with the stipulations in Articles 18 and 19 of the Provisional Regulations on Several Issues Concerning the Establishment of Foreign Invested Joint Stock Company issued by the MOFTEC (now the Ministry of Commerce) on 10 January 1995.[9]

This past situation has been dramatically changed. As pointed out by Zhou Xiaoyan, director of the regulation division of MOFTEC (now the Ministry of Commerce), M&As recently became a hot topic worldwide. Many multinational companies are paying attention to China's targets. This means firstly that foreign involved M&As have become and continue to be a hot topic in China. Establishment of the relevant systems and measures will be demanded accordingly. Secondly, it is necessary to investigate the reasons that prevented foreign involved M&As from increasing dramatically in the past. Furthermore, it is important to know whether the foreign involved

9. Ibid., pp. 16–17.

M&As will actually bring Chinese domestic enterprises a "new hope", i.e., the advantages and disadvantages need to be clearly evaluated. Thirdly, a good legal system should be established to further protect the legitimate interests of various investors.

III. OBSTACLES TO FOREIGN-INVOLVED M&AS

1. Offensive Attitude and Protection of Domestic Enterprises

On the one hand, people may see the advantages of the foreign involved M&As in terms of contributing capital, technologies, and management skills. Some listed companies see foreign involved M&As as "lifesaving straws" that can improve their achievements. On the other hand, there are many unsuccessful cases. For example, the Jinbei Motor Company established two equity joint ventures (hereinafter referred to as "EJVs") with the General Motor Company, i.e., the Jiangsheng Company and the Jinke Company. These two EJVs encountered losses and Jiangsheng alone lost profits of about ¥8.29 million. Although Jinbei was profitable in the same period, it suffered losses in the amount of ¥4.15 million, caused by Jiangsheng. Jinke's profits decreased by the amount of ¥94.61 million because of the adjustment of its product structure and reduction of price. Jinbei was directly affected in the amount of ¥30.94 million.[10]

When local governments worried about losing tax revenue because of foreign involved M&As, entrepreneurs sadly saw that most domestic enterprises disappeared because of foreign involved M&As.

2. General Legal Obstacles and Problems

The previous laws and regulations on foreign-invested enterprises (hereinafter referred to as "FIEs") emphasized the establishment of new enterprises. None of them cover foreign involved M&As. In 1999, the State Commission for Economy and Trade issued the Interim Rules Concerning M&As of the SOEs by Foreign Investors (*Waishang Shougou Guoyou Qiye de Zhanxing Guiding*) permitted foreign businesspeople to take over SOEs. Concrete and workable measures, however, were not put forward. This was understandable because both the 1993 Company Law and the 1998 Securities Law

10. Xia Zhiqiong, "Foreign Investors—Not Everything That Glitters is Gold" (*Waizi binggou bu doushi xianbing*), retrieved from http://d.wanfangdata.com.cn/Periodical_gjsc200211034.aspx on 17 October 2015.

were promulgated for the major purpose of rescuing the SOEs. In order to maintain socialist public ownership, it was resolved that State shares or legal person shares were not freely transferable.[11] Foreign investors could only realize their dreams of M&As through the subscription of B shares. In fact, it was almost impossible for foreign investors to be involved in the M&A of listed companies because listed companies were usually 80 per cent State shares and legal person shares.[12]

This situation changed after a new regulation permitted central and local governments acting for the State to be responsible for State assets as contributors. It was proposed that State shares could be transferred to employees, management personnel, non-SOEs, and foreign investors.[13] Since 2001, substantial changes have been made. The rules and regulations placed on foreign involved M&As are listed as follows.

On 5 November 2001, the Several Opinions on Several Issues concerning Foreign Investment into Listed Companies (*Guanyu Shangshi Gongsi Sheli Waishang Touzi Youguan Wenti de Ruogan Yijian*) was published by the CSRC and MOFTEC[14] jointly. This legal document permits foreign non-investment companies (using their industrial capital or commercial capital) to take over listed companies in the form of accepting non-circulated shares.

On 1 April 2002, the No. 17 Rules on Written Reports of Information Disclosures Submitted by Companies Whose Shares Are Publicly Issued—Special Rules on the Contents and Formats of Prospectuses Issued by Foreign-Invested Joint Stock Companies (*Gongkai Faxing Zhengquan de Gongsi Xinxi Pilu Bianbao Guize Di 17 Hao—Waishang Touzi Gufen Youxian Gongsi Zhaogu Shuomingshu Neirong he Geshi Tebie Guiding*) were published by the CSRC. From that time, foreign businesspeople could substantially act as promoters to establish listed companies.

Since April 2002, the Rules on Guiding Directions of Foreign Investments (*Zhidao Waishang Touzi Fangxiang Guiding*) and the Guideline Categories on Foreign Investment Industries (*Waishang Touzi Chanye Zhidao Mulu*) were officially implemented. In line with those two regulations, China has

11. Although the reduction or free transfer of state-owned shares has become a hot topic since 1994, there is no clear policy on how the reduction and free transfer could be handled. "The 15-Year Historical Process of the Reduction of State-Owned Shares" (*Shiwunian guoyougu jianchi licheng huigu*), retrieved from http://big5.xinhuanet.com/gate/big5/news.xinhuanet.com/fortune/2009-06/22/content_11578495.htm on 17 October 2015.
12. Le Jiachun, "Reorganisation of State Shares Will Be at a High Tide" (*Zhongguo guoqi gu chongzu jiang xian gaochao*), *The Shanghai Securities News Daily* (Shanghai), 15 January 2003.
13. Ibid.
14. After the Tenth National People's Congress, MOFTEC and the State Commission of Economic Trade were merged into a new organ called the Ministry of Commerce in 2003.

substantially removed limitations on foreign investments in many investment areas.

On 4 June 2002, additional rules were published by the CSRC, i.e., the Rules on Establishing Foreign Involved Securities Companies (*Waizi Cangu Zhengquan Gongsi Sheli Guize*) and the Rules on Establishing Foreign Involved Funds Management Companies (*Waizi Cangu Jijin Guanli Gongsi Sheli Guize*). These indicate that opening the financial industry to foreign investors is irrevocable.

In October 2002, the Measures Governing the Takeover of Listed Companies (*Shangshi Gongsi Shougou Guanli Banfa*) was published by the CSRC. In line with these measures, there is no limitation as to the subjects when taking over listed companies. Foreign investors enjoy the same status as local investors to participate in the takeover of A-share listed companies and purchase the State shares and legal person shares in non-listed companies.

On 1 November 2002, the Notice Concerning Several Issues of Listed Companies Transferring State Shares and Legal Person Shares to Foreign Investors (*Guanyu Xiang Waishang Zhuanrang Shangshi Gongsi Guoyou Gu he Faren Gu Youguan Wenti de Tongzhi*) and the Interim Rules on Using Foreign Capital to Reform State-Owned Enterprises (*Liyong Waizi Gaizu Guoyou Qiye de Zhanxing Guiding*) were jointly published by the CSRC, Treasury Ministry and State Commission for Economy and Trade. The notice actually removed an order not to transfer state shares and legal person shares of listed companies to foreign investors in force since September 1995. Foreign investors could officially take over listed companies.[15]

Because so many important regulations were published in 2002, this year was named the "Year of the M&A" in China.

3. Restricted Investment Areas

Despite the fact that more relevant rules and regulations will be enacted, the time to promulgate a unified M&A law by the NPC has not yet come. In particular, it is important to know that foreign investors need to overcome further legal obstacles. For example, the Rules of Foreign Investment Guidelines (*Zhidao Waishang Touzi Fangxiang Guiding*) and Guideline Catalogue of Foreign Investment Industries (*Waishang Touzi Chanye Zhidao*

15. Zeng Juan, "Reorganisation of Capital in China Moves into a New Time Period" (*Zhongguo zichan chongzu zou jin waizi binggou xin shidai*), *The Securities Newspaper* (Beijing), 4 November 2002.

Mulu), which will be amended from time to time,[16] contain limitations on shareholding control in certain listed companies. For example, under a catalogue of restrictive industries, foreign investors are basically allowed to form joint ventures and the Chinese partners shall be the controlling shareholders. However, some of the industries are now opened to foreign investors.[17] In Shanghai, foreign investors are encouraged to take over the local SOEs, but not the SOEs that are engaged in the financial industry.[18] This may trigger a break of consistency with the Chinese commitment in the service areas. On the other hand, it is predictable that the financial sector will attract more foreign involved M&As because this sector has not been thoroughly opened to foreign investors. Reports show that foreign involved M&As still occupy a lower percentage of total FDIs even though the number of M&As increases stably every year. On the other hand, statistics show that from 2004 to 2012, there were only thirty-eight foreign involved M&As in China.[19]

4. Chaotic and Inconsistent Laws and Regulations

Some conflicts between different laws and regulations may still exist. For example, Zhang Yuqing, the then head of the Law and Regulation Division of the Ministry of Commerce, disclosed that 25 per cent of foreign-invested capital in an enterprise was no longer considered as a strict bottom line for an FIE, i.e., even if 25 per cent of foreign-invested capital was not reached, the enterprise may be regarded as an FIE.[20] However, the Notice on the Tax Treatment of Foreign-invested Enterprises with Less than 25 per

16. The latest Rules of Foreign Investment Guidelines was released on 21 February 2002. The latest Guideline Catalogue of Foreign Investment Industries is the 2015 edition.
17. In accordance with the Schedule of Specific Commitments on Services List of Article 2 MFN Exemptions, foreign service suppliers will be permitted to establish joint venture value-added telecommunication enterprises with a limitation on shareholding control (first no more than 30 per cent, then no more than 50 per cent).
18. "Huang Junfeng, Shanghai Issues Detailed Rules on Foreign Involved M&A with SOEs" (*Shanghai chutai waizi binggou guoqi xize*), retrieved from http://www.cnelc.com/Article/1/AD100043577_1.html on 17 October 2015.
19. "2013 Report of Foreign Investment in China" (*Zhongguo waishang touzi baogao (2013)*), retrieved from http://images.mofcom.gov.cn/wzs/201312/20131211162942372.pdf on 17 October 2015.
20. "The Ministry of Commerce Will Publish an Interpretation of Foreign Involved M&As After the Investment Threshold of 25% Has Been Removed" (*Touzi bili 25% xianzhi jiejin, Shangwubu jiang chu waizi binggou jiedu*), retrieved from http://china.com.cn/chinese/2003/Aug/388791.htm on 17 October 2015. In addition, Article 4 of the Provisional Rules for M&A of Domestic Enterprises by Foreign Investors states that the capital contribution of the foreign investor is permitted to be under 25 per cent.

cent Foreign Investment Proportion issued on 18 April 2003 held a different view: the taxation system applicable to an FIE with less than 25 per cent in the foreign investment ratio should be treated in accordance with the taxation system applicable to PRC domestic enterprises and is not be eligible for any form of preferential treatment applicable to an FIE unless otherwise particularly required by the State Council.[21] Obviously, there is an inconsistency between the two ministries. It is fine to offer foreign-invested enterprises national treatment without giving preferential tax treatment. However, from a viewpoint of jurisprudence, it is better to change the higher level before the new change can be announced. Furthermore, the Decision of Amendments and Supplementary Rules Concerning the Interim Rules on Foreign Established Invested Companies issued by MOFTEC on 7 March 2003 (effective after thirty days) provided that those companies established by the Investment Companies should be regarded as FIEs and could enjoy tax benefits for FIEs (Article 4). This lower-level regulation may conflict with higher-level law (such as "*San zi qiye*"), under which FIEs are regarded as Chinese legal persons. Hopefully, this problem will be thoroughly resolved after the promulgation of the PRC Foreign Investment Law.

5. Complicated Procedures for M&As

There exist complicated legal procedures that defeated the original advantages of M&As and rendered their speed slower than that of FIEs. As required, foreign involved M&As should normally go through the following procedures:

- the CSRC will examine the matter of information disclosure;
- the Ministry of Commerce will examine the matter concerning identification of foreign capital and foreign involved M&As;
- the Administrative Bureau for Industry and Commerce will examine whether there is an abuse of dominant market power;
- the State-Owned Asset Supervision and Administration Commission will examine the transfer of State shares; and

21. "Notice of the State Taxation Administration on How to Handle the Taxation of Foreign-Funded Enterprises in Which the Proportion of Foreign Investment Is Lower Than 25%" (*Guojia shuiwu zongju guanyu waiguo touzizhe chuzi bili diyu 25% de waishang touzhi qiye shuiwu chuli wenti de tongzhi (Shixiao)*), retrieved from http://www.chinatax.gov.cn/n810341/n810765/n812198/n813081/c1206745/content.html on 17 October 2015.

- the National Development and Reform Commission will examine whether the project is consistent with the Guideline Categories for Foreign Investment Industries.

It is advantageous to examine all of these aspects if it can be done efficiently. Unfortunately, as pointed out previously, too much discretion exists concerning what should be examined, and there is a redundancy or overlap between various authorities.

IV. THE LEGAL ISSUES ON FOREIGN-INVOLVED M&AS

1. The Possible Consequence of Foreign-Involved M&As

The future M&A law should do more than address how to absorb foreign capital. More attention should be paid to the negative impact on society. Foreign investors do not come to rescue Chinese enterprises; rather, they intend to control certain enterprises through M&As and further control the relevant markets. It should be noted that around the world Chinese medium- and large-sized enterprises are the most attractive targets because (a) they can offer well-established channels for the purchase and sale of products, and (b) they can offer cheap but good labour. In this circumstance, it is suggested that the Chinese government should pay attention to enterprises that have close connections with the national economy and people's livelihoods, i.e., the government should use both the Rules on Foreign Investment Guidelines and the Guideline Catalogue for Foreign Investment Industrials as levers to gradually open the door to foreign involved M&As. On the other hand, there should be no violation of the WTO's obligations or the national interests.

In addition, it is important to know that the recently promulgated Chinese Anti-monopoly Law shall be used as the controlling law to decide whether foreign involved M&As should be allowed. Under the Chinese Anti-monopoly Law, foreign involved M&As shall not create market concentration or affect the national security.

In September 2008, the Ministry of Commerce received the Anti-monopoly Declaration for the Concentration of Business Operators by the Coca-Cola Company of the United States (hereinafter referred to as the "Coca-Cola Company") and the China Huiyuan Juice Group Limited (hereinafter referred to as the "China Huiyuan Juice Company"). After a half-year investigation and examination, the Ministry confirmed that the Concentration of Business Operators would lead to the following adverse influences.

(1) After the completion of the Concentration, the Coca-Cola Company will gain the ability to leverage a dominant position in the carbonated beverage market over the fruit juice market, which will have the effect of eliminating or restricting competition between the existing fruit juice beverage producers and infringe upon the legitimate rights and interests of beverage consumers.
(2) After the completion of the Concentration, the controlling force of the Coca-Cola Company over the fruit juice market will be obviously increased through its control over the two well-known fruit juice brands "Minute Maid" and "Huiyuan". In addition to the dominant position of the Coca-Cola Company in the carbonated beverage market and corresponding influence-leveraging effect, the Concentration will obviously increase the barriers for potential competitors to enter the fruit juice beverage market.
(3) The Concentration has compressed the survival space for the domestic small- and medium-sized fruit juice enterprises and restrained the domestic enterprises from participating in the competition in the fruit juice beverage market and their degree of autonomy and innovation, which will result in an adverse influence on the effective competition situation of the fruit juice beverage market in China and create an unfavourable situation for the sustained and healthy development of the China fruit juice industry.

Based on the preceding findings, the merger between Coca-Cola Company and China Huiyuan Juice Company was refused.[22]

It should be noted that one of the consequences of foreign involved M&As is that WFOEs are greatly increased. The WFOEs are the predominant type of enterprise in China because they are suitable for foreign investors to have autonomous operations on the one hand and to safely keep commercial secrets on the other hand. Because of this change, China's original intention to improve the competition capacity of domestic enterprises through foreign involved M&As may be frustrated. Also, it should be noted that further development of the WFOEs will enable foreign investors to further control relevant Chinese markets and create a potential problem of transfer price. Thus, the Chinese government should further improve the supervision system in this area.

22. Public Announcement No. 22 of 2009 of the Ministry of Commerce—On Promulgating the Result of the Anti-monopoly Declaration for Concentration of Business Operators by the Coca-Cola Company of the United States and the China Huiyuan Juice Group Limited.

2. Foreign-Involved M&As and Other Legal Systems

M&As are regular commercial decisions seen in most market economy jurisdictions. However, excessive M&As bring about the problem of monopolies, which seriously affect fair competition. In this situation, the Chinese Anti-monopoly Law is applied. In addition, it is suggested that China should pay attention to worldwide antitrust merger notification requirements and be able to establish its own antitrust merger notification system.

Many jurisdictions worldwide are tightening their merger control laws and prohibiting parties from consummating their merger transactions prior to receiving government approval. The consequence of violating pre-merger notification rules in some jurisdictions may result in the cancellation of the deal, although substantial fines are more commonly seen.

Given that China did not have a merger control regime previously, parties were not required to submit any merger filings. This situation, however, was changed after 2002, the year of the M&A, especially after the promulgation of the Chinese Anti-monopoly Law. On 3 August 2008, the State Council issued the Rules of the State Council on the Standard for Declaration of Concentration of Business Operators (hereinafter referred to as the Concentration Rules). According to the Concentration Rules, whenever a concentration reaches any of the following standards, the business operators concerned shall notify the Ministry of Commerce beforehand. Otherwise, the concentration is not allowed: (1) the worldwide business turnovers of all of the business operators involved in the concentration exceeded ¥10 billion in the last fiscal year, and the China-wide turnovers of at least two business operators among them exceeded ¥400 million separately in the last fiscal year; and (2) the China-wide business turnovers of all of the business operators involved in the concentration exceeded ¥2 billion in the last fiscal year, and the China-wide business turnovers of at least two business operators among them exceeded ¥400 million separately in the last fiscal year (Art. 3).

As discussed before, a successful M&A will definitely affect the interests of the minority shareholders of a target company and the employees of two side companies. One important issue is how to protect minority shareholders by offering them a better way out. It has been suggested that China should import the appraisal right from the United States. The appraisal right was first seen in Ohio's corporate legislation, which authorises minority shareholders to have their shares evaluated and purchased by the company when majority shareholders have voted for an M&A.[23] A similar system was

23. "Research on the System of Appraisal Rights of Minority Shareholders under the US Corporate Law" (*Meiguo gongsifa zhong yiyi gudong gufen pingguquan zhidu yanjiu*),

not provided in the 1993 Company Law, but is mentioned by Article 149 of the Required Items of Articles of Association of Companies Listed Abroad.[24] However, this provision may contain several problems: (a) it applies only to companies listed abroad; (b) it is too simple and fails to define a fair price and especially the procedures of evaluation; (c) it forces shareholders who have voted for an M&A to purchase shares of minority shareholders; and (d) it contains no judicial procedures in case an agreement of fair price has not been reached.[25] The next issue is how to permit employees to participate in the M&A decision-making process. In some jurisdictions, employees of targeting companies shall have the right to be heard or the right to vote for upcoming M&A cases.[26] Those legal issues must be resolved by future M&A law.

3. A Unified M&A Law

The existing rules and regulations concerning M&A are issued by different authorities and sometimes conflict with each other. For example, Article 9 of the Notice Concerning Several Issues of Listed Companies Transferring State Shares and Legal Person Shares to Foreign Investors states that after the State shares and legal shares of listed companies have been transferred to foreign investors, the listed companies shall not be permitted to enjoy the status of an FIE. Contrarily, the Interim Rules on Using Foreign Capital to Reform State-Owned Enterprises provides no such limitation and is more consistent with previous Chinese practice. Furthermore, the Notice Concerning Several Issues of Strengthening Administration of Approval, Registration, Foreign Currency, and Tax Collection of Foreign Investment Enterprises (*Guanyu Jiaqiang Waishang Touzi Qiye Shenpi, Dengji, Waihui ji Shuishou Guanli Youguan Wenti de Tongzhi*) issued on December 2002 jointly by MOFTEC, the National Tax Administration Bureau and the National Administration Bureau for Commerce and Industry expressly states that enterprises whose shares controlled by foreign investors are over 25 per cent of the whole will be entitled to the status of an FIE.

---

retrieved from http://www.people.com.cn/GB/paper87/5829/587528.html on 17 October 2015.

24. *Dao Jingwai Shangshi Gongsi Zhangcheng Bibei Tiaokuan*, which was issued on 27 August 1994 by the Securities Commission of the State Council and the State Commission for Reform of Economic System.
25. "Research on the System of Appraisal Rights of Minority Shareholders under the US Corporate Law", supra note 23.
26. Guan Yide, *Legal Perspectives on Taking Over Listed Companies* (*Shangshi gongsi shougou de falü toushi*), The People's Court Press (Beijing), 1999, pp. 44–45.

Similar to the idea of establishing a unified company law, it is suggested that a unified M&A law be promulgated. The proposed unified M&A law shall particularly address the following issues.

Firstly, despite the existing disclosure rules, it has been reported that the system for disclosing information is not complete or timely, especially in the case of transferring State shares.[27] Furthermore, the contents of disclosure shall be improved. For example, it shall be required that investors disclose the source of their capital.

Secondly, the concept of due diligence shall be emphasized, including due diligence in the aspects of accounting, tax, and relevant laws in order to avoid potential disputes.

Thirdly, the standard purchase price should be fixed. It is understandable that the sale of SOEs must go through asset evaluation. However, there are different evaluation methods. While Chinese evaluators emphasize book value, foreign investors may emphasize market price. In addition, attention shall be paid to the impact of non-market trade on the price and the special need for a fixed price for State assets, as well as the impact of economic reform policies from the central government to local governments on price.[28]

Fourthly, there is a need to combine A and B shares. As mentioned before, A and B shares were implemented to prevent foreign capital from dramatically pounding the newly established securities markets. Chinese people have been permitted to purchase B shares in accordance with the Notice on Several Issues concerning Domestic Individual Residents Investing in Foreign Capital Shares of Domestic Listed Companies (*Guanyu Jingnei Jumin Geren Touzi Jingnei Shangshi Waizi Gu Ruogan Wenti de Tongzhi*) since it was issued jointly by the CSRC and the National Foreign Currency Bureau on 9 July 2001. On 5 November 2002, the CSRC and the People's Bank of China jointly issued the Interim Rules on Administration of Qualified Foreign Institutional Investors Investing in Domestic Securities (*Hege Waiguo Jigou Touzi Zhe Touzi Guonei Zhengquan Guanli de Zhanxing Guiding*) and relevant rules. Since then, foreign investors have been permitted to be involved in A share markets. This strongly indicates that the combination of A and B shares will be merely a timing issue. The future unified M&A law shall prepare for this possibility.

27. Huang Xiaoping, "Too Many Problems of Transferring State Shares in China" (*Zhongguo guoqi gu zhuanrang wenti duo*), *The Securities Times* (Beijing), 3 January 2003.
28. Yang Guang, "Three Difficulties Concerning Foreign Involved M&A of Listed Companies" (*Waizi binggou shangshi gongsi shang cun san nandian*), *The China Securities News* (Beijing), 19 December 2002.

Finally, it is necessary to regulate M&A technologies. In 2003, the management buy-out (hereinafter referred to as the "MBO") was very popular in China. The MBO was originally based on the leveraged buyout (hereinafter referred to as the "LBO"). However, not long ago, the Letter in Replying to the Issues related to Reforms of State-Owned Enterprises (*Guanyu Guoyou Qiye Gaige Youguan Wenti de Fuhan*) issued by the Ministry of Finance provided that until the relevant regulations were perfected, the acceptance, examination, and approval of the management buy-out of listed and non-listed companies would be suspended.[29] Nevertheless, it is important to conduct research in advance. The MBO is exercised through agreement with the management of a targeting company. Thus, a series of company law principles will be involved. For example, issues of duties of loyalty of the management personnel and protection of minority shareholders shall be further discussed. In addition, anti-M&A methods should be further researched.

4. Equal Opportunities for Domestic Investors

On the one hand, foreign investors are asking for national treatment. On the other hand, domestic enterprises are arguing that too many special treatments are given to foreign investors and that they are thus in a worse competition situation. In fact, when China opens the door of the M&A to foreign investors, it should pay attention to the interests of domestic enterprises, especially private enterprises. China should offer financial assistance and help good quality private enterprises to become listed on the stock exchanges, as well as participate in the M&A of SOEs and listed companies.

M&As in China will become important phenomena, and thus the structure of many domestic enterprises and especially SOEs will be dramatically changed. Following the further permission for WFOEs, the unlimited shareholding status of many FIEs as well as the further development of private enterprises, China will eventually realize a formal development of various forms of economy. However, it is important to note that, on the one hand, state-owned assets shall be used or invested in important industries or key areas relevant to national security and national lifelines, i.e., the state will retain close control of these enterprises.[30] On the other hand, regular SOEs

29. "The Ministry of Finance Stops Approving the MBO in Order to Avoid the Loss of State-Owned Assets" (*Yanfang guoyou zichan liushi, Caizhengbu zanting guangliceng shougou de shenpi*), retrieved from http://news.xinhuanet.com/newscenter/2003-04/04/content_816344.htm on 17 October 2015.
30. The Resolution of the Central Party Committee on Several Issues Concerning the Perfection of the Socialist Market Economic System (*Zhonggong Zhongyang Guanyu*

will gradually disappear through M&As, bankruptcy, assets reorganization or structure adjustment. Moreover, those changes will facilitate further legal reform and the establishment of a modern property rights system, as well as the protection of private ownership.

V. FORMS OF MERGERS

As a worldwide practice, there are two forms of merger. The first form is consolidation. This refers to two or more companies together forming a new company, and the original companies no longer existing as a result. The new company takes over all of the legal duties and rights of the original companies. The second form is called a merger, i.e., one or more companies are merged into an acquiring company. There are two forms of merger: cash for stock mergers and stock for stock mergers. The former refers to a situation in which the acquiring company uses cash to buy all of the assets or shares of the acquired company. In this situation, the shareholders of the acquired company may lose their shareholder status. The latter refers to a situation in which the acquiring company issues new shares for the acquired company in return for its whole assets or shares. The shareholders of the acquired company become the shareholders of the acquiring company.

Article 172 of the Company Law provides similar forms, i.e., merger by absorption or merger by new establishment. When one company absorbs another, it is an absorption merger, and the company being absorbed shall be dissolved. When two or more companies merge to establish a new company, it is a new establishment merger, and all parties being merged shall be dissolved.

VI. ACQUISITIONS

M&As are usually used together. An acquisition can be in the form of a merger or in the form of taking control over the management powers of another company. As one author points out:

> The union of two businesses into one corporate structure can be done under statutory merger provisions, but a statutory merger needs not involve two businesses. A parent and wholly owned subsidiary can merge merely to reorganize the corporate structure of a single business. Moreover, the union of two businesses into one corporate structure

---

Wanshan Shehui Zhuyi Shichang Jingji Tizhi Ruogan Wenti de Jueding), which was passed by the Third Plenary Meeting of the Sixteenth Central Committee of the Communist Party of China on 14 October 2003.

> may not involve the union of corporate entities. All the stockholders of one corporation can exchange their stock for securities of another corporate business, converting the former into a subsidiary of the latter. The word merger, therefore, cannot always be accurately used to describe the union of two businesses, and the term acquisition is often used instead. Unfortunately, this term connotes a large, active business acquiring a smaller, passive one; but there are acquisitions in which neither is smaller or passive, i.e. a union of two independent businesses of approximately the same size.[31]

Therefore, the acquiring company may acquire part or the whole of the assets or shares of the target company. However, if the target company is a listed company, then the disclosure principle must be followed strictly. At the same time, the acquiring company should follow a tender offer method. In the United States, a bidder faces dual disclosure obligations under the Williams Act. Firstly, there is the 5 per cent threshold specified by Section 13(d), at which point Schedule 13D must be filed. Secondly, if the bidder actually commences a tender offer, it must concomitantly file a Schedule 14D–1 and provide to investors the information specified in Rule 14d–6. By filling out these two forms, the bidder shall disclose his or her identity, source of funds, and plans for the target. The disclosure remains important when the bidder is making a partial bid because such an offer is usually oversubscribed and some of the tendered shares will be returned to the target shareholders. Thus, because shareholders cannot fully liquidate their investment in the targeting company, they have a good reason to be interested in the bidder's financial condition and how it will manage the targeting company. Also, some shareholders may want to reject the offer and remain as minority shareholders in the reconstituted firm.

The information disclosure is usually addressed by the Chinese Securities Law and relevant regulations. It is noted that the information disclosure system in China is not yet perfect but is likely to be improved soon because the PRC Securities Law has been amended several times in order to provide a comprehensive list of requirements.

VII. LIMITATIONS ON M&AS

Although a merger is more or less a contractual behaviour, mergers still affect the interests of the State, creditors, workers, and so on. Therefore, many countries have provided limitations for mergers.

31. Jesse H. Choper, John C. Coffee, and C. Robert Morris, *Cases and Materials on Corporations* (3rd ed.), Little, Brown, and Company (Boston), 1989, pp. 1243–81.

(1) Anti-trust issue. If a merger exceeds certain limitations and becomes a trust, then the merger should be prohibited.
(2) Protection of special industries. The merger of special industries, such as the banking, insurance, railways, aerospace, electricity, and gas industries, must be permitted by the relevant authorities.
(3) A merger itself should not harm the interests of shareholders, creditors, and workers. For example, Swedish law provides that in cases where a merger will cause major changes to the employment conditions, the working union has the right to participate in the merger decision.
(4) Limitations on a merger between domestic companies and foreign companies. There are special limitations for this kind of merger. For example, in France, special permission is required in order for a foreign company to merge with a domestic company. In Germany, a merger between a domestic company and a foreign company is not allowed.
(5) Issue of a merger between different types of company. Some countries allow mergers only between the same types of company. Other countries may limit the nature of a newly established company.

Although the 1993 Company Law did not contain similar restrictive provisions, Article 183 stated that the merger of a JSC must be approved by the department authorized by the State Council or by the people's government at the provincial level. A reasonable interpretation is that the relevant authorities may consider the preceding limitations when they examine merger cases. However, the 2005 Company Law leaves those requirements to be stipulated by the 2005 Securities Law or other laws, and this is still the case today.

More and more jurisdictions including the United States are prohibiting parties from consummating their merger transactions prior to receiving government approval. The consequence of violating pre-merger notification rules in some jurisdictions may result in the cancellation of the deal, although substantial fines are more common.

As mentioned previously, it has been admitted that the pre-merger notification rules are scattered across various rules and regulations.[32] The systematic rules have not been established yet, but should be improved very soon.

32. For example, Article 4 of the Notice Concerning Several Issues of Listed Companies Transferring State Shares and Legal Person Shares to Foreign Investors provides the system of examination and approval. It prohibits local government from approving foreign involved M&As.

VIII. PROCEDURES FOR MERGERS

Since a merger will affect certain interests of all relevant parties, the Company Law provides several procedures that must be followed. Firstly, the parties to a merger transaction shall sign a merger agreement and formulate a balance sheet and a detailed inventory of assets (Art. 173).

Secondly, the merger of a company shall require the adoption of a special resolution by a shareholders' meeting of the company (Art. 43.2), which means that during the shareholders' meeting the resolution shall be passed by two thirds of the shareholders. A shareholder is entitled to dissent from and obtain payment of the fair value of his or her shares in the event of a merger. However, according to the US Revised Model Business Corporation Act (1984), a shareholder is entitled to dissent and to obtain payment for his or her shares under this chapter and may not challenge the corporate action creating his or her entitlement unless the action is unlawful or fraudulent with respect to the shareholder or the corporation.

Thirdly, permission must be obtained before a merger takes place. This has been especially since after the Chinese Anti-monopoly Law was promulgated.

Fourthly, the company shall inform its creditors of the intended merger within ten days following the date on which the merger resolution is adopted and make at least three announcements in the newspaper within thirty days. The creditors shall have the right to claim full repayment of their debts or provision of a corresponding guarantee from the company within 30 days from the date of receipt of the notice and within ninety days from the date of the first public announcement for those who have not received the notice. The company that fails to repay its debts in full or to provide a corresponding guarantee shall not be merged (Art. 173).

Finally, after a merger is finished, relevant re-registration shall be carried out. In other words, if the merger or division of a company involves changes in registered items, those changes shall be registered according to law with the Company Registration Authority (Art. 179).

In a cross-board M&A, the most fundamental task that foreign investors should undertake in making a successful acquisition or investment is due diligence, i.e., an investigation of the assets and liabilities of the target business. Some of the principal issues on which an investor's due diligence should focus are listed as follows.

- Credit arrangements. The investor will need a comprehensive analysis of the target's credit position. This should include a detailed assessment of any security given by the target and related corporate entities and all transactions with its principal creditors.

- Creditworthiness of the seller. Representations or warranties obtained by the investor in the transaction documentation are only as good as the creditworthiness of the party giving them. In most Asian jurisdictions, there is a provision allowing transactions that have been entered into prior to the commencement of insolvency to be set aside if they are prejudicial to the interests of the creditors.
- Employee issues. Asian companies have been far more reluctant than their Western counterparts to make extensive redundancies, although there have been some recent high-profile exceptions to this trend.
- Regulatory issues. In certain Asian jurisdictions there are controls on the level of foreign investment in domestic entities and restrictions in certain industries. For companies listed on local stock exchanges, there can be additional regulatory hurdles to consider. As a rule of thumb, the acquisition of between 25 and 35 per cent of a listed company may oblige the investor to make a general offer for all of the outstanding securities of the target company.
- Structuring the deal. At its simplest, the investment in or acquisition of the target business will typically take the form of an asset purchase, a share purchase or a combination of the two. The choice of structure will be partly driven by the tax considerations of the investor and the target. In Asia, the investor will also need to work within the foreign investment regulations and bear in mind the obligations under local securities laws and regulations, such as the general offer obligation referred to previously.[33]

IX. TAKEOVER AND CORPORATE CONTROL

1. Introduction

Takeovers provide a mechanism whereby company assets will be under the control of a person who believes the company can utilize the assets in a more efficient way than was previously the case. The offeror or bidder must generally be prepared to pay a price for the shares that exceeds the prevailing market price. This is because the purchase of large parcels of shares that affect control is generally set at a higher price than smaller, passive shareholdings. The payment of this "premium for control" will usually be justified only if the offeror is able to utilize the target company's assets more productively than the existing management personnel. This may occur

33. David Fleming, Andrew Martin, and Mark Innis, "Investing in Asia . . . The Client's Perspective", *Asian Lawyer*, Vol. 5, No. 4 (April 2000), p. 16.

because the offeror is a more efficient business manager, or it may be in a related industry where efficiencies may arise through rationalization of the offeror and targeting company's activities or economies of scale.

In addition to these economic benefits directly arising from takeovers, the threat of a takeover may offer a strong incentive to management to utilize their company's assets as efficiently as possible and to consider the interests of shareholders. It has been concluded that the most vulnerable takeover targeting companies are often asset-rich companies that generate relatively low profits. This results in a discounted market price for the company's shares relative to the value of its assets. Such companies also often pursue a conservative dividends policy that may cause shareholders to consider takeover offers favourably. Therefore, the threat of a takeover will force directors to react in a way designed to engender increased shareholder loyalty.

In practice, "the control of a company can be acquired by (a) buying its assets, (b) effecting a merger between the acquiring (or 'bidder') corporation and the acquired (or 'target') corporation, or (c) purchasing a controlling block of the target's voting shares".[34] Only the last method does not need to take care of the feeling of the targeting company. In other words, acquisitions are sometimes involved in "hostile" takeovers regardless of whether those actions are resisted by the BOD of the targeting company. It is believed that "without this last option, a prospective insurgent would first have to conduct a proxy fight to oust the board, and, such proxy contests historically have been unsuccessful".[35]

One of the advantages of the hostile takeover is its "monitoring mechanism", which unhappy shareholders or third parties may use to deter or discipline the inefficient management of the targeting company.[36]

Today, the most popular way of obtaining a controlling block of shares is a tender offer. One book describes the normal process vividly.

> The tender offeror (or "bidder") makes a public offer to the target shareholders of the class sought, offering to buy their shares at a specified price (usually at a substantial premium over the current market price) for a limited period. The bidder may offer cash (as is usual today), or it may offer to exchange a specified package of its securities for the target's voting stock (an "exchange offer"). The offer may be either for all shares of the class or only for a portion of them. In this latter case of a "partial bid", the bidder will, however, probably reserve the right to accept any "excess" shares tendered. The offer will typically be

34. Choper, Coffee, and Morris, supra note 31, p. 1051.
35. Ibid.
36. Ibid.

> subject to conditions set forth in the offering documents. For example, a minimum tender condition (i.e. 50 per cent of the class tender) is to ensure that the bidder acquire at least *de facto* voting control, or a condition that no material adverse change occurs in the target's business or financial structure. Shareholders accept this offer by depositing their shares with a depository bank that the bidder appoints as its agent. If the specified conditions entitling the bidder to cancel or reduce its offer do not arise (or are waived by the bidder), the depository bank will purchase the shares on behalf of the bidder on the expiration of the tender offer, using funds deposited with it in advance by the bidder. In contractual terms, the bidder makes the offer, and the shareholders accept it; and it is the bidder's responsibility to specify any contracting "out" with adequate precision.[37]

On the other hand, targeting companies usually defend against the bidder by adopting various structural means often seen in the United States. These companies seek:

- to sell to a third party assets coveted by the bidder ("asset lockup");
- to issue voting stock to a friendly ally ("stock lock-up");
- to adopt anti-takeover charter amendments (often called "shark repellents") if there is sufficient time;
- to repurchase the bidder's stock at a premium ("greenmail"); or
- to issue a convertible security (known as a "poison pill") that, once triggered, either dilutes the stock held by the bidder or entitles holders other than the bidder to purchase the target's stock (or some other package of the target's securities) at an attractive price below its market value.[38]

It is logical to pay serious attention to anti-takeover measures because the "insider control" phenomenon is commonly seen in Chinese listed companies. So far, there has been no systemic anti-takeover legislation and no judiciary has been given a proper chance to adjudicate any illegal anti-takeover activities.

The most important issue here is whether directors or senior management personnel have the right to decide anti-takeover measures in their own discretion. There are divided views. Opposing parties believe that directors should do everything for the best interests of the company and therefore that directors must seek prior approval from the shareholders' meeting before an anti-takeover measure can be applied. It is understandable that directors or

37. Ibid., p. 1052.
38. Ibid., p. 1054.

senior management personnel are more likely to adopt anti-takeover measures because they are afraid of losing their jobs and damaging their reputations. However, the use of improper or illegal anti-takeover measures may injure the lawful interests of the company and its minority shareholders.

Although the existing company law is silent on this issue, it is possible to learn from some of the experiences of other jurisdictions such as the United States and United Kingdom. In the United States, the relevant law gives directors the right to adopt anti-takeover measures. Obviously, in this kind of situation, the directors concerned may need to show that (1) the proposed takeover will injure the legal interests of the company, (2) the anti-takeover measure is taken to defeat the proposed takeover, and (3) the independent directors have participated in and support the decision.[39] On the other hand, however, British law requires the directors of a target company not to take any action unless the action is approved by the shareholders' meeting.

2. Takeover under the Chinese Company Law and the Chinese Securities Laws

Takeover has a relatively short history in China, so relevant laws and regulations need time to develop. The following illustrates the first takeover case in China.

On 30 September 1993, the day the Chinese people celebrated the traditional Mid-Autumn Festival, the Shanghai Stock Exchange (hereinafter referred to as the "Exchange") opened as usual. One hour later, the share price of the Shanghai Yanzhong Company (hereinafter referred to as "Yanzhong") suddenly left its regular track for the past half-month and saw an increase in share price from ¥12.05 to ¥13 per share. More and more people demanded to sell their Yanzhong shares, and within a short period the amount traded reached ¥4.2 million. At 11:15 the Exchange suspended trading because volume had exceeded the limitation of securities regulations. Shortly thereafter, another announcement made by the Shenzhen Baoan Group Shanghai Company (hereinafter referred to as "Baoan") was shown on the TV screens of the Exchange: "In accordance with Article 47 of the Interim Rules, our company proclaims that more than 5 per cent of Yanzhong's common shares have been acquired by us." In the afternoon of the same day, the Exchange resumed trading Yanzhong shares, and prices increased to ¥19.99 per share.

39. *Unocal Corp. v MESA Petroleum Co.*, 493, A2d, 946 (1985).

On 4 October, the day after the Mid-Autumn Festival concluded, the Exchange again opened for business. Baoan made a second announcement through the TV screens of the Exchange: "Our company held 17 per cent of Yanzhong's shares on 30 September." Baoan further demanded that a shareholders' meeting be held.

On 6 October, Yanzhong held a news conference, stating that it intended to block the acquisition. But Baoan continued its purchases and by the end of that trading day had acquired 19 per cent of Yanzhong's shares. The price of the shares went to ¥21.98 per share. The next day, 7 October, Yanzhong decided to defend itself by taking anti-takeover measures. The price of the shares skyrocketed, nearly doubling from ¥22.8 to ¥42.20. More than forty million Yanzhong shares were traded with a total value of ¥3.4 billion, which was an all-time record.

At the demand of Yanzhong, the securities regulatory authority investigated. On 22 October, it concluded that Baoan had violated Article 47 of the Interim Rules.[40] The Authority prohibited Baoan from buying any more Yanzhong shares until 4 November (and then to buy only in 2 per cent increments at three-day intervals). Since Baoan held more than 5 per cent of the shares, it became a major shareholder in Yanzhong and had voting power. For the violation, Baoan was fined ¥1 million.[41]

This case happened before the promulgation of the Chinese Company Law and the Chinese Securities Law. The Interim Rules were effective but still new, and the relevant experience to deal with this case was limited. Nevertheless, this case revealed several violations by Baoan. Firstly, Baoan failed to submit a written report or make an announcement to Yanzhong, the Exchange, and the securities regulatory authority in a timely manner when its holding of Yanzhong shares exceeded 5 per cent and 2 per cent. Secondly, Baoan manipulated the price of Yanzhong's shares through conspiracy and concentration of funds. Regrettably, the securities regulatory

40. Article 47 provides, "If a legal person holds, directly or indirectly, more than 5 per cent of the common shares issued by a listed company, a written report and announcement should be submitted to the listed company, the stock exchange and the CSSMC within 3 working days of the holding. However, if that part in excess is due to a later reduction of the total amount of common shares issued by the company, it is permitted to be held for a reasonable period of time. If a legal person holds more than 5 per cent of the common shares issued by a listed company, a written report and announcement should be submitted to the company, the stock exchange and the CSSMC within 3 working days starting with an increase or reduction of holding of such shares to an amount reaching 2 per cent of the total amount of the common shares issued. A legal person is not allowed to buy or sell such shares directly or indirectly before or within two working days of the submission of the above report and announcement."

41. Summary from Xue Weihong, *The Various Securities Cases* (*Xingxing sese de gupiao anjian*), The China Legal System Press (Beijing), 1994, pp. 321–27.

authority punished these violations only lightly, since it allowed Baoan to retain its shareholder status in Yanzhong.

The possibility of takeover resulted in part from the special permission allowing Yanzhong to convert its legal person shares to individual shares. When Yanzhong decided to issue shares in 1985, it planned to set up a 3:2 ratio between legal person shares and individual shares. Since there was a high demand for Yanzhong shares, Yanzhong was allowed to convert almost all of the legal person shares to individual shares, with the result that individual shares amounted to 91 per cent of the total shares. As mentioned before, legal person shares cannot usually be converted into individual shares. If the legal person shares had remained at 51 per cent, it would have been impossible for Baoan to take over Yanzhong.

Aspects of the Yanzhong transaction were questionable but, more generally, the possibility of takeover was a favourable development. In the long run, China should gradually move away from the confused classification of shares, so that each listed company will not face the challenges of a takeover if it is poorly managed.

Since then, many takeover cases have been seen in China. However, most of the cases indicate problems one way or another. The major problem is government interference and the fact that existing laws and regulations cannot be effectively enforced.

Takeovers of listed companies by foreign investors became realistic after 2002 because many relevant rules and regulations gave them permission. So far, foreign investors have taken four steps to take over listed companies.

The first step is to subscribe the non-transferable shares (such as State shares or legal person shares) of listed companies by way of takeover by agreement or to purchase transferable shares in a second market. By applying this method, foreign investors can realize their controlling shareholding status.

In the second step, listed companies issue shares or bonds (usually convertible bonds) to particular foreign investors, and the foreign investors subscribe those shares or bonds using cash, goods, shareholding rights or other assets agreed upon by the parties of both sides.

In the third step, foreign investors initially form an EJV with a listed company. The EJV then purchases the major assets of the listed company.

In the fourth step, foreign investors take over or form an EJV with the mother company of a listed company. By doing so, the foreign investors indirectly obtain the shareholding right of the listed company, thus becoming the actual controlling persons of the listed company.[42]

42. For a detailed case illustration, please read Chen Zhigang and Gu Jiong, "Four Models of Taking Over Listed Companies by Foreign Investors" (*Waizi shougou shangshi gongsi si da*

3. The Requirements under the Chinese Securities Law

(1) The Methods of Takeover

Under the existing law, the takeover of listed companies normally takes the forms of takeover by offer or takeover by agreement. In both situations, relevant duties are imposed by the Securities Law.

(2) Duty to Disclose

When an investor has held 5 per cent of the issued shares of a listed company in securities trading through the securities exchange, he or she shall, within three days (ten days in the United States) after the occurrence of this fact, report the holding in writing to the securities regulatory authority and the securities exchange, notify the listed company of the holding and proclaim it. Within the time limit prescribed previously, he or she may not continue to trade stocks of the listed company (Art. 86.1). After an investor has held 5 per cent of the shares of a listed company already issued, every time he or she increases or reduces a holding of 5 per cent of the issued shares of a listed company in the trading of securities through the securities exchanges, he or she shall report and proclaim the increase or reduction in line with the relevant provision defined by the preceding clause. Within the period of reporting and in two days after reporting and proclaiming the increase or reduction, he or she may not continue to trade stocks of the listed company (Art. 86.2).

(3) Contents of the Report and Announcement

The written report and announcement should be made if the acquisition has reached 5 per cent of the issued shares of a listed company. However, the contents of the report are not very complicated. The required information includes: (1) the name and address of the shareholders, (2) the name and quantity of the stock held, and (3) the date on which the shareholding reaches the legally required proportion, or the date on which the increase or reduction in shareholding reaches the legally required proportion (Art. 87).

In comparison, the United States law requires more detailed information. For example, the Williams Act requires the disclosure to include:

---

moshi qidi), retrieved from http://finance.sina.com.cn/roll/20030629/1536358052.shtml on 17 October 2015.

(a) the background, identity, residence, citizenship, and nature of such beneficial ownership by such person and all other persons by whom or on whose behalf the purchases have been or are to be effected;
(b) the source and amount of the funds or other considerations used or to be used in making the purchases, and if any part of the purchase price or proposed purchase price is represented or is to be represented by funds or other considerations borrowed or otherwise obtained for the purpose of acquiring, holding or trading such security, a description of the transaction, and the names of the parties thereto, except that where a source of funds is a loan made in the ordinary course of business by a bank, as defined in Section 3(a)(6) of this title, if the person filing such statement so requests, the name of the bank shall not be made available to the public;
(c) if the purpose of the purchases or prospective purchases is to acquire control of the business of the issuer of the securities, any plans or proposals that such persons may have to liquidate to such issuer, to sell its assets to or merge it with any other persons or to make any other major change in its business or corporate structure;
(d) the number of shares of such security that are beneficially owned, and the number of shares concerning which there is a right to acquire, directly or indirectly, by (i) such person and (ii) by each associate of such person, giving the background, identity, residence, and citizenship of each such associate; and
(e) information as to any contracts, arrangements or understandings with any person with respect to any securities of the issuer, including but not limited to transfer of any of the securities, joint ventures, loan or option arrangements, puts or calls, guarantees of loans, guarantees against loss or guarantees of profits, division of losses or profits or the giving or withholding of proxies, naming the persons with whom such contracts, arrangements or understandings have been entered into and giving the details thereof.

One can see that detailed information in the report and announcement is only required when the acquisition has reached 30 per cent of the issued shares of a listed company and a tender offer of acquisition shall be launched (Art. 89).

(4) Compulsory Takeover

When an investor has held 30 per cent of the issued shares of a listed company in the trading of securities through the securities exchange and plans to continue acquiring its shares, he or she shall extend an offer to all of the shareholders of the company for the acquisition of their shares (Art. 88). The Securities Law is silent on whether a bidder can apply for an exemption of the tender offer from the securities regulatory authority (normally the CSRC). In reality, some investors may not seek an exemption because it is too complicated. When an investor is not an SOE, he or she may have an especially weak chance to be exempted, or he or she may need at least 3 months to handle the necessary procedures. Thus, he or she may choose takeover by offer even though the cost is relatively higher.[43]

(5) Special Percentage of State Shares

Since some types of shares are state-owned in nature, the percentage of state shares in a company can be divided into three categories. Under the relevant Chinese rules, state shares refer to shares subscribed by government organs or institutions that are authorized to make the investment in the form of state-owned assets.[44] The state-owned legal person shares refer to shares subscribed by an SOE that makes the investment using authorized state-owned assets.[45] Since both types of shares are state-owned in nature, they could be called state shares.[46] The percentage of state shares in a company can be divided into three categories. Firstly, the state-owned shares should have the absolute controlling percentage among the total issued shares. In this case, the total percentage shall be more than 50 per cent.[47] Secondly, the state-owned shares should have a relative controlling percentage among the total issued shares. In this case, the total percentage shall range from more than 30 per cent. In any event, the holder of the state-owned shares must be the first big shareholders.[48] Finally, the state-owned shares could

43. For one example, see "Analysis of the Case of China's First Takeover by Offer" (*Zhongguo shouli yaoyue shougou anli fenxi*), retrieved from http://www.china-b.com/kaoshi/ckks/20090312/831480_1.html on 17 October 2015.
44. Article 3, the Interim Rules on Management of State-owned Assets in the Pilot Enterprises of the Joint Stock System (*Gufenzhi Shidian Qiye Guoyou Zichan Guanli Zauxing Guiding*), issued by the State Management Bureau of State-owned Assets and State Committee on Reform of the Economic System on 27 July 1992.
45. Ibid.
46. Ibid. See also page 4 of *China Law for Business* (Vol. 3, No. 6/October 1997), published by Law and Tax Asia Pacific. On that page, the term "state enterprise shares" is misleading. Instead, it should be "state shares".
47. Article 5, the Guidelines on the Rights of Holders of State-owned Shares in Joint Stock Companies (*Gufen Youxian Gongsi Guoyou Gu Gudong Xingshi Guquan Xingwei Guifan Yijian*), issued by the State Management Bureau of State-owned Assets and the State Committee on Reform of Economic System on 24 March 1997.
48. Ibid.

be any normal percentage. The relevant rules are silent on the detailed percentages.

State-owned shares are usually not allowed to be transferred to private interests.[49] In that way, the state can still retain control over companies formed by authorized government organs or institutions by using state-owned assets or by converting SOEs into corporate forms. This is also consistent with the Marxist-Leninist principle of ownership of the means of production by the people, as represented by the state.[50] For these reasons, the government pays close attention to the protection of state-owned shares and has issued two notices to urge the protection of holders of state-owned shares.[51] However, if China allows the transfer of state-owned shares, will the transfer lead to privatization of the SOEs or SOEs in corporate forms?[52] Will China develop the second biggest M&A market in the world after the United States?[53] The possible answer is that this situation changed when the Chinese government announced in November 2013 that SOEs would be

49. However, on some special occasions, the State shares were transferred. Observers of the Shanghai Exchange have stated that as of 13 November 1992, the first 13 companies listed on the Exchange "had surreptitiously put Y30 million worth of State and legal person shares into circulation. The way in which the Shanghai Exchange gave local companies special privileges and concealed the news from the mass of investors received criticism from the news media." See Fang Liufang, "China's Corporatization Experiment", *Duke Journal of Comparative & International Law*, Vol. 5, Iss. 2 (1995), pp. 149, 213, n. 142. As a result of this practice, Shanghai Yanzhong Company was taken over by Shenzhen Baoan Group Shanghai Company. See Xie Weihong (ed.), *Various Securities Law Cases (Xingxing sese de gupiao anjian)*, China Legal System Press (Beijing), 1994, pp. 321–32.

50. Xu Guangchun, spokesman for the Fifteenth Party Congress, said, "Turning State-owned enterprises into shareholding companies does not mean China promotes privatization". *South China Morning Post*, 12 September 1997, p. 12.

51. On 4 April 1994, the State Management Bureau of State-owned Assets issued the Emergent Notice regarding Protection of Interests of State-owned Shares when Issuing New Shares to Shareholders (*Guanyu Zai Shangshi Gongsi Song Pei Gu shi Weihu Guojiagu Quanyi de Jinji Tongzhi*). On 1 December of the same year, the State Management Bureau of State-owned Assets issued the Notice concerning Relevant Problems of Issuing New Shares to State-owned Shares by Listed Companies and Transfer of State-Owned Shares (*Guanyu dui Shangshi Gongsi Guojiagu Peigu ji Guquan Zhuanrang Deng Youguan Wenti de Tongzi*).

52. Since China promulgated the first national corporation law (*Zhonghua Renmin Gongheguo Gongsi Fa*) on 29 December 1993, many SOEs have been converted into corporate forms. However, "the State will maintain ultimate control and majority ownership of the largest enterprises pursuant to a policy we term 'corporatization'". Robert C. Art and Minkang Gu, "China Incorporated: The First Corporation Law of the People's Republic of China", *The Yale Journal of International Law*, Vol. 20, 1995, pp. 273, 275.

53. Laurent Gasser, "A Risky Business? The Hidden Dangers of M&A in China", *China Direct Investor*, Vol. 3, Issue 7 (April 1998), p. 20. In the article, the author announces that "since the Fifteenth National Communist Party Congress in September 1997, the green light seems to have been given by the highest authorities of the country: China State-owned enterprises are for sale". Ibid.

further reformed by adopting mixed ownership.[54] This will open the door for mergers, or at least acquisition by private investors (including foreign investors).

If future rules and regulations will open the M&A door to foreign investors, the relevant rules and regulations concerning state shares should be rewritten so that obstacles can be removed.

X. DIVISION OF COMPANIES

The division of companies occurs when one company is legally divided into two or more companies. This division can take the form of division by new establishment, i.e., one company is divided into two or more companies and the original company still exists. It can also take the form of simple division, where after the division the original company no longer exists. Basically, the legal procedures are similar to those of the merger.

Firstly, when a company decides to divide itself, it shall formulate a balance sheet and a detailed inventory of assets.

Secondly, the division of a company shall require the adoption of a resolution by a shareholders' meeting of the company. Furthermore, permission should be acquired if there is a division of a joint stock limited company.

Thirdly, the company shall inform its creditors of the intended division within 10 days following the date on which the division resolution is adopted, and make at least 3 announcements in newspapers within 30 days (Art. 175.2). Since the post-division companies shall bear several and joint liabilities for the debts of the company before its division (Art. 176), the creditors in this situation do not need to claim full repayment of their debts or ask for provision of a corresponding guarantee from the company, like they do in a merger situation (Art. 173.2).

Usually, the division of a company will result in the reduction of capital. The company shall apply to a relevant company registration authority for registration of the changes in accordance with the law (Art. 179).

54. Someone calls it "ownership diversification". See Daniel Dusek, Peter X. Huang, and Andre Zhu, "China M&A: Reform Plan Promotes Mixed Ownership of State-Owned Enterprises", retrieved from https://www.skadden.com/insights/china-ma-reform-plan-promotes-mixed-ownership-state-owned-enterprises on 17 October 2015.

12

Bankruptcy Proceedings

I. INTRODUCTION

British law may define the word "bankruptcy" for a different purpose. Thus, a company cannot be made bankrupt, but may be wound up if it is insolvent. The terms "winding up" and "liquidation" may bear the same meaning, i.e., the process by which a company's assets are collected, its debts are paid and the surplus, if any, is distributed among its members. These two terms, however, are different from the term "bankruptcy". In Hong Kong, for example, the rules of bankruptcy are contained in the Bankruptcy Ordinance (Cap. 6), whereas liquidations are governed by the Companies Ordinance.[1] Certainly, there is one major difference between "liquidation" and "bankruptcy", i.e., in a liquidation situation a company can be either solvent or insolvent, while in a bankruptcy situation a company must be insolvent. Thus, from the viewpoint of insolvency, the bankruptcy of individuals and insolvency of companies probably mean the same thing.

China adopts a similar approach to that of Hong Kong, i.e., there are separate laws governing a company's liquidation and bankruptcy. Under the Company Law, a company can be dissolved voluntarily or involuntarily (Art. 180). One thing different from Hong Kong company law is that

1. For a detailed discussion see K. Arjunan and C. K. Low, *Lipton & Herzberg's Understanding Company Law in Hong Kong*, The LBC Information Services (Sydney), 1996, p. 409. In fact, "the reforms introduced by the Companies Ordinance (Cap. 622) do not touch on the winding-up provisions of the Companies Ordinance (Cap. 32)". See Stefan H. C. Lo and Charles Z. Qu, *Law of Companies in Hong Kong*, Sweet & Maxwell (Hong Kong), 2013, p. 873.

Article 180 deals only with liquidation when a company may still be solvent: (1) the term of business operation as prescribed by the bylaw expires or any of the situations for dissolution prescribed in the company's byelaw occurs; (2) the SHM decides to dissolve the company; (3) it is necessary to dissolve the company due to a merger or a split; (4) the business licence is cancelled or the company is ordered to close down or to be dissolved according to laws; or (5) a people's court decides that the company be dissolved according to Article 183.[2]

Once a decision of liquidation is made, a liquidation committee shall be formed within fifteen days after the reason for dissolution occurs and commence the liquidation (Art. 183). It is important to note that if the liquidation committee discovers that there are insufficient assets in the company to pay off its debts, the committee shall apply to the people's court for a declaration of bankruptcy (Art. 187). It is further assumed that most companies will not consider the dissolution unless there is a serious financial problem. Therefore, the focus of this chapter is on Chinese bankruptcy proceedings.

China did not have a bankruptcy system until the later Qing dynasty. During the more than 2,000 years before 1906,[3] Chinese society was dominated by a feudal legal tradition and ideology, i.e., "The debt of a father should be paid by his son (*fu zhai zi huan*)." During that period, it was impossible for a debtor to have status equal to a creditor.[4]

The earliest Chinese bankruptcy law can be traced back to the Qing dynasty.[5] It was called the "*Pochan Lü*" and enacted in 1906.[6] However, the "*Pochan Lü*" was abolished in 1908 due to a strong protest from merchants. Later, during 1915–49, several Chinese bankruptcy laws were enacted by the Guomindang government. Interestingly, those laws became the basic structure of the current bankruptcy law in Taiwan.[7]

Within the first three decades after the People's Republic of China was established in 1949, all laws enacted by the Guomindang government were

---

2. Article 182 deals with a situation where a company has encountered "serious difficulty in its operations or management".
3. After the Opium War in 1840, the Qing feudal system was greatly shaken and the Qing government was pushed by foreign countries to reform its legal system. Furthermore, following the development of commercial activities, the Qing government had to enact modern commercial laws. In April 1806, the *Pochan Lü* was promulgated.
4. Gao Yan and Liu Lu, *Understanding and Application of Bankruptcy Law and Case Discussion*, The People's Court Press (Beijing), 1996, p. 8.
5. The last feudal empire in Chinese history.
6. Li Yan (ed.), *Commercial Law*, The Press of Central National University (Beijing), 1999, p. 497.
7. Yu Zhaoping, *Systems and Legal Practice of Bankruptcy Law*, The People's Court Press (Beijing), 1998, p. 5.

abolished. Following the adoption of the planned economy, the central government was proud of the fact that no bankruptcy case was seen in the country during that period.[8] Therefore, nobody bothered to think about the need to enact a bankruptcy law.

In addition, some other reasons might have affected the existence of bankruptcy proceedings before 1986, the year when China started to implement economic reform:

(a) There was a deeply rooted tradition of keeping one's face (*Gei Mian Zi*). There was a traditional view in China that bankruptcy was associated with the situation where both parties in disputes (usually previous business partners) lost face. Wanting to give face to their business partners, Chinese businesspeople found it difficult to accept the bankruptcy proceedings.[9]
(b) There was a strong "socialist ideology" depicting bankruptcy as an inherently capitalist product.[10] Therefore, it was impossible to associate bankruptcy with the Chinese socialist system in the past.
(c) The "iron rice bowl" (*tie fanwan*) policy had an effect in China before 1978. Under the socialist ideology, workers should be able to keep their jobs until retirement. This was termed as the "iron rice bowl" policy. It was believed that bankruptcy would ultimately affect the employment of the existing workers. Thus, bankruptcy was regarded as a contradiction to the "iron rice bowl" policy.
(d) There were other practical obstacles. The practice of bankruptcy was not long enough. The limited number of bankruptcy cases in the past indicated that governments on various levels interfered heavily because the Chinese government worried about social instability when too many workers were laid off.

8. Wang Guiguo, *Wang's Business Law of China* (3rd ed.), Butterworth Asia (Hong Kong), 1999, p. 347. The situation was the same for unemployment. For a very long time, it was believed that unemployment was only a special phenomenon in capitalist countries that would not happen in a socialist country. See Feng Hailin, "A Discussion on Unemployment Security and Re-employment Services", *The Journal of Social Security System*, No. 7, 1998, p. 24.
9. In contrast with the litigation system in Western countries, ancient China had a firmly established ideology of non-litigation. For example, in the Western Zhou dynasty (c. 11th century–771 BC), a son could not sue his father. Also, because China had a long period involving a small-scale peasant economy, family disputes were controlled under the patriarchal clan system. For detailed information, see He Qinhua et al., *The Introduction to Chinese and Western Legal Cultures*, The Fudan University Press (Shanghai), 1994, pp. 293–300.
10. Shirley S. Cho, "Continuing Economic Reform in the PRC: Bankruptcy Legislation Leads the Way", *Hastings International & Comparative Law Review*, Vol. 19, 1996, p. 743.

From the preceding introduction, one can see that China did not have bankruptcy legislation for about 40 years even though the earliest bankruptcy law appeared in China eighty years ago. Thus, before the implementation of the "open-door" policy, it would have been a big surprise for one to mention the term "bankruptcy".

However, following the implementation of the economic reform policy, which resulted in mixed economies comprising elements of both planned and market economies, and with the government's encouragement of competition among enterprises, the concept of bankruptcy was gradually accepted and recognized as an important lever for raising the productivity of enterprises.[11] Furthermore, the concept of bankruptcy became closely associated with the reform of SOEs. Due to the large-scale adoption of bankruptcy, both the Chinese government and people gradually accepted the concept of bankruptcy as a kind of economic measure.[12]

The implementation of the Old Bankruptcy Law, which was promulgated in 1986, was not so successful.[13] The central government found that the cost of bankruptcy was too high and decided to control the number and size of insolvent enterprises, while the method of merger was highly encouraged.[14] Furthermore, many problems have cropped up in the bankruptcy policy, such as too much administrative intervention, hard settlement of employees and serious local protectionism.[15] For these reasons, the new bankruptcy law was demanded for many years to replace the old one.

Around the world, a bankruptcy law usually contains the following features:

11. Wang, supra note 8, p. 347.
12. It is a difficult task to obtain the exact number of bankruptcy cases. However, it is possible to show a general picture of how many cases have been handled each year. The first source reveals that cases increased every year in 1999 (5,622 cases), 2000 (7,746 cases) and 2001 (9,110 cases). Lai Weitang, *Suggestions to Perfect the Announcement of Enterprise Bankruptcy in China (Qiantan dui woguo qiye pochan de xuangao zhidu de wanshan jianyi)*, retrieved from http://www.chinacourt.org/html/article/200706/13/251531.shtml on 18 October 2015. The second source reveals that, during the time period of 2003–2012, cases tried and concluded by all courts were reduced. There were in total 40,483 bankruptcy cases and the annual reduction rate was 12.23 per cent. Ma Jian, "Statistical Analysis of Bankruptcy Cases Handled by Chinese Court During 2003–2012" (2003–2012 *Renmin fayuan shenli pochan anjian tongji fenxi*), retrieved from http://www.legaldaily.com.cn/zbzk/content/2014-03/26/content_5401182.htm?node=25497 on 18 October 2015.
13. The whole name of the Old Bankruptcy Law is the Enterprise Bankruptcy Law of the PRC (On a Trail Basis).
14. "SOE Reform Plan Needs Rejiggering", *China Daily*, 5 May 1999.
15. Ibid.

(1) It is a procedure law, and the core issue is to maximize the recoveries for holders of legal entitlements in respect of a financially distressed debtor. However, it may be wrong to not consider the legal interests of third parties, such as employees and the general community.[16]
(2) While traditional bankruptcy law seeks to maximize the recoveries for holders of legal entitlements (creditor-oriented protection), today's bankruptcy laws tend to hold a person responsible for debt under a court-ordered repayment plan. Thus, the modern bankruptcy laws try to strike a balance between a debtor and his or her creditors.[17]
(3) Modern bankruptcy laws usually cover 10 areas, such as (i) property of the estate, (ii) claims and interests, (iii) pro rata sharing among similarly situated right-holders, (iv) the automatic stay, (v) the bankruptcy trustee's power to avoid certain pre-bankruptcy transfers, (vi) the trustee's power to reject or assume executory contracts and leases, (vii) the individual debtor's discharge and the fresh start principle, (viii) the provision for a debtor's discharge, (ix) priority claims, and (x) adequate protection for under-secured creditors.

The long-awaited new Enterprise Bankruptcy Law (hereinafter referred to as the "New Bankruptcy Law") was finally promulgated by the Twenty-third Session of the Standing Committee of the Tenth NPC and took effect on 1 June 2007. While the New Bankruptcy Law bears features similar to those of other bankruptcy laws around the world, it shows several new developments that deserve further introduction.

In part two of this chapter, the Old Bankruptcy Law as well as other regulations are examined and discussed. In addition, new developments of the New Bankruptcy Law are emphasized. The main intention of this chapter is to comment on the newly promulgated Enterprise Bankruptcy Law. In part three, this chapter addresses several remaining problems that are supposed to be improved in the near future. In the conclusion, this book points out that a unified bankruptcy law must be adopted in order to deal with various debtors.

16. Charles W. Mooney Jr, "A Normative Theory of Bankruptcy Law: Bankruptcy As (Is) Civil Procedure", *Washington and Lee Law Review*, Vol. 61, No. 3, 2004.
17. President Bush signed new legislation that was purported to be a reformation of the nation's bankruptcy law. One important feature was to make it more difficult to file for Chapter 7, which virtually writes off one's debts. On the other hand, many people file for Chapter 13, which continues to hold a person responsible for debt under a court-ordered repayment plan.

II. EVOLUTION OF BANKRUPTCY LAW

In the China, the term "bankruptcy law" contains both narrow and broad meanings. The narrow meaning of "bankruptcy law" refers to the bankruptcy and liquidation of a debtor's property (negative way). The broad meaning of "bankruptcy law" involves not only bankruptcy and liquidation, but also emphasizes the assistance given to debtors for the purpose of avoiding bankruptcy, i.e., to give debtors a chance to seek reconciliation and/or reorganize their business. Thus, the modern meaning of bankruptcy law shall contain liquidation, reconciliation, and reorganization, like that of the US Bankruptcy Law.[18] Furthermore, the broad meaning of bankruptcy law includes not only the formal law promulgated by the NPC, but also the rules and regulations issued by the State Council and judicial interpretations issued by the SPC.

On 2 December 1986, the first bankruptcy law, the Old Bankruptcy Law, was promulgated by the Eighteenth Session of the Standing Committee of the Sixth NPC. It took effect three months after the adoption of the SOE Law of the People's Republic of China on 1 November 1988. The Old Bankruptcy Law was promulgated on a trial basis and contained only forty-three articles, which indicated that at the time of the making of this Law Chinese legislators did not have any previous experience on the matter of bankruptcy and intended this legal document to be implemented on a trial basis.

The most important feature of the Old Bankruptcy Law was that it applied only to SOEs and had been implemented for more than twenty years. The bankruptcy of other enterprises including non-enterprise units; individuals were not covered by this Law. On 9 April 1991, the Civil Procedure Law of the People's Republic of China was promulgated. Chapter 19 provides bankruptcy procedures for non-SOE legal persons. Presumably, some foreign invested enterprises are not within the coverage of Chapter 19.[19]

18. Chapter 11 of the US Bankruptcy Code provides details of the reorganization. See *Bankruptcy Code, Rules and Forms*, West Publishing Company (St. Paul, MN), 1996.

19. Some scholars believe that Chapter 19 of the Civil Procedure Law applies to collectively owned enterprises, private enterprises and FIEs. See Tang Dehua (ed.), *The Interpretation of New Civil Procedure Law*, The People's Court Press (Beijing), 1991, pp. 335–36. Citing Cheng Qingbo, *Research on International Bankruptcy Law* (*Guoji pochan fa yanjiu*), The Press of Hunan Normal University (Hunan), 1995, p. 15. Furthermore, it has been noticed that Article 240 of the SPC's Opinions on Issues Concerning the Application of the Civil Procedural Law of the PRC provides that the bankrupt debtors should include "Chinese-foreign equity joint ventures, Chinese-foreign contractual joint ventures and wholly foreign-funded enterprises", but this provision does not mention whether these foreign-funded enterprises should be legal persons, since the Chinese-foreign contractual joint ventures and wholly foreign-funded enterprises may be in a non-legal person form. In the absence of relevant legal provision, does this mean that those foreign-funded

Article 206 of the Civil Procedure Law states that the provisions of Chapter 19 shall not apply to the following subjects: enterprises with no legal person status, individual industrial and commercial households, farming business households with contractual responsibility, and individual partnerships. However, in line with relevant laws and regulations on foreign invested enterprises, some foreign invested enterprises are allowed not to take legal person status.[20] If this is the case, Chapter 19 shall not apply. In practice, in handling bankruptcy cases of enterprises with no legal person status, one may assume that the court may take into consideration the procedures prescribed by the Old Bankruptcy Law and the Civil Procedure Law. On the other hand, bankruptcy and the winding up of companies are mainly governed by Chapter 8 of the 1993 Company Law.[21] However, if a company is also an SOE, one may assume that a people's court may follow the provisions of either the Bankruptcy Law or the Company Law depending on its economic situation (solvent or not).

In order for courts to successfully implement the Old Bankruptcy Law, the SPC issued the Opinions Regarding Implementation of Bankruptcy Law of People's Republic of China on 7 November 1991. On 25 October 1994, the State Council issued the Notice Regarding Trial Implementation of State-owned Enterprises in Several Cities.[22] On 2 March 1997, the State Council issued the Supplementary Notice Concerning the Trial Implementation of SOE Bankruptcy, Merger and Reemployment of Staff and Workers (the 1997 Notice). Those legal documents provided detailed instructions about how to rearrange the workers, how to dispose of a liquidating property and how to deal with the losses of banks as major creditors. In addition, the Foreign Invested Enterprises Liquidation Procedures were applied only to foreign invested enterprises.[23]

Thus, one can clearly see that the bankruptcy laws and regulations in China were in a chaotic situation in the past. This chaotic situation indicates

enterprises without legal person status may be subject to the 2002 Several Issues? With respect to this issue, further discussion shall be conducted.

20. For example, Article 50 of the Detailed Rules for the Implementation of the Law of the PRC on Sino-foreign Cooperative Enterprises states, "a cooperative enterprise without legal person status and the parties to that cooperative enterprise will bear civil liability in accordance with relevant provisions of Chinese Civil Law".
21. Subsequently, the Chinese company law was largely amended on 27 October 2005, and the liquidation of companies is covered by Chapter 10 of the existing company law.
22. In China, the SPC is delegated the power to issue a judicial interpretation for the purpose of filling in gaps while the State Council is delegated the power to issue administrative rules and regulations in order to implement national laws.
23. It was promulgated by the Ministry of Foreign Trade and Economic Co-operative on 9 July 1996.

that Chinese legislators took the precaution to experiment with the open-door policy from the very beginning. Therefore, China permitted the coexistence of different types of business enterprises governed by different sets of laws and regulations: (1) business enterprises that were based on the nature of their ownership, i.e., SOEs, collectively owned enterprises and privately owned enterprises, (2) business enterprises that were based on domestic or foreign investors, and (3) business enterprises that were similar to those in other jurisdictions, i.e., companies, partnerships and sole proprietorships.[24] The outcome of this precaution was that China could not establish a unified business law, nor could it achieve a unified bankruptcy law with its implementing rules. One may ask whether this situation will be changed soon, as it has been more than ten years since China's accession to the WTO. The answer must be positive for two important reasons. Firstly, China has started to treat foreign and domestic investors equally by unifying the enterprise income tax law.[25] Secondly, the New Bankruptcy Law will apply to all legal person enterprises regardless of whether they are established by domestic investors or foreign investors.[26] Those are considered as major steps towards the establishment of a unified business enterprise law as well as a unified bankruptcy law.

Before the goal of a unified bankruptcy law could be fully realized, the SPC made some efforts to improve this chaotic situation. On 18 July 2002, the SPC published the Several Issues on Hearing Enterprise Bankruptcy Cases (hereinafter referred to as the "2002 Several Issues"). The 2002 Several Issues are intended to clarify and streamline the bankruptcy proceedings on the one hand and to keep the principles of protecting SOEs on the other hand.[27]

The long-waiting new Enterprise Bankruptcy Law (the New Bankruptcy Law) was finally promulgated by the Twenty-third Session of the Standing

24. Gu Minkang, "Chinese Business Enterprises Law in the Twenty-first Century", in Joseph Y. S. Cheng (ed.), *China's Challenges in the Twenty-First Century*, City University of Hong Kong Press (Hong Kong), 2003, pp. 452–53.
25. The new Enterprises' Income Tax Law of the PRC was passed on 16 March 2007 by the Fifth Session of the Tenth NPC and has been effective since 1 January 2008.
26. The New Bankruptcy Law, Article 2. Furthermore, according to the SPC's Reply on Whether the Liquidation of Sole Proprietorships May Refer to the Procedure for Bankruptcy Liquidation as Prescribed in the Enterprise Bankruptcy Law issued on 11 December 2012, the liquidation of sole proprietorships could follow the New Bankruptcy Law.
27. For the first time, the 2002 Several Issues applied to legal person enterprises regardless of whether they were State owned or not. However, Article 5 of the 2002 Several Issues still required that an approval must be sought from a superior if an SOE wanted to file a bankruptcy application, which is a prima facie case of allowing government interference when an SOE is involved.

Committee of the Tenth NPC and took effect on 1 June 2007. This law was intended to replace the Old Bankruptcy Law and cover all legal person enterprises even though it still left the bankruptcy of non-legal-person enterprises to be regulated by other laws. Furthermore, the SPC issued two judicial interpretations for the purpose of implementing the New Bankruptcy Law: (1) Provisions (Part One) on Several Issues Concerning the Application of the Enterprise Bankruptcy Law of the People's Republic of China issued on 9 September 2011 and (2) Provisions (Part Two) on Several Issues Concerning the Application of the Enterprise Bankruptcy Law of the People's Republic of China (Part Two Bankruptcy Interpretations) issued on 5 September 2013. According to the SPC, all judicial interpretations made before the Part Two Bankruptcy Interpretations are still valid unless they conflict with the Part Two Bankruptcy Interpretation.[28] Thus, it is possible to say that some provisions of the 2002 Several Issues could still be treated as a valid judicial interpretation if there is no contradiction. One piece of evidence to support this argument is that the SPC issued a special judicial interpretation to explain the linkage between the application of the Old Bankruptcy Law and the New Bankruptcy Law. It, however, does not specifically announce the nullity of the 2002 Several Issues.[29]

III. DEVELOPMENTS UNDER THE NEW BANKRUPTCY LAW

1. Equal Treatment to All Legal Person Enterprises

In order for a legal person enterprise to be bankrupted, two conditions must be satisfied. Firstly, the enterprise must be unable to discharge matured liability. Secondly, the enterprise must not have sufficient assets to pay off its total debts or be obviously unable to pay off the debts.[30] These two conditions are much clearer than those provided by the Old Bankruptcy Law, which required that an enterprise incur significant losses due to inappropriate management.[31] This condition indicates clearly that the Old Bankruptcy Law was adopted to save SOEs rather than to protect the legal interest of creditors. Thus, the underlying message of the Old Bankruptcy Law was that an enterprise that did not suffer serious losses but was unable to discharge matured liability could not be bankrupted. If an enterprise suffered serious

28. The Part Two Bankruptcy Interpretations, Art. 48.
29. The Rules of the SPC on Several Issues Concerning the Application of Law to Bankruptcy Cases not yet decided when the Bankruptcy Law of the PRC is implemented, which was published by the SPC on 23 April 2007 and was taken into force on 1 June 2007.
30. The New Bankruptcy Law, Article 2.
31. The Old Bankruptcy Law, Article 3. Also, the Civil Procedure Law, Article 199.

losses because of a policy change or other reasons, the enterprise could be excused even if it was unable to discharge its matured liability. For this reason, one author pointed out that the old provision was not consistent with the international practice.[32] Furthermore, the standards for substantiating "significant" and "inappropriate" were unclear. Through comparison, it is evident that the New Bankruptcy Law intends to equally treat all legal person enterprises and that SOEs are no longer more superior to other legal person enterprises.

One achievement that has been made is that the New Bankruptcy Law eliminates the superior situation of the SOEs, where the Old Bankruptcy Law gave an exemption of bankruptcy to certain SOEs if (a) the enterprise concerned was a public enterprise or an enterprise with an important bearing on the national economy and the people's livelihood, in which case the relevant government departments would provide economic assistance or take other measures to assist in the discharge of liabilities, and (b) a guarantee was obtained and liabilities were discharged within 6 months of a bankruptcy application being lodged.[33] There are good reasons to treat all legal person enterprises equally, as all SOEs will no longer be given privilege on a policy basis (*zhengcexing pochan*). The big difference between bankruptcy on a policy basis and commercial bankruptcy (*shangyexing pochan*) is that in the former situation all bankruptcy property should be used to help the settle-down of workers rather than to pay off the creditor's debts. Furthermore, it is evident that five provinces and cities directly controlled by the central government (Beijing, Shanghai, Jiangsu, Zhejiang, and Fujian) have stopped the implementation of enterprise bankruptcy on a policy basis and started to implement enterprise bankruptcy based on commercial considerations. Finally, the central government decided that all SOEs would be bankrupted on commercial terms after 2008.[34]

2. A Convenient Venue Will Be Allowed

When a legal person enterprise is unable to discharge a matured liability, both a creditor and a debtor can apply for bankruptcy. However, in line with the Old Bankruptcy Law, the decision to be bankrupted was not in the hands of the debtor, but in the hands of its superior. This required the

32. Cheng, supra note 19, p. 93.
33. The Old Bankruptcy Law, Art. 3.
34. "The New Bankruptcy Law Forces SOEs to Say Goodbye to the Bankruptcy on Policy Basis, 'A Special Treatment'", retrieved from http://news.xinhuanet.com/fortune/2006-08/27/content_5012755.htm on 19 October 2015.

debtor to seek an approval from a higher-level department in charge before making such an application. In other words, even if an SOE suffers from a serious loss and is unable to pay matured debts, it may not be allowed to apply for bankruptcy proceedings if the higher-level department in charge disagrees. The high-level authorities may consider injecting new capital in order to rescue the SOE. This old provision definitely contradicted the relevant laws and regulations concerning the legal person status of SOEs,[35] but it was understandable because of the great social impact[36] caused by the bankruptcy proceedings and given that SOEs were not the legal owners of their assets. Thanks to the further economic reform in China, this awkward situation has been changed by the New Bankruptcy Law.

In the past, a bankruptcy case would have come within the jurisdiction of the local people's court where the debtor was located.[37] This indicated that a creditor could not apply for a debtor to declare bankruptcy in a local people's court that had no jurisdiction over the debtor regardless of how it was convenient to the creditor.

There are two points that explain this situation. Firstly, this provision complied with Chinese legal principles and practices. Article 22 of the Civil Procedure Law addresses the geographic jurisdiction (*diyu guanxia*). It states, "A civil lawsuit brought against a person shall be under the jurisdiction of the People's Court of the place where the defendant has his domicile . . . A civil lawsuit brought against a legal person or any other organization shall be under the jurisdiction of the People's Court of the place where the defendant has his domicile". Article 205 of the Civil Procedure Law also states that the debt repayment of a legal person enterprise shall be under the jurisdiction of the people's court of the place where the legal person enterprise is located. Secondly, the geographic jurisdiction will enable the people's court where the debtor is located to collect necessary evidence. However, it is important to note that in some situations the people's court where the debtor is located may have no jurisdiction over a bankruptcy case. This is because the court may have to consider the jurisdiction based on the forum level. According to the Opinions Regarding Implementation of Bankruptcy Law (Trial) of the People's Republic of China issued by the SPC, a local court has jurisdiction over a bankruptcy case if the registration of an enterprise is handled by the

35. Article 2 of the Law of the PRC on SOEs states, "The property of an enterprise shall belong to the whole people and shall be operated and managed by the enterprise with the authorization of the State, in accordance with the principle of separating ownership rights and management rights. An enterprise shall enjoy the right to possess, use and legally dispose of property which the State has authorized it to operate and manage."
36. In China, SOEs play a major role in hiring the majority of employees.
37. The Old Bankruptcy Law, Article 5(4).

administrative bureau for commerce and industry on the county level, and an intermediate people's court has a jurisdiction over a bankruptcy case if the registration of an enterprise is handled by the administrative bureau of commerce and industry on the municipal level.[38]

On the other hand, the 2002 Several Issues, for the first time, address the issue of adjustment to the geographic jurisdiction, i.e., with the approval of the joint people's court at a higher level, under a special circumstance, an adjustment may be made to the geographic jurisdiction of a particular bankruptcy case within a province, autonomous region or municipality directly under the Central Government.[39] This exception provides a legal basis for the parties in a bankruptcy case to assert "*forum non conveniens*". Although the 2002 Several Issues fail to address what are those special circumstances, one can assume that this may help to solve the big problem of local protectionism. Most significantly, this provision may play an important role in dismantling the principle of "a plaintiff following a defendant", which is deeply rooted in China.

3. A Clear List of Creditors' Rights

Following the adoption of equal treatment to all legal person enterprises, it is necessary to identify what rights of creditors shall be protected in bankruptcy proceedings. One remarkable achievement is that the 2002 Several Issues, for the first time, provide for the full scope of the creditor's rights: (a) creditor's right without a property charge arising before the declaration of bankruptcy; (b) creditor's right with a property charge before the declaration of bankruptcy, but the creditor has given up its pre-emptive right; (c) creditor's right with a property charge before the declaration of bankruptcy on the part of the amount exceeding the value of the charged property; (d) creditor's right arising from the payment or acceptance and payment by the drawee or acceptor to the holder of a negotiable instrument without knowing the fact that the issuer of the instrument has been declared bankrupt; (e) creditor's right that can be calculated in currency enjoyed by the other party according to law or contract arising from the rescission of a contract by the liquidation group; (f) creditor's right arising from the trust affairs carried out by the debtor's trustee in the interest of the debtor after the bankruptcy of the debtor; (g) creditor's right arising from the issuance of debentures; (h) creditor's right enjoyed by the debtor's guarantor that has repaid debt in lieu of the debtor and may claim reimbursement from the

38. The Opinions Regarding Implementation of the Bankruptcy Law of the PRC, Article 2.
39. The 2002 Several Issues, Article 3.

debtor; (i) creditor's right declared by the debtor's guarantor that has exercised in advance the right of reimbursement according to Article 32 of the Guaranty Law of the People's Republic of China; (j) the guaranty liability determined by an effective legal instrument to be assumed by the debtor as a guarantor before the declaration of bankruptcy; (k) the compensatory liability arising from the debtor's tort or breach of contract causing property losses to others before the declaration of bankruptcy; and (l) other creditors' rights determined by the people's court.[40] This list will definitely help to successfully implement the New Bankruptcy Law. Furthermore, this list will enable foreign investors and practising lawyers to effectively identify relevant rights in bankruptcy proceedings.

4. Administrator: A New Creation

The administrator is specially created by the New Bankruptcy Law. It has the functions similar to those of the "Enterprise Supervision Committee" (*Qiye Jianguan Zu*) created by the 2002 Several Issues for the first time in 2002. One important difference is that the administrators are professional-oriented persons, while the Enterprise Supervision Committee is still involved in administrative authorities, which may exercise administrative interference.[41] The administrator plays key roles in bankruptcy proceedings based on the powers given by the New Bankruptcy Law.[42] Therefore, the qualifications of an administrator are essential to securing their proper activities. Although the New Bankruptcy Law is silent on the qualifications, the SPC acts quickly to fill in the gap. In the Rules Concerning the Appointment of an Administrator in Hearing Bankruptcy Cases issued on 12 April 2007, the SPC excludes the following parties from being administrators:

40. Ibid., Article 55.
41. Article 18 of the 2002 Several Issues states that the members on the enterprise supervision committee should be formed by the competent higher authorities, representatives of the shareholders' meeting, management and major creditors of the enterprise.
42. Article 25 of the New Bankruptcy Law gives an administrator the following powers: (a) to take over the debtor's property, chops and books and important documents; (b) to investigate the debtor's financial condition and to make a report of the financial conditions; (c) to decide the debtor's internal administrative affairs; (d) to decide the debtor's daily expenses and other necessary expenses; (e) to decide whether to continue or to stop the debtor's business before the first creditors' meeting is held; (f) to manage and dispose of the debtor's property; (g) to participate in litigations, arbitrations or other legal proceedings on behalf of the debtor; (h) to propose to hold a creditors' meeting; and (i) to perform other duties that are considered to be proper for the administrator by the people's court.

(a) those who have been given administrative penalties or disciplinary sanctions by administrative authorities, regulatory authorities or industry self-regulatory bodies because of their intentional actions or gross negligent actions in their practices or business operations, when the time period is less than three years since the date the punishment decisions were made;
(b) those who have been investigated for their suspected violations by the relevant authorities;
(c) those who have been deleted from the administrator roster by the people's court because of improper performance of their duties or refusing acceptance of appointment by the people's court, when the time period is less than three years since the date the names were deleted;
(d) those who do not possess professional abilities required for the administrator;
(e) those who do not have a civil capacity; and
(f) other situations that, in the eye of the people's court, will affect the administrator's proper performance of duties.

An administrator will be seen as a professional and will be given attractive remuneration for fulfilling his or her duties. At this stage, an administrator will only be given remuneration on a percentage basis. This decision was made by the SPC when it issued the Rules Concerning the Remuneration for the Administrator in Hearing Bankruptcy Cases on 12 April 2007.[43] There are four reasons that justify this practice. Firstly, it is not the right time to adopt the remuneration on hourly basis because the relevant implementing system has not been established and there exists a high moral risk and a lower recognition from society. Secondly, the remuneration on a percentage basis is simple and easily operated and is easily accepted by the public. Thirdly, the remuneration on a percentage basis gives more incentive to an administrator to collect back more property, and furthermore the interests of creditors can be well protected. Fourthly, most countries and regions adopt the remuneration on a percentage basis.[44]

43. The Rules Concerning the Remuneration for the Administrator in Hearing Bankruptcy Cases, Article 2. The SPC, for the first time, announces that the administrator will be given remuneration on a percentage basis in accordance with the total amount of the property value.
44. "The SPC: The Administrator in Enterprise Bankruptcy Cases Will Not be Given Remuneration on an Hourly Basis", retrieved from http://news.xinhuanet.com/legal/2007-04/16/content_5984953.htm on 19 October 2015.

Certainly, a reasonable time period is required to evaluate the actual role and function of administrators. This may require close observation over several years.

5. Creditors' Meeting: A Proper Balance

A creditors' meeting is an important organization formed by all creditors who have registered their claims properly. Because a creditors' meeting is not a legal subject under the Chinese Civil Law, it has no right to engage in civil activities in its own name.[45] Therefore, a creditors' meeting is different from a liquidation committee or an administrator under the New Bankruptcy Law.

The 2002 Several Issues, for the first time, introduce the concept of the "committee of chairmen" of the creditors' meeting and expressly provide that the number of chairmen of the creditors' meeting may be more than one.[46] However, the New Bankruptcy Law adopts only one person as a chairman appointed by the people's court.[47] One possible explanation for this is that the committee of chairmen may create a problem of who can really chair the relevant meetings and effectively solve a problem.

Generally, only members of the creditors' meeting whose claims are not secured will enjoy voting rights. This is so because unsecured creditors are finally paid out of the bankruptcy property. If there is no bankruptcy property left, unsecured creditors receive nothing. For this reason, they need to carefully look after the debtor's property and approve a conciliation agreement. On the other hand, secured creditors have already obtained the preferential repayment rights, and presumably their interests are well protected. Thus, one may assume that secured creditors shall have no voting power unless they give up their preferential repayment rights.[48] However, this is not a true situation under the New Bankruptcy Law. According to Article 59(3), secured creditors can also vote for certain matters except for the conciliation agreement and the distribution plan for bankruptcy property.[49] This provision substantially improves the legal status of secured creditors for two reasons. Firstly, it is understandable that secured creditors will not be given voting power to the distribution plan for bankruptcy property because they will not be paid from it. Secondly, it is understandable that they cannot vote for/against the conciliation agreement because the

45. Gao and Liu, supra note 4, p. 68.
46. The 2002 Several Issues, Article 39.
47. The New Bankruptcy Law, Article 60.
48. The Old Bankruptcy Law, Article 13.
49. The New Bankruptcy Law, Articles 59(3) and 61.

conciliation agreement has a binding force only to the relevant debtor and unsecured creditors.[50] In practice, however, once the conciliation agreement has been awarded by the people's court, secured creditors can immediately exercise their rights against mortgaged property.[51] Literally speaking, to involve secured creditors in the discussion of the conciliation agreement or the distribution plan may allow unsecured creditors to be better off.

The chairman of the creditors' meeting will be appointed by the people's court from among the creditors with voting rights.[52] The first meeting shall be convened within fifteen days of the expiration of the claim declaration period. The later meetings will be convened when they are considered necessary by the people's court or may also be convened by the chairman at the request of the administrator or the creditors' committee (discussed subsequently) or by creditors whose combined holdings equal to one fourth or more of the total claims.[53]

Procedurally speaking, debtors and representatives of the working union are given an opportunity to attend the creditors' meeting and express their views.[54] In practice, however, their views are no longer meaningful for three reasons: firstly, creditors will not accept views that are not in their best interest; and secondly, only those unsecured creditors can exercise their voting right;[55] and thirdly, if an unsecured creditor believes that a resolution violates relevant legal provisions, he or she can take a legal action against this resolution.[56]

6. Reorganization and Conciliation: To Rescue Rather Than to Eliminate Debtors

Bankruptcy proceedings have a great impact on both the enterprise to be bankrupted and society in general. However, just because an enterprise is unable to pay off a debt when it is due does not mean that the enterprise

50. Ibid., Article 100.
51. Ibid., Article 96(2).
52. Ibid., Article 60.
53. Ibid., Article 62(2).
54. Article 13(3) of the Old Bankruptcy Law requires only the debtor's legal representative to attend the meeting.
55. Article 64(1) of the New Bankruptcy Law requires that the resolutions of the creditors' meeting be approved by the majority of creditors with voting rights present at the meeting, and moreover the combined amount of claims represented must equal to one half or more of the total amount of unsecured claims. Article 97 of the New Bankruptcy Law requires that the resolutions concerning the adoption of conciliation agreements must be approved by creditors whose combined holdings are equal to two thirds or more of the unsecured claims.
56. The New Bankruptcy Law, Art. 64(2).

should be bankrupted immediately. Some enterprises may still have a chance to recover their businesses. For these reasons, the New Bankruptcy Law provides two chapters to deal with conciliation and reorganization.

"*Hejie*" (conciliation) and "*chongzheng*" (reorganization) may share similarities and differences. Literally speaking, "*hejie*" refers to a negotiation made between a debtor and creditors in order to discuss a deferred schedule of payment or a reduction of debts. Once an agreement of *hejie* can be reached, the debtor can avoid a situation of being bankrupted. Nevertheless, it has been said that *hejie* cannot positively rescue the debtor because once the awarding of a *hejie* agreement is given secured creditors can exercise their rights against the mortgaged property immediately. In this situation, the debtor may have no sufficient property left for a fresh restart.[57] To some extent, this concept is quite similar to the concept of "reorganization" in the United States.[58] As one author explained below:

The "reorganization" is often more than purely financial. The debtor uses the "breathing room" provided by the automatic stay to close or sell money-losing divisions, trim excess staff, cut back on the number of company cars, and so forth. A successful Chapter 11 usually produces a smaller, leaner company with a reduced debt (and interest) burden, once again making it able to concentrate on the type of business it does well.[59]

In contrast, "*chongzheng*", which originally referred to a special plan proposed by a higher-level department in charge of the debtor in order to facilitate conciliation,[60] now refers to an independent proceeding that intends to give the debtor a chance to avoid being bankrupted and to manage and operate the enterprise under the supervision of the administrator.[61] Comparatively speaking, the purpose of *chongzheng* is to rescue those enterprises that are near the edge of being bankrupted or have a possibility of being bankrupted so that they can escape from operational difficulties.

---

57. Li Yongjun, "Differences between Forced Conciliation and Reorganisation and Value Consideration" (*Qiangzhi hejie yu chongzheng de zhidu chayi ji jiazhe kaoliang*), retrieved from http://www.flssw.com/falvlunwen/info/26886326/ on 19 October 2015.
58. In the United States, "reorganization" is a financial term. It describes a process according to which the debtor wants to "reorganize" its debt by extending the time taken to pay it and reducing the total amount to be paid. A Plan of Reorganization in Chapter 11 of the Bankruptcy Code may typically provide that the debtor will pay only 75 per cent of its bank loans and require five years to do so rather than the two-year period contemplated in the original loan agreement. For details, please see Elizabeth Warren and Jay Lawrence Westbrook, *The Law of Debtors and Creditors* (2nd ed.), Little, Brown and Company (New York) 1991, pp. 427–30.
59. Ibid., pp. 427–28.
60. The Old Bankruptcy Law, Article 17.
61. The New Bankruptcy Law, Article 73.

Furthermore, an approved plan of *chongzheng* binds all creditors, including secured creditors. Thus, one can clearly see that *hejie* focuses only on the relationship between a debtor and his or her unsecured creditors regarding a payment scheme while *chongzheng* focuses on how to improve the economic situation of the debtor in the near future.

According to the New Bankruptcy Law, *hejie* and *chongzheng* are two independent procedures. Although *hejie* is considered as a part of bankruptcy proceedings, it can render a stay of subsequent bankruptcy proceedings. Until then, the debtor can start to do *chongzheng*. For this reason, *chongzheng* cannot be considered as a part of bankruptcy proceedings.[62]

The New Bankruptcy Law is again silent on the standards, which are used by the people's court to examine and approve a *hejie* agreement. Lawmakers may want to give debtors and unsecured creditors more room to negotiate the agreement. On the other hand, secured creditors do not need to worry about a *hejie* agreement, but do have to worry about a *chongzheng* plan because in the latter situation they may be unable to seize or foreclose the security.

In past years, the application of *chongzheng* was only successful if it passed several checkpoints: the superior government, creditors, and the people's court. It was reported that the cases applying for *chongzheng* were extremely rare.[63] There are two potential reasons for this. Firstly, almost no superior department had the incentive to bear such a costly, troublesome, and sometimes risky mission. After all, it had no concern for the interests of the superior department or its officers. Secondly, creditors had no basis to trust the superior department, for the laws did not grant any means for creditors to control or influence the process of renovation, nor did it impose any responsibility upon the supervisory department for its misfeasance or failure in the process. Rather than rehabilitating the structure of the debtor enterprise, the laws sought to rearrange the relationship of debtors and creditors so that repayment could be made effectively. For these reasons, if a *chongzheng* plan did not fit such an aim, it would be rejected. Another reason was that the number of creditor-petitioned cases was very low and joint proceedings were not generally available in voluntary cases. Therefore, human factors rather than the laws played a role in deciding whether an insolvent enterprise should be saved.

Even if an enterprise is allowed to go through *chongzheng*, it will be ended and the enterprise will be declared bankrupt if three situations

62. Gao and Liu, supra note 4, p. 89.

63. Wang Weiguo, "Adopting Corporate Rescue Regimes in China: A Comparative Survey", *Australian Journal of Corporate Law*, Vol. 9, 1998, p. 238.

happen: the debtor fails to show an improvement in the financial condition, the debtor's conduct adversely affects the interests of creditors or the debtor interrupts the administrator.[64] Therefore, it is fair to say that the performance of the debtor is much more important than having a *chongzheng* agreement. Given the fact that China still has a problem with establishing "honesty and trust" (*chengxin*), creditors shall learn how to protect their legal interests effectively.

7. Liquidation: Close to International Practice

If both *hejie* and *chongzheng* do not work very well, the people's court will declare an enterprise to be bankrupted. The declaration of bankruptcy indicates that bankruptcy proceedings are in a substantial stage. Once an enterprise is declared bankrupt, the enterprise immediately loses its legal person status and has no power to dispose its property. In this situation, the administrator will take over the enterprise in order to liquidate the debtor's property.[65]

As said before, the administrator will be responsible for the liquidation proceedings. For the first time, the New Bankruptcy Law explicitly mentions that a lawyer can be appointed as the administrator.[66] Presumably, the people's court will replace the administrator if he or she is disqualified or his or her illegal activities are discovered. In addition, the administrator will be subjected to the control of the creditors' meeting. For example, the administrator shall make a plan to sell bankruptcy property immediately and submit it to the creditors' meeting for discussion and adoption. If the creditors' meeting refuses to adopt the plan, the plan shall be ruled by the people's court.[67] On the other hand, in order to speed up the bankruptcy proceedings, the 2002 Several Issues contain a remarkable provision that states, "Where the liquidation committee's property distribution plan is not adopted after deliberation twice at the creditors' meeting, the people's court shall rule on it according to law".[68] The advantage of this provision is the avoidance of an unlimited delay of the liquidation committee's property distribution plan at the creditors' meeting.[69]

64. The New Bankruptcy Law, Article 78.
65. Ibid., Article 111.
66. It was pointed out that in the past, Chinese lawyers played very little role in the bankruptcy proceedings. See Gao and Liu, supra note 4, p. 8.
67. The New Bankruptcy Law, Article 65.
68. The 2002 Several Issues, Article 44.
69. Article 30 of the SPC's Opinions on Issues Concerning the Understanding and Enforcement of the Enterprise Bankruptcy Law of the PRC (Trial) provides the following: "Where the

8. The Bankruptcy Property: Crucial to Unsecured Creditors

The bankruptcy property is ultimately important to unsecured creditors. The more bankruptcy property a debtor has, the more possible it is that the unsecured creditors will get paid. For this reason, how to count a bankruptcy property is an important topic of the Bankruptcy Law. Theoretically speaking, the bankruptcy property must contain four legal characteristics. The first legal characteristic is that the bankruptcy property must be property legally owned by a debtor. Property that does not belong to but is occupied by the debtor shall be returned to a true owner by the administrator unless doing so is prohibited by the New Bankruptcy Law.[70] The second legal characteristic is that the bankruptcy property must be disposable property. The mortgaged property cannot be considered as bankruptcy property. The third legal characteristic is that the bankruptcy property must be determined by the administrator. Although the property has been transferred to other parties by the debtor, the administrator has the right to revoke the transaction. For example, Article 31 of the New Bankruptcy Law states that if a bankrupt enterprise has carried out a fraudulent transfer within a year before the application of bankruptcy proceedings, the administrator can ask the people's court to revoke the transaction. The last legal characteristic is that the bankruptcy property must be specified by the relevant laws and regulations.[71]

Unlike the Old Bankruptcy Law, the New Bankruptcy Law provides that the term "bankruptcy property" refers to all property managed and administered by the bankrupt enterprise at the time of the bankruptcy application, as well as any property obtained after the bankruptcy application and before the end of bankruptcy proceedings.[72] Strictly speaking, the New Bankruptcy Law does not clearly outline the type of property in detail because bankruptcy property actually includes fixed assets, floating assets, and loans.

bankruptcy property distribution plan proposed by the liquidation committee fails to be adopted at the creditors' meeting after repeated discussion, the people's court shall rule on it timely according to the specific case." However, there is no specific number for the "repeated discussion", which tends to cease the abuse of this provision. In the opinion of the author, the term "twice" is clearer than the term "repeated", but considering the complexity of some bankruptcy cases, whether the term "twice" leads to a hasty decision remains to be seen in practice.

70. The New Bankruptcy Law, Article 38.
71. Gao and Liu, supra note 4, pp. 173–74.
72. The New Bankruptcy Law, Article 30. Article 28(1) of the Old Bankruptcy Law states that the bankruptcy property refers to all property managed and administered by the bankrupt enterprise at the time of the bankruptcy declaration.

The 2002 Several Issues, on the other hand, clearly define that the following items will not be treated as bankruptcy property: (a) other property possessed or used by the debtor based on a legal relationship such as warehousing, safekeeping, processing, entrusted transaction, sales on a commission basis, borrowing, consignation or leasing; (b) mortgaged property, property in lien, and pledged property, except a part of it on which the creditor has given up its pre-emptive right or a residual part of it after pre-emptive repayment of a secured creditor's right; (c) insured money, indemnity or compensation arising from the destruction or loss of a guaranty; (d) property with pre-emptive right according to law, except a part of it on which the creditor has given up its pre-emptive right or a residual part of it after pre-emptive repayment of a specific creditor's right; (e) a specific thing that has not been transferred but for which a consideration has been fully provided, in a sale of a specific thing; (f) property that has been delivered to the buyer, but the procedure for the property certificate or registration of transfer of the property has not been obtained or the ownership in the sale of the property has been retained; (g) property of which the State exclusively has the non-transferable ownership; and (h) property owned by the trade union of the bankrupt enterprise.[73]

In addition, non-bankruptcy property also includes (a) public welfare facilities such as the kindergarten, school, and hospital of the debtor,[74] and (b) housing sold to the bankrupt enterprise's employee in a housing reform, for which a contract has been entered into and payment has been made.[75]

In addition, the industry property rights obtained after the declaration of bankruptcy but before the conclusion of the bankruptcy should be treated as property rights. Finally, bankruptcy property includes the right to require shareholders to pay the contributions.

All of those provisions are so important to clearly defining the scope of bankruptcy property, even though it is evident that interests of the State and employees will get priority of protection. Certainly, creditors must be sure that, as provided by the New Bankruptcy Law, the claims established

73. The 2002 Several Issues, Article 71. On the other hand, Article 2 of the Part Two Bankruptcy Interpretations exclude the following properties from the bankruptcy property: (1) property that is possessed or used by the debtor based on the contract of storage, custody, processing, consignment, borrowing, deposit, lease or other legal relationships; (2) property that is obtained through a retention of the title sale, but the debtor has not obtained the ownership; (3) property whose ownership belongs to the State and is not transferable; and (4) other property that does not belong to the debtor in line with other laws and administrative rules. In comparison, the 2002 Several Issues are much clearer, even though Part Two Bankruptcy Interpretations are issued late.

74. Ibid., Article 82.

75. Ibid., Article 81.

before the bankruptcy declaration are bankruptcy claims. Failing to lodge claims within the time limit will be regarded as a voluntary renunciation of the claims and no right can be exercised in accordance with this Law.[76] Technically speaking, the failure of lodging claims may be good news to unsecured creditors because they may be able to get more compensation.

9. Distributing Bankruptcy Property: The Protection of Employees Is More Rational

Theoretically, when all bankruptcy property is ascertained, the unsecured creditors may have a hope to be fully compensated. But in practice, this may not be the case. Firstly, an enterprise is declared bankrupt because its debts are more than its assets and it is unable to pay the matured debts. Furthermore, parts of the assets have already been used as the security of debts. Secondly, bankruptcy property is used to cover the bankruptcy expenses in the first place. Thus, when an enterprise is declared bankrupt, unsecured creditors are never able to get full compensation. If the unsecured creditors are unlucky, they may get nothing from their debtors.

It is obvious that Chinese bankruptcy laws and regulations have adopted the idea of protecting debtors and creditors equally. When a creditor decides to loan the money to a debtor, he or she must be aware of the danger that the debtor may not be able to pay back the loan. If a creditor decides to loan the money to a debtor, the best way to protect his or her own interest is to investigate the credibility of the debtor or to become the mortgagee of the debtor's property. If a creditor wants to be an unsecured creditor, he or she would have to face the risk of getting nothing from the debtor.

Unsecured creditors may have one chance to recover or reduce their economic loss in accordance with Article 40 of the New Bankruptcy Law which states, "If a creditor also owes some debts to a bankrupt enterprise, the creditor could ask the Administrator to offset the debts before the commencement of bankruptcy liquidation". This situation is not treated as a fraudulent conveyance under Article 31. The remaining question is whether this kind of preferential treatment will effectively protect the interests of other unsecured creditors. But the supporting view is also worthy of consideration. It is believed that this preferential treatment can save the bankruptcy expenses and simplify the bankruptcy proceedings in two aspects: (a) when a creditor is allowed to offset the debts, he or she does not

76. The New Bankruptcy Law, Article 56(2). This general provision, however, does not apply to the following debts: wages, fees for medical care, allowance for injury and disability and so on. The New Bankruptcy Law, Art. 48(2).

need to participate in the bankruptcy proceedings in order to wait for the distribution of the bankruptcy property, and (b) the administrator does not need to collect the debts from the creditor and then distribute the property to the creditors again.[77]

It is an international practice that bankruptcy property is used to pay bankruptcy expenses firstly.[78] Unlike the Old Bankruptcy Law,[79] the New Bankruptcy Law names three categories of expenses as follows: (a) litigation expenses; (b) expenses for the management, sale, and distribution of the debtor's property; and (c) expenses and remunerations for the administrator and expenses for hiring other working staff.[80]

Furthermore, the New Bankruptcy Law provides that the bankruptcy property, if there is any, shall be further used to pay off new debts created after the application of bankruptcy has been accepted by the people's court. The new debts are called mutually benefited debts (*gongyi zhaiwu*), which include the following types of debts: (a) debts created due to the performance of uncompleted contractual obligations by another party at the request of the administrator or the debtor; (b) debts created due to the *negotiorum gestio* of the debtor's property; (c) debts created due to unjust enrichment by the debtor; (d) remunerations and fees for social insurance paid because the debtor wants to continue his or her operation and other debts created as a result; (e) debts created because of injuries caused by the administrator or relevant personnel when performing his or her duties; and (f) debts created because of injuries caused by the debtor.[81]

At this stage, unsecured creditors are already under a great danger of being paid nothing. If the bankruptcy property is insufficient to pay off the bankruptcy expenses, the people's court will declare the termination of bankruptcy proceedings upon the request of the administrator.[82]

---

77. Gao and Liu, supra note 4, p. 207.
78. For example, the Hong Kong Companies Ordinance provides that in a compulsory or voluntary winding up, the assets of the company are to be applied in the following order:
    a. Costs, charges and expenses properly incurred in the winding up, including the remuneration of the liquidator;
    b. Preferential creditors; and
    c. Ordinary creditors.

    See Vanessa Stott, *Hong Kong Company Law* (12th ed.), Pearson (London), 2008, p. 456.
79. Article 34 of the Old Bankruptcy Law mentions four types of expenses, i.e., (a) expenses incurred in the supervision, selling and distribution of the bankruptcy property; (b) expenses for the hiring of work personnel; (c) expenses for the bankruptcy proceedings; and (d) other expenses paid out during bankruptcy proceedings for the common benefit of creditors.
80. The New Bankruptcy Law, Article 41.
81. Ibid., Article 42.
82. Ibid., Article 43(4).

After paying the bankruptcy expenses and new debts, the bankruptcy property will be distributed in the following order: (a) wages, fees for medical care, allowances for injuries and disabilities, fees for comforting and compensating bereaved families owed to employees by the debtor, fees for basic pension insurance and basic medical insurance, and other compensations that must paid in accordance with relevant laws and regulations; (b) fees for other social insurance and taxes owed by the debtor; and (c) unsecured bankruptcy claims.[83]

The preceding order should be strictly followed. Before the wages and fees for various insurances are paid, paying the taxes or bankruptcy claims is not allowed. Furthermore, if the property is insufficient to pay fully within one category, the property will be distributed proportionally within that category.[84]

The existing question is whether the wages of employees should be paid from the bankruptcy property. Following the establishment of jobless insurance funds and other special funds, employees of bankrupt enterprises are able to get compensations from those funds. Taking Guangzhou as one example, the employees of a bankrupt enterprise are able to get economic compensations from the government, and minimum payment is ¥800 per month.[85] Before an enterprise is declared bankrupt, the enterprise has already paid those funds as required by relevant laws and regulations.[86] Therefore, when the enterprise is bankrupted, its employees should be able to get compensation and their interests are protected. If this situation could be realized, unsecured creditors would be able to get more repayment.

It is obvious that the New Bankruptcy Law pays close attention to the protection of legitimate rights and interests of employees of bankrupt enterprises in order to eliminate the possible negative effects of the bankruptcy. In fact, one of the major reasons why China could not enact a formal bankruptcy law in the past was the lack of a way to actually protect the employees of a bankrupt enterprise. On the other hand, one can easily see that the New Bankruptcy Law is trying to strike a balance between the interests of employees and secured creditors. One remarkable change is that employees' wages and other welfares are no longer paid out of the property

83. Ibid., Article 113(1).
84. Ibid., Article 113(2).
85. "Guangzhou Takes Out 1 Billion Yuan to Release the Burden of the State" (*Guangzhou nachu 10 yi wei guoqi xie baofu*), retrieved from http://www.people.com.cn/GB/channel4/964/20000623/115191.html on 19 October 2015.
86. For example, Article 6 of the Regulations on Jobless Insurance issued by the State Council on 22 January 1999 states that employer units shall pay the insurance fees in the amount of 2 per cent of the total wages of the employees.

used as security if property without security interest is not sufficient under the Old Bankruptcy Law.[87]

10. Fraudulent Conveyance: A Special Focus

A fraudulent conveyance happens when a debtor tries to obstruct the collection efforts of creditors by conveying away part or all of his or her property, usually with an intent to have it re-conveyed back to the debtor on a future date.

Chinese legislators have noticed this fraudulent conduct and provided in the New Bankruptcy Law that the following actions shall be deemed invalid if they are carried out by a bankrupt enterprise one year[88] before the case is handled by the people's court: (a) gratuitous assignment of property; (b) obviously unreasonable price of trading property; (c) supply of property security to creditors originally without property security; (d) advance discharge of non-matured liabilities; and (e) giving up its claims against others.[89]

If such fraudulent conduct is proved, the administrator shall have the right to apply to a people's court for the recovery of the property. In practice, it is not certain who should bear the duty of proof. In one case, one American court offered some guidelines which are worth considering in China in the near future: "The burden of proof to establish that a debtor's conveyance was made without fair consideration is on the creditor. However, where the evidentiary facts as to the nature and value of the consideration are within the transferee's control, the burden of coming forward with evidence on the fairness of the consideration shifts to the transferee."[90] This approach is suggested because it is fairly close to Chinese tradition.

Logically speaking, the recovered property shall become part of the bankruptcy property. However, the New Bankruptcy Law fails to provide a subsequent mechanism to prevent fraudulent conducts. Under Article 40 of the Old Bankruptcy Law, if a bankrupt enterprise carried out fraudulent conduct and the conduct was discovered within a year of the conclusion of the bankruptcy proceedings, the people's court should recover the property and a further discharge of liabilities should be carried out. Thus, within eighteen months (six months before the bankruptcy hearing and

87. "Wages of Employees Must be Given Priority to be Paid" (*Qiye pochan youxian qingchang zhigong gongzi*), retrieved from http://www.mengdeyao.com/index.php?ac=article&at=read&did=1061 on 19 October 2015.
88. The Old Bankruptcy Law requires only 6 months. See Article 35.
89. The New Bankruptcy Law, Article 31.
90. *Securities, Inc. v Rhoades*, 653 F. Supp. 1388 (S.D.N.Y. 1987).

twelve months after the bankruptcy hearing), it is possible to discover relevant fraudulent conduct. One may assume that this may be a defect of the New Bankruptcy Law.

11. Preventing False Bankruptcy Cases

In China, it is commonly recognized that being declared bankrupt is a shameful thing because an enterprise's reputation or credibility is seriously affected if it is declared bankrupt. Today, this situation has been dramatically changed. More and more people try to take advantage of bankruptcy proceedings to escape the repayment of debts. In the United States, one survey discovered that the bankruptcy system has three flaws, i.e., wantonness, indulgence, and unfairness. This problematic system helps debtors to deliberately escape the debts owed.[91] This problem also exists in China. Since 1994, the phenomenon of "false bankruptcy and true debt escape" (*jia pochan, zhen tao zhai*) has become more and more popular. Some enterprises transfer properties or even privately dispose of properties before applying for bankruptcy. In order to do so, one can divide an enterprise into two enterprises and then transfer all capital into the new enterprise. All debts are borne by the old enterprise, and then the old enterprise applies for bankruptcy. One can also keep the good parts of the enterprise in order to implement so-called "separate bankruptcy".[92] In July 2001, one large-sized SOE that included more than ten other enterprises wholly investing in it applied for bankruptcy. The people's court carefully examined the financial situation of each enterprise and discovered that one subsidiary enterprise had a poor management system, that many of its financial records were missing and that its financial situation was hard to identify. In order to avoid possible hiding or missing assets and to protect the legitimate interests of creditors, the court decided not to accept the application.[93]

In China, the biggest creditors are commercial banks. Some enterprises or even local governments believe that the money of commercial banks belongs to the State and that the State should be responsible for saving those enterprises. Therefore, the debts owed to commercial banks should be forgiven.[94]

91. Zeng Guoping, "The American Bankruptcy Law: The Umbrella of Debt Escapees", *Chinese Commercial Law*, No. 1, 1999, p. 58.
92. Zhang Qianming, "The Bankruptcy Law Shall Not be the Umbrella of Debt Escapes", *Chinese Commercial Law*, No. 3, 2000, p. 63.
93. "Shanghai Prevented From 'False Bankruptcy and True Debt Escape'", The China Industrial Newspaper (Beijing), 25 December 2003.
94. Zhang, supra note 92, p. 63.

The New Bankruptcy Law addresses the issue of "false bankruptcy and true debt escape". There are three ways to eliminate this problem. Firstly, Article 15 states that, during the time period starting from the date on which the decision to accept the bankruptcy application of a people's court is sent to a debtor until the end of bankruptcy proceedings, relevant persons of a debtor enterprise are responsible for handling the following things: (1) properly keeping the property, stamps, books, and documents possessed or managed; (2) working in accordance with the requirement of a people's court as an enterprise keeper and to answer inquiries honestly; (3) attending creditors' meetings and honestly answering the inquiries of creditors; (4) not leaving his or her residential place until permission is given by a people's court; and (5) not accepting new appointments to become directors, supervisors or senior management personnel of other enterprises. Those who fail to perform the said obligations are subjected to punishments.[95] Secondly, Article 31 provides that within one year before a bankruptcy application is accepted by a people's court, the enterprise keeper shall have the right to ask the people's court to revoke the fraudulent activities. One notable change is that the New Bankruptcy Law makes one year the duration of fraudulent transactions.[96] Presumably, the longer duration makes it more difficult for the debtors to conduct fraudulent transactions. Thirdly, the New Bankruptcy Law declares the following conduct to be invalid: (1) concealment or transfer of properties for the purpose of avoiding repayment, and (2) creation of falsified debts or acceptation of untrue debts.[97] Finally, all directors, supervisors, and senior management personnel are required by the administrator to return all abnormal incomes and possessed properties obtained using their powers.[98]

12. Sanctions against Responsible Persons: Chinese Characteristics

Because the bankruptcy of enterprises, especially SOEs, has a great impact on the social stability and interests of the State, the relevant laws and regulations have imposed liabilities on those who bear the main responsibility for the bankruptcy. Usually the punishments take the form of administrative

---

95. Article 126 of the New Bankruptcy Law states that those who fail to attend the creditors' meeting without good reason or give false statements will be fined. Article 129 states that anyone who leaves his or her residential place without reason will be fined.
96. The Old Bankruptcy Law states only six months. See Article 35 of the Old Bankruptcy Law.
97. The New Bankruptcy Law, Article 33.
98. Ibid., Article 36.

sanctions. Only in rare situations where the directors, supervisors or senior management personnel of a bankrupt enterprise or the leaders of the higher-level department in charge of the enterprises concerned cause, through neglect of their duties, the bankruptcy of the enterprises, resulting in serious losses to State property, will criminal liability be investigated.[99]

The New Bankruptcy Law, for the first time, explicitly provides civil liability. Directors, supervisors or senior management personnel who have engaged in personal interests and caused an enterprise to be bankrupted should bear civil liability.[100]

On the other hand, the enforcement of laws and regulations is also a problem. For example, the New Bankruptcy Law provides that a person shall not hold the position of company director, supervisor or senior management personnel if a period of less than three years has elapsed since an enterprise of which the person was a director, supervisor or senior management personnel was held liable for the bankruptcy because of his or her breach of the fiduciary duty and duty of care.[101] In reality, however, the enforcement of this provision is not ideal. The People's Bank did one survey and found out that the senior personnel of bankrupt enterprises were (a) assigned to be the leaders of other enterprises (26 per cent), (b) promoted to be leaders of a higher level (9 per cent), and (c) dismissed the leadership position and asked to take retirement (42 per cent). None of them bore civil or criminal liabilities.[102]

IV. FURTHER IMPROVEMENTS ARE REQUIRED

It has been said that the New Bankruptcy Law draws upon Western insolvency ideas and seeks to supply them to the particular Chinese experience in an attempt to synchronize the Chinese economy with an international standard of commerce and bankruptcy.[103] Unfortunately, the New Bankruptcy Law has not achieved this. Consider whether the objects outlined in the statement of Professor Li Shuguang, a member of the drafting panel, have been fully realized. According to Professor Li, the New Bankruptcy Law has the following five objectives:

- Significant expansion of the scope of application. The New Bankruptcy Law covers four types of subjects, i.e., enterprise legal persons;

99. Ibid., Article 131.
100. Ibid., Article 125.
101. Ibid., Article 125(2).
102. Zhang, supra note 92, p. 63.
103. Lloyds List, "Bankruptcies Soar as China Faces Up to Reality", *Westlaw*, 1995 WL 11770748.

partnership enterprises and partners; sole proprietorships and their capital contributors; and other economic entities that are legally established and operated for profits.

- Establishment and emphasis of the reorganization system. The New Bankruptcy Law takes foreign experience heavily into account and provides in detail the eligibility of reorganization, the process of application and examination, and the reorganization plan's making and enforcement.
- Sanction of fraudulent activities. The New Bankruptcy Law addresses various fraudulent activities such as hiding or illegally distributing assets, providing falsified debts or untrue debts, and directors embezzling the property of bankrupt enterprises.
- Creation of special persons in charge of managing bankruptcy. This is intended to preclude local governmental officials from participating in liquidation and to avoid local protectionism.
- Strengthening of the exemption system in order to avoid escaping debt repayment and fraud.

It is clear that the New Bankruptcy Law has not achieved its first objective because it covers only the bankruptcy of legal person enterprises. The sanction of fraudulent activities has not been seriously addressed. Regrettably, the new law did not prepare for dealing with the bankruptcy of natural persons. This ignores the reality that more and more individuals today use credit cards to buy merchandise at home and abroad. Due to the nature of credit cards, more and more individuals will spend money beyond their capacity to pay it back. It is almost the case that written laws will be developed slower than the rate of social and economic development. However, this new law fails to catch up with the new development by avoiding the bankruptcy of natural persons.

Although the New Bankruptcy Law attempts to add many provisions in accordance with international "best practices" regarding insolvency law, it is unclear whether the ideal of the corporate rescue regime has been addressed adequately, or whether it should remove the priority enjoyed by the State for unpaid taxes.

It is observed that debtors obtain benefits through bankruptcy applications, which in return encourages the debtors to declare bankruptcy when they bear so many debts. This may create a situation where the debtors obtain benefits without any effort and the creditors work without any benefit.[104] For this reason, such a reform is essential if unsecured creditors

104. Fu Zhiping, "Reconsider the Popularity of Enterprise Bankruptcy", *The Application of Law*, March 1997, p. 34.

are to have any hope of obtaining reasonable outcomes from invoking the insolvency process.[105] On the other hand, creditors must be advised to take security whenever a loan is given out.

Obviously, more training is required for judges and practitioners. Overseas training is absolutely required because the experiences of many developed countries such as the United Kingdom and United States may help to further develop Chinese insolvency legislation.

1. Liquidation of Foreign Invested Enterprises

Originally, the liquidation of foreign invested enterprises was governed by the 1996 Foreign Invested Enterprises' Liquidation Measures (hereinafter referred to as the "Measures") regardless of whether the foreign invested enterprises took the form of legal person enterprises or non-legal-person enterprises. However, it has been said that the New Bankruptcy Law establishes a uniform mechanism of bankruptcy for all legal person enterprises including foreign investment enterprises.[106] This shows a general tendency that China is going to remove special treatments from foreign investors. This position is supported by a recent change in the enterprise income tax law, which treats both domestic enterprises and foreign investment enterprises equally.[107]

The New Bankruptcy Law is silent on whether it can be applied to non-legal-person enterprises. Since many foreign invested enterprises may choose to keep their non-legal person status, it is unclear whether the bankruptcy of those foreign invested enterprises should still be controlled by the Measures. Logically speaking, it may not be a good idea to leave non-legal-person foreign invested enterprises in the dark just because legal person foreign invested enterprises are now covered by the New Bankruptcy Law. Fortunately, the SPC has taken things a step further by filling in the gap and saying that the liquidation of sole proprietorships (non-legal persons) could follow the New Bankruptcy Law.[108]

105. Roman Tomasic, "Insolvency Law Principle and the Draft Bankruptcy Law of the PRC", *Australian Journal of Corporate Law*, Vol. 9, 1998, pp. 232–33.

106. "The New Bankruptcy Law Enhances Foreigners' Investment Confidence" (*Xin pochanfa zengqiang waishang touzi xinxin*), retrieved from http://www.eeo.com.cn/2007/0628/73516.shtml on 19 October 2015.

107. The Enterprise's Income Tax Law of the PRC was adopted by the Fifth Session of the Tenth NPC on 16 March 2007. This new law took effect on 1 January 2008.

108. The SPC's Reply on Whether the Liquidation of Sole Proprietorships May Refer to the Procedure for Bankruptcy Liquidation as Prescribed in the Enterprise Bankruptcy Law, issued on 11 December 2012.

Systems such as the announcement, liquidation expense payment, payment order, and fraudulent transfer systems under the Measures are similar to those under the New Bankruptcy Law. Therefore, it is strongly suggested that a uniform bankruptcy law be adopted and applied to all enterprises, regardless of whether they are legal person enterprises or non-legal-person enterprises.

2. Bankruptcy of Listed Companies

It was said that since the promulgation of the New Bankruptcy Law, the bankruptcy of listed companies is no longer avoidable. On the one hand, it is accepted that bad listed companies should be forced to withdraw from the stock markets or to be bankrupted. In other words, listed companies cannot be treated as an "evergreen tree" and should be subject to rules of market development. On the other hand, share investors have been educated to face the risks of share investment even though they do not want to see listed companies bankrupted.[109] On 29 March 2000, the Zhengzhou Baiwen Company stopped its share trading and announced the shocking news that its creditor, the China Xinda Capital Management Company, had applied for it to be declared bankrupt by the Intermediate People's Court of Zhengzhou City.[110] This was the first listed company to declare bankruptcy in China. A survey revealed that until the end of 2005, there were a total of sixty companies listed over the Shenzhen Stock Exchange facing the risk of withdrawing from the market. Among them, thirty listed companies were in a situation where their debts were more than their capital. Another thirteen listed companies were stopped from listing because they had suffered serious losses within three consecutive years and were on the edge of being bankrupted.[111] Further data revealed that from the beginning of the implementation of the New Bankruptcy Law to July 2011, about thirty listed companies went through the *chongzheng* proceedings.[112] Certainly,

109. Gu Jisheng, "Six Questions Concerning Bankruptcy of Listed Companies: When Valuable Notes Becoming Wasted Papers is a New Fashion" (*Shangshi gongsi pochan liu wen: Dang jinzhi bian feizhi chengwei yizhong shishang*), http://finance.sina.com.cn/stock/t/20041019/07421088336.shtml on 19 October 2015.

110. Wu Tao, "Zhengzhou Baiwen is Struggling between Bankruptcy and No Bankruptcy", *Beijing Youth Newspaper*, 17 July 2000.

111. Qiu Yonghong, "Analysis of and Suggestions to Bankruptcy of Listed Companies in China", retrieved from http://www.chinalawedu.com/news/21604/21630/21652/2007/11/ji239516392951170025652-0.htm on 19 October 2015.

112. Geng Zhaoxin, "Legal Analysis of Reorganisation of China's Listed Companies" (*Guanyu Zhongguo shangshi gongsi pochan chongzheng de falü qianxi*), retrieved from http://www.insol.org/_files/Translations/Mandarin/Legal%20analysis%20on%20the%20

one has to admit that the bankruptcy of listed companies easily causes a serious social problem, i.e., a social instability. Therefore, how to deal with the bankruptcy of those listed companies may need further discussion. So far, the suggestion has been made that in order to maintain the stability of the securities markets and social order, the bankruptcy of listed companies should be done through *chongzheng* or *hejie* for the purpose of rescuing them rather simply getting rid of them.[113]

Since listed companies have emerged in China, the term "bankruptcy" has seldom been associated with them for several major reasons. Firstly, this is a phenomenon of too many Chinese people buying and selling shares, and the bankruptcy of listed company affects too many investors as well as the stability of the society. Secondly, as long as listed companies still exist, their shares in the secondary markets have certain value and can be traded. Thirdly, the bankruptcy of listed companies is not the initial goal of creditors. Creditors usually want to see that listed companies are able to survive and continue their operations.[114]

Therefore, one better solution for rescuing those listed companies is to use more mergers and acquisitions and asset restructuring (this book uses a special Chinese term: "*chongzu*"). It is believed that *chongzu* could be used to avoid listed companies disappearing from the securities markets and help listed companies that are near the edge of bankruptcy to recover, thus better protecting the interests of both shareholders and creditors. This is understandable because relevant shares would become the targets of investors and share prices would be increased substantially once the news of *chongzu* is publicized. However, on the other hand, one has to notice that many cases of *chongzu* have failed and that it is necessary to analyse the relevant reasons in order to prevent them in further *chongzu*.

(1) What Is the Failure of Chongzu?

In China, the *chongzu* of listed companies involves major asset transactions. According to the Administrative Measures of Major Asset Restructuring of Listed Companies (*Shangshi Gongsi Zhongda Zichan Chongzu Guanli Banfa*, hereinafter referred to as the "Administrative Measures"), which were issued on 18 May 2008, "major assets" refer to asset transactions done by listed

bankruptcy%20rectification%20of%20Chinese%20listed%20companies-%20by%20Zhaoxin%20Geng.pdf on 19 October 2015.

113. Qiu Yonghong, "Analysis of and Suggestions to Bankruptcy of Listed Companies in China", retrieved from http://www.chinalawedu.com/news/21604/21630/21652/2007/11/ji239516392951170025652-0.htm on 19 October 2015.

114. Ibid.

companies and their controlling shareholder companies, in addition to their daily operative activities, their buying and selling of assets and the asset transactions conducted through other means, causing major changes to the company's main business, assets, and incomes.[115] Thus, a major asset transaction refers to a transaction that causes major changes to the company's main business, assets, and incomes, and the failure of *chongzu* refers to a situation where the merger and acquisition have not been completed.[116] If the M&A is completed, it should be regarded as legally completed. Whether the listed company concerned could, after the M&A, function well is an issue beyond the legal scope of *chongzu*.

(2) *What Are the Reasons Causing the Failure of* Chongzu?

Before answering this question, it is necessary to see several public announcements made by listed companies involving *chongzu*.[117]

> S Ai Jian formally announces its failure of *chongzu* because the *chongzu* plan must be approved by the SCRC, who informs through telephone that the approval was deferred.[118]
>
> ST Qing Feng announces that due to Shanxi Renda Eco-technology Joint Stock Company failing to perform its obligation under the Agreement of Increasing Shares, Shanxi Seeds Industry Group Company has decided not to participate in *chongzu*.[119]
>
> ST Danhua Science and Technology Company discloses that Han Wang Group Company gives up participating in its *chongzu*.[120]

115. The Administrative Measures, Article 2.
116. Some scholars hold the view that a situation where the merger and acquisition have been completed but the listed company concerned cannot function well or faces serious economic difficulty should also be regarded as the failure of *chongzu*. This is certainly not a legal definition. For detailed information, see Luo Yongtai and Xu Biling, *Enterprises' Effective Chongzu and Creative Management* (*Qiye youxiao chongzu yu guanli chuangxin*), The Huawen Press (Beijing), 2003, p. 1.
117. It is required by the Administrative Measures that public announcements must be made after the decision of *chongzu* has been made by the BOD (Art. 14). If the listed company concerned decides to stop or withdraw its *chongzu* application, it should make the public announcement too (Art. 26).
118. Xu Xiaowei, "The Puzzle of *Chongzu* of S Ai Jian Company" (*S Ai Jian chongzu miju*), *The China's Securities Newspaper*, 27 August 2007.
119. Zhang Tinglong, "Shan Chemical Construction Company Engaging in *Chongzu* of *ST Qing Feng and There Is No Surprise" (*Shan Hua Jian chongzu *ST Qingfeng ji wu xuannian*), *The Economic Observer Newspaper*, 22 March 2008.
120. "Han Wang Group Company Withdraws from *Chongzu* *ST Dan Hua Suffers Expected Losses Within a Whole Year and Will Be Out of Stock Exchange" (*Han Wang jituan tuichu chongzu *ST Dan Hua quannian yukui jiang tuishi*), retrieved from http://finance.sina.com.cn/stock/s/20071102/17044133435.shtml on 19 October 2015.

The preceding news reveals that the reasons for the failure of *chongzu* can be divided into two categories. Firstly, the failure is caused by the act of a relevant authority, such as the SCRC. This is done in accordance with Article 9 of the Administrative Measures, which means that *chongzu* is regarded as the application of being a listed company and the resolution made by the SHM is not enough. Certainly, if the company concerned does not satisfy the administrative decision, it can bring the lawsuit before a people's court. Secondly, the failure is due to the agreements between parties. Certainly, the SHM has the power not to continue *chongzu*. The problem is whether the relevant decision can be made by the BOD. This book holds the view that *chongzu* should be considered as a major event and that the decision of *chongzu* must be made by the SHM. The BOD must perform its duty to disclose relevant information, but it cannot decide to stop *chongzu*. Thus, in the announcement made by the BOD, the reason that the BOD decides not to continue *chongzu* is problematic.

So far, reasons for the failure of *chongzu* can be divided into internal reasons and external reasons. As far as the internal reasons are concerned, they can be summarized as follows.

- Actual controllers or relevant parties do not have the true intent to conduct *chongzu*. What they want to do is to use the concept of *chongzu* as a tool to manipulate the share price.[121] This situation happens because the cost of making false annulments is smaller than the punishment or compensation. The fundamental reason is that the corporate governance and minority shareholders do not have a sufficient voice.
- There are too many listed companies becoming shell companies that desperately need *chongzu*, but the quality of those companies is not good enough. By the end of November 2007, both the Shanghai and Shenzhen Stock Exchanges had 175 ST companies, among which there were 107 *ST companies.[122] In July 2008, there were 82 ST companies announcing their expected losses.[123] They will be forced to withdraw from the market if they are unable to make profits within a short term. On the other hand, many companies that want to be listed companies could use this opportunity to realize their dreams. However, these

121. Chen Jie, "Because of the Failure of *Chongzu*, the Price of Jiu Fa Drops to the Decline Limit" (*Chongzu shibai Jiu Fa gufen cheng weiyi dieting gu*), retrieved from http://finance.people.com.cn/GB/6641047.html on 19 October 2015.
122. Zhong Yuan, "Before 523 Dreaming Shares There Are Two Options" (*523 Zhi Meng gupiao qianmian de liang tiao lu*), *The Money Weekly* (Guangzhou), 3 December 2007.
123. Zhao Yihui, "Among 82 ST Companies 60 Per Cent of Them Expect Middle-Term Losses" (*82 Jia ST Gongsi liu cheng yugao zhongqi yukui*), *Shanghai Securities Newspaper*, 8 July 2008.

companies have to be very careful because many listed companies are poor quality companies and hopeless. For example, the Tsingdao Zhongjin Company decided not to take over the Beijing Saidi Media Joint Stock Company that was in deep financial difficulty because the cost was too high and the risk was too big.[124]

- Big shareholders or actual controllers do not support *chongzu*. One of major reasons that listed companies become shell companies is because big shareholders abuse their power and occupy the capital of listed companies for a very long time without a legitimate reason. For example, *ST Dan Hua is on the edge of being bankrupted because its big shareholder, the Dan Hua Group Company, keeps occupying ¥700 million, causing *ST Dan Hua to stop operations.[125] Those big shareholders know very well that they may lose their leading position if their company is going through *chongzu*. They may be required to return the occupied capital after *chongzu*. Thus, they must stop *chongzu* and are able to do so by using their role as majority shareholders.
- Big shareholders cannot perform their duty under the agreement of *chongzu* within a time limit. This happens because big shareholders' shares are pledged or frozen. Although they agree with the *chongzu* plan, they are unable to dispose of their controlled shares, and this causes the failure of *chongzu*. A typical example is the *chongzu* of the ST Pijiu Hua Company in November 2007. According to the announcement made by the company, the failure of *chongzu* was due to a situation where shareholders were unable to conduct major asset transitions and there was no substantial progress.[126] In another example, the shares of *ST Qing Feng held by the Shanxi Seeds Industry Group Company were frozen by the Shanxi High People's Court due to its contractual dispute with the Jiaotong Bank Xi'an Branch Bank, which made the seeds company unable to perform its duty under the *chongzu* agreement.[127] In addition,

124. Luo Ruo, "*Chongzu* of Saidi Media Failed and Tsingdao Zhongjin Was Frustrated in Buying Shell Companies" (*Chongzu Saidi Chuanmei shibai Tsingdao Zhongjin jie ke zai shoucuo*), *21st Century Business Herald*, 3 December 2007.
125. Liu Sichen, "*ST Dan Hua: *Chongzu* Failed and Middle and Small Shareholders Want to Sue Big Shareholders" (**ST Dan Hua: Chongzu pomie, zhongxiao gudong yao gao dagudong*), *The Securities Times*, 8 November 2007.
126. Ye Miao, "The Second *Chongzu* of ST Pijiu Hua is Unsuccessful" (*ST Pijiu Hua erci chongzu shibai*), retrieved from http://finance.sina.com.cn/stock/s/20071130/11204236565.shtml on 19 October 2015.
127. Long Li, "*Chongzu* of Shanxi Seeds Company Failed and Yanchang Oil Company Has a Hope to Take Over Qingfeng Company" (*Shanxi Zhongye chongzu shibai, Yanchang Shiyou youwang jie ke Qingfeng*), *21st Century Business Herald*, 15 March 2008.

the opinions of relevant authorities play an influential role if the big shareholders are SOEs.

- Medium- and small-sized shareholders oppose *chongzu* in order to protect their own interests. On 30 December 2006, the *chongzu* plan was released, under which China Petrochemical Corporation would sell 49.977 per cent of its shares in the Wuhan Petroleum Group Company to Beijing Shengshida Real Estate Developing Company for ¥218 million. Wuhan Petroleum Group Company would sell its whole assets to China Petrochemical Corporation for ¥388 million and then would buy 90 per cent of the shares in Beijing Rongfeng Real Estate Developing Company, which were held by Beijing Shengshida Real Estate Developing Company, for ¥267 million. After the medium- and small-sized shareholders found out about this plan, they were very angry. They believed that the asset evaluation was not properly done and that their legal interests were not fully protected. In February 2007, Zhang Qiuju, a shareholder of S Wuhan Petroleum Group Company, brought a case to Wuhan Jianghan People's Court asking to stop the *chongzu* plan. Her petition was widely supported by other medium- and small-sized shareholders and attracted attention nationwide. Although Zhang Qiujue finally lost the case, the process of *chongzu* was seriously delayed.[128]

On the other hand, external reasons for the failure of *chongzu* are also worthy of serious attention. Research has found out that the first reason is changeable policies, under which the companies concerned may have to give up their *chongzu*. The second reason relates to supervisory bodies, which exercise their powers through harsh administrative orders rather than by following the legal provisions. For example, the approval of the S Aijian *Chongzu* Plan was temporally delayed by the CSRC via telephone. It did not explain why the approval should be delayed and when the delay would be over. Experts believed that the delay was due to the involvement of foreign capital and the transfer of legal person shares.[129] The third reason is the close involvement of local governments. For example, *ST Qingfeng failed its *chongzu* mainly because of improper interference of the local government.[130]

128. "The Case of a Shareholder Exercising Her Right to Avoid a Company's Resolution" (*Zhang Qiuju xingshi gudong chexiao quan an*), retrieved from http://case.mylegist.com/353/2009-05-19/2462.html on 19 October 2015.

129. Luo Xuhui, "S Aijian's *Chongzu* Failed, Who Will Continue the Takeover?" (*S Aijian chongzu shibai, mingli chuju shui jiang jiebang*), *China Times*, 1 September 2007.

130. Long Li, "*Chongzu* of Shanxi Seeds Company Failed and Yanchang Oil Company Has a Hope to Take Over Qingfeng Company" (*Shanxi Zhongye chongzu shibai, Yanchang Shiyou youwang jie ke Qingfeng*), *21st Century Business Herald*, 15 March 2008.

To many shareholders of listed companies, the failure of *chongzu* means that a relevant cost of transaction has been incurred and that their interests are affected. Therefore, the discovery of the relevant reasons is significant so that other listed companies can effectively avoid those problems when they conduct possible *chongzu*. Furthermore, it is suggested that a comprehensive preparation is required before *chongzu* can be conducted. For example, the SHM should not only decide whether *chongzu* should be started, but also assess the time arrangement, opinions of relevant authorities and risks of possible failure. In particular, the legal interests of the medium- and small-sized shareholders should be fully considered.

3. Cross-Border Bankruptcy

All of the past bankruptcy laws and regulations failed to address the issue of cross-border bankruptcy. Maybe one reason for this is that the theoretical research has not been done systematically. Another important reason is that Chinese legislators did not decide whether to apply the principle of universality or the principle of territoriality.

More than ten years after China became a member state of the World Trade Organization, the door will be widely opened to foreign investments. It is easy to predict that cross-border bankruptcy cases will increase. The New Bankruptcy Law has started to deal with this new problem. It has announced that the bankruptcy proceedings will be effective against debtors' properties that are in foreign jurisdictions. Furthermore, if there is a valid judgment or award that involves debtors' properties in the territory of China the relevant parties apply to execute that judgment or award, the relevant people's court will examine them in line with the international treaties or the principle of mutual benefit and will recognize and implement them if they comply with the relevant conditions.[131]

Another related issue is the level at which the Chinese courts will recognize or enforce a foreign judgment of bankruptcy. This may happen particularly in the situation of foreign investment in China. In practice, Chinese courts usually adopt two methods. Firstly, if the foreign country has not signed an agreement of judicial assistance with China, but the liquidators of the foreign company want to enforce the judgement against the property of the debtor in China, the foreign liquidators must make an application in a people's court where the property is located. The court will rule accordingly. Certainly, this has nothing to do with the recognition or enforcement

131. The New Bankruptcy Law, Article 5.

of a foreign judgement of bankruptcy. Secondly, if the foreign liquidators, through negotiation and mediation, reach an agreement with the debtor to transfer property in China to foreign creditors, the people's courts may or may not recognize the legal force of this agreement.[132] These methods, however, are not enough to establish some legal principles of recognizing or enforcing foreign judgements of bankruptcy. The relevant authorities should consider more flexible measures to handle this type of case in the near future.

V. CONCLUSION

The bankruptcy laws and regulations in China started with the purpose of reforming SOEs. Because the bankruptcy of SOEs affects the employment of workers, the financial situations of banks, and eventually the stability of society, the bankruptcy of SOEs is subject to administrative involvement. In this circumstance, the Old Bankruptcy Law becomes the only instrument used to make a bankruptcy announcement. On a certain level, the involvement of administration in bankruptcy proceedings has damaged the prestige of the people's courts.

The Old Bankruptcy Law has been promulgated for about twenty years and cannot fit into today's situation. Because the Old Bankruptcy Law was implemented on a trial basis, it understandably contains many problems, such as those related to the standard of bankruptcy, payment order, and protection of secured creditors. Furthermore, due to historical reasons, many important issues have not been thought out or studied.

The New Bankruptcy Law has finally been promulgated with the intention to closely follow international practice and meet the new situation of the Chinese market economy. The new law broadens the scope of application, even though it may not be wide enough. It has detailed provisions regarding simple bankruptcy proceedings, protection of creditors' interests, the system of bankruptcy administrators and the reorganization mechanism. To some extent, SOEs are no longer given preferential treatment under the new law.

Certainly, the important thing is that China should pay more attention to the serious implementation of this new law. Furthermore, it is important to note that the New Bankruptcy Law should not be used as an umbrella for some debtors escaping debts owed.

---

132. Ibid.

Following further development of the social security system, it is suggested that the issue of protecting employees should be dealt with by other laws and regulations.

Finally, it is hoped that China will adopt a unified bankruptcy law in order to effectively deal with the bankruptcies of individuals, legal person and non-legal-person enterprises, and domestic and foreign-invested enterprises. This mission must be accomplished because both the market economy and the globalization of the world economy will demand the participation of various subjects with equal footing and national treatment. Certainly, the reform of existing bankruptcy law should take into consideration the establishment of unified business enterprise laws and regulations in China.

13

Future Chinese Company Law

I. CHINESE COMPANY LAW SHOULD BE FURTHER IMPROVED

It is evident that research books and papers around the world have criticized the 1993 Company Law for being underdeveloped. Most of these comments are not groundless. However, some flaws in the 1993 Company Law should be examined by reviewing its legislative background and economic condition. During the drafting stage, the Legal Working Committee of the NPC Standing Committee sent the 1993 Company Law (Draft) to more than two hundred various government agencies, companies, enterprises, and legal research institutions in order to solicit views from them.[1] To a large extent, the view-seeking process reflects the democratic nature of law drafting and law making in China. On the other hand, however, the 1993 Company Law was virtually and unavoidably the product of various compromised interests. For example, during the drafting period, there was a debate concerning whether the 1993 Company Law should identify the role and function of the organization of the CCP. One view was that the 1993 Company Law should not include this political organization. Another view was that the 1993 Company Law should include the organization and that its role and function should be clearly identified. Eventually, the compromised approach was adopted and Article 17 of the 1993 Company Law contained a general statement: "Activities conducted by the primary organisations of the Communist Party of China through companies shall be handled in accordance with

1. The Report of the Examination Result of the NPC's Legal Committee Concerning the Chinese Company Law (Draft), issued on 17 December 1993.

the Party Constitution." Because of this, the 1993 Company Law contains inevitable internal drawbacks and was gently criticized for being "one step forward and two steps back".[2] Despite this kind of criticism, the existing Company Law still treats the CPC's primary organizations as important organizations within companies because they are able to play an active role in protecting the legal interests of workers.

The 1993 Company Law had problems in at least the following areas. Some of these problems have been resolved by the existing Company Law, but others should be further improved in due course.

Firstly, there was a serious problem with the internal structure. Under the 1993 Company Law, there was a checks-and-balances problem among the SHM, the BOD, and the BOS. Generally speaking, the SHM did take away some important functions and powers from the BOD, such as the making of business policies. The latter should routinely exercise those functions or powers in Western countries. The BOS was given the supervisory power to watch and correct the wrong behaviour of directors or managers, but in reality supervisors could hardly do anything. The legal representative of a company could represent the company to do various things without consulting the BOD or the SHM. Furthermore, he or she might have easily abused his or her powers. In the past, if a company wanted to sue someone who injured the interests of the company, the lawsuit should be filed through the legal representative. Naturally, the legal representative would not sue himself or herself. In this situation, the derivative action could be a good resolution. However, the 1993 Company Law did not provide this type of action for shareholders, especially minority shareholders. Due to its existing flaws, the 1993 Company Law could not be utilized as the general law for the foreign investment laws, even though in theory it should have been. Therefore, foreign investors preferred to choose the foreign investment laws because these laws offered more benefits to them.

Secondly, there were some technical problems under the 1993 Company Law. The term *ultra vires* is an old doctrine that closely relates to the business scope of a company. Under the 1993 Company Law, a company's business

2. Nicholas Howson, "China's Company Law: One Step Forward, Two Steps Back? A Modest Complaint", *Columbia Journal of Asian Law*, Vol. 11, No. 1, 1977. For example, before the 1993 Company Law was promulgated, there were two legal documents issued by the State Economic System Reform Committee on 15 May 1992, i.e., the "Standard Opinion Concerning Joint Stock Companies" (*Gufen Youxian Gongsi Guifan Yijian*) and "Standard Opinion Concerning Limited Liability Companies" (*Youxian Zeren Gongsi Guifan Yijian*). Article 23 of the "Standard Opinion Concerning Joint Stock Companies" provided common shares and preferred shares. Obviously, the 1993 Company Law ignores these different shares.

activities should strictly comply with the scope of business stated in the articles of association. When there was an *ultra vires* transaction made between the company and third party, the transaction was announced as invalid. The rationale behind this principle might have lain with the administrative management by the government. In practice, this principle was easily abused. One might have adopted as many business activities as there were in the articles of association in order to conduct as many business activities as possible. On the other hand, this principle might have hindered the businessperson's ambitions to expand his or her business as long as his or her business activities were lawful. Today, there is a global tendency to completely abandon the doctrine of *ultra vires*. Furthermore, the law intends to protect third parties with no knowledge of the irregularity of a company.

Although the 1993 Company Law maintained the doctrine of *ultra vires*, new legislation has paid attention to protecting the interests of a third party. The new contract law has made a substantial move towards the protection of an innocent third party if a contract is formed but the legal representative has committed an *ultra vires*.[3] The reform of the doctrine of *ultra vires* should take into consideration the national policy towards foreign investors as well.

The ownership of property was provided by Article 4 of the 1993 Company Law, which stated that "a company shall, as a legal entity, enjoy all rights over legal entity property formulated by investments from the various shareholders and shall enjoy civil rights and assume civil liability in accordance with the law". However, it also stated that "the ownership of State-owned assets in a company shall reside with the State". With regard to this language, many scholars questioned the unfairness among various shareholders. However, some scholars pointed out that the "state-owned assets" (*guoyou zichan*) especially referred to natural resources such as land, forest, and minerals. Once these resources have been invested in a company, the company acquires only operational rights but not ownership rights.[4] This is only a personal opinion and is subject to further debate. It is a well-accepted principle that a company has independent legal status after its official establishment. The company owns all of the property invested in by shareholders. Shareholders are not permitted to withdraw their invested

3. Article 50 of the Contract Law (promulgated on 15 March 1999 and effective as of 1 October 1999) states, "if the legal representative or a responsible person of a legal person or another organization acts ultra vires when concluding a contract, the act of representation is valid unless the other party knew or ought to have known that the contract was concluded ultra vires."

4. Lei Xinghu, *Research on Legal Issues of Joint Stock Companies* (*Gufen youxian gongsi falü wenti yanjiu*), Chinese Procuratorial Press (Beijing), 1998, p. 122.

property. The compensatory advantage is that they are given dividends and bonuses and enjoy limited liability towards the company's debts. If the state is permitted to retain ownership of its invested State-owned assets, a dilemma results: on the one hand, the state is the shareholder of the company and enjoys all of the benefits given to shareholders; on the other hand, the state is not liable for a company's debts, and the third-party creditors have no right to dispose of those assets. This is obviously unfair to other shareholders. Regardless of which view will prevail, the law itself should provide a clear definition of state-owned assets.

Other problems such as the verification of registered capital, the type of company, and authorized capital versus registered capital also bothered many scholars in the past.

Although many people urged the reform of the 1993 Company Law, it took more than 10 years to substantially amend it. Before this happened in 2005, the 1993 Company Law was amended in only two ways in 1999. The first amendment was a compulsory requirement to establish supervisory committees in all wholly state-owned companies.[5] In order to encourage hi-tech development and engage more people in science and technology to invest their hi-tech knowledge into companies, the second amendment allowed the percentage limitation to exceed 20 per cent of the total registered capital.[6] These two amendments were not significant. Firstly, the matter of establishing supervisory committees in all wholly state-owned companies was addressed by the State Council, which served the special rule to be followed. Secondly, Article 24 already resolved the issue of the 20 per cent rule. Thus, it is not understandable why legislators wasted so much time dealing with these two unimportant issues rather than other more important issues. Subsequently, Article 131(2) was deleted to allow the issue of shares above par without prior approval.[7] This was done in order to accommodate a relevant change in the Chinese Securities Law. Eventually, a newly proposed Chinese Company Law (hereinafter referred to as the "New Draft") was suggested by the State Council and circulated for comments and suggestions. The New Draft took into consideration China's quickly changing situation: (1) China is changing from an agricultural-oriented country to a commercial-oriented country; (2) China is changing from a society with a small-scale peasant economy to a society with a commodity economy; (3) China is changing from an identity-based society to a contract-based

5. The 1993 Company Law, Article 67.
6. Ibid., Article 229.
7. The decision to delete Article 131(2) was made by the Eleventh Session of the Tenth NPC Standing Committee on 28 August 2004.

society; (4) China is changing from recognizing mainly local rules and regulations to recognizing international customary rules and principles; and (5) China is changing from mainly using local resources to using resources from all over the world.[8] All of those changes required the Chinese company law or other laws to be compatible with new developments and international practices. Almost a year later, the 2005 Company Law was promulgated on 27 October 2005 and took effect on 1 January 2006. Furthermore, on 28 December 2013, the Standing Committee of the NPC amended the Company Law (2013 Amendment).

1. The 2005 Company Law

The 2005 Company Law made many new and remarkable changes. In order for readers to have a holistic picture of those changes, it is necessary to make the following points.

Article 4(3) of the 1993 Company Law was deleted. Originally, Article 4(3) provided that the ownership of state-owned property in companies remained with the state. This provision was heavily criticized for its inconsistency with traditional company law theory. It is widely recognized that once a company is established it obtains independent legal person status. The company then owns all of the property invested in it. As one of the shareholders in a company, the state should not be permitted to retain the ownership of investment property and enjoy the rights as a shareholder at the same time. Obviously, Article 4(3) created discriminatory treatment between the state and other shareholders because the state was not required to take any responsibility for the debt of companies.[9] Thus, one contribution of the 2005 Company Law is to adopt traditional company law theory and to formally establish the ownership system of companies and equal status among various shareholders.

Article 12(2) of the 1993 Company Law has been amended. Under Article 12(2), the accumulated total investment amount of one company in another company could not exceed 50 per cent. This provision was made due to the heavy influence of the planned economy. In accordance with the international accounting system, a long-term investment should

8. Qiu Ben, "Commercial Oriented China and Its Legal Construction" (*Shangtu Zhongguo jiqi fazhi jianshe*), *The Journal of Legal System and Social Development* (*Fazhi yu shehui fazhan*), Jilin, 2004, Vol. 4, pp. 16–34.
9. For detailed arguments, please see Gu Minkang, "Several Legal Issues of Foreign-invested Joint Stock Companies" (*Shilun waishang touzi gufen youxian gongsi*), *The Journal of International Economic Law* (Beijing), 1999, pp. 336–37.

be counted as one of the four major parts of a company's capital.[10] It is reasonably believed that this amendment[11] has laid down a legal foundation for fast-growing share-controlling companies or wholly owned subsidiary companies. It is suggested that more attention should be paid to the negative impact of this amendment. For example, it should carefully deal with the issues of affiliated companies and the duty of disclosure.[12]

The 2005 Company Law expressly requires that companies strengthen their social responsibility.[13] This new proposal reflects the new development of company law theory.[14] It tries to strike a balance between company law and human rights protection law. Thus, it can be reasonably predicted that traditional theory concerning the duties of directors will be increased in order to comply with corporate social responsibility.

The 1993 Company Law has been criticized for requiring the highest minimum amount of statutory registered capital in the world.[15] For the first time, the 2005 Company Law provides that the minimum amounts of statutory registration capital for LLCs and JSC are ¥30,000 and ¥5 million, respectively.[16] Furthermore, the 2005 Company Law has changed the paid-up capital.[17] It adopts a compromised statutory capital system, i.e., shareholders of a company should make initial capital contributions of no less than 20 per cent of the total registered capital, and the rest of the contribution should be made within 2 years after the company has been established.[18] This change has the function of unifying the registered capital system between domestic companies and foreign invested companies.

10. Liu Jipeng, "Ten Suggestions for the Amendment of the Chinese Company Law" (*Dui Gongsifa xiugai de shidian jianye*), in Guofeng and Wang Jian (eds.) *Vertical and Horizontal Discussion of Amending the Chinese Company Law* (*Gongsifa xiugai zongheng tan*), The Law Press (Beijing), 2000, p. 90.
11. The 2005 Company Law, Article 15.
12. For detailed information, please read Shi Tianshou, *Research on the Legal Issues of Affiliated Companies* (*Guanlian qiye falü wenti yanjiu*), The Law Press (Beijing), 1998, pp. 119–22.
13. The 2005 Company Law, Article 5.
14. Some Chinese scholars have started to address this issue systematically. For example, see Liu Junhai, *Corporate Social Responsibility* (*Gongsi de shehui zeren*), The Law Press (Beijing), 1999.
15. Fang Liufang, "Gain New Insights Through Restudying Old Materials: On the Issues of Amending the Chinese Company Law" (*Wenguzhixin—tan Gongsifa xiugai*), in Guofeng and Wang Jian (eds.), *Vertical and Horizontal Discussion of Amending the Chinese Company Law* (*Gongsifa xiugai zongheng tan*), The Law Press (Beijing), 2000, p. 41.
16. The 2005 Company Law, Articles 26 and 81(2). However, other laws or administrative regulations may require more than ¥30,000 as minimum registered capital for a particular LLC.
17. Ibid., Article 26.
18. Ibid. On the other hand, investment-type companies could pay the rest of the capital contribution within 5 years after the company has been established.

Although some scholars still hold the view that the Chinese Company Law should adopt the authorized capital system, which is popular in common law jurisdictions, the compromised capital system might have been the only reliable resolution in China at the time.

Article 24 of the 1993 Company Law has been amended to allow a capital contribution to take the form of intellectual property.[19] Furthermore, the 20 per cent limitation has been abolished through the provision that the total shareholders' capital contribution in cash form should not be less than 30 per cent of the total registered capital. In other words, shareholders can make other capital contributions (in the form of items in lieu, intellectual property, industrial property, non-patented technologies, land-use rights, and stock ownership) up to 70 per cent of the total registered capital. Thus, the forms of capital contribution are becoming more flexible in China.

Another major contribution of the 2005 Company Law is that it provides new rules concerning legal representatives. As discussed in the previous chapters, the 1993 Company Law could not effectively deal with the power of legal representatives, especially in situations where a legal representative refused to call and preside over the BOD meeting or SHM. According to the 2005 Company Law, the powers and functions of a legal representative should be provided by the articles of association. Furthermore, the legal representative may not necessarily be a chairman of the BOD; it can sometimes be a manager.[20] The 2005 Company Law further states that if shareholders who represent more than one tenth of the voting power or more than two thirds of directors or supervisors suggest the holding of an interim SHM, the meeting must be called.[21] A BOD meeting shall be called and presided over by the chairman. However, if the chairman is unable or refuses to exercise his or her duty, the vice-chairman shall call and preside over the meeting (there is no need to be appointed by the chairman). If the vice-chairman is unable or refuses to exercise his or her duty, more than half of the directors may elect one director to call and preside over the meeting.[22] In order to comply with the international practice, the 2005 Company Law gives the power to shareholders to remove disqualified directors whenever it is necessary.[23]

In order to change the situation where the BOS does not have sufficient power to supervise the directors, the 2005 Company Law states that the BOS

19. Ibid,, Article 27. In comparison, the New Draft has proposed that the stock ownership could also be used as a capital contribution.
20. Ibid., Article 13.
21. Ibid., Article 40.
22. Ibid., Article 41.
23. Ibid., Article 46.

can ask to hold an interim SHM. It can call and preside over the SHM if the BOD fails or refuses to do so.[24] Furthermore, in order to ensure that the BOS can exercise its duties, the 2005 Company Law provides that the BOS can carry out investigations when the operation is abnormal. If it is necessary, the BOS can hire a registered accountant firm to assist in its work, and the relevant costs should be borne by the company.[25] These changes are very helpful for improving corporate governance in China.

The 2005 Company Law contains an independent chapter that systemically addresses the duty of loyalty, which should be fulfilled by directors. It further states that the civil liabilities should be imposed in a case where directors, supervisors, managers, and other senior management personnel violate the legal provisions and cause damage to the company. One of the achievements is that the 2005 Company Law formally adopts the derivative action, which is popular in common law jurisdictions.[26] Those provisions can effectively force senior management personnel to work for their companies with heart and soul. Furthermore, it seems that the emphasis on senior management personnel is a new feature of the 2005 Company Law. Although the 2005 Company Law fails to specifically address the role and function of company secretaries, it does mention that company secretaries are within the category of senior management personnel[27] and have the duty of loyalty imposed on them.

According to Article 58 of the 2005 Company Law, a "one-person limited liability company" refers to an LLC that has only one natural person shareholder or a legal person shareholder. To allow the establishment of one-person LLCs would rapidly stimulate the quick development of the market economy. Many Western countries used to hold a negative attitude towards one-person LLCs because of their obvious flaws, including the lack of a checks-and-balances mechanism, the easy mixture of shareholders' own property with the company's property, the abuse of corporate legal person status, and so on. That is why company laws in the United Kingdom and other jurisdictions provide the doctrine of lifting the corporate veil. In fact, one-person LLCs are becoming widely adopted by more and more countries. This shows the existing value of this type of company. It is further believed that following the perfection of the corporate system, it is possible to prevent this type of company from being largely abused.

24. Ibid., Article 41(3).
25. Ibid., Article 57.
26. Ibid., Article 152.
27. Ibid., Article 217(1).

The 2005 Company Law states that JSCs can adopt the accumulative voting system instead of the "one share, one vote" system.[28] It has been concluded that under the traditional "one share, one vote" system, big shareholders may easily control the voting result and choose all of the directors who will act on their behalf. Thus, minority shareholders do not have a proper chance to elect their reliable persons to be directors. The accumulative voting system was firstly created in the United States. It was intended to protect the legal interests of minority shareholders and it has since been widely adopted.

The 2005 Company Law contains new provisions regulating the transfer of shares by special persons. Article 142 provides that promoters cannot transfer their shares of the company within 1 year after the company has been established (The 1993 Company Law stated that promoters could not transfer their shares within three years). Under the 2005 Company Law, directors, supervisors, managers, and other senior management personnel are now permitted to transfer their shares during the terms of their positions. However, the transfer of shares may still be subjected to several limitations: (1) they should report the total amount of shares held and changes; (2) each year their share transfer shall not exceed 25 per cent of the total shares held; (3) they cannot transfer their shares within one year after the shares of their company have been listed and traded over the stock exchanges; and (4) within half a year after they leave their positions, they cannot transfer their shares. Those new provisions eliminate the differences between the Chinese company law and the Chinese securities law. On the other hand, it is not clear why the 2005 Company Law does not accept the proposal made by the New Draft, i.e., for companies whose shares are listed and traded over the stock exchanges, shareholders cannot transfer their shares within 1 year after the shares have been listed.[29]

Article 167 of the 2005 Company Law provides only the allocation of profit to the statutory accumulative fund. That means that the allocation of profit to the statutory provident fund is no longer mandatory. It further requires that after-tax profits shall be distributed to shareholders in line with their share amounts. Thus, shareholders are given legitimate expectations of their dividends. On the other hand, however, it remains a question whether companies should continue to take care of the collective welfare of workers, since the statutory provident fund is no longer mentioned. In comparison, the New Draft proposes to strike a balance between the interests of shareholders and workers. Article 207 of the New Draft provides that when

28. Ibid., Article 106.
29. The New Draft, Article 177.

a company distributes the current-year after-tax profit, it may allocate a part to the provident fund to be used only for collective welfare.

The 2005 Company Law has one independent chapter to deal with the legal liability of various violations. It generally follows the model of the original Company Law to provide only administrative sanctions and criminal punishments. One remarkable change is that the amount of fines under the 2005 Company Law has generally been increased. For example, Article 199 provides administrative sanctions to conduct such as falsely declaring registered capital, submitting false documentation and adopting other deceptive means to conceal important facts. Where a company has falsely declared its capital, a fine of 5 per cent to 15 per cent (originally a fine of 5 per cent to 10 per cent) of the amount of registered capital falsely declared shall be imposed; where a company has submitted false documentation or has adopted other deceptive means to conceal important facts, a fine of ¥50,000 to ¥500,000 (originally a fine of ¥10,000 to ¥100,000) shall be imposed. This may indicate that the previous amount of fines has not served its proper function of deterrence.

In accordance with traditional company law theory, a company must operate its business within its scope of business; otherwise, the transaction concerned will be deemed *ultra vires*. The purpose of this doctrine is to protect shareholders and creditors. The current international tendency is to abolish the doctrine of *ultra vires* so that the interest of a *bona fide* third party will be better protected and companies will be able to take the chance to adjust their operational direction as quickly as possible. For example, Hong Kong gives companies discretion to decide whether to provide a scope of business in the articles of association. Contrarily, Article 11(3) of the 1993 Company Law required that companies should engage in their business activities within the registered scope of business. Although companies may be able to alter their scope of business, the modification must go through legal procedures in order to be valid. Article 69 of the Regulations on Administration of a Company's Registration (2014 Amendment) provides relevant punishments if a company's business activity exceeds the scope of business. These two provisions reflect the idea of strict control of enterprises under the original planned economy. In reality, some changes have been made. For example, Article 50 of the Chinese Contract Law expressly treats a contract as valid even if there is an *ultra vires*. It should be noted that the Chinese Contract Law was adopted by the National People's Congress while the Chinese Company Law was adopted by the Standing Committee of the National People's Congress. It can be argued that the Chinese Contract Law is a higher-level law than the Chinese Company Law. In this situation, it can be argued that the *ultra vires* doctrine has been technically abolished.

Although the New Draft kept the *ultra vires* doctrine, the 2005 Company Law reflects the abolition of this doctrine and no longer requires that "a company shall conduct operational activities within the registered scope of its business activities". However, the 2005 Company Law does not go far enough to relax the content related to scope of business, even though one can see this relaxation has been practised. On 12 February 2004, the Administrative Bureau for Industry and Commerce of the Beijing Municipal Government published the Several Opinions on Reforming the System of Market Access and Perfecting the Economic Development Environment. In accordance with this document, the Administrative Bureau, starting from 15 February 2004, no longer restricts a detailed scope of business unless some commodities or industries are especially reserved for particular enterprises or they must be approved. In other words, the general scope of business has been abolished in Beijing.[30] Therefore, one can predict that further relaxation will happen in China in the near future.

It has been recognized in common law jurisdictions that a company is a separate legal entity that can be used as a "shelter" to protect shareholders from being directly sued. However, when a company is used as a vehicle for fraud committed by some shareholders, the courts will permit a lifting of the corporate veil to impose liabilities on those shareholders. The 2005 Company Law adopted this doctrine. Article 20(3) provided that if a shareholder abuses the principle of the separate legal entity of a company and the limited liability of the shareholder in order to escape debt obligations, and the interest of the creditors concerned has been seriously injured, he or she shall bear a joint liability. Thus, in practice, creditors could bring a civil case against the shareholder concerned directly.

Under the 1993 Company Law, only JSCs, wholly state-owned companies, and LLCs established with investment by two or more SOEs or by two or more state-owned investment bodies could issue corporate bonds. Other LLCs that were desperate for capital were denied an opportunity to raise funds from the public. This was certainly not good for fair competition among various companies. The 2005 Company Law permits all companies to issue corporate bonds once they have satisfied relevant conditions, which could be considered as a meaningful change.

Under the 2005 Company Law, companies could decide on the matters of mergers and divisions by themselves. This was a concrete reflection of China's intention to adopt a "big market and small government" situation.

30. "New Domestic Companies Established in Beijing Will Not Be Restricted in Scope of Business" (*Beijing buzai heding neizi qiye juti jingying fanwei*), retrieved from http://www.lawtime.cn/info/gongsi/jyfw/2008102632270.html on 20 October 2015.

However, the system of pre-merger approval had proved to be a good system and had to be clearly mentioned. The 2005 Company Law contained one independent chapter to systematically deal with issues of takeover, reorganization, bankruptcy, and liquidation. State wholly-owned companies were still regulated by the 2005 Company Law. One new change was that the 2005 Company Law required that the minimum number of the BOS shall be 5 and that the minimum proportion of employee representatives shall not be less than one third. Thus, at least two employee representatives could be members of the BOS to protect the legitimate interests of employees. For the first time, the 2005 Company Law stated that the number of promoters shall be two to two hundred and that a one-half majority of the promoters must have their domicile within the territory of China.[31] The 2005 Company Law also no longer required the share offer method if a SOE transforms into a JSC. One would assume that the major mission that the 1993 Company Law set out to rescue SOEs had been completed.

2. The 2013 Company Law

The 2013 Company Law has basically kept the major changes made by the 2005 Company Law with slightly different numbering. One revolutionary change made by the 2013 Company Law is the abolishment of both the statutory registered capital system and compromised registered capital system and the adoption of the capital contribution subscription system. Since this new system does not require shareholders to make full capital contributions, it is laterally called the "zero capital" system. Furthermore, this new change applies to foreign-invested enterprises with some limitations.

3. Remaining Problems

Although both the 2005 Company Law and the 2013 Company Law made remarkable changes, it is important to note that the existing Company Law cannot be perfected all at once. Some important issues have not yet been addressed.

(1) Does the Company Law Need Guiding Ideologies?

Guiding ideologies can be regarded as the soul of a law because they help to make, understand, and implement that law. Chinese people may use

31. The 2005 Company Law, Article 79.

guiding ideologies, guiding thoughts, and legislative purposes interchangeably. In this situation, it seems that the Company Law contains guiding ideologies in Article 1, which says that "this Law is enacted for the purposes of regulating the organization and operation of companies, protecting the legitimate rights and interests of companies, shareholders and creditors, **maintaining the socialist economic order, and promoting the development of the socialist market economy**". Now, let us compare this provision with Article 1 of the PRC Securities Law, which states that "the present Law is formulated in order to standardize the issuance and trading of securities, protect the legitimate rights and interests of investors, **safeguard the economic order and public interests of the society and promote the development of the socialist market economy**". Through this comparison, we can see that the guiding ideologies of these two laws are similar and too general to offer concert guidance. Thus, it is meaningful to discuss two issues in the future: (1) whether the Company Law needs specific guiding ideologies, and (2) which guiding ideologies should be included in the Company Law.

In order to answer the first question, it is necessary to look at company laws in other jurisdictions. In the United States, the two legislations have been chosen: neither the Delaware General Corporation Law nor the US Model Business Corporation Act has guiding ideologies. In Germany, neither the Stock Corporation Act nor the Limited Liability Company Law has guiding ideologies. In France, neither IX of the French Civil Code nor the French Commercial Code has guiding ideologies. In Japan, neither the Japanese Law of Limited Liability Companies nor the Japanese Law of Joint Stock Company has guiding ideologies. The Hong Kong Companies Ordinance has no guiding ideology. Thus, it seems that one characteristic of Chinese laws is that they contain guiding ideologies. In fact, it is fine to adopt guiding ideologies. However, the next question is: what should be included in those guiding ideologies? Jiang Daxing suggests two guiding ideologies: (1) to meet the needs of international competition and to comprehensively enhance the competitiveness of enterprises (thus, a company law should follow the ideologies of free market and giving more freedom to enterprises), and (2) to have sufficient legislation to deal with companies so that companies can follow detailed laws.[32] Enlightened by his wisdom, this book proposes that the guiding ideologies should contain the following three aspects: (1) the Chinese company law should show more respect

32. Sun Min, "The Company Law Opens up the Time of Corporate Autonomy", retrieved from http://www.dffyw.com/faxuejieti/ms/200511/20051111122516.htm on 6 November 2015.

for the effectiveness of articles of association and shareholders' agreements; (2) in terms of corporate governance structure, the Chinese company law should allow a company to choose a one- or two-tier system through its articles of association; and (3) the Chinese company law should fully respect the spirit of freedom of a contract. If those are acceptable guiding ideologies, it is possible to review whether the existing provisions of the Chinese Company Law are compatible. For example, Article 15 states, "a company may invest in other enterprises. However, unless it is otherwise provided for by any law, it shall not become a capital contributor that shall bear several and joint liabilities for the debts of the enterprises in which it invests." Liu Junhai criticizes this provision for taking away the autonomy of the company. In his view, the shareholders in the company should decide this matter. If the shareholders do not want the company to become a general partner, they can prevent it from becoming so through the articles of association or by resolution at the SHM with two thirds of the voting rights.[33]

(2) State-Owned Companies: Can the Government Be Separated from SOEs?

The idea of separating the government from SOEs emerged at the beginning of the economic reform and is still discussed today. In China, the relationship between the two always presents a dilemma: on the one hand, the government still pays attention to keeping or adding the value of state-owned assets based on various reasons and wears different hats (after the reform, the representatives of state-owned assets were created) to interfere with the activities of SOEs; on the other hand, the representative of the state does not perform the duties well due to the restriction of information, interests or manpower. Due to this reason, many state-owned assets leave state control or are lost.

Advocators of separation believe that asset ownership and operation rights should be separated so that SOEs can be independent enough to engage in autonomic operation and implement self-development and self-regulation. If the ownership relationship is the basis for clarifying the relationship between administration and enterprises, can it be said that once there is a clear ownership relationship, true separation can be realized? Or does the creation of a new ownership system suit the purpose of engaging

33. Liu Junhai, "Several Disputed Issues Relating to Amendment of the Company Law", retrieved from http://www.jcrb.com/xueshu/zt/200806/t20080613_22822.html on 6 November 2015.

in a deep reform of the enterprise system? One has to consider the following points in order to answer these questions. First, so long as SOEs exist, the separation is not consistent with company law theory; as an investor, the state must have a say in the operation of SOEs. The State Assets Management Authority (hereinafter referred to as "SAMA") is derived from the government and has a close connection with the government. Thus, SOEs cannot be free from government interference. SAMA, through the CPC system, is directly involved in the activities of SOEs. In fact, only private enterprises can truly realize the separation for one simple reason: the ownership of the enterprises is theirs and has nothing to do with the government. The government will supervise them within the framework of the law. On the other hand, SOEs cannot be separated from the government because their ownership is with the state. Thus, it is unrealistic to separate the government from SOEs.[34] Second, the core part of power, i.e., the appointment right of senior management personnel, is still controlled by the government and thus any major decision should be approved by SAMA. So far, about 124 giant SOEs are directly under the supervision of the central government.[35] Unlike other government organs such as the National Development and Reform Commission and State Administration for Industry and Commerce, which have the general authority to guide the development of enterprises, SAMA is representing the state to exercise the shareholder's right, which is similar to the agent of the principal.[36] Certainly, the lack of separation of government and SOEs may present a potential problem under other laws. For example, under the Chinese Competition Law, it would be regarded as an administrative monopoly if the government were to give benefits or preference to SOEs, which is an issue beyond the scope of this book.

34. Zhu Xiaoquan, "It is Difficult to Reform SOEs Without Changing the Property Ownership", retrieved from http://finance.ifeng.com/opinion/zjgc/20121123/7338090.shtml on 7 November 2015.

35. Fang Gang and others, "The Role of SOEs in China's Economy", retrieved from http://www.chinausfocus.com/2022/china/wp-content/uploads/Part-02-Chapter-16_SC.pdf on 7 November 2015.

36. This conclusion can be further supported by Article 57 of the PRC Property Law, which states that "the authority performing the duties of administration and supervision over State-owned property and its staff members shall, according to law, exercise vigorous administration and supervision over State-owned property, promote the preservation and increase of the value of such property, and prevent its loss; and where losses are caused to State-owned property due to their abuse of power or dereliction of their duties, they shall bear legal liability according to law".

(3) Should the Protection of Human Rights Extend to Legal Persons?

Should a legal person have moral rights (personality rights)? In order to answer this question, it is necessary to define three things: (1) a legal person, (2) moral rights, and (3) a legal person's moral rights.

It has been generally recognized that the theory of the artificial person (*Fiktionstheorie*) appeared during the period of Roman law.[37] According to this theory, an enterprise is a legal person in that it is an artificial natural person and thus has acquired moral rights. The 1896 German Civil Code, for the first time, adopted the term "legal person" (juristic person). Article 36 of the General Principles of the PRC Civil Law states that a legal person shall be an organization that has a capacity for civil rights and civil conduct and can independently enjoy civil rights and assume civil obligations in accordance with the law. China adopts the concept of the legal person based on this comparison and summarized from various concepts.

However, some scholars argue that a legal person does not have personality rights because it is created by law and is a legal concept only. "Legal person" is merely a technical legal term established for the purpose of conferring the entitlement to equality in law on citizens to participate in civil activities. It lacks specific properties such as rationality, awareness, ethics, and morality that are attributed only to natural persons.[38] Others believe that it is an important corporate development to treat a company as a natural person.[39] According to relevant research, companies in the United States are protected under the Constitution as "persons" and are given such rights as the freedom to contact and freedom of speech and are subject to proper procedures.[40] In Europe, the human rights of legal persons developed a bit late. In March 1952, the European Convention on Human Rights, for the first time, stated that legal persons were the subjects of human rights. In addition, the European Court of Human Rights, through case discussions, protects companies' fundamental economic rights and freedoms.[41] If this is a tendency, it is reasonable to examine several issues. First, is the phrase "the business license shall be revoked" under Articles 198, 207, 211,

37. Huang Wenxi, "The Nature of the Personality Rights of Natural Persons and Legal Persons", retrieved from http://old.civillaw.com.cn/wqf/weizhang.asp?id=56391 on 8 November 2015.
38. Ibid.
39. Ma Yi, "Research on Corporate Human Rights", retrieved from http://cdmd.cnki.com.cn/Article/CDMD-10652-2008202117.htm on 8 November 2015.
40. Ibid.
41. Ibid.

and 213 equivalent to a death penalty?[42] If the answer is yes, then should the revocation of a business licence be decided by a court following due process? Secondly, should a legal person be entitled to spiritual damages? Article 120 of the General Principles of Civil Law states that if a citizen's right of personal name, portrait, reputation or honour is infringed upon, he or she shall have the right to demand that the infringement be stopped, his or her reputation be rehabilitated, the ill effects be eliminated and an apology be made; he or she may also demand compensation for losses. This provision shall also apply to infringement on a legal person's right of name, reputation or honour. However, the SPC, in its Interpretation on Problems concerning the Ascertainment of Compensation Liability for Emotional Damages in Civil Torts (2001), refused to give emotional damages to legal persons. All of these issues deserve further research and debate.

(4) Is the Definition of the Articles of Association Unclear?

Traditional company law theory considers the articles of association as a contract between a company and its shareholders as well as between shareholders.[43] Other employees such as non-shareholder directors and company lawyers cannot sue on the basis of violating the articles of association.[44] The 1993 Company Law stated that the articles of association had a binding force over the company and its shareholders, directors, supervisors, and managers.[45] This provision has been debated for years. However, the existing Company Law not only retains the position of the 1993 Company Law, but also extends its binding force to other senior management personnel. It is

42. Certainly, there are divided views on whether the revocation of a business licence is equal to the death penalty (termination). According to the General Principles of Civil Law, a legal person's capacity for civil rights and capacity for civil conduct shall begin when the legal person is established and shall end when the legal person is terminated (Art. 36.2). Furthermore, an enterprise as legal person shall terminate for any of the following reasons: "if it is dissolved by law" (Art. 45). However, in the Reply Letter to Hebei Higher People's Court in 2000, the SPC stated that even though the business license of a legal person may be revoked, it is an administrative sanction. The operation qualification is deprived by legal force, but this does not mean that the enterprise loses its ability to engage in operations, nor does it mean that the legal person is eliminated immediately. The enterprise is stopped from doing anything that is outside the scope of liquidation. Only after the liquidation can the enterprise be completed eliminated.
43. For example, articles of association under the Hong Kong Companies Ordinance (Cap. 622).
44. Vanessa Stott, *Hong Kong Company Law* (12th ed.), Pearson (Hong Kong), 2008, pp. 64–65.
45. The 1993 Company Law, Article 11.

debatable whether this provision is a sign of progress or a sign of theoretical confusion.

(5) Unsolved Problem of Article 18 of the 1993 Company Law

Article 18 of the 1993 Company Law stated that the Law also covered LLCs with foreign investors. It failed to address foreign-invested JSCs. Thus, in theory, the 1993 Company Law did not apply to foreign-invested JSCs. This problem was resolved on 10 January 1995, when the Interim Rules on Several Issues Concerning the Establishment of Foreign Invested Joint Stock Companies were promulgated.[46] It was expected that the existing Company Law would address its relationship with all foreign-invested companies. However, Article 217 of the Company Law basically repeats the 1993 Company Law by stating that although the LLCs and JSCs invested in by foreign investors shall be governed by this law, priority shall be given to other laws regarding foreign investment if the provisions of other laws are different. Thus, one may expect that within a reasonable period of time the existing Company Law and other laws concerning foreign-invested companies will remain separate.

(6) The Provision of One-Person Companies Is Too Simple

The existing Company Law has seven provisions to deal with one-person LLCs. The Law states that other provisions concerning LLCs can be used as a reference.[47] However, it is not sure whether other provisions concerning LLCs can apply to one-person companies. For example, the provisions concerning corporate governance obviously cannot be applied to one-person companies. Furthermore, it is necessary to address in detail how to prevent one-person companies from being abused, especially given that the existing Company Law has abolished minimum registered capital for one-person companies.[48] China may need a special law to deal with one-person companies in the near future.

46. For a detailed discussion, please see Gu Minkang, "Several Legal Issues Concerning Foreign-invested Joint Stock Companies" (*Shilun waishang touzi gufen youxian gongsi*), *The Journal of International Economic Law*, The Law Press (Beijing), 1999, Vol. 2, pp. 327–42.
47. The Company Law, Article 57.
48. Before the 2013 Company Law was released, scholars suggested that one-person companies should be subjected to the following requirements: (1) restrictive registration and public announcement; (2) minimum registered capital and maintenance of capital; (3) special supervision of financial records; and (4) prohibition of self-dealing. Obviously,

Another issue is the possibility of allowing the establishment of one-person JSCs. Professor Liu Junhai once suggested that Chinese legislators should permit one-person JSCs and at the same time raise the member ceiling of LLCs to more than 50 persons.[49] So far, there are four types of legislation concerning the one-person company: (1) both one-person LLCs and JSCs are allowed (e.g., Canada, Holland, Germany, and Japan); (2) only one-person LLCs are allowed (e.g., the United Kingdom); (3) one-person companies are not allowed (e.g., France, Denmark, and Belgium); (4) one-person companies are generally not allowed, however, after a company is established and only one shareholder is left, the company is not required to dissolve and the shareholder is not liable (e.g., Austria and Swaziland); (5) one-person companies are not allowed, and if all of the shares of a company are in the hand of one person, the company must be closed or the shareholder bears joint liability (e.g., Greece, Ireland, Italy, and Spain). Although legislation is not the same around the world, the general tendency is clear: one-person companies will gradually be recognized. The 2013 Company Law does not accept the one-person JSC. It may require more research and discussion.

(7) Issue of the Independent Director

Professor Jiang Ping has written one article to discuss whether the Company Law should adopt the independent director system. He suggests that the independent director system should be adopted. But he points out that it is not proper to simply make it mandatory or discretionary. He then suggests that the following three types of companies should adopt the independent director system: (1) wholly state-owned companies, (2) listed companies, and (3) investment fund companies.[50] However, the Company Law provides the independent director system only for listed companies.[51] Whether this is a proper approach is questionable and should be subject to further research. Furthermore, it is important to handle the relationship between

---

the suggestion of minimum registered capital is no longer valid. Wang Zhaohua and Wang Li, "Legal Mechanism to Deal with the Negative Impact of One-person Companies" (*Lun yiren gongsi de fumian xiaoying de falü guizhi*), retrieved from http://fanwen.glzhe800.com/?fl/HTML/fl_20061124194322_6215.html on 20 October 2015.

49. Liu Junhai, "Six Debated Issues during the Implementation of the New Company Law" (*Xin Gongsifa shishi zhong de liu da zhengdian*), retrieved from http://finance.sina.com.cn/review/20061124/15463107843.shtml on 3 November 2015.

50. "Famous Scholar Jiang Ping's Analysis of the Company Law: Six Tough Questions Should Be Resolved" (*Faxue taidou Jiang Ping puxi Gongsifa: Xu jiejue liu da nanti*), retrieved from http://finance.sina.com.cn/roll/20040408/0447707850.shtml on 20 October 2015.

51. The Company Law, Article 122.

independent directors and the BOS.[52] The important thing is to adopt the independent director system on the basis of improving the role and function of the BOS. For this reason, it is proper to consider the viewpoints of Professor Zhu. Firstly, the role of two institutions should be clearly defined in order to avoid the cost of supervision becoming too high. Secondly, the companies that have imported the independent director system should focus on perfecting this system. On the other hand, the companies that have not imported this system should focus on perfecting the BOS system.[53]

(8) New Concept of the Affiliated Relationship

The concept of the "affiliated relationship" was not provided in the 1993 Company Law despite the fact that in reality some scholars have addressed it. The existing Company Law adopts this concept. Thus, "affiliated relationships" refer to the relationships between the controlling shareholders, actual controllers, directors, supervisors and senior management personnel, and the enterprises, which are controlled directly or indirectly by those persons, or any other special relationship that may result in the transfer of the company's interests.[54] However, the Company Law states in Article 124 only that a director of a listed company shall not exercise his or her voting right to a resolution made by the BOD if the resolution affects a particular enterprise that has an affiliated relationship with him or her. One may infer from this provision that directors of non-listed companies shall not worry about this matter. In comparison, the New Draft contains a better proposal: any shareholders or directors shall not exercise their voting power if the matter to be voted on concerns an enterprise in which they have an affiliated relationship. Otherwise, the company concerned shall have the right to appeal to a people's court to rescind relevant contracts, transactions, and arrangements within three months after the resolutions have been made.[55]

(9) Other Problems

Although Article 4 of the existing Company Law solves the problem of Article 4(3) of the 1993 Company Law, it also deletes one important

52. For a detailed discussion, please see Gu Minkang, "Questioning the Independent Director System of Listed Companies" (*Zhiyi shangshi gongsi de duli dongshi zhidu*), *The Journal of the Rule of Law* (*Fazhi luncong*), Shanghai, 2003, Vol. 3, pp. 92–95.
53. Lei Fang, *The Company Law Should Be Amended Greatly* (*Gongsifa ying da xiugai*), The Chinese Aviation Newspaper (*Zhongguo minhang bao*), 28 July 2004, p. 9.
54. The Company Law, Article 216(4).
55. The New Draft, Articles 43 and 52.

statement under Article 4(2): "a company shall, as a legal entity, enjoy all rights over legal entity property formulated by investments from the various shareholders and shall enjoy civil rights and assume civil liability in accordance with the law". In fact, this statement articulates an important concept: that companies shall assume unlimited liability towards creditors even though shareholders' liability is limited. Another problem remains under Article 112 of the Company Law: where a director is unable to attend a board meeting due to special circumstances, he or she may commission in writing another director to act on his or her behalf, and the letter of proxy shall stipulate the scope of authority. This provision fails to address a situation where "another director" refuses to act on his or her behalf and whether other means could be used.

4. Short Summary

Nothing is 100 per cent perfect. China may need more time to experiment with the market economy to accumulate rich experience. The Company Law has made remarkable achievements in various aspects. One important thing is that the existing Company Law tries to get rid of the bad image that the main purpose of the 1993 Company Law was to rescue SOEs. It also sends out a new message that the Chinese government has a firm intention to move towards a market economy. Thus, it is optimistic to expect that a more perfect Company Law will promote more healthy business development in China.

II. CHINA SHOULD ADOPT A UNIFIED COMPANY LAW

1. Existing Situation

After 1978, the Third Plenary Meeting of the Eleventh CPC Congress officially endorsed an open-door policy and economic reform in China. The major task in rescuing the SOEs was to expand their autonomy and management powers. In order to do so, many laws and regulations were published during 1979 and 1988. The most important one was the Law of the PRC for State-owned Enterprises, promulgated in 1988.[56] This Law intended to establish a principle of "separation of property rights and operational rights",

56. Other laws and regulations include Regulations on Factory Heads, Regulations on the Representative Assembly of Staff and Workers, Regulations on the Grassroots Level Organization of the Chinese Communist Party, Provisional Regulations on the Contract Responsibility System and Provisional Regulations on the Leasing System for a Small Size Enterprise.

i.e., the property of an enterprise shall belong to the whole people and shall be operated and managed by the enterprises based on authorizations of the state. An enterprise shall enjoy the right to possess, use, and legally dispose of property that the state has authorized it to operate and manage.[57] For the first time, this law defines fourteen autonomous rights of SOEs:

(1) the right to arrange the business and to make decisions;
(2) the right to fix the price for products and services;
(3) the right to sell products that are not subject to mandatory plans;
(4) the right to order products that are not subject to mandatory plans;
(5) the right to import and export;
(6) the right to make investment decisions;
(7) the right to allocate and use its retained funds;
(8) the right to dispose of the State property;
(9) the right to conduct joint cooperation and mergers with other enterprises;
(10) the right to recruit and dismiss workers;
(11) the right to determine its own structure;
(12) the right to determine a wage system and bonus distribution;
(13) the right to determine its own personnel system; and
(14) the right to refuse the apportionment.[58]

This law, however, was still influenced by the idea of a planned economy, and many provisions required SOEs to be under the guidance of state plans.[59]

One further step taken was to permit the establishment of private and foreign-invested enterprises. Furthermore, the 1993 Company Law was promulgated to restructure SOEs on international capitalist models and to legitimate a much smaller private sector.[60]

The individual and private business enterprises were re-established in China through seven stages.

(1) From 1978 to August 1982, the individual economy was officially recognized. The Eleventh Party Congress declared that a state-owned economy and collective economy were the basic economic forms in

57. Law of the PRC for State-owned Enterprises, Article 2.
58. Ibid., Articles 22–34.
59. Article 22 of the Law of the PRC for State-owned Enterprises states, "An enterprise, under the guidance of the State plan, shall have the right to arrange by itself the production of goods required by society or the provision of services for society".
60. Robert C. Art and Minkang Gu, "China Incorporated: The First Corporation Law on the People's Republic of China", *Yale Journal of International Law*, Vol. 20, No. 2, 1995, p. 282.

China, while the limited individual economy was the necessary supplement to the public economy.

(2) In September 1982, the individual economy was written into the Constitution amended by the Fifth National People's Congress. Article 11 states, "the individual economy of urban and rural working people, operating within the limits prescribed by law, is a complement to the socialist public economy. The State protects the lawful rights and interests of the individual economy."

(3) In 1987, the term "private enterprise" appeared in the CPC's documents for the first time.

(4) In November 1987, the Thirteenth Party Congress encouraged the development of a private economy.

(5) In 1988, the Seventh NPC passed the Constitution (Amendment) and the private economy was written into the Constitution for the first time.

(6) In 1992, the Fourteenth Party Congress recognized not only the legal status of the individual economy, private economy, and foreign investment economy, but also the cooperation among different economic forms.

(7) The Fifteenth Party Congress officially recognized the role of the non-public economy in the socialist market economy.[61]

Law and regulations particularly concerning individual and private business enterprises have gradually been developed. The initial regulations dealt with individual household businesses that were far from recognized as business enterprises.[62] In fact, the first regulations concerning private enterprises were the Provisional Regulations on Privately-run Enterprises of the PRC issued on 25 June 1988 by the State Council.[63] Subsequently, the Partnership Enterprises Law of the PRC[64] was promulgated on 23 February 1997 in order to accommodate joint cooperative business among individuals. The formal law regarding sole ownership (sole proprietorship)

61. For detailed information, see Li Zhenjie, *The Perspective of Private Enterprises* (*Siying qiye toushi*), The Economic Management Press (Beijing), 1999, pp. 25–29.

62. On 5 August 1987, the State Council issued the Provisional Regulations Governing Individual Households in Cities and Townships (*Chengxiang Geti Gongshanghu Guanli Zanxing Guiding*). The Regulations do not interpret the individual households as enterprises.

63. See *Zhonghua Renmin Gongheguo Siying Qiye Zanxing Tiaoli*. Under those regulations, private enterprises were divided into three categories, i.e., sole ownership enterprises, partnership enterprises, and LLCs. This is a typical example of mixing business forms under a planned economic system with business forms under a market economic system.

64. See *Zhonghua Renmin Gongheguo Hehuo Qiye Fa*.

enterprises was eventually promulgated on 30 August 1999 and took effect on 1 January 2000.[65]

Foreign investment in China has developed dramatically since 1979. Foreign investments in China have gone through several stages.

The initial stage was from 1979 to 1985.[66] During this period, China established the special economic zones in Guangdong and Fujian. Furthermore, these two provinces were given wider "law"-making powers to promulgate rules and regulations provided they did not contradict the Chinese Constitution, national laws, and relevant regulations.[67] The second stage was from 1986 to 1989. During this period, the number of foreign investments rose rapidly because of the improved legal environment.[68] The third stage was from 1989 to 2000. During this period, there was an Asian financial crisis that affected foreign investments in China. During the period from January to July 1999, contracted overseas investments dropped 20 per cent.[69] After 2000, foreign investment in China increased again. Among 500 biggest multinational companies worldwide, about 400 companies have invested in China in more than 2,000 projects.[70]

So far, the laws and regulations on foreign-invested enterprises are too numerous and confusing. The following list contains the laws and regulations that are most relevant to business enterprises:

(1) The Law of the PRC on Sino-Foreign Joint Equity Enterprises[71]
(2) The Law of the PRC on Sino-Foreign Cooperative Enterprises[72]

---

65. The Sole Proprietorship Enterprise Law of the PRC (*Zhonghua Renmin Gongheguo Geren Duzi Qiye Fa*).
66. H. Sun, "Macro-economic Impact of Direct Foreign Investment in China: 1979–1996", *The World Economy*, Vol. 21, No. 5, July 1998, p. 676.
67. The Resolution of the NPCSC to Give Legislative Powers to the Provincial Congresses and Their Standing Committees of Guangdong and Fujian in Making Special Economic Laws for their Special Economic Zones was issued on 26 November 1981.
68. H. Sun, "Macro-economic Impact of Direct Foreign Investment in China: 1979–1996", *The World Economy*, Vol. 21, No. 5, July 1998, p. 677.
69. "China: Uphill Battle to Keep Overseas Funds Flowing In", *China Daily*, 9 October 1999.
70. Zhang Yi, "400 Multinational Companies Have Invested in More than 2,000 Projects in China", *Xinhua Daily Electronic News*, 3 October 2001.
71. *Zhonghua Renmin Gongheguo Zhongwai Hezi Jingying Qiye Fa*, which was passed on 1 July 1979 by the First Session of the Fifth NPC; the first amendment made by the Decision Regarding the Revision of "the Law of the PRC on Sino-foreign Equity Joint Venture Law", adopted at the Third Session of the Seventh NPC on 4 April 1990; and the second amendment made by the Decision Regarding the Revision of "Law of the PRC on Sino-Foreign Equity Joint Venture Law", adopted at the Fourth Session of the Ninth NPC on 15 March 2001.
72. *Zhonghua Renmin Gongheguo Zhongwai Hezuo Jingying Qiye Fa*, which was passed on 13 April 1988 by the First Session of the Seventh NPC, amended by the Decision Regarding the Revision of "the Law of the PRC on Sino-Foreign Cooperative Joint Venture

(3) The Law of the PRC on Wholly Foreign-owned Enterprises[73]
(4) The Provisional Regulations on Several Issues Concerning the Establishment of Foreign-investment Companies Limited by Shares[74]
(5) The Provisional Measures on the Trial Establishment of Sino-Foreign Joint Equity Foreign Trade Companies[75]
(6) The Pilot Projects for Commercial Enterprises with Foreign Investment Procedures[76]
(7) Provisional Regulations Governing the Establishment of Investment-Type Companies by Foreign Business Investment[77]
(8) The Merger and Division of Foreign Investment Enterprises Provisions[78]

Many foreign-invested enterprises have taken the form of LLCs. However, they are not subject to control by the existing Company Law. China may need to fix the problems of foreign investment gradually. At the very beginning, there was a dilemma: China needed foreign capital, but was afraid of foreign capital. There was a worry that foreign capital would endanger the security and stability of the Chinese society and economy.[79]

2. Chaotic Problem

From the preceding brief introduction, it is evident that there are two situations in China. On the one hand, various forms of business enterprises have been established because of the open-door policy and creation of relevant

Law", adopted at the Eighteenth Session of the Standing Committee of the Ninth NPC on 31 October 2000.

73. *Zhonghua Renmin Gongheguo Waizi Qiye Fa*, which was passed on 12 April 1986 by the Fourth Session of the Sixth NPC, revised in the Amendment to "the Law of the PRC on Wholly Foreign-owned Enterprise Law" Decision on 31 October 2000 by the Standing Committee of the Eighteenth Session of the Ninth NPC.
74. *Guanyu Sheli Waishang Touzi Gufen Youxian Gongsi Ruogan Wenti de Zanxing Guiding*, which was issued on 10 January 1995 by the Ministry of Foreign Trade and Economic Cooperation.
75. *Guanyu Sheli Zhongwai Hezi Duiwai Maoyi Gongsi Shidian Zanxing Banfa*, which was issued on 30 September 1996 by the Ministry of Foreign Trade and Economic Cooperation.
76. *Waishang Touzi Shangye Qiye Shidian Banfa*, which was issued on 25 June 1999 by the State Economic and Trade Commission and the Ministry of Foreign Trade and Economic Cooperation.
77. *Guanyu Waishang Touzi Juban Touzixing Gongsi de Zanxing Guiding*, which was issued on 4 April 1995 by the Ministry of Foreign Trade and Economic Cooperation.
78. *Guanyu Waishang Touzi Qiye Hebing yu Fenli de Guiding*, which was issued by the Ministry of Foreign Trade and Economic Cooperation and the State Administration for Industry and Commerce on 23 September 1999 and effective as of 1 November 1999.
79. Zhang Shaofeng, "Restructuring Legislation for Foreign Investment Enterprises" (*Waishang touzi qiye lifa de chonggou*), paper submitted to the 1999 Annual Conference for the International Economic Law Society, unpublished, p. 4.

rules and regulations. On the other hand, China took the precaution of experimenting with the open-door policy from the very beginning. Thus, it permitted the coexistence of business enterprises, which are governed by three different series of laws and regulations.

The first series of laws and regulations govern business enterprises based on their nature of ownership, such as SOEs, collectively owned enterprises, and privately owned enterprises. The second series of laws and regulations govern business enterprises that are compatible with internationally recognized enterprises, such as companies, partnerships, and sole proprietorships. The third series of laws and regulations govern business enterprises because they involve foreign investors, such as equity joint ventures, contractual joint ventures and wholly foreign-owned enterprises. The coexistence of these laws and regulations causes several problems. The first problem is due to the impression of the rule of law in China. In an extreme situation, it would seem that one business enterprise may be governed concurrently by three different series of laws and regulations. In this situation, confusion arises when applying the laws and regulations. The second problem is due to the different treatment of different enterprises in the past. However, both domestic investors and foreign investors are basically given the same treatment. The time to discuss unified law has almost arrived.

Furthermore, China should consider how to establish a mechanism to support medium- and small-sized enterprises. Medium- and small-sized enterprises are an important part of the national economy and cannot be replaced by large-sized enterprises. In the past, SOEs had a predominant position and no one paid serious attention to medium- and small-sized enterprises, especially when they were non-state owned. In comparison with large-sized enterprises, medium- and small-sized enterprises have problems with insufficient capital and financing difficulties. Fortunately, the relevant Chinese authority announced that the Law on Promoting Medium and Small-Sized Enterprises was promulgated in 2002.[80] This indicates that the method of supporting medium- and small-sized enterprises will be a good research topic in the future and that considerable good experience should be learned from abroad.

Many scholars in China demand reform to existing business enterprise laws and regulations. Through their research and examination, they have indicated that the existing business enterprise laws and regulations have two major problems. Firstly, there are conflicts between various laws

80. Wang Fu, "China Will Promulgate the Law on Promoting Medium- and Small-Sized Enterprises in 2002" (*Zhongguo Zhongxiao Qiye Fa youwang yu 2002 nian chutai*), *China Market Economy News* (Beijing), 5 November 2001.

and regulations because different authorities promulgate those laws and regulations, especially in the fields of foreign investment laws and regulations, where they overlap each other. Taking equity joint venture law, contractual joint venture law, and wholly foreign-owned enterprise law as examples, about 50 per cent of them overlap.[81] Secondly, the existing laws and regulations are not consistent with WTO rules and principles. On the one hand, the WTO demands that every member have transparent laws and regulations instead of complicated or internal rules and regulations, so investors from other member countries or regions can rely on those transparent laws and regulations. On the other hand, the WTO requires each member to offer "national treatment" to other members. The implementation of this principle will eventually narrow the distance between domestic investors and foreign investors.[82] Thus, China will eventually move away from the three series of business enterprise laws and regulations and adopt unified business enterprises laws and regulations.

3. Possible Solutions

Enterprises with different ownerships, domestic enterprises, and foreign-invested enterprises can be identified in accordance with modern business laws and regulations, i.e., company law, partnership law, and sole proprietorship law (from legal persons to non-legal persons). Most foreign investments in China take the form of legal persons. For this reason, all foreign investment laws and regulations have a close relationship with the 1993 Company Law or the existing Company Law.[83] A few foreign-invested enterprises, which intend not to take legal person status, may elect business forms that are compatible with partnerships and sole proprietorships. This is the same situation where domestic business enterprises (regardless of their ownership nature) can be formed in line with company law, partnership law or sole proprietorship law. If this theory could be established, the next bold suggestion would be to abolish or restructure existing foreign investment

81. Xu Chongli and Lin Zhong, *Chinese Foreign Investment Law*, Joint Publishing (Hong Kong), 1997, p. 62.
82. It is necessary to point out that even after China's accession to the WTO, China may still give favourable support to domestic enterprises. For example, Beijing made an announcement not long ago that any enterprise formed jointly by Hong Kong investors and domestic investors should be treated as "domestic enterprises" and will be given financial support or favourable tax treatment. *Ming Pao*, 24 October 2001.
83. In China, special laws prevail over general laws. See Article 83 of the Legislative Law of the PRC (*Zhonghua Renmin Gongheguo Lifafa*), which was promulgated on 15 March 2000.

laws and regulations, as well as the laws and regulations for domestic enterprises based on ownership nature, i.e., SOEs, collectively owned enterprises, and private enterprises.[84]

To restructure the existing foreign investment laws and regulations has a twofold meaning. On the one hand, many of them should be abolished since logically, under the tendency of national treatment endorsed by the WTO, the concept of "foreign investors" will be dramatically diluted or ignored eventually.[85] Thus, foreign investors should go only to the registry authorities to handle the establishment of their business enterprises in accordance with company law, partnership law or sole proprietorship law. On the other hand, it has been recognized that foreign investors may nevertheless enquire about their legal status or benefits. In this regard, it is proposed that a new law called "Foreign Investment Guidelines" be tentatively adopted to include all issues such as investment percentages, investment areas, tax benefits, and administrative matters.[86] It is further proposed that the foreign investment guidelines should be unified on a national level in order to prevent local protectionism. The central government should make its best effort to formulate unified policies for all WTO members, including investors from Hong Kong and Macao. Such an effort will be consistent with the WTO's spirit and principles.[87] In addition, the central

---

84. For example, the Provisional Regulations on Privately-run Enterprises of the PRC issued on 25 June 1988 permit private enterprises to adopt three business forms, i.e., sole proprietorships, partnerships, and LLCs. After the Company Law, partnership law and sole proprietorship law were promulgated, the Provisional Regulations were virtually abandoned.
85. This is the typical situation in the European Union today. The Treaty for Establishing the European Community endorses the following freedoms: free movement of goods (Articles 23–24); free movement of persons, services and capital (Articles 39–42); and freedom of establishment (Articles 43–48). Thus, "restrictions on the freedom of establishment of nationals of a Member State in the territory of another Member State shall be prohibited". This implies that the investors from one Member State shall have the right to invest in the territory of another Member State without being regarded as a "foreign investor".
86. The existing Provisional Regulations on Foreign Investment Guidelines mainly focus on foreign investment projects that are encouraged, permitted, restricted or prohibited. The proposed foreign investment guidelines should have wider coverage.
87. It was reported that the mayor of Beijing announced on 23 October 2001 that investors from Hong Kong would be given special treatment. For example, if Hong Kong investors form a joint venture with domestic enterprises in Beijing, the joint venture will be treated as a "domestic enterprise" and be given tax and loan benefits. For detailed information, see *Ming Pao*, 24 October 2001. This announcement was criticized for giving special treatment to Hong Kong investors but not to other WTO members. In response to this criticism, one of the vice-mayors of Beijing explained that this was a local policy for Hong Kong investors and had nothing to do with national policy. Perhaps this explanation has no grounds.

government is in a better position to give preferential treatment to investors who invest in remote or poor areas.

In addition to future national treatment, China has successfully implemented unified laws and regulations in other areas. Firstly, the new Law on Enterprise Income Tax was promulgated in 2007, and the different tax treatments had been eliminated within five years. Secondly, the newly promulgated Contract Law clearly states that the original economic contract law, foreign economic contract law, and law on technology transfer were abolished. Thus, the Contract Law applies to both domestic contracts and foreign-related contracts. Those are good examples to support the idea of establishing unified business enterprise laws and regulations in China.

Index

www.ingramcontent.com/pod-product-compliance
Ingram Content Group UK Ltd.
Pitfield, Milton Keynes, MK11 3LW, UK
UKHW021835100926
8556IPUK00004B/364

9 789888 390526